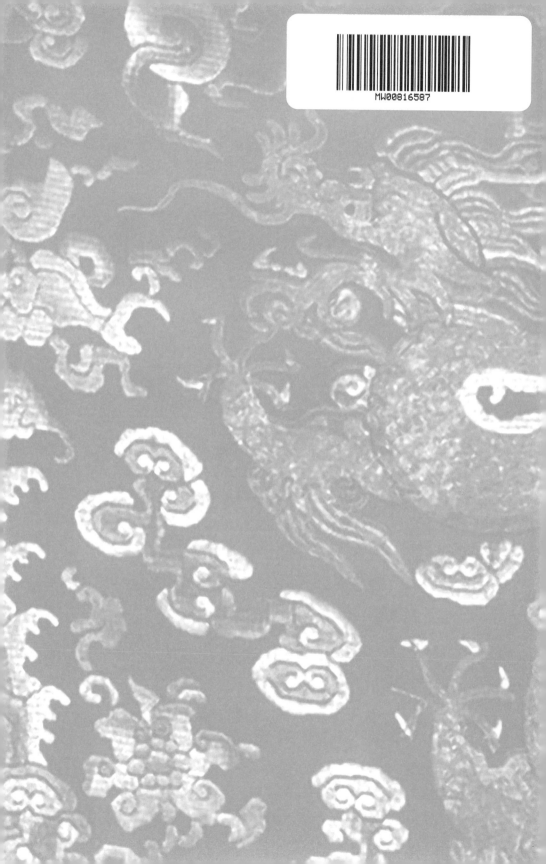

IMPERIAL MASQUERADE

Princess Der Ling

IMPERIAL MASQUERADE

The Legend of Princess Der Ling

GRANT HAYTER-MENZIES

With a foreword by PAMELA KYLE CROSSLEY

香港大學出版社

HONG KONG UNIVERSITY PRESS

Hong Kong University Press
14/F Hing Wai Centre
7 Tin Wan Praya Road
Aberdeen
Hong Kong

© Hong Kong University Press 2008

ISBN 978-962-209-881-7

Secure On-line Ordering
http://www.hkupress.org

British Library Cataloguing-in-Publication Data
A catalogue copy for this book is available from the British Library

Printed and bound by United League Graphic & Printing Co. Ltd. in Hong Kong, China

To Pamela Kyle Crossley,
for her belief in this book.

To Christopher Ives,
for his belief in Der Ling.

To "Han Liangxi,"
for his belief in me.

Se non è vero, è ben trovato.
— Italian proverb

Contents

Illustrations

(Following p. 147)

1. Thomas Allom engraving of how a typical Chinese mandarin lived early in the reign of Queen Victoria, following the first "Opium War." It was images like this that fed occidental appetites for oriental plunder, not to mention romantic Western misconceptions of Chinese reality. Author's collection.

2. Rong Ling and sister Der Ling, dressed for Carneval in Paris, circa 1900, photographed by Charles Chusseau-Flaviens. This and the following two photographs have never been identified until now with Der Ling or her family. George Eastman House.

3. Xinling, one of two brothers of Der Ling, dressed for Carneval in Paris, circa 1900, photographed by Chusseau-Flaviens, circa 1900. George Eastman House.

4. Possible image of Yu Keng, Der Ling's father, in his office as Chinese minister to France, circa 1900, photographed in Paris by Chusseau-Flaviens. George Eastman House.

5. Li Hongzhang (1823–1901), statesman, friend and protector of Yu Keng. Author's collection.

18. The Guangxu Emperor and his father Prince Chun. Guangxu was described as having a voice like the faint buzz of a mosquito. Author's collection.

19. Der Ling and Cixi, with eunuch Cui Yugui holding umbrella, standing on Peony Hill at the Summer Palace. Der Ling is visibly cold here, but the Empress Dowager was a great lover of outdoor activity in all weathers. Photographed by Xunling, circa 1904. Collection of Arthur M. Sackler Gallery/Freer Gallery, Washington, D.C.

20. Cixi with Rong Ling, Fourth Princess and eunuch attendants on the Lotus Lake at the Summer Palace. Photographed by Xunling. Author's collection.

21. Cixi and her female court, from left to right: Lustrous Concubine (sister of Guangxu's beloved the Pearl Concubine), Rong Ling, Empress Dowager Cixi, Der Ling, Louisa, and the Young Empress, consort of the Guangxu Emperor, by Xunling. Author's collection.

22. A rare image of Cixi showing the smile described by so many who met her. "She must have been taking in her teens!" exclaimed Sir Robert Hart, inspector general of customs. Photographed by Xunling. Collection of Arthur M. Sackler Gallery/Freer Gallery, Washington, D.C.

23. Cixi wearing her famous cape made of over 3,000 pearls. This photo was evidently taken after Cixi's stroke in 1903–04. Photographed by Xunling. Author's collection.

24. Cixi attended by eunuchs while Der Ling poses demurely to one side. Photographed by Xunling. Collection of Arthur M. Sackler Gallery/Freer Gallery, Washington, D.C.

25. Cixi, Rong Ling, Der Ling and Louisa on Peony Hill at the Summer Palace. Photographed by Xunling. Collection of Arthur M. Sackler Gallery/Freer Gallery, Washington, D.C.

26. Cixi, Fourth Princess and eunuchs in the snow at the Summer Palace, photographed by Xunling. Neither this nor the following photograph has ever been published before. Collection of Arthur M. Sackler Gallery/Freer Gallery, Washington, D.C.

27. Cixi, Fourth Princess and eunuchs in the snow at the Summer Palace, photographed by Xunling. This photograph has not been

Foreword

Der Ling is one of those figures who have been sifted out of the pure sand of respectable history. *Two Years in the Forbidden City*, her memoir of life in attendance on the self-caricaturing Empress Dowager Cixi, her eunuchs, dogs and toys, is usually brushed off as a historically illiterate farrago of poorly remembered vignettes and ill-considered comment. It may be that. Der Ling is commended to the historian's attention not for her literary efforts but for her true oeuvre, her performance. She was handed scraps cut from *fin de siècle* Paris and *ancien regime* Beijing, from an American ancestor and putative Qing nobility, and wove from it a robe that cast a brief spell over an international audience. It was an age in which tall tales were welcome and affectation was not interfered with. Archie Belaney's solemn masquerade as Grey Owl was reverently received, Frank T. Hopkins' stories of incredible racing and endurance feats for himself and his intrepid horse Hidalgo were accepted with delirious credulity, Anna Anderson could claim to be Anastasia Nikolaevna miraculously saved from the savage murder that befell the real Anastasia and her family. Edmund Backhouse fabricated a Manchu aristocrat's diary and fooled the world. Reginald Johnston retired to an island in Scotland and built a Chinese folly palace for himself that enveloped all viewers in a fantastic China that never was. American fascination with European and with Asian royalty in the early twentieth century would have invented Der Ling if she had not existed. But she did exist, she did come to America, where she rode the upwellings and collapsed in the downdrafts of fame.

Der Ling ended as an obscure teacher of Chinese to students born long after the twilight era of the great empires which had given her both a passage of reflected glamor and her true claim on our attention. As exotic as Der Ling appeared to the Americans who devoured her writings and her lectures when the twentieth century was fresh, her story hid the coherence of the last years of the Qing empire beneath the cross-hatching of mask, costume, and script. She claimed to be a Manchu princess. But the facts were the sort that our modern vocabulary does not accommodate easily, demanding simplification and distortion to fit the mold that American and European readers wanted then and often want now.

Der Ling's father, Yu Keng, was not a Manchu. Neither was he Chinese. He belonged to the old and misunderstood Chinese-martial caste of mixed origins who conquered China alongside the Manchus in the seventeenth century. To Chinese civilians the entire conquest elite was "Manchu," despite a range of cultures and family histories. Yu Keng was a member of the elite ranks within the empire's hereditary Eight Banner force, recruited as many mid-nineteenth bannermen were for the diplomatic corps that was forced upon the Qing after their repeated losses to European navies and marines. Yu Keng dressed in the robes of the traditional Qing official, even when based in Paris, and was in the political clique of the Empress Dowager Cixi. Yet in his politics he was a reformer, a progressive, a student of international affairs (as Cixi was herself in earlier life). To those seeing Cixi as the emblem of all that was corrupt, small-minded, self-centered and reactionary at the late Qing court, Yu Keng may appear to be a contradiction. In fact, he was typical of a certain group of Manchu and Bannermen progressives, who lost out to the forces of radicalism on both the loyalist and nationalist sides. After the revolution of 1911 they were as lost to history as the Chinese-martial people themselves.

So, her presentation of herself to Americans knowing nothing of the complexities of Qing imperial ranks and identities as a "Manchu princess" was in many ways a playful exploitation of the limitations of the modern imagination. It was shorthand for the intolerable ambiguities that, in the hands of the right author, make our understanding of Der Ling and her times more precise. She had an American grandfather, something she tended to suppress as distracting for her American audiences and posing a certain deflationary threat to her exotic themes. Yet, Eurasians were not extremely rare in the generation of Der Ling's mother. Chinese laborers in the USA and its territories frequently had children at both ends of the journey, and in some unusual instances took American wives home to their villages. Yung Wing, who in the mid-nineteenth century became the first Chinese to graduate from an American university, married a white woman who traveled with him to China and bore him two sons. Robert Hart, the British Inspector General of the Imperial Maritime Customs service, had three sons by his Chinese common-law spouse. Most of the European and American merchants in China — many, like Der Ling's ancestors, active in the tea and opium trades — had extra-legal Chinese families. It was not a history that Der Ling's era took for granted, and it is one we still need to naturalize in our understanding of the late nineteenth-century world. Like the transmutation of Der Ling's Chinese-martial heritage into a "Manchu" one, like her father's elite banner status translated into royalty, Der Ling's American roots made her uncommon among Chinese but an authentic reflection of the larger world in her time.

Grant Hayter-Menzies has put some of our assumptions about Der Ling's exaggerations and fabrications to one side to better reveal the unwieldy truths about China, America and the world of the early twentieth century. He completes the story Der Ling partly narrated herself, but never finished: personal, meandering, delighting in costume and masquerade, sumptuous in detail, replete with the scenery and the dramatis personae of the world when it staggered away from its imperial pasts and toward the inconstancies of modernity. Just as the Empress Dowager once commanded the young Der Ling to appear at her side in the unlikely guise of a traditional lady-in-waiting, foreign readers and audiences demanded she appear in the guise of a survivor of the rarified, secluded, pampered, eternally foreign world of "oriental" imperiality. As sternly as Der Ling sometimes demanded that her audience surrender all skepticism, her smile too easily betrays her awareness that she was the authentic princess of the empire of ignorant bliss.

Pamela Kyle Crossley
Norwich, Vermont

Preface

While reading *Isadora: A Sensational Life*, Peter Kurth's 2001 account of the twentieth century's most influential dance reformer, I encountered a Chinese woman named Princess Der Ling who as a teenager had studied with Isadora in Paris between 1899 and 1903. Kurth quoted several piquant remarks on Duncan made by this writer, who seemed to admire Duncan's blithe disregard for wearing the heavy clothes of the era (and her scorn for clothes in general), and who relished her many feminist declarations. For all her youth, and considering she came from a culture to which Western dance and women's rights were foreign territory, Der Ling seemed remarkably aware of Duncan's artistic genius and modern outlook.

Later on, when I read *Dragon Lady*, Sterling Seagrave's 1992 biography of Empress Dowager Cixi, I met Der Ling again. I discovered that while making an effort to rehabilitate the Empress Dowager, Seagrave also addressed the denigration (by many of the same sources) of Der Ling and her contributions to late Qing historiography. Seagrave's book led me to find and read all of Der Ling's books, along with her several published articles. Through chance references to her in the memoirs, diaries and travel writings contemporary with her time frame of late Qing, early Republic China that I read subsequently, I occasionally found doubts about her facts (or the way in which she related them) and especially about her title, and realized from the beginning that Der Ling was nothing if not a figure of controversy. I saw her as a fascinating human battleground of conflicting identities, a victim of the hallucinogenic effects of too much publicity, much of it prompted by Der Ling herself, and a figure whose life provides a glimpse into one woman's experience of living not just between two cultures — that of China and the West — but among many different worlds: social, religious, moral, political.

In writing about Der Ling I faced two challenges: I do not read Chinese, and thus sources in Chinese have had to be translated for me. And there is the matter of what to believe and what not. I concur with others who have identified the essential challenge of Der Ling's *oeuvre* — there is little if any chance of proving everything she describes of the court of the Empress Dowager Cixi and the Guangxu Emperor. What can be corroborated in English-language sources (those well-known, and others I have unearthed) I have used in writing this book; where there has been criticism in Chinese sources, I have used translations of these. Where I feel doubt is warranted, I make my own reservations clear. What I do not want to do, as some commentators have done in the past, is dismiss her out of hand.

Der Ling has been called many things. Some of these criticisms are just, some deliberate slander: that she was a fantasist, a self-publicist (a trait that disgusted many of her relatives and friends in China), even an outright liar. She has yet to be proven the latter, but of the two former traits she partook liberal helpings. A cursory reading of her writings conjures a person who was likeable and funny, also a snob and an egoist, and at the same time sensitive and talented, maybe a reliable witness to history and friend of important historical figures, and maybe not. But the legend that was "Princess" Der Ling does not end there, as her detractors may have hoped — it actually just begins. In my research I found that not everything Der Ling wrote was a lie and that much of what she wrote about the court of the Empress Dowager and Beijing society is either provable from other sources or so plausible it is not worth the trouble to unpick all her literary needlework. And I found evidence that some of the detractors who dogged her in her lifetime bent the truth themselves in order to present an image of her that closely matched their version of another controversial woman central to her story, the Empress Dowager Cixi, in order to make their own versions of Cixi and her court more competitive in the marketplace. Through my research and that of others seeking to set the record straight on the Empress Dowager I found that many of these revered "China hands," such as J. O. P. Bland, Edmund Backhouse, Sir Reginald Johnston and George Morrison, did systematically disparage Der Ling's and other women's accounts of the Empress Dowager in favor of their own casting of her as the quintessence of Asian female evil. This character type and the lurid tales of her murders and mayhem sells books, after all — it was not just easy for Westerners to believe Cixi capable of the worst, it was titillating for them to obsess on the topic, particularly on her alleged sexual enormities. In old China, Sinophile Westerners had gained the same upper hand as Western entrepreneurs; it was they who claimed authority not just over the Chinese economy, but more significantly, over Chinese culture and history. The Chinese themselves, like the hungry ghosts of abandoned ancestors, wandered over their own land, unable to take part in or alter its destiny. Der Ling, at least at first, tried to present a balanced picture of the feared and hated Cixi, perhaps bending the truth herself from time to time, but achieving what was the first intimate glimpse of the Empress Dowager and her court written by a woman of Cixi's own race. For this act alone, Der Ling merits the attention of scholars and ethnohistorians alike.

What many who discount Der Ling's perspective on Cixi fail to realize is that she is not the only source for evidence of the Empress Dowager's humanity. We have the unimpeachable diaries of Sarah Conger, wife of the American minister in Beijing and an acquaintance of Der Ling's and her mother's but very much an independent thinker who formed her own opinions. We have painter Katherine Carl's *With the Empress Dowager of China* (1905), the earliest first-hand English-language memoir, by a Western woman, of court life with Cixi. We also have the earnest and careful recollections of Dr. Headland, wife of Professor Isaac Taylor Headland, who for twenty years served as physician to the Empress Dowager. The problem, and the opportunity, for men like

Johnston, Bland, Backhouse and Morrison was that these accounts were written by females. Easy enough for them to look askance at the writings of an Asian woman — easier still to include all women's recollections of Cixi under the category of wishful thinking, and their own accounts of a woman these men had never met as the authoritative voice. As alluded to above, it did not hurt sales at the bookstore.

For all her efforts to disappear into oriental mists, like clouded mountains in a Chinese scroll painting, the facts for "Princess" Der Ling are the same as for any other mortal. She was born on June 8, 1885, in Beijing (as she claims in her memoirs, or in Tianjin, given as her birthplace in a ship's manifest from 1927), daughter of a Manchu official of non-Manchu origins and an Amerasian woman born in Western-dominated Shanghai. Der Ling married an American, Thaddeus Cohu White, in May 1907 in Shanghai, and with him had a son, Thaddeus Raymond White, who died tragically young — age twenty — of pneumonia in New York City. Der Ling herself died in Berkeley, on November 21, 1944, struck by a grocery van in a freak accident at the corner of Bancroft Way and Telegraph Avenue, while on her way to lecture in Chinese language on the campus of the University of California, Berkeley. She died that night, before midnight. She was fifty-nine years old, and was described in a *Time Magazine* obituary (directly above the obituary of another self-made woman and publicity seeker, would-be "opera singer" Florence Foster Jenkins) as the "first high-born Chinese woman to marry a foreigner." The mysterious glamor of her origins and the rule-breaking habits of her early life pursued her, as she undoubtedly planned, till the end.[1] The driver who killed her, one Lloyd James Chevalier, drove on, claiming when he was brought in a week later for the inquest that he had been unaware he had hit anyone. I have walked the intersection where the accident occurred, and while it remains a busy area, the heaviest traffic is that of students going to and from the south gate of U. C. Berkeley, which opens at the T of the Bancroft/Telegraph intersection. Standing there amid the rowdy high spirits of college students, I had to ponder whether this woman who had obsessively tried to place herself at the heart of crucial events of a century ago, in Europe and China, had not become a physical example of her brief, forgotten fame — as invisible in 1944 as her name and title had been ubiquitous on three continents two decades before.

Der Ling's husband, a shadowy figure at best, did not contest the judge's acquittal. A picture taken of the couple in 1935 seems to show a loving bond, but events after her death raise questions about what held this pair together. In his will, probated in 1953, White listed two warehouses of Chinese art objects, three hundred books, a house in Joshua Tree, California, and "the ashes of my wife, which are now stored in the Chapel of the Chimes" in Oakland. Nearly a decade after her death, Der Ling's mortal remains were still in storage, like her dust-gathering *objets d'art*. But these screens, tables, porcelains, scrolls, robes and ivories were at least in the same city as her husband. Der Ling was on the margins, in death as in life.[2]

Shadows cling to Der Ling, too, many of them accidentally or intentionally self-generated. With the exception of her first book, the refreshingly detached *Two Years in the Forbidden City*, Der Ling does herself no favors in her subsequent literary efforts. Much of the writing and reportage in Der Ling's remaining seven books and in her articles is artless, even shallow, when compared to the output of such Chinese-European women writers as Sui Sin Far or, later, Han Suyin, women who approached head-on their seesawing experiences of belonging to and yet being no real part of different worlds. Unlike Sarah Conger or Katherine Carl, who took pains to make their accounts of Cixi as serious as possible because they were aware that the Empress Dowager and her court were a source for bad press, Der Ling's writing grew increasingly sensationalist, to the point where she was running out of material and padding where truth ran thin.

She is accused of making things up, and perhaps she did; but one thing no one has ever called her on until now is the fact that she never once, despite repeated opportunities to do so, told the world about her own American ancestry. When she was living in Beijing in the 1920s, Der Ling was told by a foreign woman that she did not "look" Chinese. "You are almost as white as I am!" "Does one require a special face," Der Ling wrote, "with which to speak English?" Yet she never admitted that part of the "whiteness" so obvious in her features came from being less than 100 percent Asian. This descent through her mother from the Pierson family of Boston, Massachusetts, furnished an ideal starting point for Der Ling to explain some of her own "American" nature — her flapper attitude, her love of slang and the freedoms American women were the first to experience, even her amused recounting to breathless American reporters of her famous Thanksgiving turkey dinners (with the Chinese Kitchen God looking on from over the modern stove). Yet for reasons known only to her, she never mentioned her mother's Amerasian origins or how she dealt with the difficulties which are handled so eloquently by writers of her own day and after. Consider the confession of half-Belgian Han Suyin:

> It is rather frightening to be so many different people, with so many dissimilar and equally compelling emotions, affections, ideas, *élans*, apprehensions . . . always so aware of shades of meaning that life becomes occasionally unbearable.[3]

Strangely comfortable, even manipulative, with her ambiguity, Der Ling always seemed happier floating like Cixi in her Summer Palace pagoda boats, on the calm surface of that turbid lake of subdivided identity, refusing to belong to any world at all. Perhaps for this reason she also refused to pin herself down as an "Asian American," preferring the enigmatic, anachronistic identity of being "Manchu," with all the permutations of definition that implied. Unlike Cixi, however, who did not have to answer to anyone, as self-appointed historian of this most infamous ruler's court, Der Ling did bear the responsibility for answering the many questions her assertions raised. Her silences on matters crucial to our understanding of her own background cast doubt over her recollections of Cixi. Because where she withholds in one area, why should she not in others?

In the end, Der Ling became what she seems to have striven for — a European romantic, and as such hers was a romantic China, fueled by scroll paintings of misted mountains and serene temples, the China that had raised refinement of mind and setting to an art form. It was not the gritty China of her childhood, with its institutionalized graft, its suppression of women and bilking of peasantry, its state-sponsored racial segregation and its willful reluctance to learn how to survive in a contemporary world, surrounded by the red-fanged tigers of foreign commercial interests. She openly deplored China's ugly realities and declared herself all for changing and improving them, but ultimately she preferred living in China's dream. She had lived for less than the two years of her most famous book's title at the very heart of its dream, which was also the heart of the Empress Dowager's mystique: the Summer Palace and the Forbidden City, where a talented but paranoid woman had seized power from feckless men and held it tightly in her long-nailed hands; where a court, its personnel and its rituals moved in ineluctable orbit around her dragon throne as planets skirting the sun. Perhaps, as she crossed the street that November day in 1944, thirty-nine years after she had left that dream-world for good, it was to that world that Der Ling was casting her mind, comparing pleasant, bland Berkeley with the violence and beauty of crimson-walled, golden-roofed Beijing, comparing her peripatetic life to that of friends and family who had remained behind. Perhaps, indeed, much of her was already absent from the present. Like the Ming dynasty poet Ming-Y, in Lafcadio Hearn's romantic ghost story, who wandered back in time during an afternoon stroll into the life and the love of a Tang dynasty courtesan, Der Ling had been checking out of reality for years — it might not have taken much for a truck driver to run her down as if she were not even there.

However unstable, unreliable, self-dramatizing and certainly self-aggrandizing, the personality and legacy that emerged from my study convinced me that Der Ling was a unique twentieth century woman, as gifted as she was flawed. In this biography I have made every effort to let her speak in her own voice. As in the days when she was the toast of the New York publishing world and smiling back at readers of the *New York Times* from the society columns, it is up to the reader to judge of her. As she said herself, "Each writer has his own China." However much Der Ling wanted others to believe what she told them, it is in dialogue with her own uncertain identity that she fascinates us with a journey far more colorful than any trip she took by land or sea, and a personality at least as intriguing as that of her hero, the Empress Dowager of China.

Grant Hayter-Menzies
Sidney, BC

Acknowledgements

In the several years of research needed to write Der Ling's life, I leaned on some people more heavily than on others. Of immense help to me was the convening at Dartmouth College, in May 2005, of a discussion seminar around the manuscript of this book. Prof. Pamela Kyle Crossley brought together Prof. Laurence Davies (now at the University of Glasgow) and Prof. Roland L. Higgins to read and ponder my effort to explore and understand the several different lives of the woman known variously as The Princess Der Ling, Mrs. Thaddeus C. White, and Elizabeth Antoinette Yu. If I have succeeded in making the phenomenon that was Princess Der Ling flicker even briefly to life, it is due to the searching questions and supportive commentary of these people — of Prof. Crossley in particular: since my first communication with her in course of my research, she has devoted hours of her time and her scholarship to educating me in the Manchu context Der Ling claimed for her own, as well as in seeking out the many facets of this complicated woman who had as many faces as she did names.

I would be remiss indeed if I did not also thank the following friends and colleagues (a by-no-means-complete list) for their unflagging support and enthusiasm when my own quest for the real Der Ling (an impossible task to set oneself) would have wearied and defeated lesser beings:

The late Rosario Aglioloro, executive director of the Northwest China Council in Portland, Oregon; John Bonath; David and Victoria Bouchard; Dr. Dennis Cunniff; Dr. Colin Day, Hong Kong University Press; Dr. Shiou-yun Fang; Robert Hall; Les Hayter; Clara Ho; Christopher Ives; Peter Kurth; Prof. Luke S. K. Kwong, University of Lethbridge; William Luce; Emily McPhail; Stephen Markbreiter; Scott Menzies; Sean William Menzies; Noreen O'Rinn; Alexey Panchenko; Michael James Redmond; Sterling and Peggy Seagrave; Eddie Song; Barry Till, Art Gallery of Greater Victoria; Mark Trawka; Kuo-chiu Tsai; Hubert Vos; Prof. Stephen Wadley, Portland State University; Prof. Juwen Zhang, Willamette University; and Willow Zheng, Northwest China Council, Portland, Oregon.

And though they have gone to the Yellow Springs nearly three decades, I must not fail to acknowledge my grandparents, John and Gertrude Menzies. These Western Europeans transmitted to their American grandson their respect and admiration for past times and ancient peoples. I like to think they knew, when they showed me walls built by nineteenth-century Chinese laborers, which still snake elegantly across fields in central California, and listened patiently to my excited theories about the Chinese coins I occasionally unearthed in my garden, that what they loved, I would love, too.

PART I

At heart, I was a foreigner.

— Princess Der Ling

1
"The marriage, I believe, was a *love* affair . . ."

In 1885, when the future Princess Der Ling was born, the Chinese empire was like a once-priceless blue and white vase — repeatedly fractured and repaired, it now tottered, as on an unsteady curio shelf, on the verge of radical reform. The Guangxu Emperor, aged fourteen, had been nominal emperor of China since the age of ten. He and China were governed by his aunt the Empress Dowager Cixi, a vigorous, intelligent, shrewd and luxury-loving woman of fifty who had started as a low-ranking concubine of the Xianfeng Emperor and ended as Empress Dowager. Her love-hate relationship with the West and with Westerners had not yet born full fruit but would do so during Der Ling's girlhood, imprinting her personality — rumoured and real — on the child's eager mind.

The power and splendor of Cixi's world and that of the Qing dynasty, so fascinating to Der Ling when viewed from afar, did not bear close inspection — it was merely the rich veneer covering more than a century of political and societal disintegration. And while a part of this disappearing old world, Der Ling's family was also instrumental in its dissolution. In fact, her parents were a case study in the modern changes creeping over Chinese society — her father, Yu Keng, was a Manchu, of the minority ruling class that had governed China since the seventeenth century; her mother, born Louisa Pierson in Shanghai, was a Chinese-American woman of mysterious antecedents. In this way and many others, theirs was a home that would serve as a model of how to live for a woman who would one day be famed, and defamed, for her own breaking of what few shards remained of the old Chinese ways.

In nineteenth-century China, a Manchu official like Yu Keng did not so blithely abrogate the rules of strictly stratified, overtly racist Qing society by marrying not just out of his proper class but out of his own ethnicity, without repercussions, even if the latter were restricted to tea-house gossip. Miscegenation in Qing China was regulated with the same vigor as the Manchu directive against Han Chinese foot binding, an ancient practice which Manchu rulers held to be abhorrent in the extreme. But Yu Keng had chosen a very different path from most of his peers, as his daughter Der Ling would do after him: he had chosen a spouse who was not paternally Chinese, but the daughter of a Boston-born American merchant based in Shanghai. In marrying Miss Pierson, who was not just what conservative Chinese termed a "foreign devil," but also that worse thing, a half-caste Chinese, Yu Keng proclaimed himself a new kind of man — the very opposite of what made a man's fortune, or protected what fortune he had, in Qing China. Yet for all his radical ways, Yu Keng enjoyed the sort of immunity that made him an object of curiosity and envy, as his daughter was to be at Cixi's court a generation later.

Ulster-born Sir Robert Hart, Inspector General of Customs in Beijing, had a word to say about Yu Keng's marriage to the pretty, petite, foreign-featured Louisa. "Mrs. Yü is the Eurasian daughter of a small American storekeeper who used to be at S'[hang]hai," he wrote to his associate Campbell in England, "and as far as *Yü* was concerned, the marriage, I believe, was a *love* affair."[1] Yu Keng's marriage had indeed broken that other stiff rule of Chinese life: he had chosen his wife for reasons of affection rather than family or property. (Unlike many upper-class Chinese males, he seems never to have taken a secondary wife or mistress.) Not that Sir Robert had not done much the same thing as Yu Keng, but marriage was never part of his plan. Prior to wedding prim

Hester Bredon, Hart had kept for years a Chinese mistress named Ayaou, by whom he had three children who, like Louisa Pierson, bore their father's surname. But Hart evidently held his position in both British and Chinese society to be far more valuable than the children of a faithful woman. All three were sent to England for education and safe distance after their mother's early death. Having assured that they were provided for, Hart never laid eyes on them again.

Perhaps Hart's own well-kept secrets, which moved him in his elderly years to expunge great tracts of his diaries, kept him on the *qui vive* for the sort of hearsay that made him write of Yu Keng: "The Yü Keng family are not thought well of anywhere, but the old man himself has powerful backing — I don't know why."[2] As Hart's comment indicates, Yu Keng was not immune to the calumny that sifted through Beijing like dust from the Gobi Desert, and it may have been his own vaguely unsettled origins that formed the source of this. In *Kow Tow*, her memoir of her early childhood, Der Ling describes her father as a Manchu noble, a high-ranking bannerman of the prestigious Manchu Plain White Banner corps — one of only three corps, with the Plain and Bordered Yellow, which answered to the emperor himself as his personal property. She goes on to claim for herself, through him, descent from the Aisin-Gioro, the Manchu clan which burst into northern China in 1644 and founded China's last dynasty. She was even to one day sign a copy of one of her books with the imperial-sounding moniker "Der Ling of the Manchu Dynasty," an absurdity not likely to register suspicion on the part of the royalty-mad American public which gave her most of her renown.

Der Ling records a girlhood discussion she had with her father, when Yu Keng pointed out to her that though he was a Manchu "Lord" by birth, the statesman Li Hongzhang, as a mere conferred marquis, a Chinese and scion of petty provincial gentry, was much more powerful. (If this is a sample of the kind of thing Yu Keng regularly told his daughter, it is no wonder she developed the habit of self-aggrandizement which was to cost her so dearly in the future.) "My rank is hereditary," Der Ling was told, "and I do not use it to advance myself. I am a Manchu. He is Chinese, and his title is bestowed upon him . . ." Yu Keng and Li differed in another important way, too: both were avid for reform, but Li was much more of a nationalist than he. "I am more like a foreigner," admitted Yu Keng, echoing what would become his daughter's proud motto in later years.[3]

Even as Der Ling was more "foreigner" than she ever publicly admitted, her father was less "Manchu" than stated in all her published writings, and his claim to any sort of title scarcely more durable than her own. A record from the *Chronological Tables of the Newly Established Offices of the Qing Period*, listing all bannermen of high rank, places Yu Keng not in the Manchu but in the *Chinese Martial* Plain White Banner.[4] The distinction is no less significant for being a matter of terminology rather than ethnicity: from the beginning, the term "Manchu" was always more an administrative designation than a racial one — or, more properly, a designation of caste. There were Manchus who were of Jurchen or Mongolian ancestry, whose roaming ancestors had settled in the area northeast of Beijing, which came to be called Manchuria, and who came south with the conquering armies in 1644. But there were also Chinese subjects woven of a variety of ethnic threads — provincial officials and military operatives of the failing Ming government, exiled scholars, colonists, adventurers — who had lived in northern China for generations. Many of these people joined the Manchus on their journey southward or after their triumph, and though they came under the term *hanjun* (which Dartmouth College historian Pamela Kyle Crossley translates as "Chinese-martial"), as opposed to non-banner Chinese, called *hanren*, they in time were considered and considered themselves bannermen on a par with the Manchu banners.[5]

There is nothing untruthful *per se* in Der Ling declaring herself Manchu: all Manchus were *qiren* or bannermen by affiliation; and *hanjun* were held to as strict a code of non-exogamy as Manchus and Mongolians, making them part of the same exclusive group. But banner membership was hereditary, and Yu Keng was a member of the Chinese Martial Plain White Banner. "The 'Han-chun' were a separate cultural group," says Crossley, "that has got mangled in our modern terminology of race and ethnicity." A member of the "Chinese banners" need not necessarily be Chinese, and "nobody would willingly identify himself as a 'Chinese bannerman' in the late nineteenth or early twentieth centuries," Crossley continues. The stigma that still attached to *hanjun* as Han who "treacherously" served the Manchus still obtained in Yu Keng's lifetime and in the wrong company could prove dangerous to life and limb. "Since they could only choose between 'Manchu' (meaning bannerman) and 'Chinese' (meaning civilian), Manchu was in fact the more accurate." For Der Ling to attempt to explain all this to foreigners was expecting too much even of the self-styled ambassadress of all things Chinese — it is possible that Yu Keng had as many Manchu ancestors as anyone with the legal right to call himself Manchu. And as Crossley also points out, it likely served Der Ling, her sister and family to play to the foreign romanticization of the Manchus. More suspicious is Yu Keng's claim that he was descended from the Aisin-Gioro, the Manchu clan from which came the Qing, the last imperial dynasty of China. His daughter is our informant on this, and to give her the benefit of the doubt it is possible that Der Ling, who was only twenty when her father died in 1905, misheard or misunderstood his account of the family history, which may have been as full of exaggeration as her own memories of her past would be. (Her erroneous belief that Chinese titles were hereditary was probably a result of her European education.) Perhaps the descent was genuine and came by way of a distant Aisin-Gioro ancestress. Marriages did take place between high-ranking Aisin-Gioro and *hanjun*. It is possible that after the family's Beijing house burnt during the Boxer Uprising in 1900, Der Ling was functioning only on memories of what she had glimpsed among some old papers — genealogies leading to greatness being something that would interest her.[6]

Yu Keng's name and rank pose a greater mystery. Der Ling describes his surname as "Yü," but the character "yu" used in Yu Keng's name is not the one normally found in a Chinese surname. Maybe it was a rare usage or a Chinese transliteration of an adopted Manchu name. The name could also be, as Der Ling seems to suggest, Yu Keng's surname and personal name — the practice was to retain both surname and personal name when the latter contained one syllable. But assuming that "Yu Keng" was just the double-barreled form commonly used among Manchus, combining two given names without the clan name, still does not tie up the loose ends.

Further confusing matters, Der Ling claims for her father the title of "duke" (*kong*), a hereditary rank for which *hanjun* bannermen like Yu Keng were not eligible. (Nor is there any evidence on record that Yu Keng was granted such a title.) According to another family tradition relayed by Der Ling's niece, this title was connected to the province (or prefecture) of Xuzhou, north of Nanjing, which she claims was given by descendants of Nurhachi to Yu Keng's ancestor for taking part in the 1644 invasion. But there is no conclusive proof for this story, either. In China there was no European-style hereditary nobility. Under Han or Manchu, China was more of a meritocracy than anything else, where even a peasant's bright son could take the state examinations and rise to become a power in the land. In any case, *kong* was a title inherited by the male descendants of a *beitzu*, or prince of the fourth, most junior class, who in turn was downgraded from his father's rank of *beile* or prince of the third class, who would have been a prince of the first or second class and son or grandson of a reigning Manchu emperor. Despite his daughter's best efforts to place him always cosily connected to central figures of power, and hinting at special rank and privileges he enjoyed, Der Ling leaves us with no more clarity about who Yu Keng really was than she does the details of why the Qianlong Emperor, one of the greatest of the Qing dynasty's rulers, would have given Der Ling's ancestors the gifts later listed as such among her *objets d'art* auctioned after her death. With Der Ling and, perhaps, her father, all that mattered was one's assertion of rank — never mind the evidence for it. After all, the Empress Dowager Cixi would one day tell Der Ling that because of the Manchu court clothing she had given her, she "had become Manchu once more." Perhaps it was indeed a case of clothes making the Manchu.[7]

Pamela Kyle Crossley's work on the ambivalence of Manchu and Chinese Martial identity and their interconnectedness shows how possible it was for a *hanjun* family to consider itself Manchu, even to petition to be registered as Manchu, once the designation gained in political weight and a certain glamor in the late eighteenth and early nineteenth centuries. Der Ling's emphasis on her Manchu roots in the years after the 1911 revolution (during which many Manchus were killed because of their origins) was clearly a reflection of this glamor, perhaps even a flirtation with the sort of danger she confessed she found exciting. Whoever or whatever he was, where the details can be confirmed one thing is clear: there was something different about Der Ling's father, whether as private citizen or as Qing official, a difference Yu Keng seems to have exploited whenever possible. From the beginning, when he fought alongside and was befriended by the progressive Yixin, Prince Gong, half-brother of the Xianfeng Emperor, in the Second Opium War of 1860, Yu Keng allied himself with important Westward-leaning personages, with Viceroy Li Hongzhang forming the most influential jewel in this crown of alliances. He was probably educated in one of the banner schools (and likely picked up English and baptism from missionaries), which though founded to ensure that all upper-rank bannermen had at least the rudiments of the Manchu language, came by Yu Keng's time to serve as a forcing shed for future members of the Chinese foreign diplomatic corps. Yu Keng's obvious, possibly deliberate courting of Westernizers and Westerners and the controversy that accompanied them and such overtures in China became not an object of concern or shame to his daughter, but a desideratum to aspire to. If anything, it was her "Manchu" father and not her half-American mother whom Der Ling sought most to emulate.[8]

None of Der Ling's books includes a portrait of this man she considered the most important influence on her life. Other than a photograph of a courtly Chinese official who may or may not be Yu Keng, taken by Charles Chusseau-Flaviens, the globe-trotting French photographer who took many pictures of Der Ling, her sister, her brothers and legation staff, in which the elegantly robed middle-aged sitter poses comfortably at a desk in what appears to be the Chinese legation in Paris, we have only Der Ling's words to go by. "My father was a big man," she wrote, "with shoulders broad enough to bear the burdens of many who needed his help," as well as to carry the six-year-old Der Ling on occasion, "one arm encircling Father's head, dragging his cap askew," that cap on which she remembered the ruby button of a mandarin of the first class gleaming. He had a good sense of humor, "always given to belittling even the biggest trouble." He wore a beard "and an uneven moustache, below a strong nose flanked by piercing, wise eyes."[9]

From Der Ling's earliest childhood till her young womanhood, Yu Keng and his wisdom permeate nearly every page. Her memoir *Kow Tow* opens in summer 1891, with her father described first among the family seated at the breakfast table (enjoying a foreign-style morning meal). Der Ling amusedly focuses on his forbearance of her chatter, a trait which was to protect her, while her father was alive, from the criticism drawn by her "unfeminine," "un-Chinese" energy and initiative. Der Ling also establishes from the start just how novel her father was for his insistence that she and her sister Rong Ling apply themselves to all the same studies that their two older brothers were engaged in, even to sharing the same tutor. According to the Book of Rites [*Li ji*], after the age of five boys and girls, even brothers and sisters, were never to "sit together or share a meal" — one of many Confucian rules broken in Yu Keng's household. Clearly, Yu Keng would have scoffed at the Ming era dictum: "Woman without talent is indeed a virtue."[10]

Der Ling claims that as a small child she had been literally exposed to a whole new world outside China, about which few Chinese adults could say they knew much more than hearsay, when the family had spent time in France. This would have been before Yu Keng was posted to the Yangzi River town of Shashi to become inspector of the *likin* tax system, some time in the early 1890s. Why Yu Keng would have been sent to France is not explained, either by Der Ling or the known history of Chinese diplomacy in Europe; he is not, for example, listed among Chinese diplomatic staff in any *Almanachs de Gotha* prior to his appointment to the Chinese Legation in Paris in 1900. Der Ling did learn French, however, whether through living in France, from her mother, or from one of the missionary teachers the children had. Again we see Yu Keng's effort to set his children outside the pale of ordinary Chinese childhood expectations, not to mention ordinary Chinese childhood experience. It was an uneasy situation for all concerned, but per Der Ling Yu Keng was a remarkably tolerant and understanding Chinese father. Where Der Ling recalls her mother as a "stickler for the proper 'form'" (a character-trait often noted in Eurasians, who among both Asians and Westerners were held as being outside polite society), she constantly reports how Yu Keng would amusedly intercede for his eldest daughter, even when she was at her brattiest — which, according to Der Ling (and which we have no trouble imagining), was often.

Yu Keng also provided for her and her siblings beautiful surroundings in which to grow up, perhaps a part of that sense of aristocratic entitlement, that striving for the finer things of life, inherited by his daughter. In provincial Shashi, where the streets were "inexcusably rough, almost impassable . . .", remembered Der Ling, Yu Keng's family lived in relative splendor. Their house boasted a walled garden swaying with willow trees, stocked with statuary of animals natural and mythological, a rockery studded with "scholar's stones," on which Confucian aphorisms were carved in the style of various famous calligraphers, and intricately paved paths meandering beside a pond full of goldfish, on which a little boat always floated.

The worst punishment Yu Keng ever imposed on her, Der Ling remembered, after she had quarreled with her strict nanny Hung-fang, or refused to pay attention to her uninspiring tutor of Chinese classics (whose name, when translated into English, came out frighteningly as "skin them alive"), was to banish her to this garden. She usually used the opportunity get into even more trouble, climbing trees just at the moment when silk-robed dignitaries arrived to confer with Yu Keng, or tumbling into the shallow pond and being fished out by her laughing father. Even when she once shattered what she remembered being a priceless Song dynasty fishbowl during an argument with Hung-fang, Der Ling was not whipped — the very least any other child could expect under the circumstances. Instead, she was taken on her father's knee and patiently given an explanation of why the bowl was priceless, why what is priceless deserves to be honored and protected whatever the mood of the moment. Having seen the destruction caused by the Taiping Rebellion and the Opium Wars, Yu Keng knew well of what he spoke. It was advice which Der Ling would increasingly come to treasure, and which would one day to help her understand some of the more puzzling traits of the Empress Dowager Cixi.

"There had been a bond of love between father and daughter that both knew," Der Ling wrote later, "something as deep as parental love mingled with that different kind of love which the American word 'pal' evokes in the minds of folk who are pals, and have them." Yu Keng was, Der Ling recalled, "kindness and understanding personified." This kindness and understanding was directed not just to his daughter but to everyone, Der Ling insists. This and what we may assume was a powerful charm and an ability to stick close to those in power would stand Yu Keng in good stead when, in later years, denunciations from the radical right surrounding the Empress Dowager rained down on his head, and Cixi consistently refused to give credit to charges filed against such a loyal official. Yu Keng, after all, had named his favorite child with the character for "virtue." This would be a quality which Der Ling would struggle to live up to in years to come.[11]

The West-leaning atmosphere of Yu Keng's household extended to allowing a good deal more permissiveness to the children than was usually the case during the late nineteenth century. As a result, Yu Keng's offspring must have been a handful. Sir Robert Hart met them in 1899, just before Yu Keng was posted to France, when the girls were approaching their teens and the boys were well into them, and described them as "a noisy family of English-speaking children."[12] By Der Ling's own account, she and her siblings even tried their father's patience during official receptions, hiding behind the carved teakwood screens in the Shashi *yamen*'s audience hall and giggling at the often histrionic personal characteristics of waiting provincial magistrates, much the way English children in pinafores and sailor suits might have done toward the native sari-wrapped and turbaned guests arriving at some hill-station in Raj India.

What Der Ling loved most about hiding behind the screens was the chance it gave her of seeing her father in official kit. A handsome man no matter what he wore, according to Der Ling, Yu Keng's natural dignity was enhanced by the ceremonial splendors of formal Chinese court clothes. Yu Keng would enter the hall where his guest sat awaiting him, wearing a long red gown, over which he wore a plum-colored coat, its "horse-hoof" cuffs covering his hands, its breast emblazoned with the *buzi* or breast badge of official rank. As Der Ling remembered it, Yu Keng's badge featured a stork embroidered in gold and silver (designating him a first-class civil official). His black satin boots were stuffed into blue silk trousers, his necklace of 108 amber mandarin beads, emulating the Lamaist Buddhist rosary, swung from his neck, and on his head he wore his peacock-plumed hat with its bright ruby button. This ensemble, Der

Ling remembered, made her father look "even larger, broader shouldered, more dignified and commanding than he really was." It was an early sign of Der Ling's most deeply held trait: her love for the lovely outward appurtenances of old China, which was as strong as her distaste for its less attractive realities.[13]

She encountered one of these realities very young, and her reaction to it as a little girl was no different from what it would be in her early twenties, when she would have to face down the Empress Dowager instead of a meddling household servant. Though under ten and still playing with her dolls — foreign-made ones that caused her slave girl Hung-fang to snort in disgust — Der Ling found herself one afternoon being considered for possible wifehood.

Per memoirs left by Chinese and Westerners alike, it would appear servants in old China comprised a sort of subterranean government. Old amahs, ancient cooks or menservants, who had been with a family through two or three generations, tending successive waves of children and wives, emptying chamber pots and brewing health tonics, would sometimes take it upon themselves to effect all sorts of events more properly the preserve of the family itself. Marriage and descendants being of utmost significance in Confucian society — for who would sweep the master's grave if there were no descendants, and might a servant not be blamed and pursued by an angry master's hungry ghost for not having taken the initiative when it arose? — old family retainers might take that initiative in plotting alliances between their master's children and those of the respectable family on the other side of the garden wall. This might achieve positive results that the family itself might not have been able to obtain, and might equally achieve results that the most comic of Beijing opera plots could not do justice to.

In Der Ling's case, when her amah was sounded out by the servants of a neighboring magistrate as a possible future wife for the magistrate's little son, the old woman hissed a refusal. Her master, Yu Keng, was a mandarin of the first rank, a far cry from the magistrate's petty status. "The child of your master will not do!" she cackled. Perhaps having expected this response, the little boy's amah, a Han Chinese tottering on bound feet, had ammunition up her sleeve. As if Der Ling were not standing a few feet away, the amah turned the tables, acerbically adding up all the reasons why Yu Keng's daughter would not be a fitting mate for her honorable master's son. Not only was the girl's father an alien Manchu (pronounced, remembered Der Ling, as if she were saying the word "devil"), and not of the good Chinese family of her master the magistrate, but she had also heard that Der Ling and her siblings were being brought up to learn "foreign devil" ways. "She doesn't act like a Chinese girl at all," scoffed the amah. "She is forward, laughs immoderately, even at her guests." And the worst of it? "She has big feet!" (Manchu girls never had their feet bound.)

To the young Der Ling, all of this was more amusing than frightening, because she already knew that her father had other plans for her than those that could be expected by the typical Chinese girl. "While he was intensely patriotic," wrote Yu Keng's daughter, "he did not believe in arranged marriages, in which the love of the two individuals most concerned was not considered." Sir Robert Hart had, after all, described Yu Keng's own marriage to Louisa as a well-known "love-match"; his especial notice of the fact shows how uncommon it was in Chinese society. "And he believed that women should be educated," Der Ling recalled, "at least his girl-children." This was very different from the beliefs held by conservative Chinese males, and went far toward helping Der Ling believe that she did indeed have a destiny before her that was completely different from that of most other Chinese girls.[14]

2
Culture clash

Growing up in an unusual household in remote Shashi seems to have given Yu Keng's children a sense of perpetually being on stage. Yet while they were encouraged to feel proud of their uniqueness, the sisters and their brothers were also highly protected — in their classroom, in the walled garden, and by their parents, from too close contact with the things and people whose homogeneousness was most apt to point up the children's differences, those traits that Yu Keng intended to nurture.

Yu Keng's protectiveness included keeping his children apart from the turmoils big and little that ranged across the countryside as famine brought on uprisings, and uprisings official retaliation, and all was kept simmering by the universal Chinese irritation under the "improving" efforts of foreign missionaries and merchants, whose activities were not often distinct from one another. But in summer 1891, the reality of Yu Keng's heavy responsibilities, and the reality of his determination to carry them out even beyond the call of duty, was brought home to the family's walled compound, when Methodist missionaries at Wuxi, a river town several days' journey east down the Yangzi, were attacked and murdered by anti-foreign, anti-Christian rioters. What was worse, in the eyes of horrified foreigners, who suspected the Chinese capable of every demonic torment, was that the rebels took several of the foreign missionaries hostage and refused to give them up or to parley.

Hearing of the violence, Sir Robert Hart blamed it on the *Ko-lao-hui* or "Society of Brothers and Elders," a secret insurrectionary organization with an anti-missionary (and anti-Manchu) program, which had been armed through the rabble-rousing services of Charles Welsh Mason, a British subject and ex-employee of Customs at Zhenjiang. Hart believed the uprising to be "incipient rebellion rather than hostility to either foreigners or Christianity," but the fact that those killed and held hostage comprised people answering to both descriptions shows he was not aware of all the facts (or chose to ignore them). For reasons which have never been completely clarified, Mason sought the overthrow of the Qing government and joined the *Ko-lao-hui* to that end, recruiting Chinese and purchasing arms and ammunition for the organization. The rebellion, which flared not just in Wuxi but also in Wuhu and other Yangzi River towns, was eventually put down by the foreign-friendly Governor-General of Jiangxi, Liu Kunyi; he would later prove his nerve further during the Boxer troubles of 1900 by sealing off southern China from the violent uprisings which, finding no purchase there, moved north to tear Beijing to pieces. Following Liu's quashing of the Yangzi valley uprising, Mason was arrested later that fall and put on trial. Sir Robert Hart would liken the "thousand hostilities [the uprising and its aftermath] has set in motion" to "Mrs. Shelley's Frankenstein," that creature built up out of the remnants of the dead. Even Frankenstein was vanquished in the end, but Hart obviously had fears that where this uprising had failed, others would rise from more fertile soil in the near future.[1]

Soon after the Wuxi news broke, the house was filled with visitors who crowded into Yu Keng's office, all eager to discuss the uprising and trade various strengths of hearsay and condemnation, mostly of the foreign victims — according to Der Ling, Yu Keng's talent as mediator was known to everyone and his opinion on so critical a situation was valued even by those who disagreed with him. Der Ling remembered how she escaped from Hung-fang's grip and slipped into her father's office, with its stiff blackwood chairs and tables, where Yu Keng stood surrounded by chattering Shashi officials. Viceroy Zhang Zhidong, Yu

Keng's superior, obviously also held his *likin* inspector's mediating abilities in high esteem, because as Der Ling overheard, the viceroy asked her father to go to Wuxi and negotiate with the rioters. Yu Keng's agreement to do so had raised objections from everyone in town. Der Ling's account is so vivid that we can envision her head, its pig-tails tied with red yarn, pivoting from robed figure to robed figure, trying to hear everything that was being shouted. Why should Yu Keng risk his own life to save those of some foreign devils, the men demanded, foreigners who moreover had no business to be in China? Why should he, the father of a family, a respected official, risk his life (and, most importantly, face) by helping such people? After all, in China it was accepted that no married man with children would ever be blamed for not diving into a river or lake to rescue someone else's drowning child.

So went the chorus of advice from the men who stood between Der Ling and her father. "They will not harm me," Yu Keng insisted. "I am going. It is my duty!" He probably enjoyed the controversy as much as he did taking on the responsibility for rescuing the foreigners.

As a girl child in a proper Chinese home, Der Ling should have been secreted away in the women's quarters on the edge of some far courtyard, far from the important affairs of grown men. But at the sound of her father's voice, she pushed through the crowd and ran to where he stood, and demanded to know why he must go away. "You are too young to understand it," Yu Keng told her. He might just as well have said the same to the adults who were crowded into his study. Though they were part of the fabric of ancient China, a civilization that made the rest of the civilized world seem still in infancy, yet these men were treating a situation which encapsulated all that had always been wrong between East and West — the refusal to interfere, to sully one's self by touching anything foreign — in the same unthinking, hotly emotional way a teenager might handle a matter requiring solemn judgment. Yu Keng's concern for the foreigners at Wuxi must have been activated not only by common human care for his fellow man, but also as a step toward proving what would be a hard and fast principle in all his acts as an official of the Qing government: that the only way to promote harmony with the outside world which had been beating down China's doors for centuries, and to demystify it in the process, was to treat all people and their various religions as equal, to show that it took more courage to cooperate with and try to understand the foreigners in China than it did to hide behind xenophobia and superstition. Seeing her father calmly explaining his position to the frowning men in his study, Der Ling had an object lesson — one she would have to turn to her own uses in the very near future — in how not just to endure being different but how to turn it to constructive ends.

As he left the house that day to embark on the steamer waiting for him at the Yangzi docks, Yu Keng did not prevent his daughter from riding with him in his ornate tassel-hung sedan chair. Der Ling remembered sitting on her father's lap while he diverted her with dramatic explanations of the scenery passing by the sedan chair's windows: the dike embankments around Shashi and how they kept the town safe for its citizens from the encroaching floods of the Yangzi, of why his sedan chair was covered with green broadcloth, and laughingly explaining why it was unlucky for it to pass beneath a woman's trousers. (Servants accompanying an official's sedan chair frequently used bamboo poles to knock down laundry hanging over the twisting thoroughfares because a man who passed beneath women's pants was believed to have unsexed himself, a sad commentary on the status of women in Qing China.) The one thing they did not talk about were the dead and imprisoned missionaries at Wuxi, that awful place where Yu Keng would soon be. Der Ling tried to be brave, but after she had watched the steamer take her father away she cried all the way home in the jolting sedan chair. Only later in life, when she knew all the facts of what Yu Keng proposed to do for the missionaries — blowing his own horn, at least publicly, was not a Yu Keng trait — did Der Ling discover that his efforts at Wuxi had resulted in the rescue of all the hostages held by the rioters, including a group of Swedes, for which he received a decoration from Swedish King Oscar II.

His involvement with the Wuxi incident would not be Yu Keng's last public bucking of both popular sentiment and received custom. But at least it did not prevent him from being offered a promotion by the imperial court, according to Der Ling, a job change which took the family from Shashi's narrow, laundry-hung streets to the larger town of Wuchang, across the Yangzi River from Hankou: as Treasurer of Hubei province. He left Shashi garlanded with what Der Ling was told was the highest honor the municipality was able to bestow — the so-called "Ten Thousand Men" umbrellas, a pair of which, fringed in multicolored silk ribbons printed with the names of ten thousand men, was presented to the outgoing Inspector of Likin and mediator of Wuxi.

Before even reaching his new post, Yu Keng had decided that because his *yamen* residence was located in Wuchang, Louisa and the children would reside across the river, in Hankou, where it would be easier for the children to study with the Englishwoman who had been engaged to teach them. Yu Keng would come to visit them twice each day, crossing the Yangzi in his official vessel. Though the arrangement made sense to the family, it did not do so to local officialdom, for whom it was shocking that a husband and father should not have his family living with him at his *yamen*. It was bad enough that Yu Keng's sons were left without the constant discipline of their father, but for the two daughters to be left under the supervision of only their mother seemed careless and even dangerous. Making things worse, the residence Yu Keng chose for his family in Hankou turned out to be a Western-style house, located in the foreign settlement. If Yu Keng was blamed for abdicating his traditional role as head of the family, Louisa was looked at as something even worse: a disobedient wife. It could not have failed to negatively impress certain of the other Wuchang officials' wives when it became known that Louisa was unwilling to live in the "cold and cheerless" *yamen* residence, preferring the Hankou house for its comfort and convenience — a sure mark of the foreignized Chinese woman. Given the fact that a proper Chinese lady was supposed to put her husband first, this reversal of roles, achieved with Yu Keng's blessing, would have also sat ill with Wuchang's conservative male society.

The family's progress from Shashi to Wuchang seems to have taken place in royal style. According to Der Ling, the trip required a total of eight boats. First there was a houseboat for the family, with sleeping and living quarters, "all the conveniences except bathrooms," which Der Ling might have added were not usually available even in most luxurious

Chinese houses. Then another houseboat carried Yu Keng's secretary and his family and retainers, while another provided transport for the family's many servants. A flatboat held the family's sedan chairs, and then came what Der Ling smilingly refers to as a "flotilla" of gunboats, meant to ward off attackers but far more useful for the maintenance of "face" so important in old China. Der Ling found it particularly amusing that instead of preceding her father's boat, all four remained just behind it. Each gunboat flew a white flag Der Ling describes as bearing the characters representing Yu Keng's rank and his name (she clearly states that "Yu" was his family name), and on the decking of each stood drums that were beaten five times each day, finishing off at nine in the evening, at which time the guns were also let off. And every boat in the little fleet was punted up the canal by several coolies armed with thin but thickly ribbed bamboo poles, digging into the muddy bottom to drag the boats forward, then running back along the decks to get in line again. This smooth, slow ride gave those aboard plenty of time to enjoy the scenery, which was breaking into spring.

Inquisitive as ever, Der Ling watched the honors paid to her father during the journey and could not help but notice that he always sent instructions ahead that no one was to kowtow to him. Unlike her father, "who never ceased to be amused, and at times bored, over all the attention that was paid him," Der Ling had an early love of ceremonial splendor that remained with her the rest of her life, and enjoyed watching and participating in what her father referred to as "the fuss and the feathers." Yu Keng responded to his daughter's query with a smile and a secret: he did not ask visitors to kowtow to him because this action required a response from him in kind, "and it is a very distinct effort," said Yu Keng, who was far past middle age (and, according to Sir Robert Hart, had trouble with his eyesight and hearing, a factor which could have made the harmless kowtow a flirtation with physical injury). "And besides," he added, "it's rather a silly custom, anyway, don't you think?" — another version of a remark Isadora Duncan would make to Der Ling years later.[2]

Had Der Ling only been old enough to realize it, her father's amused indifference to time-honored Chinese ceremonial, as funny as it seemed to her in childhood, should have given her pause, since the matters he held so lightly were taken by Chinese officialdom with all the seriousness of religious ritual. Omitting to follow any of the customs validated since time immemorial, as showing honor to the gods, one's emperor and the ancestors to whom one was indebted for existence, was to place one's own honor in a questionable light — a risk not without danger in a society that made a cult out of the hypocrisy of "face," another Chinese custom Yu Keng regarded with a Westerner's smiling rationality (or, to the Chinese witnessing it, blatant lack of respect).

True to form, Der Ling spent no concerned thought on this boring topic of whether one kowtowed or not. Instead, she gave everyone a fright by jumping from the family houseboat to the deck of the gunboat, where her father stood chatting with the crew. Between the boats lay a "chasm with yellow water," but she knew no fear: "I thought and acted at the same time." It was an early example, one of many, of her intense need to be at the center of any situation that seemed to her crucial or exciting. Der Ling remembered how, after her leap, she came running to Yu Keng, laughing, and how the crew sucked in their breath, registering to a man just what very bad luck it was for a female to come aboard a gunboat. (And probably their relief that the girl had not fallen into the river.) Yu Keng took the child to him and assured the captain that while it was true that the presence of most females aboard his male-only vessel might cause all manner of disasters, nothing of the kind would occur because of little Der Ling: "She is different from all other women, and girl-children!"

"A very cryptic utterance of my father," Der Ling recalled, relishing the attention and in retrospect her future career as breaker of Chinese customs, "which became the keynote of all my training in years to come."[3]

3
"A noisy family of English-speaking children ..."

It was Yu Keng's unusual view of educating his daughters not only in foreign languages but in the Chinese classics, as well as the fact that his family did not live with him in the *yamen* residence, that brought about a visit of enquiry from the Viceroy of Hubei, Zhang Zhidong.

In his fifties at the time of his visit to Yu Keng's Wuchang *yamen*, Zhang was a curious mixture of progressive and traditional China. A descendant of high-ranking Chinese magistrates, Zhang not only achieved the prestigious *jinshi* degree in the state examinations but did so by focusing his essay on current issues and writing in a style outside the conventions of Chinese literary tradition. A reformer at heart, he used a succession of government positions to clean up abuses in the examination system, tax-collection, and engaged as secretaries a number of young men who had been outside China. He was responsible for opening China's first modern mint, laying the groundwork for railway systems, and in a nation where "squeeze" made the fortunes of everyone from imperial cabinet ministers down to lowly palace eunuchs, Zhang bequeathed no money on his death in 1909. Some of this may have had to do with his well-known passion for collecting jade, which Der Ling admired when visiting his house in Wuchang. She was amused to note that Zhang left his jade in its rough state, as hewn from the rock, with the best specimens under glass. He never allowed these to be used for making jewelry for his wife or his concubines.[1] On the other hand, though he had originally sympathized with the men behind the "100 days reforms" of the Guangxu Emperor, when Cixi cracked down on her young nephew and his followers, Zhang wisely but traitorously disassociated himself from them. He would go on to tread the fine line between pleasing the dowager and keeping his stock in good order with his friendly connections in the foreign legations during the Boxer Uprising and its aftermath some two years later.

Fluttering and clacking in his silks and feathers and mandarin beads, as Der Ling remembered him, on arriving at Yu Keng's *yamen* Zhang must have realized that some of the rumors about his colleague were true, when Yu Keng allowed Der Ling to remain in the room during the interview: well-bred Chinese children, particularly girls, were to be neither seen nor heard. Pretending that Der Ling in fact did not exist (an attitude he was to affect on another occasion a decade later), Zhang sat down with Yu Keng and the questions began. Was Yu Keng aware that rumors were rife about him and the way in which he and his family lived? Did he know that people were saying that he allowed his daughters Der Ling and Rong Ling to study the Chinese classics, that preserve of male scholars alone? That he allowed the girls to learn foreign languages and foreign ways, and to consort with foreign persons in the process? Had he no fears that with these languages and customs, the girls would also imbibe evil foreign habits and beliefs and prove hateful to the spirits of their ancestors?

Der Ling says her father heard Zhang out, and was just as frank in his reply. Yu Keng believed, he told Zhang, that his daughters were destined to do great things. They could not accomplish them if they were not educated, not just in the Chinese classics but in foreign languages and ways. "I am ambitious for them!" Yu Keng said, ambition being the very air Der Ling breathed. According to Der Ling, Zhang grew severe at hearing this (possibly annoyed, too, that one of the daughters in question was still hanging about the room). "If you persist in educating your daughters," he warned, "your own people might even rise up and kill you!" Besides which, the foreigner-hating Cixi would surely have him decapitated. That would be hard for her to do, replied Yu Keng. Because Her Majesty the Empress Dowager Cixi did not even know that he had any daughters. If Zhang had not yet sucked in a shocked breath by this point, this was certainly his cue to do so. "I did not register my daughters when they were born," Yu Keng explained. Had he done so, he insisted, his daughters would become eligible when it came time to make selections for the Guangxu Emperor's inner household. "I do not care for such honor as might be mine through allowing either or both of my daughters to become playthings of any man," Der Ling heard her father say, "whether Emperor or commoner!"

Here lies another mystery of Der Ling's background, which she does nothing to clarify; or possibly, she knew too little about to explain. Since the early years of the Qing dynasty, detailed genealogical records had been kept of all bannermen, in a two-pronged effort to ensure that all banner members and their families were accounted for and would receive their due stipend from the government, and to keep the records of clans and their marriages clarified. In a society where intermarriage between conquerors and conquered was officially forbidden, such genealogical surveillance played a very important role. According to Der Ling and to a few other sources, these records also afforded an easily accessible list of potential concubines for the use of the Qing court. "It was from these registrations that His Majesty was accustomed to pick the names of girl-children of his highest ranking officials," Der Ling explains in her memoirs. The Empress Dowager Cixi had been selected from such a list of Manchu and Mongol adolescent maidens, educated for four years in the ways of the imperial court, and only then selected by the then Empress Dowager, the stepmother of the Xianfeng Emperor, to be a concubine to the emperor (who never made the selection himself) in the Forbidden City. Only by dint of the fact that Cixi had borne the emperor a son, the short-lived Tongzhi, had she been lifted from the harem and into the secondary wife category, and from there to empress dowager. What Der Ling is not telling us is that *hanjun* girls like herself and Rong Ling were not eligible to be called up as concubines. To give Der Ling the benefit of the doubt, it is possible the family had enough Aisin-Gioro connections to waive the usual rule, but again, we simply do not know enough about Yu Keng's family to say one way or the other. And again, given Der Ling's other errors (her father's title, for example), being wrong about this would fit in with the rest of the misinformation she reported as fact.[2]

"My father's perpetual fight to educate his children," Der Ling wrote, "was one of the things that made him great, at least to me." What would have required even greater courage, however, was something that Yu Keng dared not confess to so powerful a personage as his superior officer Zhang Zhidong: that not only were his daughters being educated in foreign languages and in the Chinese classics, just like their brothers, and taught such foreign arts as playing the piano and singing foreign songs, but that all his children had been baptized as Christians, by no less than the bushy-bearded Bishop Favier of Beijing. It was another of those undercover efforts at living outside the rules that Yu Keng would pursue throughout his life not only at his own risk but that of his family as well.[3]

What Der Ling could not know at the time was that in less than a decade, she would be encountering both anti-Christian and anti-foreign sentiments not from a provincial viceroy, in the safety of her father's presence, but without any protection whatsoever, and that the person directing these sentiments her way would be the woman who had held the reins of China's wild horses for over a quarter century, trying to outrun the invasions of the outside world: the feared Empress Dowager Cixi. Like her father, Der Ling would have to learn, under pressure she would never have believed she could withstand, that what one did *not* say in Qing China was far more important than what one *did* say. That, in fact, one's survival depended on it.

Der Ling had seen something of the world outside China, and even picked up the rudiments of a couple of its languages. But she had never yet been to Beijing, the city of her birth, where her father had a sprawling mansion in the Tartar City, almost within the tantalizing shadow of the Forbidden City's patchy vermilion walls. Now she would see it at last, but only briefly, and then through the blur of a storm that for a change had its source not in the Gobi Desert but to the east, where war was brewing on the Korean Peninsula, between the tiny, future-focused empire of Japan and the immense, past-proud empire of China. Between the grinding stones of these two Asian powers lay the Hermit Kingdom of Korea, a nation over which China had long claimed vassalship but which Japan, ostensibly because she wished to modernize the country as had been done in Japan under the Meiji restoration, desired to bring into line with the same principles.

In 1875, China had given the nod to Japan to recognize Korea's independence, but Japan intended to gain something quite a bit more. Unspoken but well understood by both Chinese and Japanese politicians was Japan's hunger for hegemony over such territories outside its islands as would make the word "empire" a fitting one to use, and redress what the Japanese saw as a power imbalance between it and China, as well as a source of leverage against the might of imperial Russia. Unfortunately for China, the Qing government set itself up for a future confrontation by reasserting its former authority over Korea, giving Japan *carte blanche* for reactionary measures to assert similar claims; and when the pro-Japanese reformist Kim Ok-Yün of Korea was done to death in Shanghai in 1894, provoking an uprising by the uncompromising Korean religious sect known as the Tonghak, China was called in by the weak Korean monarch to help.

Unfortunately, though the Japanese government made gestures of encouragement toward the Chinese, they then sent a military force to Korea which allegedly was to assist the Korean reformists, but which ended up securing a foothold by means of which they seized the palace of mild King Kojong in early June, abrogating restrictions against such actions laid out in the 1860 Treaty of Tianjin. War between Japan and China broke out officially on August 1, and what followed was a series of Chinese skirmishes and then defeats. Mrs. Archibald Little, a Western witness to the military buildup and aftermath in China, saw the soldiers sailing off "To the butchery! To the butchery! Float on, Chinese soldiers, all unconscious of your doom, and convinced beyond the power of argument and canon that there is no race like the Chinese race, and that all other nations are your subjects born," choosing for illustrations beside her text photographs of two surly soldiers, their queues bound around their heads, looking more like unhappy boys posing for a festival.[4]

The poor performance against the Japanese of men like these and their commanding officers resulted in a Chinese suit for peace and the Treaty of Shimonoseki in April of 1895. Japan had pressed as far into China as Manchuria — long a piece of territory in their sights — and the Liaodong Peninsula as well. What they got in addition was a massive indemnity from China of 200 million taels, the opening of several treaty ports not already on the long list of ports opened (by force) through the Treaty of Tianjin, and the worst defeat of all: the perpetual cession of Taiwan, then called Formosa, the Liaodong Peninsula — which Russia, France and Germany eventually forced them to return to China, having interests in it themselves — and the Pescadores islands to Japan. In addition, Korea was made a Japanese protectorate.[5] Little wonder that Yu Keng, though a patient parent, could spare no time to explain the complex situation to an importuning nine-year-old daughter, unlike other girl-children though she was.

The frustration of not knowing what the war meant or why her father's life had been turned upside down by it was ameliorated by the news that the family would be leaving Wuchang for Beijing. Imperial China's capital was to Der Ling "the center of the Universe," where she would "see wonderful things, and might even have a chance to steal a glimpse of the great Empress Dowager."[6] The thought of what she would see in Beijing kept Der Ling from brooding, as her mother was doing, over the wartime confusion of the Wuchang/Hankou docks, where the family watched while their things were packed and sent ahead — furniture, kitchen and tableware included — and from which finally they, too, set forth, boarding the merchant steamer *Chiang Yung* for the trip down the Yangzi to the port city of Shanghai. Der Ling does not describe her reaction to the the city already famed as the "Paris of the Orient," but Shanghai's modern, Westernized skyline, its foreign flags flying overhead, its streets that were a vivid patchwork of foreigner and Asian, its quay crowded with Chinese junks and sampans and foreign vessels for business and pleasure, its peddlers and priests, whores and officials, merchants and beggars, must have greatly impressed the girl from the backwaters of Shashi.

The dockside chaos in Shanghai had been so great that a misunderstanding almost left the family stranded on deck for the duration of the voyage. When Yu Keng's family boarded the *Chiang Yung*, they found their cabin already taken by another official — it turned out that his enterprising servant had removed the card stating that the cabin was Yu Keng's and replaced it with his master's. A ruckus between the servants began — one foreign passenger, an official, poked his head into the argument to ask rudely whether "you blamed Chinks [are] going to argue till tomorrow morning?" Order was restored when the captain was summoned and a witness was found who had seen Yu Keng's servant place the family's red card first on the cabin door. The usurping official and his family were summarily turned out and Yu Keng and family were able to move into a cabin that Der Ling remembered (like some precious *memsahib*) as "unclean and ill-smelling," but at least gave them a place to rest while they chugged downstream. There they picked up the steamer *Hsing Fung* for Tianjin, the port of Beijing. The sail north was rough, but Der Ling had to admit she did not know what rough was until, after disembarking from the houseboats the family and retinue had taken up the Baihe River, she got into the two-wheeled, springless, canopied Beijing cart awaiting her and her sister, for the sixteen-mile ride overland from Tongzhou to the capital.

British travel writer Mrs. Archibald Little devotes almost a whole chapter of her book *Intimate China* to describing just the kind of journey Yu Keng's family made to Beijing — first boating up the "ever-wriggling" Baihe ("white river," now called the Hai), where along the windless reverse reaches the house-boats had to be towed, in a trip that took from Thursday to Sunday to reach Tongzhou. Though as disapproving of time wastage as any vigorous English governess, Mrs. Little had to admit after a day or so of gently gliding toward Beijing that "after all there is a charm about this exceedingly slow method of progression." Not that she found much alongside the river to amuse her eagle eye. "There is nothing to be seen upon the road that cannot be seen as well elsewhere," she writes airily — "sandhills, millet- and sorghum-fields with poor crops, fairly nice trees, fences gay with convolvulus flowers, mud houses, mud roofs, and level mudbanks crowded with all the disreputable refuse of a poor Chinese village."[7]

As Der Ling would discover for herself, a trip overland in a Beijing cart would shatter the somnolence of the river journey, as well as threaten to do the same to her bones and her nerves. Riding in a Beijing cart (which, like Mrs. Little, Der Ling claims she had up to now never seen before or ridden in) meant having to clamber in from the front, being careful not to bump your head on the low curved ceiling, where you then half-lay, half-squatted for the duration of the journey, just behind the driver. "The road was paved with huge stones," Der Ling recalled of her first journey over this highway, "some of which thrust themselves up more than a foot above the roughest road I have ever traveled," while others sank into the roadbed in large pits. As Der Ling could come to discover, the one well-paved road in all of northern China was the route used by the Empress Dowager Cixi and her court to travel between Beijing and the Summer Palace.

Sharing those sixteen miles and several hours of jolting discomfort were Louisa, ensconced in the hardly more comfortable conveyance of a sedan chair, and Yu Keng, who with his two sons rode donkeys alongside. It was the brothers who finally took pity on the girls midway through the trip and urged them to ride donkey-back like themselves. Thus it was from behind a pair of floppy ears that Der Ling first saw Beijing, the city which was to become one of several stages of adventure and tragedy in her future life. "The sun was hovering just above the huge wall surrounding Peking when we approached the city of my dreams," Der Ling recalled.[8] The family entered the city via the Qihuamen (now Chaoyangmen) the main eastern gate leading directly into the North or Tartar City. Yu Keng's house stood north of the famous *DongsiPailou* or "East Four Archways," which framed the intersection of Hatamen Street, the city's main commercial thoroughfare, and the east-west road leading from the Qihuamen.

On first seeing the city an American journalist wrote:

> The approach to Peking is tremendously impressive. Lying in an arid plain, the great, gray walls, with their magnificent towers, rise dignified and majestic. Over the tops of the walls nothing is to be seen . . . The street are marvelous. Those in the Legation Quarter are well paved, European and stupid; but those in the Chinese and Tartar cities are full of excitement. A few are wide, but the majority are narrow, winding alleys, and all alike are

packed and crowded with people and animals and vehicles of all
kinds. Walking is a matter of shoving oneself through the throng,
dodging under camels' noses, avoiding wheelbarrows, bumping
against donkeys, standing aside to let officials' carriages go by . . . [9]

Just a one-hour trip by train away from the Great Wall, Beijing had been
shaped and beautified by a succession of brilliant dynasties — Mongol
Yuan, Chinese Ming and Manchu Qing — since the thirteenth century,
when it was first built by Kublai Khan. The locale had served as China's
capital since the time of the Norman Conquest, under a variety of names:
Yenching, Chi, Chungtu, Tatu (Khanbalik), Peiping and finally Peking
(more correctly, Beijing). Though the city, which was substantially rebuilt
by the Ming Yongle Emperor in the early fifteenth century, was laid out
on an orderly north-south axis across a table-flat landscape, and no one
but the emperor could build a house more than one story high, Beijing
was no flattened pueblo but a rolling sea of green trees, brightly tiled
roofs, and the fragile bell-hung towers of pagodas, hemmed in by forty
foot-thick walls of rammed earth and brick. To those who went to the
trouble of climbing to the top of the well-guarded wall or some other
high place, the combination of curved rooflines and leafy trees made for
an enchanting sight.

Chinese writer Lin Yutang, who knew Beijing as well as Der Ling
would one day know it, believed the best view was to be had from
atop the so-called Coal Hill, or *Mei Shan*, a triple-peaked man-made
promontory which stood to the north of the imperial palace. If one stood
in the pavilion at the apex of the central hill, it was possible to see the
city spread out like a fantastic carpet: "Its symmetrical lay-out along a
central axis is unique, and contained in it is a jewel-like city within a
city," wrote Lin, "its scintillating heavy golden-yellow roofs set off by the
luxuriant green of the great park areas." And at the observer's feet lay the
Forbidden City, "with its mass of glazed, shining roofs, surrounded by yet
another square of pink, crenellated walls."[10]

Yu Keng's cavalcade of donkeys, sedan chair and carts, surrounded
and followed by the various grades of servants, slowly made its way into
the three-mile stretch of Hatamen Street. Der Ling saw there not the
jade-and-gold paving stones Beijing's glamorous reputation would lead

a child to expect but the class-stratified byways of an ancient capital, streets seventy-feet broad, with a high section in the center for the sedan chairs and carts of the well-to-do, rising some four feet above pathways alongside crowded with basket-bearing peddlers, pedestrians, beggars, and countless variations on these themes, all kicking up the "ankle-deep dust" that the northward desert provided for every square inch of the city at windy nightfall, and which, as Der Ling records, coolies carrying large buckets were trying in vain to lay low by splashing about with ladlesful of water. Dust was always a problem in Beijing, but more so in winter, when, as one Manchu writer described it, "The blue sky became a yellow sky, and it rained yellow dust. The blackish soil combined with horse piss and donkey dung was wafted up to the sky where it cavorted gaily with chicken feathers and garlic peels."[11]

Amid the garlic peels and chicken feathers, on her first day back in Beijing, Der Ling would have seen a populace largely dressed in the dusky blue cotton robes favored by and affordable to the common class, interspersed with silk-clad grand officials passing by in their sedan chairs — green for officials of the first rank, like her father. She would have seen few women of her mother's class, because Chinese ladies of rank did not show themselves on the open streets, and when they did travel did not raise the curtains of their sedan chairs lest they be seen by men. A welter of dialects would have greeted Der Ling — the colorful slang of Beijing street people, the guttural tones of Guangzhou traders, the cries of peddlers offering a fantastic array of sweets, steamed bread, fruit, toys and a welter of gadgetry, cries broken now and then by the strange honking bray of camels carrying coal, or the strange shouts from coolies carrying coal, balanced in baskets on either end of poles stretched across sweating shoulders. But it was the tangle of multicolored shop signs that drew her special attention: "Whole forests of them . . . Shop fronts done in gold, and silver, and lacquer. Shop fronts of rare beauty, because China of the Empire was rich." With its numerous foreign concessions benefitting foreign rather than Chinese interests and its numerous indemnities for wars it had not caused, imperial China was constantly on the verge of bankruptcy, but to see these signs and the richness of the goods within the shops, one would never know it.

Because Yu Keng's family had arrived in Beijing in the late afternoon, it was dark by the time they had reached the crimson arches of the *Dongsi Pailou* gates, and they watched while lamplighters scurried through the streets, touching flames to small brick towers topped by paper-paned lanterns that, as Der Ling amusedly noted, "served [more] as beacons, eyes through the night, than illumination."[12] The notorious Beijing night winds picked up, scattering more of the fine dust than even Der Ling's donkey could stir. The family was dead tired and distracted: Louisa by concerns for getting the children fed and to bed, Yu Keng by what awaited him on awakening tomorrow. But in Der Ling's young mind, like the lanterns along the dark, tree-lined streets, one thing stood out, past her weariness and the dust and her rumbling belly — the image of the Empress Dowager Cixi, glowing serenely, fascinating as a new star in the night sky, as a great gilded statue of the Buddha shining in a dark temple. Already, Der Ling could say she felt a sort of distant worship for this woman about whom she had heard so much, this powerful empress who ordered China just as easily as she did the miniature universe of Beijing, yet who — maddeningly to Der Ling — did not even know that young Der Ling had even been born.

4
Beijing to Tokyo

As it turned out, Yu Keng's mansion was not to be the place where the family would live during their stay in the city. What Der Ling describes as a half-European, half-Chinese compound of 175 rooms had been lent to a friend of the family's, who despite a half year's forewarning was still not ready to leave it. So the family was lent the house of another acquaintance (possibly Li Hongzhang, who owned many such properties in Beijing), "a magnificent place," Der Ling remembered, but a lonely one for her.

After her father departed next morning for an unexplained and urgent meeting with Prince Gong, brother-in-law of the Empress Dowager Cixi, Der Ling wandered the house's gardens, with its high walls shutting out the noise from the streets, its rockeries and fish pools overhung by willows that seemed to the out of sorts Der Ling like women suffering in tears. She did not like the walls surrounding the garden — "I always resented . . . seclusion, always desired to try my wings," she insisted. Even at nine, Der Ling was questioning the old Chinese tradition by which a man's home was his palace and a woman's her prison.[1]

Prince Gong's summoning of Yu Keng was not merely to pass the time of day with an old friend and colleague returned to the capital.

Beijing had been the forcing ground for Gong's political education as far back as the 1860 Opium War, when allied troops threatened the city, sending the Xianfeng Emperor fleeing with his Empress Cian, secondary wife Cixi, and toddler heir Tongzhi into the wastes of northern China and leaving Gong behind in abandoned Beijing to negotiate out of the mess what he could. A sturdily handsome man with long nails as sharp as his disapproving gaze — even his personal seal gave back a hard stare, with its motto "No Private Heart"[2] — Gong had been something of a playboy prince before circumstances swooped down to transform him into a statesman at only twenty-seven years of age. For the past thirty years he had been involved in one way or another with securing Beijing against foreign invasion, via military or, given the Chinese army's typically poor showing, diplomatic means. With the emperor and court in flight to the imperial hunting lodge of Jehol (Chengde), that ultimate getaway resort, with its miniature Potala palace in the backyard and pavilions scattered about the arid valley bearing names like "Hall of Refreshing Waves and Mists," Prince Gong faced the allied invaders alone, sometimes playing along with the foreigners and sometimes upbraiding them for their lack of manners. Unfortunately, seeking short-term safety and sanity, he developed a *Realpolitik* style which tended to accede to the invaders whatever they asked, particularly when these requests seemed the easily granted ones of cash indemnities and the opening to trade of more Chinese ports. Expedient these concessions may have been, but they would create long-term headaches both for the Qing empire and the Chinese republic that followed it. By the end of his long life, in 1898, Prince Gong had seen too many upheavals and retreated to the "private heart" he had earlier claimed not to possess. As Fang Chao-ying wrote of Gong, in his old age "[he] was filled with resentment against the entire Court . . . and spent most of his last days in his garden, Lang-jun Yüan."[3]

As Der Ling discovered later, what Prince Gong wanted to discuss with her father was the prospect of becoming his second-in-command in a newly created Department of Military Affairs, which the Empress Dowager had commanded to be formed soon after the outbreak of fighting between the Qing and Meiji regimes. The department's purpose was to develop defense plans for China. While Yu Keng was all for keeping China safe, he had no illusions about the outcome of battle between China and Japan — in fact, it was probably his sober view on the matter that moved Prince Gong to ask Yu Keng to be part of the department. "We are a peaceful nation, knowing nothing whatever about war, while Japan knows much," Der Ling recalled her father saying. "That we will go down to defeat [against the Japanese] is a foregone conclusion." Yu Keng based his gloomy but realistic prediction not only on China's technical unreadiness for the sort of war Japan's modern war machine would wage against her, but also on the ignorant and outdated mindset of many officials at the very top of the government, ironically in the new war department. He told Louisa about one of them, an elderly man who knew the Chinese classic backwards but nothing about the military milieu which was his portfolio. What he did claim to know was that the close-fitting trousers worn by foreigners were a consequence of the latter possessing unbendable knees, and that the best sort of weapon for the Chinese army would be simple bamboo poles — all they need do on the battlefield was push the stiff-legged Japanese infantry over on their backs, like so many tin soldiers.

This level of ignorance could be laughed at, but not the other kind, which moved one member of the new department to suggest that Chinese merchant vessels, armed and staffed with naval personnel, could easily take on and defeat the Japanese navy. The vessels in question were mere market produce tubs, plying the coast with minimal crew; the notion of stocking them with armaments and expecting them to make any headway against the known ironclad superiority of the Japanese navy was not ludicrous, it was insane. It was because Yu Keng could not resist speaking out when faced with these continued proofs of China's direful need for reform that, according to his daughter, he made himself increasingly unpopular among the conservative set of Beijing. Ominously enough, Der Ling also records that it was at this time that Yu Keng and his family began to be addressed by a term which, during the Boxer Uprising, would take on a far more sinister tone: "*er mao tzu.*" This meant either Chinese foreigners, Chinese Christians, or Chinese who worked for foreigners, and had the effect of marginalizing the family from mainstream Chinese, something the house of Yu Keng hardly needed at this time.

As Der Ling remembered it, official mismanagement was endemic, and if it proved a waste of time and money it was also often quite comic. All during the Sino-Japanese War, the house was crowded not just with staff — most of whom could never all be used for the purposes intended — but also with other, less official personages who were in for the ride. "The visitors move across the retina of my memory like fantastic figures on some quaint frieze," Der Ling wrote. How many of her father's retainers, paid up to $100 Mexican silver each month, were useless to him — interpreters who could not speak proper Chinese, illiterate secretaries, diplomats who stepped on toes and tripped over their own, clerks whose sole work was to show up for their stipend. It is important to remember that Der Ling always took a severe view of servants and especially those retainers she believed took advantage of her father, in an age-old Asian custom of client-patron interaction that she despised as being antiquated and ignorant. But we can be certain she did see a fair amount of this sort of acceptable abuse of the system.[4]

Yu Keng found no fault with these ancient ways on the surface, but inside he was, according to Der Ling, a frustrated man, who sat impatiently through the circumlocution of a visitor when he knew all along why the man had come to see him, and yet was too polite to demand the frank Western ways of talking business which he preferred. Instead, Yu Keng devoted his energies to reform of the larger structures on which this kind of human society stood, hoping that by improving the big picture the small one would take care of itself. Der Ling tells us he made efforts to reorganize the postal service along efficient European lines and to develop a workable tax system. He befriended "foreign devils" like American diplomat Colonel Charles Denby, who with his tall, broad-shouldered, angular-faced handsomeness sounds like Yu Keng's European counterpart; like Yu Keng, Denby was also an enthusiastic admirer of the Empress Dowager Cixi, and was later taken to task in the American press, during the Boxer Uprising, for his friendliness toward Cixi. Yu Keng made sure that Denby and other Beijing Americans knew how grateful he was to them for America's intercession in the ending of what was looking like a war that would never end, in which the Chinese would keep losing and the Japanese keep winning.

These reforms and these relations with foreign officials seemed to please, or at least amuse, only two people in the Qing government. One of them was Prince Gong, who despite his distrust of foreign powers and his alliance with the Empress Dowager's conservative policies, could not but see good in improving the way China managed its mail and tax structures. The other was the Empress Dowager Cixi, who despite all the memorials being sent across her desk, sometimes several a day, criticizing Yu Keng and demanding his removal, preserved the patient watchfulness that had earned her the respectful nickname "Old Buddha": she acted on none of them. As the old lady would later tell Louisa, when she and her daughters were in service at court, "I never believed [the denunciations]. Yü Kêng was recommended by Ronglu, and is as faithful as Ronglu."[5]

Something of Yu Keng's concept of religious faith may be seen in his manner of handling the problems his liberal belief caused him. A secret Christian who also had about him a certain Daoist mysticism, Yu Keng's lenient approach to his fellow men seemed to follow the most important tenet of Laozi's philosophy: "to discover the unity underlying all diversity . . . the eternal principle of the universe."[6] Where both strict Confucians and staunch Christians secretly feared that unity, Yu Keng not only welcomed it but practiced it in his own home and among his friends, acquaintances, even among his enemies. And like a true Daoist, he was willing, even happy, to take the accompanying risks, because with any journey into the unknown came valuable knowledge.

In Cixi's world of ever-shifting allegiances and power struggles, her support was invaluable. If Yu Keng had to have only two people in all China on his side, it was best to have Prince Gong and Cixi, particularly when he opposed what Der Ling describes as "an insane idea," advanced by one or another of the radical conservatives in the War Department, that the department use the Sino-Japanese War as a pretext for driving all foreigners out of China — a notion which would rise again only five years later during the events of the Boxer Uprising. When news of Yu Keng's "foreign sympathies" leaked out — and Der Ling assures her reader on every other page that in the China of her day, there were no secrets — not even Prince Gong's protection could shield him from censure. Which is why Yu Keng's third friend in China, Ronglu, appeared on the doorstep of the rented house, his serious expression announcing the need for a serious discussion.

Born in 1836 into the Manchu Plain White Banner, Ronglu was a hardened soldier descended both from the famed chieftain Fiongdon, who led Manchu troops in their first sortie with Ming soldiers in 1618 and after his death two years later was given the colorful posthumous title "Duke of Unswerving Uprightness," and from Nurhachi, founder of the Qing dynasty.[7] Reputedly a distant cousin of the Empress Dowager's, Ronglu had known her since her childhood in the *hutongs* (alleyways) of Beijing. He stood by her every step of her subsequent career, from powerless secondary wife to powerful Empress Dowager. He saved her neck on a few crucial occasions — notably when the Gang of Eight tried to have her assassinated, following the Xianfeng Emperor's death in 1861; and he was believed by some (including Der Ling, who makes much of the now questioned romance in her biography of Cixi) to have enjoyed an unrequited love affair with her.

Though Ronglu naturally tended to side with the dowager in all her policies, he was not completely in the camp of the anti-foreigners who so often swayed Cixi, as would prove especially fortuitous for the besieged foreign legation residents in the summer of 1900. This in turn also helped bind him to the liberal Yu Keng. His proximity to the throne, as well as his position as head of the Beijing police force, gave him a special insight into the secret tides turning against his friend, not to mention the likely outcome once they had reached peak surge. Hence his impromptu visit to Yu Keng, to warn him of the increasing number of memorials against him, and to suggest a solution that would at one and the same time put Yu Keng and his family out of harm's way and place a known reformer at the head of Japan's first post-war Chinese legation: that Yu Keng assume control of the Chinese Legation in Tokyo as the new post-war minister. Prince Gong and even the busy Empress Dowager would take heart, Ronglu insisted, that a man of such principle and vision was in charge of this important foreign office at such a sensitive time. "China is not ready for your ideas," Ronglu told Yu Keng. Leaving China would help settle the simmering criticism of him and his ideas. In fact, the Empress Dowager had already given her blessing to the appointment. With that extra push, Yu Keng could not but accept.

The position, for all its importance, was a dangerous one, posted in a nation with whom China had just been at war, filled with anti-China sentiments. There would also be a huge backlog of work since the original legation staff had dropped everything and fled at outbreak of the war.

As his daughter points out, Yu Keng would have no idea of just what an Augean stable he had taken on until he actually got to Tokyo and saw the situation for himself. But the offer, Der Ling says, stirred his patriotism, his desire to build bridges again between the two great Asian nations, and his ever-present wish to please the imperial woman who continued to place trust in an official with whose ideas she did not always agree. It may also have made it all the easier for him to communicate with reformist Chinese living in Japan — and if some of the dots do connect as they appear to do, perhaps, too, with highly placed Japanese who were working against China in the interests of a united Asia and, most of all, a more powerful Japan.[8]

5
Samurai in pinstripes

The Japan and the China of 1895 could not have been more opposite, starting with the troublous subject of reform and modernization.

When Mutsuhito, the Meiji Emperor, came to the throne as Japan's 122nd emperor (according to Japan's founding myth) in 1868, he and his powerful regents ended over two centuries of peaceful but cloistered Tokugawa shogun rule of Japan, and immediately began instituting changes in government. They started with a representative Diet, moved on to manufacturing, laying the foundations for Japan's great role as an importer of goods; and then dealt with society, that of both court and commoner. These reforms sat well with Japan's progressives and badly with the old-fashioned, particularly those of the old samurai class whose feudalism, in the words of samurai descendant and first female Diet member Baroness Shidzue Ishimoto, "was being undermined by Western materialism." The samurai revulsion toward work that led to material compensation led some hungry warriors, per Baroness Ishimoto, to sit at tables before plates filled with carved wooden fish, picking their teeth as if they had had their fill.[1]

This was a hard-nosed conservatism that would have seemed familiar to impoverished Manchu bannermen, forbidden as they were from engaging in trade and thus reduced to living on credit, all to retain the necessary "face." This self-destructive clinging to ways that were not just antiquated but harmful to the state and the individual was something many progressive Chinese would also have found familiar and in need of immediate change. But when it came to dealings with the outside world, Japan had been far more accommodating than China. Where the latter had been pried open by the Western powers in a series of painful and expensive wars, and continued to suffer upheavals inflamed by anti-foreign feeling, Japan had learned its lesson early, not just in terms of opening its doors to the West but in taking whatever the West could do and doing it better and more cheaply, and selling it back to them.

This revolution, as it certainly was, affected commerce as much as it did the arts, the latter even more so when Japanese cultural treasures were given the spotlight at the 1876 Philadelphia Centennial Exposition as well as at the Chicago World's Fair almost twenty years later. Porcelains, silks, furniture, lacquer, *cloisonné* — all the accoutrements of Japanese artistic genius, poured adroitly into Western-inspired forms, were shown off in all their splendor, sparking a worldwide fascination with things Asian that bypassed connoisseurship and went straight to what middle-class taste and budget could afford.

China's emperor rarely showed himself — his gaze was believed blinding to any who met it, whether commoner or minister — and when he did, at times of great ceremonial and never to the general public, he was always dressed in the robes and regalia of his predecessors of centuries before. Japan's Meiji Emperor, however, rapidly divested himself of the complex garments that went with his semi-divine station and took to wearing uniforms that smacked of officers at the court of France's Emperor Napoleon III — not only that, he took to growing the moustache and goatee that also distinguished that bourgeois French ruler, and maintained the look for many years after it went out of style elsewhere, adding more medals to his tunic front as time went on. His empress, too, often attended openings of girls' schools, in full view of foreign men as well as women, wearing the latest Paris fashions. No Chinese empress had been seen in public as far back as anyone in Beijing could remember, but residents of Tokyo could say that on at least one or two occasions they had seen their beautiful, willowy empress somewhere or other.

Not that the emperor was completely sold on all things European and American: he preserved as many of Japan's traditions as interlocked within his structure of reform, including all the rites and ceremonies long revered in Japanese life. But his move to unite Japan under one power and a single-minded push to place Japan among the world's most modern nations gave the island empire an army that would beat much larger China in 1895 and go on to crush even larger Russia in 1905.

Baroness Ishimoto remembered turn-of-the-century Tokyo as a city filled with flowers, from the "cherries fringing the imperial moats along the red brick buildings" of the British Embassy, to the fugitive manicured perspectives captured from the windows of one of the modern electric trains operating through Ueno Park: "White, pink and rose tree-peonies, purple and white bunches of wisteria, red and white camellia, white magnolia and yellow yamabuki [the so-called 'Japanese yellow rose] decorate the capital, in private gardens, in the parks and in the numerous temple courts . . ."[2]

As the daughter of the first Chinese minister to set foot on Japanese soil since the end of hostilities, Der Ling would receive a very different first impression of Japan's tidy but bustling capital. Just getting there, Der Ling recalled, was a nightmare. Not only the expected household upheaval of preparing luggage and paperwork for a four-year sojourn in another country, but the chaos attendant on any kind of official promotion in China dogged the family well after they boarded the *S. S. Oceana* in Shanghai. People Yu Keng had never met appeared out of the woodwork, asking for favors in China or preferred places in Japan, busybodies who counseled proper behavior for a Chinese minister posted to foreign parts, and always those troublemaking personages affiliated with the Board of Censors, noting any damning foreign predisposition on the Yu Keng family's part. And the suite required to accompany the new Chinese minister to his post in Tokyo was gargantuan by any measure: three secretaries, each with his family; two writers of whose work Der Ling had her habitual poor opinion; a couple of military attachés and two naval attachés who she claims had never been to sea; two doctors with cases packed full of Chinese herbs; three very good cooks; two barbers (for Yu Keng, his sons, and the other queue-wearing males of the retinue); a Number One houseboy, with a

Number Two in tow; two boys for odd jobs in Yu Keng's office; four Han amahs whose bound feet barely allowed them to walk; and "seven slave girls who did nothing but interfere with people who really wished to do something"[3] Ultimately, fifty people, with luggage and chattels, wended over the uneven roadway from Beijing to Tongzhou, from where they would be hauled down the Baihe in white-pennanted houseboats.

"[I]t was a never ending thrill," recalled Der Ling, "for me to look back along the trail where there were curves, and see the cavalcade stretched out behind us, like a great serpent."[4] When the party reached Tianjin, Yu Keng decided all should spend a few days of rest (which he probably needed more than anyone else, considering his poor health) before boarding their ship for Shanghai, whence they would ship out for Japan on a steam liner. Here, past custom and present exigencies clashed again. Per tradition, when a celebrated individual entered a city, its grateful officials would put its finest temple at the visitor's disposal. Unlike houses of worship of most faiths around the world, Chinese temples were capable of being equipped as living quarters for guests of high rank; temples in the Western Hills near Beijing were often rented out in summer by their priests to foreigners and upper-class Chinese seeking relief from the heat of town or a place, as Der Ling cattily pointed out in later years, to carry on extramarital assignations undisturbed.

Not to be thought lacking in the niceties of form, Tianjin's high-ups offered their finest temple building for the family to live in while they were in town. Unfortunately, when Yu Keng went to see where they would be staying, he took one look at the damp and musty rooms, turned about face and headed for the well-appointed, British-style Astor Hotel (which would also shelter such celebrated guests as Dr. Sun Yat-sen, Emperor Puyi, and the Beijing Opera actor Mei Lanfang), where he booked suites for his family and retinue. No sooner had everyone been installed there, however, but a high official of the city came to call. Der Ling, as always, was there with her father when the man approached him. "Yu Keng, Yu Keng!" he cried. "This is a foreign-devil hotel!" When Yu Keng explained why he had decided to put up at the Astor, the official continued to splutter. There would be criticism, much criticism of his choice, so fatal for a newly appointed minister! Her Majesty would be furious and might order decapitation! "I think the custom is silly," replied

Yu Keng, referring to the rule of staying in the city's temple. "I like this hotel, pay for it, and am going to stay here!"

Though the Astor was a cosmopolitan hotel, with visitors of every nation parading under the palm leaves and fringed draperies of its lobby, the ways of its elegant microcosm were definitely those of Europe. Hence Yu Keng's request to his servants that they inform any Chinese visitors come to see him that they must respectfully refrain from the kowtow. According to Chinese custom, says Der Ling, if such a visitor kowtowed to you, you had to kowtow in return, lest you rob the other man of "face," and Yu Keng evidently believed that this was bound to cause a flutter of unwanted attention from the sleek foreigners in the lobby. Considering the fact that the Astor had been in operation since the 1860s, in the port that served Beijing, with all manner of Chinese officialdom coursing its corridors, the kowtow should have been a gesture more familiar to foreigners than Yu Keng evidently imagined it was. In any event, when a Chinese visitor of Yu Keng's happened to slip through the phalanx of servants and, on finding him in the lobby, kowtowed to him, he and his family had to get down on the Persian-carpeted floor and return the sentiment. The laughter of a naïve foreigner shot over the hubbub. Others gathered in the lobby tittered behind gloved hands. It must have occurred to Yu Keng and his children that the mildewed temple might have been a better place to stay after all.[5]

Chinese backwardness had its own moment of infamy. When the family and retinue boarded their ship at Shanghai, it became embarrassingly evident that everyone except Yu Keng's family had underestimated the sanitary accommodations available on a modern ocean liner — Der Ling recalled how each servant had brought his or her own chamber pot, carried under their arms as they went up the gangplank. Yu Keng could find this sort of thing funny, but not Louisa, with her mix of high ideals about proper behavior and the need to show that she was as up to date as any Western woman on the ship. Galvanizing her household, she ordered all the servants' rooms cleared of the offending antique toilet receptacles. Der Ling remembered looking down from the deck at the men in the sampan-tenders below, who had brought her and her family out to the *Oceana*, watching their amazed expressions as chamber pots were jettisoned from one porthole after another. They bobbed briefly in the chocolate-brown Huangpu River until they sank with a succession of bubbling gulps to the depths below.

"I hadn't known till now," she recalled, "that I had been dissatisfied with life in China . . . I was ready for any voyage, to any country, and Japan was as good as any other." This attitude of hers was not to change much over the next forty-nine years.[6]

When war was declared between China and Japan in August 1894, the personnel of the Chinese legation had fled their posts, seeking the quickest route home. As Yu Keng discovered, after picking his way through the unkempt front garden of the foreign-built mansion that had served as China's legation, they had literally dropped everything they were carrying and walked out the door, like "rats deserting the ship," Der Ling remarked tartly. She, too, traversed the "sea of weeds" as she followed her father up the front steps of the house, which had been abandoned so suddenly it was left unlocked.

It was as much a mess inside as outside. Furniture, much of it broken, had been shoved around the rooms. The Chinese had left so precipitately that they had dropped clothes and shoes all over the floors, where they had quietly mildewed. The dining room was the worst scene of all: there the family found leavings of unfinished meals caked to dusty plates, mummified tea leaves in stained teacups. After the family had walked through all the rooms, holding kerchiefs to their faces as they peered into closets and offices, they concluded they could not possibly live here until the building was scoured from top to bottom and put into order again.

Chan chan bo zu, literally meaning, says Der Ling, "Slaves with tails," were the first Japanese words the family heard the moment they got off the *Oceana* in Kobe. Because the sea journey to Yokohama was rumored to be rough going, Yu Keng had decided to take his family and retinue overland, and had hired two train cars to convey everyone. These cars were, however, not like those of European trains, with seats facing frontward, but with long banquettes on each side of the car and a wide corridor between. All through the journey to Yokohama, Yu Keng's family and their staff were harassed by curious Japanese, who boarded the train, saw the great number of Chinese, and could not resist staring at and commenting on the presence of people who only shortly before had been their mortal enemy. On discovering what the hostile Japanese were saying to her father, "It was very much as though queue-wearing folk out of old China were to visit America," Der Ling wrote, "and be trailed by mischievous boys, yelling, 'Chinks! Chinks! Chinks!'"[7]

When they disembarked in the Tokyo station and got into the landau that would take them to their lodgings at the Second Empire-style Imperial Hotel, there was more to worry about, because a large crowd had gathered. To guard the family four policemen, each in his own bicycle-propelled *jinriksha*, had been appointed to follow their carriage closely through the streets. "It was my first venture into hostile territory, and I must admit that it all thrilled me," recalled Der Ling.[8] Like Japan's people (and already, like Der Ling herself), who could seem one thing while being another, the country itself began to fascinate her from her first glimpse of it. Here it was, a tiny Asian nation which had modeled its government and its military on Bismarckian Prussia and outfitted its former samurai in pinstripes, and yet it had managed to preserve the inimitably fragile charms of its gardens, its complex, rainbow-colored costumes, and its tiny, doll-like women in their click-clacking getas, moving along the tidy streets with paper parasols floating in a dozen pastel hues over their glossy bent heads.

Der Ling was even taken by the way Japanese who talked to her or her father drew in their breath, lest it should offend him or her whom they addressed, yet which made them sound, in her description, like so many hissing snakes, adding to the sense of weird danger that gave her such pleasure. And though it could not have come as a surprise to the authorities that a crowd would be at the station to greet the new Chinese minister with less than friendly commentary, an eventuality they clearly did nothing to prevent, yet someone had had enough respect for Yu Keng to arrange for the police escort, but for which the stones and insults might have grown far more violent. It was a start, Der Ling noted hopefully.

While Yu Keng settled into his responsibilities, the family remained at the mansard-roofed Imperial Hotel for two weeks while the Chinese legation was cleaned and repaired. Yu Keng supervised the latter, and had no easy time of it, because he dealt with architects and carpenters who, says Der Ling, could not speak either Chinese or English, and seemed to be saddled with the same inept Chinese translators Der Ling had so deplored. Louisa, for example, had asked that a room in the mansion be partitioned, a simple request that should have given no difficulties. But when the family visited the legation to see how the work was coming on, they found that not only was the partition wall completely at variance with what Louisa had asked for, but had been put up in a completely different room.[9]

Things were no better at the Imperial Hotel, where Der Ling reports there was a better than 50/50 chance that a request for ice water would gain you a slice of watermelon. But for Der Ling, while impatiently awaiting the move to the shined-up grandeur of the Chinese legation, there was the constant fascination of visitors from the other foreign legations, who came to pay courtesy calls on Yu Keng. Years later she remembered them all, her recollection salted by a grown woman's sharper criticism: Sir Ernest Satow, British minister, who spoke perfect Japanese and had a winning sense of humor ("A thorough gentleman," wrote Der Ling); Monsieur Harmond, the French minister, who reminded Yu Keng of a butcher yet who with his buxom wife put on great airs, refusing to speak anything but French, with a daughter whose only dream was to marry a wealthy man; Prince Khitrovo, from Russia, who though elderly was still handsome, made much of Der Ling, and had an even more handsome and linguistically talented son besides; Count Orfini, the Italian minister, who despite his "tuft of hair on the back of his head," managed to enjoy the attentions of most of the legation ladies; the multilingual Monsieur Lisboa, from Brazil, whose elegant wife and accomplished children drew Der Ling's immediate interest; Señor de Carcer of the Spanish Legation, who later became Spain's minister in Beijing, remained a blur to Der Ling and might have been completely forgotten had he not had a charming daughter who became a good friend of Der Ling's — Der Ling would later see Carmen and her mother again at the Empress Dowager's garden parties at the Summer Palace.

Germany's minister, the Freiherr von Gutschmidt, was all too memorable for Der Ling and Yu Keng both, thanks to a lack of tact he raised to a kind of art form. (Even German Chancellor von Bülow, who had plenty to deal with in the eccentric personality department where his master Kaiser Wilhelm II was concerned, once described Gutschmidt as "an irritable and incompetent agent," who regularly "exceeded his instructions.") In her memoirs Der Ling relates an early interview her father had with Gutschmidt, in which the latter shooed away the interpreters, declaring he could well talk to Yu Keng without them. He then launched into a flood of semi-intelligible pidgin English, which was so poor the baffled Yu Keng at first took it for German. "Oh, my savee!" spluttered Gutschmidt, in Der Ling's recollection, when Yu Keng turned to his own translator to ask whether His Excellency the Baron could not switch to English or French so that he could understand him. "You no savee English talkee. Well, my no savee Chinaman talkee!" During his Japanese tenure, Gutschmidt was to favor Yu Keng with several such instances of what apparently passed for good manners in the halls of power at Berlin.[10]

After the family moved to the Chinese legation, the language that would prove most troublesome for all concerned turned out to be Japanese. If Der Ling is to be believed, none of her father's Chinese translators could perform their jobs satisfactorily, and Louisa's efforts at hiring bilingual butlers came to grief when language-related fights broke out between Japanese and Chinese servants. With the single-minded ease of a child, and a particularly willful one at that, Der Ling set herself to learning Japanese, and claims she became not just official interpreter between Yu Keng's household and the Japanese world outside it, but also served as translator for much official business in her father's study. If true, this work stood her in good stead when she would be called on to translate official business, including newspapers in French and English, for Empress Dowager Cixi in time to come.

Not that these heavy new responsibilities did much to shorten Der Ling's childhood. In her memoirs, she describes with the relish of bratty pre-pubescence how she annoyed her father's uptight secretary by climbing the legation's flagpole, to which the yellow flag with its white-scaled blue dragon was affixed, and refused to come down when ordered to do so. "I wish to inform you that this is *my* legation!" Der Ling retorted from on high. The secretary spluttered that it was unlucky for girls to climb flagpoles, probably referring to some obscure rule of *fengshui* tinctured with misogynistic Confucianism. Der Ling slid down the pole, gathered pebbles from the driveway in her pockets, and before the man could catch her hoisted herself back up the pole. With the silken symbol of imperial China flapping in the wind over her head, she began to pelt the secretary with the stones, while her siblings and other children who had gathered screamed with laughter. Reading Der Ling's admission of such conduct, Sir Robert Hart's remark about Yu Keng's "noisy family of English-speaking children" begins to take on three very vivid dimensions.

But there were also times when Der Ling could enjoy the utter solitude she craved. One place where she loved to be alone was a part of the garden where a miniature Japanese town (an outdoor version of the *bon-kei* tray landscape) had been built by the legation's Japanese gardener, atop a knoll around the base of a spreading pine tree. "There were little Japanese houses, no bigger than the hand of a child," she remembered, "little Japanese pagodas hanging precariously to the sides of hills no higher than my own ankles." Miniature walkways trailed alongside ponds where goldfish darted. Der Ling spent hours standing under the broad low-hanging branches, imagining the lives of the townsfolk below. In her mind, all of them were the Chinese, French, English and Japanese people she had known, all as multilingual as her own family — symbolic of Der Ling's own future, where only in places that were as multicultural, multiethnic and multilingual as this little world would she ever be happy.[11]

Meanwhile, the newly restored legation began to light up at night with all the receptions and balls that Louisa so well knew how to organize. As the guests arrived of an evening, wearing their silks and jewels, Der Ling and her sister would hide behind the Japanese screens in the hall to watch them, absorbing all the details hungrily. Misunderstanding many of the same foreign ways that so fascinated Der Ling was to bring Yu Keng's servants so much unhappiness that they almost abandoned the legation en masse. Der Ling, who like many upper-class children spent much of her time around the family servants, happened to overhear their arguments, and discovered what they were angry about. In China, when guests came to stay at the master's house, they left liberal tips for the Number One Boy or major domo to share out to them equally, typically on one of the many festival days that dotted the calendar. In Japan, where the moral principles of *bushido* made the naked proffering of cash a vulgar gesture (special decorative envelopes called *shugi-bukuro* were developed to conceal such cash transactions), tipping domestics was not the custom, so that when all Yu Keng's servants received were their wages, their "visions of unheard of riches" they had thought to gain in wealthy Japan went up in smoke. Even after the Japanese custom was explained to them they failed to see the point of its foggy niceties — one of several points where backward China functioned on a better footing with reality than modernizing Japan.

One of the older servants, the bound-foot amah who had declared Der Ling too good for the Chinese magistrate's boy in the garden at Shashi, hinted darkly that if they were all obliged to remain in "barbarous" Japan for four long years, who knew what other terrible changes might be required of them? There was no harm in that, replied the Number One Boy, who had also worked for Yu Keng in China. Who had ever seen Yu Keng worship at his ancestral tablets before, anyway? How could foreigners change him when he was changed before he ever set foot in Japan? "Father had no special religion," Der Ling wrote, "living mostly by his own equivalent of the Golden Rule." That Yu Keng did not worship at his ancestral tablets is a revealing bit of information which Der Ling, as shown above, did nothing to enlarge upon. Why Der Ling, who claims to have known her father through and through, expected him to react angrily to her report of the below-stairs chatter, she does not explain. Yu Keng only smiled and said that he had no intention of breaking the family tablets. But like the pioneer he was, he also had no intention of bowing before them every day (in fact, nowhere in her memoirs does Der Ling ever record bowing before them herself, or even their presence in any household her father and mother lived in). Der Ling observed her father's brazenly modern thinking with all the acuity she devoted to the manners and mores of foreign visitors to the legation, firming up her own pressing need to prove that one could be Chinese, French, Japanese — a true citizen of the world — just like the happy imaginary people in her miniature garden village, and still enjoy the benefits of each culture. There would be rude awakenings on that score in the not too distant future.[12]

6
Chrysanthemums and politics

Each spring, a festival of cherry blossoms was convened at the O-hama Detached Palace, also known as the Shinjuku Palace (in autumn, a chrysanthemum party was held at the European-style Aksaka Palace). The O-Hama Palace had pleasure gardens dating from the period of the Tokugawa shoguns, in which they had enjoyed picnics and other outdoor amusements amid the carefully cultivated setting. Baroness Shidzue Ishimoto remembered going to the O-Hama for the cherry blossom festival as a young student from the Western-style Peeress' School. The vast park was enclosed by stands of old pine trees, which parted on the south side to a cliff that looked over Tokyo Bay. The garden featured a lake in its center; the grass was trimmed so perfectly it might have been green velvet, and the glory of the garden, the cherry trees, stood all about, "heavily laden with pale pink blossoms [calling] attention to their dark gray trunks, lustrous skins between the pinkish mists, reflected on the water."[1]

Despite her youth, Der Ling had become fast friends with a young woman, Countess Tokugawa, who served as first lady-in-waiting to the Empress Haruko, wife of Emperor Meiji, and a frequent caller at the Chinese legation. It is perhaps to Countess Tokugawa that we may attribute what was to become for Der Ling an overwhelming fascination with the culture and structure of imperial courts and a hunger to be a part of them — a trial run for the court of the Empress Dowager Cixi. "I often listened as [Louisa and Countess Tokugawa] talked over the gossip of the Japanese court," Der Ling recalled. How wonderful it must be, Der Ling concluded, to be what Countess Tokugawa was: a court lady, a proximity to power which the daughter of Yu Keng naturally found irresistible.[2] It was probably through the good offices of Countess Tokugawa that Der Ling found herself invited with her parents to the O-Hama Palace cherry blossom festival. The young woman's father, Count Tokugawa, was to serve as master of ceremonies for the event, and to Der Ling's delight it was announced that the emperor and empress would make a brief appearance during the festivities.

The day the invitation arrived, Louisa — that stickler for all that was proper — took one look at the suggestion that "the young lady Yü" also attend, and put her foot down: Der Ling, at 11, was far too young to be present at such a gathering of the greats of the land. As Der Ling relates in her memoirs, on hearing this she was on the point of hysterics until her father stepped in. "Tush! Tush!" Yu Keng said to Louisa. "This isn't China!" In Japan, Der Ling could have a taste of what life was like for a European girl, with all the freedoms included.

Dressed in their embroidered silk robes and jewelry, even to wearing high embroidered Manchu clogs, Louisa and Der Ling entered the gardens of the O-Hama Palace in company with Yu Keng, announced by Countess Tokugawa's father at the gateway. Masses of people had gathered around the entrance to the garden, which was guarded by soldiers "dressed in their gaudiest uniforms," their swords gleaming in the afternoon sunshine as they lifted them in salute to each arriving diplomat and celebrity. "I bowed and smiled," Der Ling remembered, "as though the salute had been for me."[3]

Among the many dignitaries present, there were foreign guests who, remembered Der Ling, "made remarks about everything as though they believed everyone deaf, dumb and blind, ignorant of English, or did not care what impressions they made. Disparaging remarks were spoken loudly and freely, with overbearing superiority." This was behavior she would encounter in later years, not just in Tokyo or Beijing but in New York and Los Angeles.

It was not till around four o'clock, when the spring sun had begun to slant through the pink and white clouds of blossom, that a stir rippled through the crowds of guests, and Count Tokugawa announced: "Their Majesties are coming!" Der Ling remembered that there was an instant scramble for places, so that the walkway along which the imperial pair were to make their progress was "banked solid" with diplomats and their wives, standing in order of their seniority. Der Ling, who was never to be very tall, even while wearing three-inch high clogs, realized she would not be able to see the emperor and empress arrive under these circumstances, and promptly forgot her rule about giving the best possible impression of China by brazenly moving out ahead of the diplomatic array, where she planted herself right in front of the Belgian minister, Baron d'Anethan. A short man himself, and native of a nation notoriously sensitive about its dignity, the baron threw up a fuss at the impudence of this eleven-year-old Chinese girl. "You have no right to be here!" he hissed. "I can't see a thing!"

As Der Ling later recalled, "I refused to be cheated of my thrills by even the Minister of the Belgians," and she stayed where she was, eager to see as much of the imperial couple as possible. But as the emperor and empress came near, Der Ling's excitement flagged. Romantic even at eleven, she had envisioned the emperor and empress dressed in full Japanese court regalia, attended by ladies in stiff silk kimonos and gorgeous jade hair ornaments. However, the imperial pair only donned traditional garb when performing ceremonials in strict seclusion. When Emperor Meiji and Empress Haruko stepped down the garden path, they did so in European dress that would not have been out of place in the Bois de Boulogne. Emperor Meiji, recalled Der Ling, was wearing a suit that fitted him so loosely it seemed to hang on his body — the emperor, who constantly waged battle with weight, must have been at the end of one of his diets.[4]

Empress Haruko preferred European clothes to Japanese, and appeared at most public functions wearing them, looking svelte and chic in the puffed sleeves and trailing trains of the day. A daughter of Prince Ichijo, Haruko was a tiny, slender beauty, the proverbial "Japanese doll."

But she had a strong sense of personal style, remembered by Baroness Ishimoto as a pristine presence in hat and veil who "sat on her throne motionless except for an occasional smile," sometimes smoking a golden pipe, offered to her by a lady-in-waiting, and lifting her veil each time, "just enough for three short puffs."[5]

The emperor and empress were not the only ones wearing what to Der Ling seemed ill-fitting European clothes: "Imitative Japan was adopting Western modes of dress, and passing through the throes of sartorial evolution with a vengeance." Clearly, it had not been worthwhile trumping the minister from Belgium just to see something she could have watched from behind the screen at the Chinese legation. Yet the magic of the imperial presences still seized her. Emperor Meiji and his empress bowed and smiled their way past the diplomatic corps, entering a pavilion tent set up on the lawn nearby, where they would formally receive and greet each dignitary in their turn. Der Ling's thrill increased as she, Yu Keng and Louisa drew nearer the pavilion, and then stood under its pitched roof which by now was powdered with pink cherry blossom petals. Count Tokugawa called out their names. After Yu Keng and Louisa had bowed before the imperial presences, Countess Tokugawa brought Der Ling forward. The kindly young Countess "told Their Majesties about me, and that I was studying Japanese," Der Ling recalled, "and both Their Majesties said that was very nice, and a distinct compliment to Japan!" Though the custom was not to present daughters under the age of sixteen, Der Ling had managed it at eleven going on twelve, assisted by her Manchu court shoes and an indomitable desire to join the charmed circle that sparkled around royal courts. Little did she know that in a half-dozen years' time she would have her place in the sun, at the court of one of the most famous female rulers ever to occupy a throne.[6]

Her presentation to the Emperor Meiji and Empress Haruko was the last time Der Ling was allowed to mingle so freely with the diplomatic corps. (Perhaps Baron d'Anethan had had a terse word with Yu Keng about his willful eldest daughter.) When her father and mother began entertaining foreign dignitaries at the redecorated legation mansion, Der Ling had to be satisfied with watching the goings-on from behind the screens in the entrance hall. This, however, was an education in itself, as she observed her father work his charm on diplomats and Japanese excellencies not predisposed to friendliness with any representative of China.

Yu Keng's predecessors had been all but inscrutable to the Japanese, accepting invitations to court functions, the homes of dignitaries and to other foreign legations, but never returning the favor, in a diplomatic version of the same "sufficient unto oneself" policy which, on the international stage, had led the West to gatecrash Chinese ports and whip up grievous wars earlier in the century. Because he had no fear of foreigners and in fact went out of his way to court them, and because of his belief that only by dispelling that fear would East and West ever come to see one another as they really were, Yu Keng had a very different attitude to his duties in Tokyo (probably seconded by Louisa, whose taste for official splendor she bequeathed to both her daughters). As such, there were few evenings when the Chinese legation's drawing room, decorated by Louisa in a Franco-Japanese style of blue and gold brocade, crystal chandeliers, and display tables full of Japanese porcelains, bronzes and enamels, did not sparkle with the diamonds and feathers of ladies foreign and Japanese, the medals and braid of their husbands, and diplomatic *causerie* in a complex web-work of languages.

Der Ling loved this drawing room so much, she writes, that when no one was about, she would prance the length of it, acting the *grande dame*, murmuring polite nothings to her guests as she leaned on the arm of an imaginary gentleman, who probably had the same features and style of a Japanese officer named Major Hijikata, son of Count Hijikata Hisamoto, Minister of the Imperial Household. Hijikata the younger was very handsome. Educated in Germany, he twirled his waxed mustache and habitually clicked heels as he bowed to ladies. Der Ling thought he looked like he was wearing a corset, but she nonetheless fell in love with him. Sitting behind the screen in the glittering hallway, Der Ling watched ladies pass wearing gowns with trains, their hair piled high with diamonds and feathers. The true magic for Der Ling occurred once the guests removed to the ball room. She knew the room by heart — as with the blue and gold drawing room, Der Ling would sometimes creep into the empty ballroom, her footsteps echoing as she danced across its wide shining floor, the four chandeliers over her head glistening even in darkness, wondering as she twirled how the ladies danced so gracefully in their long trains, and hoping she would soon have an opportunity of learning to do the same. During her parents' grand receptions, all she could see from behind the Japanese screen in the hall was whirling figures crossing the open doorway, blotting out and at times appearing to blend in with a large Chinese scroll painting that dominated the facing wall. Despite the feathers and frills, diamonds and swords, the polkas, lancers, waltzes, and schottisches and the laughter and chatter that were part of them, the elegant painting remained coolly, indomitably itself, penetrating her dreams at night with visions of dancers circling beneath glittering crystal fixtures, against a backdrop of stylized but serene Chinese mountains, clouds and waterfalls.

She wanted to be one of those grand ladies — not a Chinese lady in stiff brocades, hidden away, but a free-wheeling Western woman, able to take a kiss on the hand or dance around a ballroom without consequences. Even for a girl of her progressive upbringing, this was a tall order.

In the middle of this Sino-Japanese social flowering at the Chinese legation, Der Ling had the privilege of meeting one of the greats of China for a change — Viceroy Li Hongzhang. In his mid-seventies at the time of his 1896 visit to Yokohama, aboard the Pacific Mail Steamer *S.S. City of Peking* (on which Rudyard Kipling would travel to San Francisco a few years later), Li had already lived the equivalent of several lifetimes. Son of a vice-president of the Board of Punishments who had achieved the highest possible academic degree in China (*jinshi*) and was one of the hundred top officials in the country, Li came from a family of provincial gentry in Anwei, due west of Shanghai, which would be his headquarters of choice on and off for the rest of his life.[7]

In 1847, Li himself attained to the *jinshi* degree (one of the few achievements for which Der Ling makes no claim for her father) and was made a member of the Hanlin Academy in Beijing, the prestigious library located near the imperial precincts of the Forbidden City; scholars from the Hanlin were held in such esteem they frequently wrote the proclamations issued under emperors' names. When the future Empress Dowager Cixi became secondary wife to the Xianfeng Emperor, she knew very little of reading and writing, and it was scholars from the Hanlin Academy who helped her attain the skills she later was wont to brag about to Der Ling.[8] Li might well have remained in these comfortable scholarly surroundings but for the outbreak of an uprising in Guangxi province in 1850, which within a few years had spread down the Yangzi Valley like wildfire and overtaken the city of Nanjing in the name of a quasi-Christian religious movement called *Taiping Tianguo* or "Heavenly Kingdom of Great Peace." Begun by a Christian convert named Hong Xiuquan, a failure at the state examinations whose visionary episodes convinced him that he was the brother of Jesus Christ and must reform China of its sins, the Taiping Rebellion was largely born out of Hong's disgust (shared by many Chinese) of the perceived and real strictures of Qing society, including its exclusion of women from service to the state, and the many hoops it made even its brightest jump through, with no promise of a reward for their effort.[9]

It was the Taiping unrest that brought Li back home to Anwei province in 1853, effectively altering the course of his career: from scholar to military leader, at a single bound. Standing over six feet tall, with a face made solemnly handsome by a mustache and goatee and coolly sparkling black eyes which one writer has vividly described as "warm as a pawnbroker's balls,"[10] and a temper which another who knew him chalked up to the fact that "like ginger [with age, Li] became hotter," Li was tailor-made for the military.[11] Joining forces with General Zeng Guofan, a fellow *jinshi* who in contrast to Li looked much more the retiring scholar but proved remarkably equipped to deal with the Taiping rebels, Li became Zeng's protégé in innumerable ways, most significantly in learning the tactics that would serve him well on and off the battlefield: razor-sharp cunning, the techniques of ambush and the uses of preemptive attack to remove present or potential rivals. Upper-class Li had had to learn these ways, but not so the outsiders and roustabouts with which he populated his armies.

By the end of the Taiping campaign, with the "Emperor" Hong dead by suicide, and after Li's wily mentor Zeng had neatly stepped out of the way, at the young age of forty-nine Li was named Viceroy of Zhili, placing him in a seat of power rivaled only by that held in Beijing by the dowager empresses Cixi and Cian. It was the protection of the former, especially, that kept Li hermetically sealed from his many enemies, though it was also a fact that when Cixi was displeased with him, she just as easily withdrew the emoluments and sent him off to do conservancy inspections along one of China's troublous rivers, only to restore him to grandeur when needed. A reformer who tended to make use of undercover means not generally relied upon in the West (or at least not admitted as such) but characteristic of China's corruption-riddled governing structure, Li also leaned on the advice of upright foreigners such as the unimpeachable Sir Robert Hart. As the author of his biography in *Eminent Chinese of the Ch'ing Period* writes, "Always progressive, yet patient and conciliatory, it was [Li's] fate to bear the blame for failures which might have been avoided if he had had his way," though it is also true that policies constructed by Li for dealing with Russia helped make the road all the smoother for the Russo-Japanese War of 1905, not to mention many other troubles, particularly in Manchuria, that followed in its wake.[12]

Li had had a stroke in 1888, followed by the death of his wife four years later, and these shocks combined with the uncontrollable *mêlée* that was the Sino-Japanese War, including an assassination attempt in Japan which had wounded him in the face, had had their doleful effect on his physical and emotional well-being. Still to come was the Boxer Uprising, which would literally put the final nail in his coffin. But in 1896, following the May coronation in Moscow of Tsar Nicholas II, at which Li was present, the aged statesman decided to take a goodwill trip around the world, meeting everyone from Kaiser Wilhelm II to Queen Victoria to President Grover Cleveland in Washington D.C. His stop in Yokohama was the last leg in an exhausting diplomatic whirlwind. While some Chinese sources state that Li did not go ashore, Der Ling reports that he did, and to give her the benefit of the doubt it is characteristic of Li to have made an effort to check in with Yu Keng, one of his most successful protégés, as it was like Yu Keng to have made the trip to

Yokohama just to see the old man and make sure he was comfortable for his brief stay, and perhaps to report on undercover matters unknown to us today. Der Ling says her father arranged for Li to pass the time in what she describes as "gorgeous rooms" in the Hotel Metropole, which certainly sounds like the sort of splendid lodgings Yu Keng regularly arranged for his own family.[13]

"Many strange stories were told about this man," Der Ling remembered, having heard them in both the kitchen and in the drawing room. Li was said to be highly eccentric, with such a terror of dying abroad that he carried a Chinese coffin with him everywhere he went.[14] Der Ling accepted this as one of the trappings of his great power, as well as being symbolic of reformist Li's essential foundation in old Chinese tradition, according to which a man's coffin was as important as — and often far more expensive than — a fine piece of household furniture. But when Der Ling and Yu Keng reached Yokohama and were ushered in to meet the famous Li, Der Ling's idealistic vision of the statesman took a generous splash of cold water. Li must have looked every bit his age, being tired from his round-the-world journey, and he obviously had not bothered to freshen up for the visit because Der Ling beheld him "dressed in a huge Chinese padded gown, padded boots . . . a great ungainly bundle of a man." With his long gray beard, Li had something of regality about him, yet Der Ling was struck by how rumpled he looked: "Just an ordinary old man," she recalled. She also could not help noticing that every time he answered her father, he cleared his throat with a phlegmy "rasping" sound.

Li was the first Chinese official Der Ling had encountered since the family had been living in comparatively Westernized Japan, and she remembered thinking him uncouth. He had some bad habits, allowing burning ash from his water pipe to singe the fine carpeting in his hotel room, spitting continually, and passing gas freely. But Li's servants were worse. According to Der Ling, they did not understand how to turn spigots and so broke them off to get water, flooding Li's suite; they, too, smoked, and burnt holes in the carpeting. In the several hours of Li's stay, they had managed to ruin the hotel room. Perhaps it gave Yu Keng some comfort to discover later from the Chinese minister to Washington that Li's servants had similarly trashed a luxury hotel in New York City. But

Der Ling tells us that when the Metropole's staff presented Yu Keng a bill for damages to the tune of $800, her father paid it without a word to Li. Clearly, he owed Li for more than a few past and perhaps present favors.[15]

With the irony that attends all events of high state import, it came about that not long after Li Hongzhang's visit to Japan, another Chinese visitor wended his way to its shores, one known not only to both Li and Yu Keng but to most of China's highest officials and police force. This fugitive, whose arrival was kept under strictest secrecy, would one day wield far more power, even after his early death, than even the Empress Dowager at her most indomitable — the power to unmake the Qing empire that Cixi and Li had worked most of their lives to hold together. He was Dr. Sun Yat-sen.

Ironically, it was because of this sought-after enemy of all that the Qing court stood for that Yu Keng, one of the most loyal and honest of the Empress Dowager's officials, would find himself at the mercy of his own countrymen, within the walls of the Tokyo legation itself. The problem was that Yu Keng's pro-Western reputation had preceded him. When an order arrived suddenly from Beijing in summer 1897, allegedly from the Empress Dowager herself, commanding him to seek out and arrest the revolutionary Sun Yat-sen, Yu Keng himself took the matter objectively, while his first secretary, an excitable man of conservative bent, approached the situation as if the Empress Dowager herself had stood in the office doorway, demanding instant action on her decree.

Aside from the first secretary's obvious motivation for following the Beijing decree to the letter — if we can believe Der Ling, Yu Keng was surrounded by such martinets, always with an eye out for increasing their own stock at his expense — Sun Yat-sen's whereabouts were of understandable importance to the government he sought to overthrow. Born to a poor family in South China, not far from Macao, Sun Yat-sen (also known as Sun Wen) had had the luck of having a brother whose immigration to Hawaii had resulted in enough material gain to send money home to his family. He was eventually to bring the younger Sun over to the islands, where he attended an Anglican school in Honolulu. But along with medicine and politics, Sun flirted with Christianity, alarming his brother, who promptly sent him back to the backwater whence he had come, with consequent hardening of the young man's resolve to reform not just the low-lying ignorance of China's country culture but also the highest peaks of her governing powers.

Fleeing to Hong Kong after an incident in which he and some other secret society brethren had desecrated a village idol, Sun was baptized and received from his patron the name Yixian, which in the angular dialect of Guangzhou became Yat-sen. The newly reborn Sun Yat-sen graduated from the Hong Kong Medical School for Chinese in 1892, only to find that his diploma did not meet British standards. So he opened a herbal shop and continued his underground activities, until a nagging itch for testing the potential of his belief system moved him to write an epistle to none other than Li Hongzhang himself, urging the harried viceroy to make use of China's own talents in moving the rusted-out hulk of the Qing empire toward the same sort of Western modernization that Japan had so successfully achieved over the past quarter century. Li, with problems of his own, probably never saw Dr. Sun's letter. But a step had been taken; Sun soon took more.

By this time, Dr. Sun had made friends with the American-educated Guangzhou-born Charlie Soong, whose clan was to produce an epic's worth of revolutionaries, financiers, politicians, and assorted larger-than-life personalities that could well hold its own against the most colorful of China's real royal dynasties. By the time Dr. Sun made his way to Japan in July 1897, he had overseen and escaped the consequences of a failed revolutionary conspiracy, which left several of his co-conspirators beaten, sliced to death and beheaded, and had escaped — thanks to the power of the press — from being kidnapped and held at the Chinese legation in London, where he had been recognized as a fugitive due to his own carelessness in allowing himself to be photographed while drumming up nationalist support in San Francisco. Once in Japan, Dr. Sun was welcomed by powerful Japanese supporters, who not only wished to behead the power of China's Qing dynasty and all its officialdom but to expunge Asia of all traces of the West. After the fall of the Qing in 1911 and the declaration of the republic, Dr. Sun would briefly serve as provisional president of China before turning the reins over to Yuan Shikai, who was not only more suited to the harsh demands of the seat of power but moved by far more self-interest.[16]

Thus when Yu Keng's first secretary demanded that the Chinese legation act instantly on the arrest orders, his tension can be understood. In the China of the time, failure to act on an imperial order, like giving offense to a high official, could cost a functionary his head. But something more was motivating the man's reaction. Yu Keng knew that the order had not come from the Empress Dowager, and used this assessment in defense of his cautionary response to the order. "Produce Sun Yat-sen," he told the secretary, "or bring me proof that he is in Japan, and where he is hiding, and I will take the necessary steps; but on mere rumor I can do nothing." Nothing, that is, according to the Western legal view that to arrest a man wanted in one country while he has taken refuge in another, without a proper extradition decree, was to cheapen and undermine the very authority requesting the arrest. Yu Keng was probably also thinking of the public relations aspect. He knew that a failed attempt at capturing Sun, at the Chinese legation in London, had hurt the Qing government far more than it had Dr. Sun, and in fact had enabled him to escape amid a huge amount of publicity that did nothing to improve the world's baleful view of imperial China and its methods of silencing opposition.

Der Ling claims that her father did not know whether or not Dr. Sun was in Japan at the time. However there is no reason to assume that Yu Keng was not aware of Sun's whereabouts, given his uncommonly friendly relations with Japan's most powerful men, many of whom put heavy stock in Sun's anti-Qing credo. As for the first secretary, there cannot have been much for Yu Keng be astonished at when the Empress Dowager's brother-in-law, his old friend Prince Gong, forwarded to him a letter the secretary had sent to the throne, denouncing Yu Keng in the strongest of language: that he had "cast aside old Chinese customs, adopting Japanese ways," was a "traitor," who treated the Japanese as equals; that he knew that Sun Yat-sen was in Japan and would do nothing about it because he, in fact, was a follower of Sun's revolutionary party and was assisting him in hiding.[17] This was probably mostly true.

In her memoirs, Der Ling claims that her father did receive a visit from Sun Yat-sen in Paris, shortly before the family returned to China in 1903. According to Der Ling's account, Dr. Sun was not just known to her father but was considered a friend with whose ideals Yu Keng was in agreement; and she recalls that her father had the foresight to meet with Dr. Sun in the family's private apartments rather than in the legation office itself. Yu Keng knew, Der Ling insists, that by meeting with Dr. Sun he had risked his own life, should the information about the visit ever reach China, and she records her father's summing up of the occasion: that while Dr. Sun must never come to see Yu Keng, he was willing to meet him on safer neutral territory. When Dr. Sun came to Japan during Yu Keng's ambassadorship in Tokyo, the latter must have known more about his whereabouts and his connections than he let on to the Chinese government.[18]

One of Dr. Sun's avid supporters, the strongly Westward-leaning constitutionalist Count Okuma Shigenobu, was (according to Der Ling) a close friend and colleague of Yu Keng's, which makes it at least possible that he knew more about Sun's whereabouts than he admitted. That the anti-Sun group in China never had much evidence of Yu Keng's friendship with the man is clear from the next big denunciation to the throne, a silly matter of form that must have made the Empress Dowager laugh. While Yu Keng and two court functionaries were meeting with Count Okuma, Yu Keng removed his peacock feather and bright-buttoned cap and placed it beside his chair — a gesture European gentlemen performed all the time, as Der Ling points out. The visiting Chinese, one of whom was Li Muchai, sent to Japan to study its finance system, and his first secretary Wong Tachih, regarded this as *lèse-majesté*, and promptly sent memorials to the throne advising Yu Keng's recall. Der Ling is probably exaggerating things for maximum dramatic benefit, as usual, but it is not impossible that Li and Wong were in Japan more to spy on Yu Keng's legation than to learn about foreign budgetary methods. (Yu Keng himself had been charged with the task of covertly gathering information on Japanese military and naval schools, which was later put to good use for Beijing's Imperial College.)[19] As Der Ling recalled, "[I]n spite of Li Mu-chai, Wong Ta-chih, and his own vindictive first secretary, [Yu Keng] went calmly on his way, doing the best he knew, as always."

"I do what I think is right," Yu Keng told his critics. "Her Majesty may always recall me if I do not please her." They were words that could have come out of the mouth of any official serving a European crown, or even in the cabinet of an American president; but considering the power of the reactionary conservatism of the China of Yu Keng's day, they were brave words coming from a representative of the Chinese throne. But then, if Yu Keng was as close to Cixi's mortal enemy Dr. Sun as Der Ling says, bravery was something he knew quite a bit about.

7
Back to China, forward to France

Li Muchai did get something for his pains. Despite his treatment of Yu Keng, when it came time for Yu Keng's ambassadorship to wind down, he offered to recommend Li to the post at Tokyo, and the recommendation resulted in Li's appointment. In part, it is possible Yu Keng did this to quiet the denouncers at the Board of Censors, who (says Der Ling) in the wake of the elderly Prince Gong's death in late May of 1898 had again impeached Yu Keng to the throne. Between him and disaster now stood only old Ronglu and the Empress Dowager Cixi.

"Father liked excitement," Der Ling tells us (she did, too), so when news reached Tokyo of the reforms that seemed to tumble off the young Guangxu Emperor's desk in a cataract of paper and ink, toppling all that most conservative Manchus and Chinese held nearest and dearest, it seemed that China was not such a dreary place to return to after Japan. Yu Keng's excitement — which may possibly have been activated as much by clandestine involvement in the events leading to the changes as the changes themselves — was felt by many reform-minded Chinese, in and out of the government; the wide-ranging reforms proposed and implemented by the young Guangxu Emperor were like so many rays of hope coming up over the horizon of what had become a dark landscape of discontent. It was not to last, for two significant reasons: the characters of the Emperor and Empress Dowager themselves.

Since 1861, first for her son Tongzhi and then for her nephew Guangxu, the Empress Dowager Cixi had ruled from behind the curtain — the only place for a woman in Confucian China, even if she was the Empress Dowager — and though she had given Guangxu nominal use of the reins of his office, shortly after his marriage to a cousin, the future empress dowager Longyu, in 1889, and retired to the magnificence of her Summer Palace on Lake Kunming outside the city, she still had eyes watching, ears listening, and hands taking notes on his activities, and received regular visits from him. There would always be fundamental differences between the two, differences which went deeper than conflicting ideas of government: they were entire opposites, a situation which must form the basis of Cixi's continued vigilance over the young man's activities in running the government on his own. Where she was healthy as an ox, he was sickly and temperamental. Where Cixi was strong but cautious, Guangxu was headstrong but weak; where she was willing to coddle distasteful elements of the court, like the eunuchs, who could be of most use to her, Guangxu alienated them with violent punishment and hyper-vigilance.

It is often stated that the Empress Dowager worked against her nephew's reforms, but in fact there is no lack of evidence that she was not only well aware of most of what Guangxu was doing that spring and summer of 1898 but was supportive of reform, as observed by astute foreigners like Yu Keng's American friend, Colonel Charles Denby.[1]

Guangxu's connection with the reformer Kang Youwei who, despite his known feminist sympathies circulated intensely misogynistic writings about the dowager, was far more tenuous than the latter would ever admit (all Kang got out of the meeting was the offer of a low-level flunky position in the Zongli Yamen). It would cast disproportionate shadows as Kang's exilic reformist reputation and the "discussion groups" he gathered to further its aims waxed on, while the emperor's influence, cut off by an alarmed and reinstalled Empress Dowager, waned in the isolation to which Cixi's resumption of power committed him.

It was with Cixi's approval that the young emperor promulgated the first of his reforms to an anxious empire, on June 11, a rambling document in which he pushed the need for all Chinese subjects, be they mandarins or *ricksha* boys, to open their minds to the sort of practical, self-advancing knowledge needed by the contemporary world, while still maintaining the essential Golden Rules of Confucian teaching. This overoptimistic belief that you could sift China of all that was backward and bad while retaining all that was classic and good was a notion Der Ling (and Kang Youwei) would continue to espouse publicly for some time. But for many, it was the only place to begin the long uphill climb to reform.

As Der Ling would write after moving to America, "Life in China is a long song played softly in a low, tranquil key,"[2] and it was this long, low song, made up of variations on a theme of fatalism and superstition, that was interrupted as by a Sousa brass band by the Guangxu Emperor's impatient decrees, some fifty in all, issued over the course of the next 102 days. Nothing remained untouched by the fragile monarch's steely reforms, whether in the realms of education, commerce, the military, dealings with foreign nations, and the like. On all of these reforms the Empress Dowager was consulted, with Guangxu making frequent trips to see her at the Summer Palace when she was not coming to Beijing to meet with him. Cixi was far more the realist than her detractors were willing to give her credit for; not only that, she was deeply concerned about China and its people, feeling what Der Ling would later observe to be a literal sense of the weight of her office. Significantly, the dowager was never accused of the treachery and conspicuous consumption at China's expense that later became synonymous with her name until, in the aftermath of her reining in of her nephew's reforms, Kang Youwei escaped and spent his time traveling, writing poetry, and fund-raising (sometimes spending the latter on his travels), and publishing increasingly ugly screeds against Cixi. "The False One," he wrote in one open letter which was actually published in a Chinese newspaper, "attempted to introduce avarice and licentiousness into the Palace, in order to tempt our Sovereign [Guangxu] to destruction." Cixi was "the antitype of those vile and licentious ancient Empresses Lü and Wu," who "poisoned the Eastern Empress-Consort of Hien Fêng; she murdered with poisoned wine the Empress of Tung Chih; and by her acts made the late Emperor Hien Fêng die of spleen and indignation." It was writings like these that became attached to

Cixi's reign and memory, effacing all trace of and, indeed, need for, the less sensational truth.[3]

While Yu Keng was champing at the bit in Tokyo to return to an ever-changing Beijing, the mood in China was high if slightly delirious — so many reforms were coming at once, many of which undermined China's most basic traditions, including some that predated the Qing dynasty. But by the time Yu Keng and his family had returned to China, to take up residence once again in their house in the Tartar City — Der Ling dragging her feet all the way — the excitement had turned to frustration for some and fear for others. Kang Youwei had managed to stir up a storm. But the flash point for Guangxu's overthrow by Cixi was, significantly enough, a meeting with bearded Prince Ito Hirobumi, architect of the Meiji restoration and one of the real powers behind the puppet who was the Meiji Emperor, to discuss at a formal audience all the ins and outs of the sort of reforms which had made Japan the nascent Asian superpower it was to become. That these reforms had helped Japan defeat China militarily in the recent past was a huge elephant in the parlor to Chinese patriots who believed that even having Prince Ito within the precincts of the Forbidden City was wanton sacrilege.

It was in this atmosphere sulphurous with rumor that Cixi had gotten wind of details of an alleged plot against her. Her informant was Ronglu, who on hearing the outline of the plot had come to Beijing from his viceregal office in Tianjin to tell what he knew. It turned out his informant was the slithery Yuan Shikai, who had played the reformers' game long enough to discover their plans. According to the story Yuan told Ronglu, Guangxu, abetted by Kang Youwei and his circle, intended to place Cixi under house arrest at the Summer Palace, so as to better carry out his present and future reforms. Kang, of course, would remain at his side as advisor. For all the accounts of her frantic reaction to this tale, the Empress Dowager cannot have been terribly impressed by what she heard. By this stage of her life Cixi had survived her fair share of plots, directed at her by assassins far more dangerous than her inexperienced 27-year-old nephew — just how cool her reception of the rumored plot was can be seen in the unhurried visit she made to the Forbidden City. Ostensibly this trip was made so that she could be present behind the curtain for Guangxu's audience with Prince Ito. But it was also a sample of how Cixi did her best work: by watching and waiting. If anyone had reason to be afraid, it was Guangxu.

After the meeting and the banquet that followed, Cixi remained calm. She called Yuan to her palace in the western precincts of the Forbidden City complex later to hear about the planned coup directly from him. Only after she had determined that what he said accorded with Ronglu's account, and questioned him on further details, did she take Prince Qing and other ministers into consultation. Cixi seems to have concluded in the end that while she had very little to fear from the emperor, he had allowed himself alliances with troublemaking characters like Kang Youwei, who *was* someone to fear — who knew what else Kang would make the emperor do? For all her *sang froid*, it could not have been hard for Cixi to surmise what her own fate would be had this plot been successful.

It was at this point, in late September, that the Empress Dowager resumed governance in her nephew's name. Per all known evidence, Guangxu gave in without a fight. "Moved by a deep regard for the welfare of the nation," Guangxu wrote (or was dictated to write) in his edict of September 21, "I have repeatedly implored Her Majesty to be graciously pleased to advise me in government, and have received her assent."[4] After a brief vacation, Cixi was back in the saddle again. Guangxu then went into a forty-eight hour retreat to the delicately beautiful Yingtai Pavilion, set in the middle of the Forbidden City's South Sea Lake and connected by causeway to the shore. While this situation in some ways symbolized what was to be Guangxu's restricted role for the rest of his short life, Yingtai was not a prison. It had been used in happier days by both the emperor and his aunt as a shared office. While it is clear that the Empress Dowager was too sensible to think she could benefit from letting her nephew wander the kingdom at will, Guangxu was not held by her under lock and key. To a great degree, both Cixi and her nephew, by virtue of their imperial rank, were always prisoners of their own courts.

The rumor of Guangxu's being subjected to a European-style, classically medieval deposition, a Chinese Man in the Iron Mask, started not in the Forbidden City but in the foreign legations, where the young emperor's two-day retreat was exaggerated into confinement to a dank prison, made the more horrible by the European imagination of what a Chinese prison must be like (forgetting the dank prisons of Spain, Germany, and the United States of America). It was even rumored that the emperor, too modern for his own good, had been executed outright. As a result, Cixi was done more public relations harm than her actions warranted or deserved, particularly as after she resumed the "regency" she saw to it that many of the same reforms were carried out as planned, but according to a more realistic timetable.[5]

It was not this that people remembered but the emperor's strange "disappearance," the public executions of Kang Youwei's cohorts (though not Kang; like many ringleaders who incite violence, he was to die a natural death), and the stringent tightening of control that had always characterized the Empress Dowager's rule, all of which worked to fill in any gaps in the popular perception of her as a serpentine tyrant. And the press, in time-honored fashion, made much hay from the incident. Cruel caricatures of the dowager — like the one on the cover of *Le Rire* magazine from shortly before the Boxer Uprising, showing her shriveled and fanged, a bloody knife in one hand, a fragile fan in the other, and a shishkabob of gory skulls behind her — helped spread the legend of her inhuman (and "unsexed") nature far and wide.[6]

In his absence from Beijing, Yu Keng's enemies had become a good deal more dangerous than they were before. Der Ling records that the conservative Manchu faction, which had never wished her father well, was now provided with additional hot air by the leadership of a belligerent member of the imperial family named Prince Tuan (Zaiyi). A grandson of the Daoguang Emperor, Tuan used the fortune and rank of a prince (*beile*) of the third degree to carry out a variety of schemes in support of the status quo. In addition to the usual emoluments of high birth was his marriage to a niece of the Empress Dowager, which bound him to her in a way that would cause enormous difficulties during and after the Boxer Uprising. Though Tuan had allied himself with Cixi after the coup of 1898, in most ways he out-did her in his adamant conservatism.

Why Tuan was such a favorite of the Empress Dowager's, to the point of his son, Pujun, called the "Da-e-ge" (literally, "eldest brother"), being named heir-apparent to Guangxu, remains a mystery. But contrary to popular belief, Cixi was far from being as autonomous as people believed. There is more to be said for her weakness in this case than her strength, because she was quite capable of giving in to a stronger, more resolute (and in Tuan's case, more violent) character than her own. Far from being an extroverted tyrant, the Queen of Hearts image to which she was compared by so many uninformed foreigner observers, she was much more a watcher and a waiter. She had always had to be; such was the secret of her rise to power. Prince Tuan, as he would prove in 1900, was willing neither to watch nor to wait, and he went far toward showing his hand shortly after Yu Keng's return to Beijing in 1899. Der Ling remembered the prince's strange visit to her father's house in the Tartar City. It was a visit ostensibly made out of friendship, but no one was completely taken aback when Tuan abused the freedom accorded a guest to a Chinese home by his request that he be shown all over the house — not just its principal rooms but everywhere, as if he were looking for something.

Yu Keng's mansion was undoubtedly an object of much curiosity in Beijing, reflecting as it did the East-West mixture of the family itself. "When we bought the place," Der Ling explained, "there was a very fine but old Chinese house, the palace of a Duke, standing on the ground, and by some clever re-arrangement and building on, it was transformed into a beautiful foreign style house with all the fine hardwood carving of the old house worked into it." When finished, Der Ling says, the house and gardens covered some ten acres of prime Tartar City real estate. Tuan's own mansion, incidentally, lay not far to the east of the family's compound. It was a proximity that was to prove ominous in the near future.[7] "I remember Prince Tuan very well," wrote Der Ling. "He was an evil-visaged man; his face was marked by smallpox scars, his eyes small and ferret-like."[8] In his way he was as much an outsider as her father, but in the opposite direction. Disliking, or professing to dislike, his own class, he spent his time with low-level people, many of whom, Der Ling believed, were outright crooks. Not only was his visit to Yu Keng's mansion to case all of its foreign-built details and furnishings. Der Ling claimed that Tuan suspected that her family were *ermaozi* or Christian Chinese, and his visit was, therefore, also a mission to unmask the family for what they were.[9]

On this occasion Tuan found nothing untoward, but that did not mean that he would not try again. Der Ling tells us that it was not long after the prince's visit that Ronglu invited Yu Keng to meet with him, and laid the cards on the table with his typical gruff honesty: "Prince Tuan is your deadly enemy!" As Der Ling was told later, her father had at first scoffed at this threat. "I know you are not afraid," Ronglu told his friend, "but you must think of your family!" Yu Keng did think of his family in all his decisions, but he was also a man with a strong belief in doing things according to principle. Instead of seeking another escape route from China Yu Keng had accepted an extremely visible position, that of Minister of Foreign Affairs in the Zongli Yamen, a job which would only serve to give his anti-foreign adversaries like Prince Tuan even more ammunition to blow him up with. We know Yu Keng stayed in office a little over half a year — a mere moment of time compared to long-serving officials, but a very long period indeed for a man in such danger that he had to post guards around his home, and keep an eye over one shoulder as he tried to carry out his duties.

Since returning to China, Der Ling had moped about the family's garden, missing Japan intensely — or what she thought was Japan. What she really missed was the world outside China — as she might have said, any world, so long as it was not China. "I found that as a child, and even later," she wrote, "if I wished for anything, and wished with all my might, I always got my wish" — probably aided by a great deal of playing on her father's weakness for her whims. She had wished that her family would only have to be in China a short while, that her father would receive another foreign appointment, to Europe or to the United States. As it happened, Ronglu had recently told Yu Keng that the Chinese minister to France, Ching-ch'ang, was to be recalled soon, and he offered to recommend the post to Yu Keng. The latter said he would think about it, but it was Der Ling who actually went on cogitating over the idea.

When Der Ling's fourteenth birthday, on June 8, came around, with a "shower of presents" befitting the foreign style in which the family lived, she remembered the good things which had happened on her other birthdays — leaving Shashi for Wuchang, and Wuchang for Tokyo. "Couldn't we leave China again?" was her *leitmotiv*. "Couldn't we go to Europe, to America?" Yu Keng would merely smile and say, "Perhaps."

On Der Ling's birthday, while her father was still at the Zongli Yamen, the miracle Der Ling wished for came through. The lazy heat of the early June day, remembered vividly by Der Ling, was shattered by running feet and a voice shouting congratulations in the courtyard. One of the four guards posted around Yu Keng's residence had been handed a note to pass on to his master. "He has been appointed Minister to France!"

When Yu Keng returned home, he had already been apprised of the news, and he smiled at his thrilled daughter. "You are my lucky child!" he told her simply. They were luckier than they knew. Exactly one year later, the house in which they stood celebrating Yu Keng's promotion would be looted and burned to the ground, under special orders from a certain former guest of the family's named Prince Tuan.[10]

8
La ville lumière

"The Chinese Legation at Paris was located in an excellent apartment house on Avenue Hoche," wrote Der Ling; and the five story structure, with its classical pilastered façade, was excellent from without in all respects.[1] With its broad, high rococo-paneled reception rooms hung with massive chandeliers, the Chinese Legation should have provided a fitting welcome to Yu Keng, his family and their staff, after a journey from China which had been royal in every detail. But nothing prepared them for the disappointment they were to encounter on arriving in Paris.

Boarding a French steamer in Shanghai, the family put in briefly at Hong Kong, then moved on to Saigon, where Der Ling says the bearded Governor-General of Indochina, Paul Doumer, entertained them lavishly. Yu Keng and family moved on to Singapore, where they were greeted by the Chinese consul and British protectorate officials, then to Colombo, Sri Lanka, and up the Red Sea — there Der Ling and her sister had a wicked laugh when their father's first secretary stated that all foreigners were liars: They called this the Red Sea, and it was not the *least* bit crimson. The ship put into Port Said, where smiling people in skiffs pulled up alongside the steamer and sang to the passengers; then the vessel moved on to the Mediterranean, the blue of which dazzled Der Ling, with her unhappy memories of China's river-muddied seas. "I gloried in every minute we spent cruising over her deep blue bosom."[2] From Egypt, the steamer took the family northwest to the teeming port of Marseilles, where Der Ling says they were met by staff members from the Chinese legation in Paris, as well as by the mayor and various other officials of the city.

Der Ling claimed that while this parade of welcome committees, plumes and gold-lace gave her what we are not surprised to learn were "many ideas of my own personal importance,"[3] her father took it all in stride. Yu Keng was wise not to build up any great expectations. When he and Louisa stepped into the Chinese Legation at 4, Avenue Hoche, they must have been reminded in certain ways of their first glimpse of the abandoned Chinese Legation mansion in Tokyo. There was no broken furniture, meals left to dessicate on plates, broken windows or the other unseemly sights in Tokyo. But the impression was negative; the lovely rooms looked to Der Ling to have been "furnished from some rummage sale." None of the furniture matched, in style or quality; the floors were carpeted in red while the walls were a sickly blue, with draperies of a sicklier green. (It should be pointed out that, based on photographic evidence, most attempts on the part of foreign-influenced Chinese to decorate their dwellings with a mixture of East and West resulted in much the mélange that greeted Der Ling's parents on stepping into the Paris legation.)

All of Louisa's insistence on not just elegance but propriety rose up at the sight of the place, which according to Der Ling had barely been made ready for the family's occupation by Yu Keng's predecessor, the Manchu minister Ching-Ch'ang.[4] The girls, who had just been laughing at their Chinese servants' terror of the building's elevators shortly before, now joined their parents in gazing solemnly on all the work that had to be done before the legation could be opened for business. They did not stand there for long. With her customary force, Louisa set out to look for an interior decorator and, having found one, set him to work, using silks and embroideries she had brought from China. Soon the Chinese legation would be an eye-catching riot of floral patterned carpet and figured silk upholstery, amid which coolly composed Chinese landscapes and tapestries hung from the paneled walls like vertical pools of calm.

The girls, too, were in for a makeover. A French friend of Louisa's, knowing the mother was overwhelmed with making the legation a fitting place for Yu Keng's receptions as well as with accompanying her husband on the introductory diplomatic rounds, took Der Ling and Rong Ling to be outfitted as proper diplomat's daughters by the small but fashionable Paris couture firm of Stamler and Jeanne. Stamler and Jeanne would keep the family's female division in the latest fashions for the next four years, and it would be in Stamler and Jeanne gowns that Der Ling and her sister would be presented at the court of Empress Dowager Cixi in 1903.

For all its problems of interior décor, the Avenue Hoche apartment building was well situated. One of the dozen thoroughfares spoking out from the Arc de Triomphe in west Paris, Avenue Hoche ran northerly toward the fantastical Parc de Monceau a few blocks away. Laid out for a member of the French royal family before the 1789 revolution, the Parc de Monceau, with its elegant gilded wrought iron gates, was one of the world's first public theme parks, studded with picturesque follies: ruins, arches, a pyramid and a minaret, a windmill, and even some structures Chinese in inspiration if not in fidelity, all surrounded by the narrow canyons of mansard-roofed apartment buildings. There was also room for Der Ling's brothers to ride their horses in the park, where they were captured by the celebrity-stalking photographer Chusseau-Flaviens. (He had already taken pictures of Der Ling in Tokyo, dressed in Japanese clothing and posing like a demure Madame Butterfly beside a sorry example of *ikebana*, or flower arranging.)

"What a noisy place Paris was then!" Der Ling recalled. Though the automobile had not proliferated as heavily as it would do in another few years, the cobbled streets were crowded with carriages; their ringing wheels and the clatter of horses' hooves were a constant background din. Making Paris even noisier were the preparations, already underway when the family reached the Avenue Hoche legation, for the Paris Exposition, scheduled to open in the spring. The Paris of 1900 was never more ready for such a grand public works affair; however brief in duration, like that monument from the 1889 Exposition, the Eiffel Tower, the Exposition was calculated to have a longer shelf life in the memories of those who came to participate in it and those who could only enjoy it from afar. "In London," writes Vincent Cronin, "Crown and Court set the tone. In Paris, no longer a royal city, the tone was set by higher civil servants," who made much of their civilized mode of living but likely "did not own a comfortable armchair."[5]

But the world of the incoming twentieth century had something else to proclaim besides the pleasures of well-padded furniture, with all the bourgeois limitations that image conveys. The new century's new men and women — scientists, discoverers, artists — meant to show that the rapids of progress, coursing madly toward the future, were not too dangerous for the French to hazard them. The 1900 Exposition was meant to demonstrate that audacity to the rest of the world. Strasbourg-born Alfred Picard, who made steelworks his specialty, had organized the 1889 Exposition and was chosen by President Émile Loubet to outdo himself for 1900's celebration of progress, but specifically that peculiar to France, in the world's most gargantuan international exposition to date. By January of the new year, along the banks of the Seine began to arise a world in miniature, with Turkish mosque, English manor house and Russian Kremlin cheek by jowl, the iron exclamation point of the Eiffel Tower overlooking the two and a half mile-wide grounds from nearby. There would be electric trams to transport visitors, exhibitions of the fine and performing arts, and after-dark lightshows of thousands of bulbs twinkling on every curlicued cornice and window casing.

The 1900 Exhibition would be a success in almost every way, launching the careers of new artists, designers and craftsmen — the birth of *le style Art Nouveau* is clocked from this exhibition — as well as the birth of the film age. And a 22-year-old dancer from San Francisco, Isadora Duncan, would not only find Auguste Rodin's sensual realism of form an inspiration for entirely new theories of movement, but the whole Exhibition itself an expression of the sort of changed world she believed was necessary for the acceptance of those ideas.

Although she would miss most of the 1900 Exposition, due to an upheaval in China which gained the entire world's attention all summer long and into the following year, it was through Duncan that Der Ling would come to share in all the excitement of the new age, and would come to feel that, like the salutes in the O-Hama Palace gardens, it was an age made for herself alone.[6]

In her memoirs, Der Ling says that her first year in Paris passed like a dream. For a Chinese girl used to the restrictions of Beijing and the hardly less demanding regulations of Meiji Japan, free-wheeling Paris, bright with the International Exposition, must have seemed far more fantasy than reality — a city modern in all the ways of technology as well as in its easy acceptance of an Asian girl and her delirious love for every new sight, sound and freedom that Paris had to offer. But halfway through the year the reverie was rudely interrupted when Der Ling came home from the Sacre Coeur Convent School, an institution for the daughters of prominent families located at 77 Rue de Varenne, to find that the China her family had just left was on the verge of an explosion. And that distant though China was, the explosion it was about to touch off would rumble the Avenue Hoche legation just as if it lay not halfway around the world but right next door.

While her memory of just how long the family had been in Paris at this point is somewhat sketchy (Yu Keng was appointed Chinese minister on June 20, 1899 and the family had arrived later that summer, so Der Ling's holiday would have fallen in the following spring of 1900, making the Paris sojourn at that point only some six or seven months in duration rather than a full year), it is possible that Der Ling was registered at Sacre Coeur some time during winter 1900. She did not have many clear memories of the place, other than some fleeting impressions recorded in an article she wrote for the January 1931 issue of *Pictorial Review*: "Girls hustled into shapeless blue uniforms with darker blue pinafores over them, donned white collars and cuffs and heavy-looking black shoes, snatching hasty glances at themselves in the one inadequate mirror that the convent boasted." Der Ling was, she says, "not particularly religious," and soon grew weary of uniforms, "routine, of sameness." That was about to all change on a grand scale of drama even she could not have hoped for.

Der Ling admits that being away at school accounted for the fact that she was "not so closely in touch with affairs as I had always been before," hence the alarming sight that greeted her on her return at Easter break — her usually sunny father sat brooding over a strange telegram that had been sent to him from Beijing. As always, he shared its contents with her. "You are recalled," it said flatly. "Return to China at once with your family." The sender signed himself "Prince Tuan." The fact that Prince Tuan, who had no authority to do so, would take it upon himself to issue China's minister to France an abrupt recall notice, struck Yu Keng as something more than just evidence of Tuan's ignorance of protocol.

"There is a certain formality in recalling a minister," Yu Keng told Louisa in Der Ling's presence. Tuan's telegram lacked that formality as much as it lacked an explanation for why Yu Keng was being recalled. Louisa urged Yu Keng to cable Ronglu in Beijing, quoting Tuan's note and asking for confirmation. Ronglu himself had advised Yu Keng to take his family out of China by accepting the Paris appointment, because he feared that Tuan was up to something; perhaps it was Ronglu who could now explain the telegram. Der Ling noted that her father and Ronglu had agreed to use a secret code, which would prevent people like Tuan from being able to read the telegram even if he managed to intercept it. The code worked, because Ronglu did receive Yu Keng's telegram, and sent a return cable instantly to Paris: Yu Keng was not to move an inch. The court was unaware of any recall order. "It means evil days for China," Yu Keng concluded grimly.

How evil they would prove to be nobody yet had a clue — not even the nameless rustics who were setting events in motion in China, where a charismatic village cult from Shandong province, whose pugilistic ritual exercises earned them the fateful nickname "Boxers," and whose faith in god-given invincibility powered a hatred for the *fengshui*-disturbing, god-offending activities of Christians foreign and Chinese, was rising up from the warm soil like shoots of bamboo. Far from being merely one of the many local cults that arose in China when drought or political unrest seemed to point up the gods' dissatisfaction, the Boxers grew in strength and influence, not just in muddy villages but within the precincts of Beijing itself — which was hardly surprising, since several hard-line princes of the Manchu dynasty were backing them all the way. A letter from an obviously worried Ronglu, arriving a month later, left little to

Yu Keng's fraught imagination. The court was in an uproar; it would be dangerous for Yu Keng to return, particularly since Cixi was being pressed by Prince Tuan to receive the Boxers. Ronglu added that for the first time since he had known Cixi — going on nearly forty years at this point — he could not influence her.[7]

A stronger character dominated the court now; and if Prince Tuan thought the old lady should receive the Boxers, there was not much he had to do to convince her that see them she must. It is not impossible that one of the attractions the Boxers had for Cixi was their entertainment value. The post-revolutionary writer Chen Duxiu actually blamed Beijing opera, along with Buddhism, Daoism and Confucianism, as factors directly responsible for the Boxer Uprising.[8] Der Ling believed that Cixi's obsession with theatre had indeed left her open to Boxer influence. "The Boxers, from time immemorial, were jugglers, mountebanks, purveyors of strange medicines and charms, and their number was legion," wrote Der Ling. The Chinese term for these people, "*mai yi te*," she tells us, translated approximately to "doers of stunts," and these they performed, "under grimy awnings," while also selling folk remedies and stealing from their customers' pockets as they entertained them.[9]

With their built-in distrust of foreigners (many Chinese even expressed disgust at the way Westerners smelled), and their deeply held beliefs that foreigners and their Christian religion had angered the gods of China to so great a degree that the latter had turned away from protecting the interests of the Middle Kingdom, the Boxers found a friend in Prince Tuan, who despite his royal birth shared much with these lower-class sectarians. According to Der Ling, it was Tuan who "undertook to weld the Boxers into a fighting organization" for his personal amusement than for any other reason, and only later seized upon the idea of using them to drive out the foreigners.[10] Cixi, says Der Ling, disliked Prince Tuan's perpetual involvement with "the riffraff of China," but here was a perfect scheme for proving to the old lady that Tuan had not just been playing peasant all these years — he had actually been stirring up a grassroots army to rid China of the foreign element that both he and the Empress Dowager loathed. Behind all this public fulminating against foreigners was a hidden reality: that the Boxers from the start had been as anti-Qing as they were anti-foreigner. Using the

Boxers to declare war against a common enemy would keep the emperor and empress dowager safely in situ. Cixi, convinced that the Guangxu Emperor would produce no heirs, had nominated Prince Tuan's son, Pujun, to be Guangxu's heir-apparent. This nomination only increased Tuan's territorial attitude toward the throne. Little wonder, then, that Cixi, who for all her reputation as an icy tyrant actually was ruled far more by heart than head, fell into the trap Tuan had set for her. It was a trap she was not to see as such till it was too late to escape it. As Der Ling described her in later years, "She had strong emotions, but her will was stronger . . . and yet she liked people to sympathize with her."[11] That susceptibility came at a price.

Where the Empress Dowager and Prince Tuan parted company was the personal nature of Cixi's feelings on the matter of foreigners in China. For Tuan, the ousting of the foreign powers from China was clearly just a step in eventually removing all obstacles on his son's route to the throne and the power Tuan would hold as father to the emperor. To Cixi, with her longer experience and more complex reasoning, the foreign merchants who had pushed opium down Chinese throats, destroying families and economy, were much the worse for having sent their armies to invade Beijing and destroy the glorious Old Summer Palace, which Cixi, her husband the Xianfeng Emperor and their son Tongzhi, the Empress Cian and the court retinue had had to abandon to the flames. In poor health when he fled to the hunting palace at Jehol, Xianfeng's condition had worsened traveling over rough terrain; it was also distressing to watch from afar as concessions were wrung from his brother Prince Gong by the victorious foreign commanders. The emperor's death was just an added mortification for everyone concerned, but especially for his secondary consort.

Considering this background, Cixi could be forgiven for blaming the foreigners for having killed not just her happiness as a woman of influence at one of the world's most luxurious courts, but for killing her husband into the bargain. Perhaps by striking at the foreigners when and how she did, through the convenient agency of Prince Tuan, the old lady was putting all the strength of a bereaved widow into the blow. One might say she used none of her famous reason, and all of her infamous passion, in backing Tuan's scheme.

"People in Europe will never quite understand the East," wrote acerbic Englishman Bertram Lenox Simpson, who would survive to write at length about the siege of the legations, "for the East is ruled by things which are impossible in a temperate climate."[12] Unfortunately, the Boxers showed that China's was not just a temperate climate permissive of the bending, even breaking, of rules held dear by the foreign community at large, but was also easily capable of rising to blistering heat — not the heat of the summer sun so much as that of wildfire. Fire was one of the tools used by the Boxers, particularly by their female contingent, the Red Lanterns, young women who were believed capable of flight and other superhuman acts, perhaps one of the few instances in China where women were accorded powers equal to their men. During their levitations, it was rumored, they would set fire to buildings using their namesake candle lanterns. (They were also allegedly able to set fire to a house simply by waving a fan.)[13] Understandably, of all the weapons used by the Boxers to eradicate foreigner and foreignized Chinese, flame was the most potent and most dreaded.

It was, in fact, the fiery rampage the Boxers went on during the days of June 13–16, following their entry into Beijing, that convinced the court hardliners, among them Prince Tuan and the Empress Dowager, that letting these men and women run around like children in a toy store was to risk having the whole scheme turn from scaring the foreigners out of China to burning down the entire Imperial City. In those three days of mayhem, great sections of Beijing were set fire to and pillaged, but not entirely at random: it is clear that certain buildings owned by certain people were targeted for special attention. British journalist George Lynch, who entered Beijing with the relieving allied forces in August, had an account from a Manchu witness named Chuan-Sen that confirms this:

> In the evening, shortly after my arrival at my house, large numbers of persons, carts and horses were running eastward from the main street inside the Hai-Tai Gate [Hatamen]; all the men of the shops were hurried to shut their doors; some one cried out

that the Boxers had entered the Hai-Tai Gate. After a moment some concentrated smoke rose to a great height, and a noise of firing guns was heard. By judging the noise and direction of the smoke, I knew it was the American missionary building near the entrance to [the] Hu-Tung [or alley], inside the Hai-Tai Gate, which was burnt down by the Boxers. The Boxers as they were walking northward ordered every shop to burn incense. Then the English hospital, *the house of Yu-Keng, present Chinese minister in France*, all the shops thence southward to the entrance of Teng-Shi-Ko [Lantern Market Street], the American Church in Teng-Shi-Ko, the French church at Pa-Mien-Tsao, the dwellings of the professors of the Imperial College were burnt one after another. [Italics added][14]

Writing from burning Beijing to a cosmopolitan Paris caught up in the swirl of the International Exposition, Ronglu broke the heavy news to Yu Keng in a halting telegram: "Your house destroyed in Peking." As Der Ling later explained, on this occasion cases of heirlooms brought to Beijing by Yu Keng's ancestors were either stolen or burned. Only after Yu Keng returned to China several years later did he hear from Ronglu just what had happened. According to Der Ling, Tuan himself said to Ronglu the following day that his only regret in the matter was that Yu Keng and his family were not inside the house when his Boxer bravos torched it. Tuan had managed, however, Der Ling adds, to wreak his vengeance on relatives of her father's, some of whom had committed suicide rather than face torture and execution.[15]

Thus, after the mayhem of June 13–16, the imperial court made a decision. Beijing was full of the Muslim troops of General Dong Fuxiang, who had accompanied the Empress Dowager from the Summer Palace to the Forbidden City, along with four other Chinese military contingents. What happened was a simple act of mercenary absorption: vigorous young Boxers were taken into Dong's army, while the older ones who were causing the most trouble in Beijing were sent outside the city to form a sort of "human shield against foreign troops" who were slowly heading toward the city to rescue the legationers. To sweeten the pill of conscription, both General Dong's men and the Boxer recruits were granted allotments of rice and payments of silver. The only Boxer mob which was left to its own devices was the one attacking the siege-worthy North Cathedral, where Bishop Favier, clergy and converts were being protected by a tiny group of officers and the building's strong walls.

As a recent historian points out, just when "the famous Boxer siege is said to have begun, the Boxers ceased to have anything to do with it, and ceased to exist." Why? "Now that war with the Foreign Powers was a matter of fact, there was no reason to continue the pretense that the Boxers were a peasant uprising for which the government had no responsibility."[16] Thus the many accounts left by diarists within the legations of seeing no crimson Boxer bandanas among the bright-silked imperial and Muslim troops surrounding the distant walls of the British legation, and the fact that most of their shots not only went wide of the mark but seemed suspiciously like the cracking of fireworks (which, in fact, most of them were). And it was Ronglu who, having been told by the Empress Dowager to protect the safety of the barricaded foreigners, and trying in vain to secure a cease-fire with the understandably hysterical legationers, wrote the following letter to Viceroy Zhang Zhidong, Yu Keng's critical superior from Hubei province:

> After the death of the German Minister [von Ketteler, whose violence and foolhardiness had made him an early Boxer target], the British Minister [Sir Claude MacDonald] had Prince Su driven out of his palace and ordered thousands of Chinese converts to live there. The various legations were united and daily fired their rifles and guns, killing innumerable officials and people. It was therefore impossible for the Headquarters Army and Tung Fu-hsiang's troops not to defend their positions and make counterattacks ... On June 25 I had a notice written in big characters saying that in accordance with the [Empress Dowager's] Imperial decree we will protect the legations, that shooting is forbidden, and that we should communicate with each other. [The legations] not only paid no attention, but [opened fire] ...[17]

Communication was not just problematic, it was nonexistent. Chinese court officials and military officers came bearing truce and were immediately shot at or killed, and with their telegraphic connection to the outside world cut off, the legationers had nothing but their instincts to rely on, with all the paranoia that that implies. Ronglu had his own double game to play. The only troops from whom much was to be realistically feared were those of General Dong, with their mix of Muslim and ex-Boxer fighters, functioning according to the dictates of pockmarked Prince Tuan.

Ronglu, on the other hand, kept his men close to only a few perimeter points, and made them understand that the Empress Dowager's directive regarding protecting the legationers was to be followed to the letter, while still shooting off enough ammunition and firecrackers to satisfy the aggression of the court conservatives. Within the accidental miscommunications were other miscommunications of a more deliberate nature. Ultimately, none of it did any good. Before the month was out, delicate ministers' wives would be sitting for hours at sewing machines, flinching under the rattle of constant shellfire as they stitched into sandbags the bolts of silk given to them by the Empress Dowager the year before.

9
Chinese powder keg

It was miscommunication about the fate of the man who had been a kind of Gallic Cassandra in the Legation Quarter just prior to the Boxer violence that put Yu Keng, his staff and family in danger, in faraway Paris. The French minister in Beijing, Stephen Jean-Marie Pichon was a plump, excitable little man with a snobbish wife, who was given to what the high-nosed British scoffed at as typical overwrought "Continental" behavior.

But Pichon was a friend of Bishop Favier, who had been frank with the French minister about where things were headed. The bishop had warned Pichon in mid-May that with the recent Boxer-related violence a mere forty miles outside Beijing, he had no doubt that the cult and its followers would be in the capital, where no measures were being taken to defuse or defend against them. The bishop also claimed to have heard that the date for an actual attack on the Beitang or Northern Cathedral had been fixed. The Boxers had in fact set July 1900 for an attack, basing the schedule on auspiciousness of the moon or month and the year; and at least one Chinese servant in legation employ insisted she had known of the Boxer plans fully a year before, "but had dared not tell [her master] for fear of losing [her place]."[1]

No doomsayer is welcome, but admittedly Pichon made himself more annoying than was necessary, with his moanings of "*Nous sommes perdus!*" accompanied by much wringing of his chubby hands. He envisioned a replay of the horrors of the 1871 Prussian siege of Paris and the Commune which had followed. Soon other legationers would come to see his point, though where a Frenchman would have nightmares about a replay of the Siege of Paris, Britishers felt chills at the thought of another Sepoy Mutiny. In either case, the Chinese outside the walls of the Legation Quarter were assumed capable of unimaginable barbarity. Therein would lie much of the misconception of just what it was that happened next.

As would be discovered when the legationers had to start eating everything from horsemeat to sparrows, Pichon was not far off the mark. But his warnings were unnerving and annoying to the other ministers, most of whom subscribed to the approved British stiff upper lip school of disaster response. One of the ministers in particular, the German Baron von Ketteler, made a habit of taking Western aggression to the extreme, picking off "Boxers" (any Chinese would do) like pheasants winging it over an *Ostpreussen* heath. He had already made himself a target by attacking a Boxer boy he had found idling in the street, afterward taking him captive. American artist Cecile Payen, who had come to Beijing with Sarah Conger, the wife of American minister Edwin Conger, recalled seeing Ketteler follow German soldiers who had taken a pair of alleged Boxers captive, hitting the young Chinese men relentlessly with his cane.[2]

When on June 19 officials of the Zongli Yamen issued a request to the ministers, sealed in eleven red envelopes, to leave Beijing voluntarily for Tianjin within twenty-four hours, all of the ministers except Ketteler wanted to take the chance to get out. They requested a meeting with the Yamen the following morning to discuss the details, but a response came that infuriated the bellicose Ketteler: the officials were happy to discuss the situation, but in view of the riots and mayhem of the past several days could not guarantee the safety of any foreigner on the way to the Yamen. Unfortunately for Ketteler, he declared prior to this letter's arrival, with a bang of his fist on the table top, that he would head for the Yamen then and there and wait for the officials to show up for parley. Not only did he enter the street against the advice of all present, but did so in the ostentatious green and red sedan chair betokening his rank. He never made it to the Zongli Yamen — in fact, did not make it very far down Hatamen Street, before he was shot point blank in the head and killed by a Boxer brave named Enhai. Now it was obvious even to the most delusional that it was not safe to leave the legations, and the ministers, their families and staffs not only stayed put, but had to make room for the other foreigners and the Chinese Christians who quickly came running to them for safety. Of all of these, it would ultimately be the latter group that suffered the most during the two months of siege that followed.

The furor over Ketteler's death, kicked off by the racist ravings of German Kaiser Wilhelm II, soon inflamed all parts of the world; and it was in the fictional penny-dreadful press reports that cropped up in the wake of the real events that the news hit Paris that not only had Ketteler been killed, but that all the ministers had been massacred by slavering Chinese fiends. Among them would have been Minister Pichon, whose imagined death French newspapers seized on with zeal and gallons of ink: **MINISTER PICHON ASSASSINATED IN PEKING!** screamed the headlines of all the papers that lay about Yu Keng's ministerial offices in the Avenue Hoche. Amusingly enough, rather than having been assassinated, in the days after the flight of the imperial court from and the entry of allied troops into Beijing, Pichon would be photographed sitting sententiously on Guangxu's own throne, surrounded by grinning Westerners giddy from larking in the abandoned imperial apartments.

"Father was perhaps the only calm and collected member of our family," Der Ling recalled. Given Yu Keng's past experience fighting the Taipings and his subsequent sparring with officialdom in high places, this coolness could be taken for granted. But even Yu Keng's iron control under pressure would be challenged by French reaction to the alleged assassination. First, Der Ling reports, came a message from the French foreign minister, Théophile Delcassé, advising him to come to his ministry to receive "protected alien status," enabling the family to stay in France until the Boxer issue was sorted out. Louisa lost her composure at reading this message and forbade her husband to go to the foreign ministry. "You will be killed as you go along the streets!" she cried. It was still not known whether or not Pichon had actually been murdered, but she was right to be concerned — perhaps Yu Keng might travel with semi-safety wearing Western clothing, but he would not put off his Manchu tunic, trousers and peacock-plumed cap, and under the circumstances anyone with Chinese features was fair game on the streets of Paris.

"I am not afraid," said Yu Keng. "I have done France no harm. Why should France want to harm me?" Besides, Der Ling heard her father say, with his habitual quiet reason, France was too modern a nation to emulate the madness sweeping over China by attacking him for something he did not do. And he had many friends in France. He would, he insisted, go to see Minister Delcassé as requested. It was his duty. Just as Yu Keng was on his way out the door, the family's Number One Boy (chief majordomo) came rushing into the room, crying out that a mob had surrounded the building. Word from the street was that these crowds were seeking a leader to help them smash into the legation. If they thought the Number One Boy was overreacting, they had only to listen, wrote Der Ling, because from Avenue Hoche below came a roar of voices, drawing nearer. From a window Der Ling saw that "[t]he street before the legation was packed with the riffraff of Paris," most of them carrying weapons of various kinds. Yu Keng shared his daughter's opinion of the "riffraff," and perhaps her enjoyment of the excitement. "A few fools see in this excitement a chance to attract attention," he said dismissively. With that, Yu Keng put on his hat and swept out of the building.

"There were no words which hinted of what we should do in case he failed to return," Der Ling wrote of being left in the silent room, surrounded by her mother, siblings and servants. "He went down to the street, and at that moment, as never before, I understood exactly how proud I was of that Manchu father of mine." After all, was Yu Keng not doing what Der Ling herself would have done — pulling out all the stops in a performance no one would forget? At Yu Keng's appearance in the street, Der Ling remembered, the protesters surged toward him, screaming and gesturing with sticks and firearms. Yu Keng looked neither right nor left, but walked straight into the mob. As the family looked down from above, the crowds began to separate for the dignified Chinese official. "He did not even look back," Der Ling remembered. The shouting died away.

Rather anticlimactically, the crowds were gone when Yu Keng came back to Avenue Hoche; he returned just as safely from Delcassé's office as he had gone there, now armed with the ministry's official protection. The threats, however, continued. In the days that followed Der Ling says there were snarling telephone calls, which tried the legation secretary's nerves on an hourly basis. A madman from Portugal invaded the neighborhood, running around the legation's apartment block shouting, "Pichon is dead! We must have revenge! Kill the Chinese Minister!" Orders went out that no unidentified persons were to enter the Avenue Hoche building above the ground floor, yet one man somehow managed to penetrate as far as the family's own residence door. When guards took him into custody they found a note in his pocket, scrawled with the warning that he had mined the basement of the apartment house with explosives. None were found, but after the incident no one breathed easy.

The increasing tensions hampered the freedom not just of the members of the Chinese legation but of all the people living in the apartment house. Yet some of the residents showed not just typical French *sang froid* but typical French humor when they told Louisa, "You know, it is as much as one's life is worth to live in the same house with you people at this time!" Yu Keng shared their humor. A little friend of Der Ling's whose parents had an apartment in the building came to her one day, quite excited, and told her that she had heard that someone had offered to kill Yu Keng for ten thousand francs, and fifty thousand for the entire family. Yu Keng was only amused by the news: "At last, I discover how much I am worth!"[3]

As gossip regarding the fate of the foreign legations proliferated and it became less wise for the Chinese legation staff to leave their offices, it was necessary to hire policemen on horseback to accompany staff or family on the rare occasions when they had to go into the outside world. The 1900 Exposition was waltzing its way gaily up and down the Seine, but Yu Keng's family saw no part of it — it was dangerous enough just stepping out the door. Not only that, but it had become dangerous for Yu Keng to open his mouth to the Paris press. In mid-November 1900, *Le Matin* published an interview of Yu Keng in which hardly a word he allegedly spoke was not set forth in language which at the very least would have branded him a traitor toward the Chinese imperial throne:

> Let the powers bring back the Emperor to Peking, whether he will or not, and rescue him from the disastrous guardianship of the Empress. Whenever my master, who has been dethroned for attempted reforms, becomes free and independent, Europe will have found its most loyal auxiliary and its most certain pledge.

He is further alleged to have suggested that in gratitude for European friendship, Guangxu would remove all anti-foreign officials and commit mass executions of Boxers found to exist in any of China's provinces. Whether Yu Keng actually spoke these words is unknown. But the comments he is reported to have made are foreign to those Der Ling records from her father, whom she paints as first and foremost a supporter of the Empress Dowager and her efforts at reform. Up to this point, Yu Keng had appeared in the press only as emissary of the Imperial Chinese court, dutifully reporting on telegrams received from Beijing (all of which correctly state that the foreigners in the legations, "with the exception of the German Minister," are safe and sound and would be protected) and keeping his own opinions out of the press entirely. But that he should suddenly step forward with a message virtually the same as that being touted in the Western press — the evil Empress Dowager, the persecuted Guangxu, whose return to sole reign would usher in glory days for both China and the Western powers — and endanger not just himself but his family by doing so, is suspicious to say the least. There was some doubt on the matter from the other side of the Atlantic. In December, while quoting from parts of the *Matin* interview, the *New York Times* pointed out at the top of the article that on the day after Yu Keng's interview appeared, "the Minister sent his secretary flying about Paris from one newspaper office to another with an expurgated copy of the interview, which limits and qualifies the alleged original statements. Later *Le Temps* printed an authorized interview which on all essential points confirms *Le Matin*'s interview, but which is expressed in more guarded language." Clearly, the secretary sent running about Paris was only able to make a little headway. But at least Yu Keng could insert those "qualifiers" that took some of the edge off the words attributed to him.[4]

Probably just as much as for reasons of personal and familial safety, this dangerous tangling with the Parisian press must have played a part in Yu Keng's decision to quit France until the dark clouds blew over. Yu Keng's stipend from China had dried up, according to Der Ling, and he paid servants and staff from his own pocket. Despite this, she claims, he assumed the cost of taking not only his family but the staff to Geneva, Switzerland, where he had rented a villa. At least there would be no bomb threats or troublemaking journalists in the Alps.

Just before their departure, Yu Keng received one last message from China: the allied troops had entered Beijing and freed the legationers. It was August 14, 1900, that month of Beijing's finest weather, when in happier times, "The late summer fruits have been harvested [and are] on display on stands and stalls in the streets, dressing the early fall markets in a rainbow of colours."[5] While American Cecile Payen was standing on the shell-pocked Tartar Wall, gazing at the sunset and remembering that "the sight of ruined Peking will forever be impressed into my memory," the Empress Dowager Cixi, with the Guangxu Emperor and hordes of officials and servants, was fleeing north and then southwest in sedan chairs and carts, toward the ancient imperial capital of Xian. Their exile, which began ragged enough, would stretch over a period of two years and quickly regain both equilibrium and splendor under the dowager's command.[6]

"Her Majesty will never again see Peking," Der Ling heard her mother say ruefully, when the news of Cixi's flight reached Paris. Yu Keng knew the old lady much better than his wife did. "I will lay you a wager," he said, "that she does return to Peking," and when she did she would resume her power as if nothing had happened. Yu Keng, who may have been speaking more from admiration of Cixi's famed bravery than any other reason, was more perspicacious than he realized. Not only had Cixi fled like an empress — as she was to tell Der Ling in later years, she had not, as rumor had it, disguised herself as a peasant woman, though when the official Wu Yung first met her when she stopped in his westerly jurisdiction of Huailai, he recalled her lamenting that she looked "like an old country woman now."[7] But even in exile Cixi would continue to live like a ruler, issuing edicts and receiving audiences at the various stations of her baggage-laden journey away from Beijing. And when she did return to the capital, she would do so as an empress — serene, indomitable, and well-dressed as ever.

10
Dancing with Isadora

Before coming to Paris in 1900, where she was wafted along on the heady breeze of French culture and first discovered what she termed "the crater of motor power," 22-year-old Isadora Duncan had survived a California childhood of feast and famine, semi-starvation as a young hoofer in Chicago, and a hotel fire in New York, where her name first began to appear in newspapers and on the lips of astounded patrons of the dance.

Now she was hoping to make her name in Paris, *la ville lumière*, though she must have first made plenty of heads turn with her dashes about the Louvre galleries with her long-haired, Grecophile brother Raymond, exclaiming over mythological figures incised on vases, and by her spirited defense of Rodin's *oeuvre* at the Rodin Pavilion at the 1900 Exposition. In 1901 Duncan, her accompanist mother, and her brother took up residence in an apartment in the eighth *arondissement*, at 45, Avenue de Villiers, which would serve as a combination laboratory and instruction studio for expounding her ideas of the truth of the dance. Certain fashionable upper-class hostesses of Paris, notably American heiresses Winnaretta Singer (the princesse de Polignac), Anna de Castellane (née Gould, later duchesse de Talleyrand) and Clara de

Caraman-Chimay (née Ward of Detroit), were drawn to the free-flowing moves of this plucky girl from their homeland, and Isadora was invited to perform in their drawing rooms, where she was observed and approved by a mixed crowd of artists, writers, composers and countesses. "I . . . sought the source of the spiritual expression to flow into the channels of the body," Duncan wrote later, "filling it with vibrating light — the centrifugal force reflecting the spirit's vision." And it was only great music — not the dizzy, pizzicati-dotted tunes of ballet scores, but the symphonies of Beethoven, the mazurkas of Chopin, and the fugues of Bach — that could "start the motor in my soul."[1]

By the time Duncan was beginning to impart her precepts in her Rue de Villiers studio, on the walls of which Raymond had painted pretentious Grecian-style pilasters, Der Ling and her family had returned from Switzerland and moved back into the apartment on Avenue Hoche. After the dust-covers came off the furniture and the chandeliers, and the necessary business of the Chinese legation had begun again (the backlog of paperwork resulting from the now extinguished Boxer incident had overflowed from file boxes onto desk tops and down to the floor), Louisa began to take her daughters, much to their delight, on her social rounds. It was the first time they had been able to move freely in Paris since before summer 1900.

According to Der Ling, Louisa had many friends among the vaguely demimonde artist-aristocrat circles that could flippantly make dinner partners of the flamboyant transvestite, the Comte de Montesquiou, and the reserved, mystical composer Claude Debussy. Thanks to Paris society's wide-ranging net Louisa and the girls also came to know the Académie Julian-trained American artist, Katherine Carl, who would become a friend of Der Ling's and would later paint both her and the Empress Dowager's portraits in Beijing. They also met the travel writer Eliza Ruhamah Scidmore, who had just published a perceptive if derogatory book about China, pointing out that "There is little sympathy, no kinship nor common feeling, and never affection possible between the Anglo-Saxon and the Chinese," and painting yet another foreign portrait of the Empress Dowager as she-devil.[2]

It was at one of these parties that Louisa must have first met Isadora Duncan. Der Ling had been as fascinated by Loie Fuller's "butterfly dance," demonstrated at the Paris Exposition, as Isadora would be when she first saw Loie perform in Berlin in 1901, and had begun to stretch her own creative wings. Der Ling knew she wanted to be a performer — an actress or a dancer, she had not made up her mind which. She and her siblings were already delighting in dressing up in costumes, as evidenced by the Carneval pictures taken of them by French society photographer Chusseau-Flaviens. She also knew that aspiring to either of these professions, while not immediately frowned upon by her parents, would have lowered the full weight of conservative Chinese censure on her head, should the news ever get back to Beijing — and it was likely that, sooner or later, it would. In old China, aspiring to be an actress was the same as aspiring to be a prostitute — there were no female actors in China, all female roles being taken by male performers like the brilliant Mei Lanfang.

Even being in up-to-date Paris was not enough to secure the "Mlles Yu Keng" (as Der Ling and Rong Ling were called by the French) against the censure of certain portions of respectable Western society. When Louisa arranged for Der Ling and Rong Ling to join Duncan's small dance class in the Rue de Villiers studio, several of her society friends threw up their hands. "You should never let those innocent children go to such a shameless creature!" they warned Louisa. She wore white robes that were so thin you could see her naked body underneath![3] This attitude toward Duncan was not confined to Paris drawing rooms — Loie Fuller was no prude, but when she sponsored a Duncan performance in Vienna's Hotel Bristol, she gave the excuse to shocked patronesses in white gloves and feathers that the scantily clad Isadora had lost her costume and perforce had to dance in her skimpy undergarment, when in fact what looked like a chemise *was* Isadora's costume. But Louisa was not fazed one bit, Der Ling writes. She understood that once her daughters returned to China, all such options as were offered by Paris would be cancelled, and she wanted her girls to experience everything up-to-date and fashionable in Western society.

Of course, Der Ling had been nursing a very different idea of what constituted a wonderful dancer, much the way Russian diarist and artist Marie Bashkirtseff had romanticized what she took to be the glamorous lives of courtesans in Nice. Der Ling was very impressed by the flamboyant actress (and royal courtesan) Belle Otéro, who "sported fine carriages, wonderful horses, and dressed to [her] roles." Otéro could be seen riding through the Bois de Boulogne, decked out in full glamor and accompanied by neatly liveried maids and footmen. The writer Colette described Otéro's "blue Mercedes, with a hat-box for aigrettes and ostrich feathers which was so narrow and high that when it rounded a corner it drooped and sank gently on its side." The occupation that brought her these riches was conveniently ignored by Der Ling.[4]

This excess was not Duncan's style, at least not early in her career. "When I first saw her," Der Ling wrote, "she was dressed all in black. A black, plain, tailor-made suit . . . too plain, somehow suggesting poverty or mediocrity." She wore a schoolmarmish white lace collar, high and boned, decorated merely with black ribbons sewn with tiny rhinestone bows. The Duncan of silken tunics and prominent cleavage would come with increased fame, but Isadora was already of a mind about the needlessness of "proper" garb. It was all very different from the time Der Ling had seen her perform in public, when she stood in bare feet, her body draped in transparent white and under the drapings a flesh-colored leotard clinging to her body. "I do not live in ordinary dress," she told Der Ling. "I cover my body because the law demands it. Silly, the law!"

Duncan's studio reflected her indifference to the trappings of empty adornment. It was echoing and huge as a barn, with a "bare and large" stage at the end. There was what to Der Ling seemed a peculiar rostrum-like construction, with a flight of steps leading up to it. A pulpit was hardly out of character for the precincts of the fiery reformer of dance, but Duncan told Der Ling the stairs were for another reason. Few women knew how to walk up steps gracefully, Duncan said. Der Ling and her sister would learn this rare feat from her. Graceful carriage would stand Der Ling and her sister in good stead in a few years, when they were daily climbing the several throne-dais stairs of Empress Dowager Cixi, wearing unwieldy three-inch high Manchu clogs.[5]

Duncan's strongest teaching tool was her own self. "I find it difficult not to go into rhapsodies over the glorious body of Duncan," Der Ling remembered. Isadora looked at the Yu Keng sisters "as a scientist studies the antics of newly discovered creatures," and soon made her pronouncements. Rong Ling, though younger, was taller, more willowy and more conventionally beautiful than Der Ling, who resembled her mother in a certain plump prettiness. Rong Ling was more appropriate for Duncan's "Greek interpretations," as Der Ling calls them, whereas Duncan had other plans for Der Ling. She should burst onto the stage dressed as a Pan-like figure, her head thrown back and her hair flowing as she played a panpipe.[6]

The lessons, which were attended by two other girls, lasted an hour and a half, three times each week. Classes were broken out into three sections, and Isadora's redoubtable mother, herself dressed in black, sat at the piano churning out music hour after hour, a "stumpy and persevering" figure, whose playing made little impression on Der Ling: "Thump! Thump! Thumpety-thump!" was all she would remember of her, as well as her habit of smacking each of the girls with a kiss, whether they wanted it or not. Each girl, says Der Ling, had her errors or her virtues explained to her patiently. To dance and pose beautifully, Duncan insisted to all of them, "means to practice, practice . . . until the head aches and the heart aches, and even the soul perspires with the endless effort."[7]

When not drilling the girls like a master sergeant, Duncan would take them on field-trips to the Louvre to study the same Greek sculpture and vases which had delighted her on her arrival in Paris. According to Der Ling, Duncan even took the girls to Versailles, where she wandered with them not through the palace itself but through the broad parterres and vistas of the gardens. On this occasion, Der Ling and Isadora happened to pause before the Temple of Love, the twelve-columned marble structure, commissioned by Marie Antoinette in 1778. Der Ling admired the statuary under the temple's dome, and told Isadora she wished she could see her taking their place. With her characteristic humor, Duncan pulled a wry smile. If only it were possible to dispense with clothing altogether, she replied.[8]

Der Ling would be privy, however, to less than classical behavior on Isadora's part. A certain French count whom Der Ling does not name had fallen in love with Duncan after she had attended a fancy dress ball at the American Embassy, costumed as Cleopatra. Der Ling says she was present at the ball, and remembered the count kissing Isadora's hand and fawning over her before the other guests. Things only got more heated when Isadora performed a dance to Mozart's "Turkish March." At the conclusion of this ecumenical blend of Ptolemaic Egypt and Habsburg Vienna, the count abased himself at Isadora's feet, tears streaming down. Thereafter, he made every effort he could to see and be with her, even gate-crashing her dance classes. As the girls taking part in the classes were all clad in what amounted to their nightgowns, the appearance of a dapper French gentleman of well-known hyperemotional romantic tastes did not sit well with the pupils' mothers and chaperones. Isadora had to send the count away, but she did so without too much reluctance, if Der Ling's recollection is accurate. One afternoon Der Ling was with Duncan in the studio when a huge box of roses was delivered. Duncan signed for them, opened the box and expressed her delight over the beautiful flowers, only to become "suddenly and insanely furious." The roses had come from her importuning comital admirer. Did Miss Duncan not care for the count, Der Ling asked her. "Oh, he's all right, I suppose," Isadora responded. But he had ulterior motives. Rather than looking at Isadora he was looking toward her future, when she would be earning large figures and he could marry her and live off her bounty — a scenario which, despite Duncan's vigilance, was to become a reality in all too many cases. "[I]f I marry him I'll have to pay for the flowers!"

Isadora then took the box, flowers still inside, to a second-story window, and tipped it over the edge. Moments later, the old janitor, who had found the box in the courtyard below, brought it upstairs, only to stare as the peculiar Mademoiselle Duncan pitched the box out the window again. The janitor, no doubt as appreciative as most Frenchmen of the significance of a box of costly roses, remained standing in awe as Duncan and Der Ling burst out laughing.[9]

11
"The golden goddess of tragedy"

"One of my youthful dreams was to study ballet dancing," Der Ling wrote. Significantly enough, it was an actress who dissuaded Der Ling from switching from the Rue de Villiers studio of Isadora Duncan to the mirrored *barre* of a ballet practice room. And not just any actress but a woman who was arguably the greatest performer and personality of the nineteenth and early twentieth centuries — Sarah Bernhardt.

What is perhaps fitting, considering the overt drama of Bernhardt's life on and off the stage, is what Der Ling says was her first encounter with the actress on the day of one of Paris' worst theatre disasters. On March 8, 1900, a charity bazaar was being held in the foyer of the columned Neoclassical *Théâtre Français*, concurrently with a matinée performance in the theatre itself, and Der Ling and her sister were wandering about the crowded space, selling nosegays of roses from ribboned baskets held over their arms. "I was doing quite well and gentlemen were buying my flowers freely for their buttonholes," Der Ling recalled, "when the whisper, electric and startling, went through the crowd . . . 'Madame Sarah Bernhardt is here!'"

Fifty-four years old but capable of appearing half her real age, Bernhardt entered the foyer dressed from head to toe in purple velvet, her curly, dark auburn hair cushioning a large picture hat that sprouted purple and gold ostrich plumes. Bernhardt stood straight as a soldier, Der Ling remembered, but she also was struck by how old Bernhardt looked close to: having only seen the actress from a distance, it seemed inconceivable that she was anything but a youthful sylph, an illusion assisted by the long, lean lines of her body, her dislike of the florid frou-frou that was *de rigueur* for the fashions of the time, and the head held ever erect. Der Ling's eye was also caught by a strangely Chinese detail of Bernhardt's very simple jewelry — a gold ring on her left thumb, like the jade archery rings worn by princes of the imperial Manchu house.

Der Ling was drawn immediately to the goddess in purple velvet: "How I wished I could go boldly up and address her!" But the hostess of the bazaar summoned Der Ling away. It was close to noon. Chastened but not defeated — "[I] promised myself I would make an opportunity to see her again, and if possible speak to her" — Der Ling returned to making rounds with her basket when she heard the most riveting word that can be called out in a theatre: "Fire!" Panic broke out as the crowds began to scatter from the area around the theatre's entrance. Der Ling lost sight of the long purple figure of Bernhardt. Rong Ling had by now joined her sister, and both gaped through the open theatre doors, at the fragile figure, dressed in white, of the actress Jeanne Henriot, standing alone on the stage. Whether she was trying to calm her audience or find a way off the stage, the sisters never knew. The gentleman to whom Der Ling had been selling flowers took both her and Rong Ling and pulled them toward the street entrance, trailed by the rancid stench of burning wood and fabric. Patrons and stage hands, actors and actresses, leapt from windows. Newspaper artists would have a field day sketching ladies being handed down from smoking casements by sturdy firemen, their skirts blowing up to reveal shapely calves to gentlemen on the sidewalks below, but it was not funny: many died in the process. Henriot's burned body lay unrecognized at the morgue before being identified by a theatre friend.[1]

In the aftermath, Der Ling's desire to speak to the great Madame Bernhardt grew more pressing. The atmosphere of funerals of the fire's victims must have seemed to Louisa an unsuitable backdrop at best to

Der Ling's continued importunings, but the fact that Der Ling thought she could gain the famous Bernhardt's time and attention just by asking for it seemed to her even more absurd. "Madame Bernhardt is a great artist!" admonished Louisa. She had no time for children. Der Ling was not convinced. "I meant to have my way," she noted coolly.

Between lovers, admirers, an illegitimate son she adored and a busy career Bernhardt had managed to carve out just for herself an exquisite little house on the corner of the Rue Fortuny and Avenue de Villiers, the same street in which Isadora Duncan had her studio, north of the Parc de Monceau and thus a few blocks from the Chinese legation. Designed by the architect Félix Escalier, the house's interior was finished off with original artwork by several of Bernhardt's artist friends: Abbéma, Jadin and Clairin (the latter had painted murals for the Paris Opera House). The house was run by a staff of eight, and in the end cost her half a million francs. The guest list for her five o'clock afternoons reads like a tablet of the immortals of art, literature, science and politics, ranging from Victor Hugo to Gabriele d'Annunzio, Oscar Wilde to Charles Gounod, Louis Pasteur and Dumas *fils*. It was this world and this living legend that Der Ling was prepared to take on, with or without her mother's approval.[2]

"My sister and I were making social calls with Mother," Der Ling wrote, "and Madame Bernhardt was at one of the homes we visited." Der Ling made an immediate beeline for the actress, who on this occasion was a vision in black, the starkness livened by a ruff of white lace at the neck and thick lace cuffs that hid her slender hands. Only a rope of pearls and an onyx thumb ring served for jewelry. Louisa introduced Bernhardt to her daughters, and Der Ling began chatting with her in French. Bernhardt complimented the girl on her fluency and pronunciation, and appeared surprised that a young Chinese girl should be able to speak the language so fluently.

Der Ling told Bernhardt that she was taking singing lessons along with piano (from the well-known pianist Clémence Fulcran, a colleague of Henri Casadesus and Pierre Monteux), and that though she was studying dance with Isadora Duncan, she wanted more than anything else to become a real ballet dancer. She said she was also learning to recite French poetry. "She smiled at me, rather pityingly, I thought," recalled Der Ling. But then Bernhardt said in her purring tones that she would like very much to hear Der Ling recite for her. "[T]o me that seemed a promise for the very next day," but Louisa quashed the idea, Der Ling recalled; it was best to let Bernhardt make a proper invitation. Der Ling could not accept this, and suffered. Resourceful as ever, however, she talked Louisa into taking her to see Bernhardt in *L'Aiglon*, which opened in the Théâtre Sarah Bernhardt on March 17, 1900.

"What a boy she made!" Der Ling remembered. "White kid breeches and black boots reaching almost to the knee, with golden trimmings. Gorgeous!" But it was Bernhardt's voice that captured Der Ling's imagination most alluringly. Even into middle age, and worlds away from the Théâtre Sarah Bernhardt, Der Ling was to remember that crystalline voice, calling out, as the Duc de Reichstadt does to his servant toward the end of the play, "Flambeau! Flambeau!" Der Ling was also mesmerized by the final death scene, in which the actress playing the young duke's mother, Marie Louise, hands him a bouquet of violets, which to Der Ling seemed to draw the very color out of Bernhardt's sunken face. In her biography of Bernhardt, Cornelia Otis Skinner quotes a witness as describing L'Aiglon as "dying as angels would die if they were allowed to." Der Ling could not have put it better.[3]

For all her friends in the theatre, Louisa was a martinet about what she would expose her daughters to in terms of entertainment, and when Bernhardt reprised her famous role as the soulful courtesan Marguerite Gautier in *La dame aux caméllias* later on, she refused to let Der Ling attend. But Der Ling managed to learn the plot anyway. In her mind she imagined Bernhardt's dashing but doomed Marguerite, and swore to herself she would see her sometime, someday, in the role. She was never to do so, but her perseverance to know as much about Bernhardt as possible was rewarded one day on her return to the Avenue Hoche legation, when Der Ling walked into a buzz of whisperings from both the French and the Chinese servants. A most distinguished guest had come to visit the legation. It was the divine Madame Bernhardt herself.

"She had been received at the embassy as though she had been a queen of France," Der Ling recalled, and was talking to Louisa in the drawing room. Der Ling was permitted to enter, speak a few words to Bernhardt, curtsey in the approved graceful style, and depart. "[C]hildren were to be seen and not heard," recalled Der Ling years later with still-fresh annoyance.[4]

A few weeks later, Der Ling was rehearsing a play — Arthur Wing Pinero's *Sweet Lavender*, an old-fashioned gushy romantic comedy that Der Ling had chosen over the same author's farce, *The Magistrate*. Since its 1888 premiere in London, *Sweet Lavender* had become a piece of oft-performed fluff most suitable for school performances, its cast replete with London barristers, a young man from America, a laundress' daughter named Lavender, and various schematic and romantic improbabilities. While the young people rehearsed, people came and went, and some stood to watch. When Der Ling glanced up she saw that Bernhardt was among them. Though the play was in English, Bernhardt knew the plot well enough to follow the action. After the rehearsal, the actress gestured to Der Ling to come speak to her. If we are to believe Der Ling, Bernhardt said to her: "You did it very well — but there are a number of faults that should be corrected. Let me teach you! Come to me and I will give you some tips." Bernhardt had barely finished before Der Ling found herself saying, "When?" "Tomorrow at four!" Bernhardt purred.

It says something for Louisa's basic trust of both Bernhardt and her daughter, and certainly her daring, that she allowed Der Ling to make her way to the actress' *hôtel particulier* north of the Parc de Monceau, accompanied only by her Chinese maid and the Chinese coachman who drove them there. Most fashionable Paris mothers of fewer scruples than hers would rather have locked their daughters up than seen them enter the house of the scandalous Bernhardt. Perhaps Louisa was impressed that the actress would be interested in Der Ling, and secretly enjoyed the reflective glow of that interest. Perhaps Yu Keng, who also had a yen for courting celebrity, played a role in the decision.

Der Ling recalls that she stood for a moment looking up at the two-story façade of Bernhardt's gray stone house, with its balcony above the door and bright geraniums in baskets, not quite sure she was ready for an adventure she had pursued for herself. The butler who answered was punctilious and hesitated to let Der Ling enter, asking for her card. As a girl who had not yet made her debut, she did not have a calling card, but when it was cleared up that Madame Sarah was expecting her, Der Ling was let into a hall lined with mirrors, in each of which Der Ling saw multiple reflections of a blushing young woman and her staring Chinese maid. Bernhardt's maid entered to usher Der Ling into a drawing room filled with Louis XV gilt and yellow satin, more mirrors on every wall. The maid then asked Der Ling to follow her upstairs to Bernhardt's boudoir.

Even in an age of potted palms, fringed draperies, and loud patterned velvets, Bernhardt's taste in décor was overblown. According to Der Ling, the walls of her boudoir were lined with "[b]lack satin wall panels, with golden buttons in the center of each . . . the ceiling . . . covered with gold and black brocade, shirred all around," which formed in the middle in a star shape. Der Ling would recollect the details so clearly that, years later, after her marriage to Thaddeus White in Shanghai, she would try to copy them in her own home. Beckoning Der Ling into this shimmering world, Bernhardt lay dressed to match it in golden gauze trimmed with gold lace upon a gilded *chaise longue*, beside a table where the tea things stood ready. She handed Der Ling a gold-rimmed cup; on the gold-rimmed saucer lay a gold spoon. Befitting her offbeat tastes, she also served a sort of garlic mousse, which Der Ling found delicious.

The lesson began without further ado. "Remember when you cross the stage from the right that the audience is on your left," lectured Bernhardt. Step with your foot away from the audience; never show the palms of your hands. Most important of all, Der Ling was not to "forget the audience and that the audience wishes to see everything you do." Bernhardt put her finger on what was Der Ling's essential problem. Der Ling had told her she wanted to dance ballet, and she also wanted to be an actress, and a singer, and several other things besides. "Learn one thing well," Bernhardt told her, "and specialize on that one thing no matter how tiresome it may become." She also advised Der Ling to continue her studies with Isadora Duncan. One day, she predicted, "she will be a great artist," because she danced from the soul, as all great artists should do.

With Bernhardt at the keyboard, Der Ling then stood beside the piano and recited, in a genuine coaching session full of stops and starts, with Bernhardt giving advice and suggestions, urging her to continue and improve. Afterward Der Ling confessed to Bernhardt that it was highly unlikely that her father would ever allow her to go on the stage, and to her surprise Bernhardt agreed. "Your father, my dear child, is perfectly right!" Bernhardt replied. Whatever she chose to do, she must do it for love, she assured Der Ling, and she was sure to succeed.[5]

One afternoon not long afterward, Der Ling and Rong Ling were in the Bois de Boulogne, in a carriage driven by their Chinese coachman, when Bernhardt drove toward them in her sparkling equipage. She was hard to miss, dressed in pristine white, with a single pink camellia on her bosom. Like the celebrity-chasing Marie Bashkirtseff whom she so resembled, Der Ling directed the coachman to pull up close enough to the great lady to be recognized. Bernhardt bowed to her with a smile as she glided along and then was out of sight again. "Parisian traffic assumed the role of fate," she recalled — as did the crafty Chinese coachman — "when we turned again and passed once more." The gracious (and perhaps resigned) actress called out from under her white parasol: "Let us go to the Château Madrid. I will meet you there!"

No sooner had they reached the café and ordered tea but Bernhardt's presence began to attract attention — to Der Ling's delight, but not to Madame's. "I do not like to come to a place like this," Bernhardt said, perversely, since she had made the arrangements. Having people stare at her when she was on stage and in a public place like this were two different things. Der Ling enthused (not to her readers' surprise) that she would love to always be the center of attention. "My dear," Bernhardt intoned, "you may think so now, but later you would grow to hate it!" Conversation ceased and Der Ling and her sister did what everyone else in the café was doing: they stared at the aging but fascinating face of the greatest actress of their time. It is curious to ponder whether it was not Der Ling's insignificance rather than her talents that allowed Bernhardt to mother her to this degree. In any case, Der Ling never appears to have questioned the matter; she remained blinded by the glow of Bernhardt's glamor till the end.[6]

12
Scandal

For the present, Yu Keng had no objection to Der Ling performing in the little production of *Sweet Lavender*, which was soon to be staged at the legation.

"My father thought it would amuse and interest me," she wrote. Blinded by her dreams of following in the footsteps of Bernhardt, Der Ling also knew that performing in a play, even if before friends, was likely to draw criticism from the conservative members of her father's staff. She had noticed, the day of the rehearsal, when Bernhardt had beckoned to her afterward, that the wife of Yu Keng's secretary had spirited her ten-year-old son out of the room after watching Der Ling and a boy actor embrace in innocent sentimentality. During this scene, not even prim and proper Louisa had stepped forward to stop the proceedings — it was a Pinero play, after all. This was not, however, how the secretary's wife saw it. In fact, from this time, when Der Ling was in her sixteenth year, we can date the creation of a reputation she may have done little to avoid, but which she certainly did not deserve — that of Westernized Chinese sex-pot.

But this trouble began with the death in January 1901 of Queen Victoria. Her son acceded to the throne as King Edward VII, his coronation scheduled for June 1902. Illness made it necessary to postpone the ceremonies till August. To attend the celebrations in London, a party of high-born and prominent Chinese was sent from Beijing: 26-year-old Prince Zaizhen, the handsome, scandal-attracted son of Prince Qing; Sir Chengtung Liang-Cheng, a Guangzhou native knighted by the British Crown in 1897; and "Jack" Wang, one of the earliest Chinese graduates from an Ivy League United States university (Yale), along with a suite of some seven or eight officials and ten servants.

The party was to embark at Shanghai on April 22, with projected arrival by the end of May or early June in London, where they were being put up at the Hotel Cecil.[1] En route to the coronation, Prince Zaizhen and his party had been entertained by Yu Keng at Marseilles, and on their return from London they stopped in Paris, where they began to spend time at the Chinese legation. It is obvious that both Sir Chengtung Liang-Cheng and Prince Zaizhen were quite taken with both Der Ling and Rong Ling — Liang reported back to China that both girls "would quite fascinate the Empress Dowager if they go to Peking." One source indicates that Cixi may already have been interested in having Louisa and her daughters at court a few years before this.[2]

"My sister and I liked Prince Zaizhen immensely," Der Ling remembered. "He was little more than a boy [perhaps meant figuratively; Zaizhen was over ten years Der Ling's senior], very handsome, well educated, and his tastes were the same as ours in many things." She adds that while she and the prince were prone to quarrel, Zaizhen paid court to her softer, prettier sister. Sir Chengtung Liang-Cheng also found himself drawn to Rong Ling. A widower since 1900, Liang was even linked with Rong Ling by the venerable but gossipy Sir Robert Hart, according to whose rumor sources "Sir Liang . . . is to remarry and . . . the bride will be one of the daughters of Yu Keng (Paris)." Der Ling confirms that Liang's interest lay not with her but with her sister, and a *New York Times* article from March 30, 1903, when the family was already back in China, maintained that "Miss Nellie Yu-Keng" was to marry Sir Chengtung Liang-Cheng and "can hardly fail to be a popular acquisition to diplomatic society in Washington."[3]

Der Ling, Rong Ling, Sir Chengtung Liang-Cheng and Prince Zaizhen appeared together as dance partners at the Chinese legation and elsewhere. (It was useful to Zaizhen that Der Ling and her sister spoke fluent French, as he himself knew only Chinese.)[4] Yu Keng's daughters were eager to show their fellow Manchus all the sights of Paris — sights the flashy novelties of which delighted the prince and his educated retinue but shocked the Confucian sensibilities of many of their staff. Der Ling does not seem to have been entirely unaware of Zaizhen's frowning functionaries, but her judgment was very much that of a teenage girl seeking to please and impress. When she invited Prince Zaizhen, Liang and Jack Wang, along with her own friends, to partake of a special dance evening at the legation — in which Der Ling and Rong Ling would perform — she and Zaizhen left his Chinese staff off the guest list. This preemptive action caused more trouble than anyone had planned.

Wong Ta-chih, the uptight mandarin who had made trouble for Yu Keng in Japan, had resurfaced (probably not by accident) as part of Prince Zaizhen's retinue. While his annoyance at being excluded from the ballet is understandable, his indignation went far beyond the pale. This man, who had funneled back to Beijing so many rumors about Yu Keng's activities in Tokyo, now attacked Der Ling. As Der Ling wrote later, not only did Wong report to China that Prince Zaizhen spent most of his time at the Chinese legation with the minister's shameless daughters, but that he gallivanted about Paris with them, touching them in public (while dancing, of course), ruining their reputations and his own. Not only that — Yu Keng's eldest daughter, he claimed, had fully descended into disgrace by dancing naked for the pleasure of the prince and guests in a ballet of her own devising.

It did not take long for Zaizhen to get wind of the rumors filtering via back-draft from Beijing. He "instantly realized his responsibilities to my sister and me," recalled Der Ling. The prince talked the matter over with Sir Chengtung Liang and, finally, with Yu Keng, and it was agreed that the coronation party should return to China.

Considering that his daughters' virtue was at stake, bandied about the officialdom of the court at Beijing, Yu Keng had dealt with the situation with all his customary reason and calm. Possibly he knew that whatever punishment he could mete out to Wong Ta-chih would be visited on the man twicefold once Prince Zaizhen got him back to China. But a mighty anger was hidden beneath his impassive exterior. One day shortly after the coronation party had departed, a staff member came to Yu Keng's office. This man had heard Yu Keng's secretary, husband of the lady who had fled the rehearsal of *Sweet Lavender*, making remarks about Der Ling that he felt Yu Keng should know about. It appeared that the secretary's wife had come running to him with the news that Yu Keng's daughter had allowed a male not just to touch her but to kiss her in front of everyone. Before several witnesses, including the staff member who carried the story to Yu Keng, the secretary threatened to get the Board of Censors in Beijing to denounce Yu Keng to the throne for allowing his daughter to "take part in a bedroom scene." What made the man's reaction all the more puzzling was that he had served Yu Keng as secretary for many years, was well acquainted with his progressive ideas about bringing up his children, and besides was a man old enough (almost Yu Keng's age) to know better.

Yu Keng sent for the man instantly. Der Ling says she was present in her father's office when the secretary arrived. Not only did he confirm everything but added a few more critical opinions of Yu Keng's laxity toward his daughter. He added that perhaps what his wife saw was not all there was to be known about the scandal. Der Ling was speechless, but not so her father. "I do not care what you say about me," cried Yu Keng, "but if ever you mention another word that is derogatory about one of my daughters I will kill you if I am decapitated for it!" The secretary attempted to apologize but Yu Keng silenced him. He demanded that the secretary bow to Der Ling in abject apology. Der Ling was well into her teens at the time, and noted the man's astonishment at being asked to bow to a "mere child."

"Did you think of her as a mere child," Yu Keng growled, "when you tried to ruin her reputation?" As requested, the old secretary dropped heavily down on the French carpeting of Yu Keng's office, and performed the kowtow at Der Ling's feet. Unfortunately for Der Ling and her reputation for the future, this was closing the barn door after the horses had already run away.

The clashing of West and East under Yu Keng's own roof were trying enough for a man no longer young. But the accumulated stresses of the Boxer Uprising and its aftermath — the deaths of family and the destruction of his home in Beijing, the heightened security and the threats which had prompted it — had undermined the Chinese minister's physical and mental health. "He felt," says Der Ling, "that all these things were poor reward for a lifetime of service to his country." It is possible that Yu Keng was already suffering from the lingering illness that eventually killed him, which may have been type 2 diabetes.[5] Yu Keng's European doctors were consulted, and their recommendation was that he take a leave of absence from his duties in Paris. Yu Keng seized the chance to get away from the legation and show his children something of the world they were soon to leave behind.

What followed was a whirlwind trip of some two and a half months, taking the family all the way from Spain to Germany, Italy to Russia. In Madrid, Der Ling tried to talk her father into arranging an audience with the young King Alphonso XIII of Spain, with whose handsome looks she seems to have been taken and who was at the time one of Europe's most eligible royal bachelors. Yu Keng rarely denied his daughter anything, "but he refused because of the fact that he did not wish to be bothered with official duties of any nature whatsoever," possibly also safeguarding Der Ling, one year older than Alphonso but much less mature, from the king's well-known lady-killing charms.

The family moved on to Rome, where Yu Keng agreed to just one audience, arranged by bushy-bearded Bishop Favier of Beijing, with Pope Leo XIII. Der Ling remembered that the pope bestowed an unnamed decoration on her father (possibly, again, at the urging of Bishop Favier) and that when she knelt before him and made reverence, the old pontiff "patted my head and told me I would be a great woman. He was a great man," Der Ling adds wryly, "but not an especially inspired prophet!" Yu Keng and family spent two weeks in Rome, leaving it to explore other parts of the country before heading north to Germany, where they spent a month in Berlin as guests of Lu Hai-huan, the Chinese minister, who was a boyhood friend of Yu Keng's. From Berlin, the family journeyed to St. Petersburg, of which, Der Ling admits, "I have but the haziest memories." It is possible that Yu Keng went there for political as well as recreational ends — there may have been loose ends to tie up in the recently deceased Li Hongzhang's Sino-Russian policy. Perhaps because Asians like Yu Keng were taken for granted in upper-class Russian society, as they seldom were elsewhere in Europe, thus created no exciting stir, Der Ling lost interest in the sights and sounds of the imperial capital which was so soon to be the stage of a revolution.

Der Ling's hazy memory may also have as much to do with the fact that her father was not feeling much better than when he had left Paris. Ominously, when the new Chinese minister, the tall, handsome Sun Baoqi arrived at the Avenue Hoche legation, he did not warm to his predecessor. Der Ling claims he even issued orders to the legation's permanent staff that when he took over they were to do everything in the traditional way, accusing Yu Keng of being a traitor who had sold China to the foreigners. Der Ling's whole reading of the transfer and the otherwise statesman-like Sun Baoqi's alleged high-handedness was probably skewed by her unhappiness at leaving Paris and her father's loss of the prestige of being Chinese minister, and cannot be taken as fact. One thing is clear: the freedom Yu Keng's children had enjoyed for the past three years was coming to an end.

One day, Yu Keng asked Der Ling to come see him — she notes that when he spoke in English to her, he used her Christian name, Elizabeth. Had he been in better health, he said, he would have applied for the Chinese ministership to Washington, which would have been the natural progression in his career. But he confided to Der Ling that he felt he would never leave China once he had returned there. However, Yu Keng had a consolation prize for his daughter. Because she would so soon lose the freedoms he had encouraged her and her sister to enjoy, "I wish, if you wish it, for you to make your official début." She was free to arrange everything as she would like it to be.

Yu Keng was crafty — he had left Louisa out of this discussion, the reason for which soon became clear. When Louisa came to hear that Der Ling had been given *carte blanche* to throw her own début party, she objected: Der Ling was still too young for a début. The fact that Der Ling, at seventeen, was still considered too young to formally enter society shows just how high Louisa's standards of protection for her were. Yu Keng overrode Louisa's refusal. "[A]nd so I made my formal entrance to society," wrote Der Ling.

There would be one final highpoint for the young girl who had started out life in laundry-hung Shashi. At a reception given by French President Emile Loubet, honoring King Oscar of Sweden, Der Ling was presented to the elderly monarch, who took her hand gently in his own. "You are the first Chinese young lady I have ever met!" said King Oscar in florid French. He bowed to her, adding: "My homage to you!" It was the last sliver of light before the door between Paris and Beijing, China and the rest of the world, shut completely. But Der Ling and her sister little knew that the door to a wholly different and even stranger world was just about to swing wide to receive them, a world which, as she would write later, made her feel "as out of place as Mark Twain's Connecticut Yankee at the court of King Arthur" — far more out of place than she ever felt in the West.[6]

PART II

Women, when they are old enough to have done with the business of women, and can let loose their strength, may be the most powerful creatures in the world.

— Isak Dinesen

13
Empress Dowager Cixi

It was the beginning of January 1903, and the frigid weather echoed everything Der Ling was feeling as she got into the launch and steadied herself against the choppy waters.

The last Der Ling had seen, and so heartily loathed, of the China to which she was now returning were the churning yellow waters of her silt-laden rivers. Compared to these, the bright Mediterranean and even the limpid grey Seine seemed dazzlingly beautiful, full of a magic never to be recovered. (As the West-loving ex-emperor, Puyi, would confide to his memoirs, "A stick of Spearmint chewing-gum or a Bayer aspirin would be enough to make me sigh at the utter doltishness of the Chinese," a perspective with which Der Ling would have found much reason to sympathize.)[1]

Gone was the orderly life they had known in Paris. As when they had left for Japan years before, the family was faced with assistants and servants who could not be depended on, who lost the keys to the luggage, who had to be told what to do next every step of the way and then did not fulfill their tasks as ordered. And as before, Louisa, fresh from playing the grand diplomat's wife in the Avenue Hoche, had to roll up her sleeves and sort out all the messes before putting a foot on shore. Der Ling and Rong Ling were morose, their mother was frantic, Yu Keng was ill, and the *Daotai* (intendant of circuit) of Shanghai offered the family the hospitality of the same damp temple compound they had rejected on their previous Shanghai sojourn prior to leaving for Japan. Once again, Yu Keng had to mollify these same unhappy officials while booking more comfortable rooms in the Hôtel des Colonies, in the French Concession.

Telegrams began to arrive from Beijing, ordering Yu Keng to return to the capital. The river route to Tianjin, Beijing's port, was frozen solid, and the only other route to Beijing, over land, was long and arduous. Doctors advising Yu Keng vetoed any notion of his roughing it to get to Beijing, which probably made a few officials at court mutter in their beards. At least, for the duration of the family's stay in Shanghai, Yu Keng had access to the foreign doctors he preferred.

By the third week in February the family was ready to be on the move again. On their arrival in Tianjin, Yuan Shikai, the Viceroy of Zhili province who had his offices in the city, accompanied Yu Keng in full court regalia to worship at the city's *Wan Shou Gong* or Ten Thousand Years Palace, where obeisance was made to the Emperor of Peace, in form of imperial tablets dedicated to the Guangxu Emperor and the Empress Dowager Cixi. Der Ling describes how her ill father had to kneel painfully before the tablets and say, "Your servant gives you greeting," followed by a formal enquiry of Viceroy Yuan as to the rulers' state of health. It took three days in Tianjin for Yu Keng to recover enough to set forth on the bumpy road to Beijing. Then his first action on arriving in the city was to request from the Empress Dowager four months' leave of absence from his duties, so that he could recover in peace. Cixi, who knew enough about poor health to sympathize, granted his request immediately.[2]

The Beijing Yu Keng and family returned to at the end of February was almost a different city from the one they had left four years earlier. Most of the Legation Quarter was still in ruins from the Boxer mayhem; the few Christian churches and missions that remained were battered almost beyond recognition. Yu Keng's house north of Lantern Market Street was little more than rubble. "The loss sustained by having this house burned," noted Der Ling, "we never recovered, as my father, being an official in the Government, it would have been very bad form to have tried to recover this money." Property losses totaled some 100,000 *taels* (about $150,000 at the time). The loss of the family's heirlooms to theft and fire was, of course, incalculable.[3]

Knowing his house was in ruins, Yu Keng had arranged while still in Shanghai for a place to live. It turned out that the house found for the family was none other than the Temple of the Loyal and Virtuous, a property of the late Li Hongzhang's, which his American secretary, William Pethick, also deceased, had used as his residence in the city.[4] Not only had the temple been used for the signing of the treaties with the foreign powers following the end of the Boxer troubles, but it had been where Li had died. No one had lived in the place since then, fearing they would see Li's ghost. The Yu Keng family had no such qualms, Der Ling reports.

It is fatiguing to read Der Ling's account of these exhausting days, particularly as it appears the family had no real chance to rest after the hard trip from the south. On March 1, a mere day after the family had arrived at the house (and a day of especial auspiciousness to the Qing dynasty),[5] Der Ling records that a pair of princely visitors arrived to speak with Yu Keng, men well known to both him and to his daughters. It was the now old and frail Prince Qing, who had assisted Li at the treaty parley and signings in this very building and his son, jolly Prince Zaizhen, who had danced with Der Ling in Paris. The princes had not come just to socialize. Prince Zaizhen and Sir Chengtung Liang had done their work, because it appeared that the Empress Dowager Cixi not only desired to meet Louisa and her daughters but wanted them at the Summer Palace by six o'clock the following morning. What this bombshell meant to women who had yet to unpack all their trunks, let alone move properly into their new home, can only be imagined. Louisa seems to have risen to the occasion, however. She told Prince Qing that she and her daughters would be pleased to wait on Her Majesty as requested, but pointed out they had no Manchu court clothing to wear. "[Prince Qing] replied that he had told Her Majesty all about us," Der Ling remembered, "and also mentioned that he had seen us in European attire," and that Cixi had said she especially wanted to see the ladies in their foreign garb.[6]

To make it easier for Cixi to rebuild the ruined bridges between herself and the foreign community — diplomatically and linguistically — it had become important to her to have women at her court who were Chinese but capable of welcoming and talking to the foreign ladies at the dowager's teas and garden parties, women who were conversant not just in foreign languages but in foreign manners and customs. It was for all these reasons that, in the end, she sent for Louisa and her daughters. Liang and Prince Zaizhen would also have mentioned that besides being accomplished, Yu Keng's daughters were lovely to look upon, which also drove up their stock with the dowager — for all her ferocious reputation, Cixi loved beauty the way a poet loves words. In short, the daughters satisfied all of her criteria.

After the princes left, Louisa began to get ready, worried more about leaving her husband than which hat to wear to the Summer Palace. The girls, however, could think of nothing else. "My mother had always made us dress exactly alike, ever since we were little girls," Der Ling recalled. Rong Ling wanted to wear pale blue velvet, which she felt suited her features and complexion, while Der Ling had her eye on red velvet, with plumed hats and shoes to match, thinking that red, the color of happiness, would garner favor with the old empress. "After a long discussion, I had my way," she notes coolly.

"It had been the dream of my life to go to the Palace," wrote Der Ling, thinking of her childhood fantasies of how glorious it must be to be Empress of China, which had been discouraged by Yu Keng. Looking over the service of Hebei silver Yu Keng had prepared to send as his gift for Cixi's sixtieth birthday, Der Ling had exclaimed how wonderful it must be to be Empress of China. Yu Keng had pulled her up short: "I would much rather have you here, asking me questions about these gifts, dreaming dreams of greatness which never materialize, than to know you were Empress Dowager of China. Here you are happy, there you could not be!"[7]

The girls went to bed that night, barely able to sleep from excitement as well as worry — what did the Empress Dowager want from them? Having to get up in time to dress and leave by 3 a.m., in order to make the six o'clock arrival time, would have played no insignificant part in the tension not only of the daughters but also of their mother, who was leaving the sick Yu Keng behind.

The Summer Palace lay not more than ten miles from where the family was living in central Beijing, but because they had to travel there via sedan chair, the trip would take at least three hours to complete. After awaking and donning their gowns and gloves, Der Ling, Rong Ling and Louisa had to pick their way through the dark courtyard and each cram their trains into the small compartment of a four-man sedan chair, their hat plumes brushing the low ceiling. Per Der Ling, the distance required two dozen chair-bearers, to carry in relays, along with carts to transport the fresh bearers and a military officer to accompany each chair. "This made a cavalcade of forty-five men, nine horses and three carts," Der Ling noted with satisfaction.

For all the pomp Der Ling so enjoyed, riding in a sedan chair was not much fun. No one who had not ridden in a sedan chair, Der Ling declared, could have any doubt as to its essential faults as a conveyance, primary of which was the need to constantly sit bolt upright and never move from that position, lest the coolies misinterpret the tilt and trip or drop the chair. The women were jounced through the darkness, the silence broken by the calls of the bearers, which Der Ling had heard from earliest childhood: " 'Wa!' said the coolies who carried the forward end of the chair . . . [conveying] the following meaning: 'Hole in the road! Cobblestone missing! Watch your step!'. . . 'Ugh!' [said the rear coolies], which meant nothing either, as a word, but which might have been interpreted as follows: 'I heard you! I am watching!' "[8]

In this ancient form of transportation, exhausting for bearers and for passengers, Louisa and her two daughters headed for the summer residence of a semi-sacred ruler, infamous for her distrust of things and people foreign, swathed in fashions bought in a European city which had just celebrated the virtues of all that was most modern.

"I thought of the many experiences of my short life," remembered Der Ling, "but this was by far the strangest of them all."[9]

14
Garden of Nurtured Harmony

Louisa and her daughters may have thought themselves prepared for anything, but the importance of the occasion seems to have sunk in, per Der Ling, when they passed through the western city gate and were saluted by a contingent of uniformed guards on the way. Beijing's gates were normally closed at seven o'clock in the evening and not opened until sunup, barring certain special occasions; this was clearly one of those special exceptions. Sitting back carefully in her chair for the ride that lay ahead, Der Ling mused on what the future might bring. "We were told that probably we would be asked to stay at the Court," she recalled, "and I thought that if that came to pass, I would possibly be able to influence Her Majesty in favor of reform and so be of valuable assistance to China." These were democratic aspirations for a teenage girl who had recently been fawning over the young king of Spain in Madrid and fancying herself material for marrying him, a spoiled debutante for whom servants were a barely human nuisance.[1]

Why Der Ling thought she would be any more successful than the Empress Dowager's own nephew, not to mention numerous other statesmen, in bringing China up to the standards of the Western world remains something of a mystery, if for no other reason than that Der Ling herself is never clear on what reforms she sought to inspire. Reformer Kang Youwei, with whom Der Ling shared many aspirations for China, had a laser eye for what was wrong with his nation, and we can infer exactly what from his memorials, as well as from the Guangxu Emperor's reforms based on them enacted during the Hundred Days of 1898. China needed to increase domestic revenue, which in the mid-1890s was only at some seventy million silver taels per year, hardly enough to make a dent in the indemnity from the Sino-Japanese War, let alone the indemnities claimed by foreign nations after the Boxer Uprising; devise a national system of railways, which would provide a needed transfusion for domestic and foreign commerce, assist in developing more places for the country's burgeoning population to live and work, and give a foot up for the woefully backward military. The military and commercial interests were starving for lack of modern technology; the currency was outmoded and unstable; and the postal system, which Der Ling describes as having been Yu Keng's concern for years, was still not so much in a medieval state as not extant at all. Another of Kang's radical ideas was women's rights, a belief to which Der Ling had subscribed, through her father, since girlhood.

Kang's main concern, he claimed, was the plight of the people of China: "Our nation is founded upon people — if we cannot think how to foster those people, then we ourselves destroy our own foundation."[2] Some of these desiderata Der Ling had taken to heart since the nursery, because they were issues important to her father and were simply in the air she breathed. But it is likely that the reform possibilities reeling through her head as she trundled toward the Summer Palace that dark March morning were far more abstract, and probably quite personal, starting with the freeing of young ladies like herself from the strictures of Chinese societal regulations, proto-feminist ideas being explored by very few Chinese women in the China of 1903. Only after she had lived within the Empress Dowager's close circle would Der Ling see how implausible many of her individualist ideals were. In a misogynistic nation that tolerated a woman on its throne, Der Ling would find that even that supposedly all-powerful woman was as bound up in etiquette and the rules of "a woman's place" as the feet of Han Chinese ladies, and would hurt just as much to unbind.

As she sat thinking, Der Ling recalled, she noticed for the first time "a faint red line appeared on the horizon heralding the coming of a most perfect day." Through the crimson early spring light, she could see her surroundings: a "high red wall which zigzagged from hill to hill," four miles of it in total, along with pagodas and small outbuildings here and there, the tops of which "were covered with yellow and green tiles" that sparkled in the morning sun — such tiles being a sign that the cavalcade had passed into imperial territory. Der Ling began to feel a little royal herself, particularly when, on passing through a village less than a mile from the gates of the Palace, she heard some children in the street say, "Those ladies are going to the Palace to become Empresses."[3]

What she then saw was a great triple roofed *pailou* or arch gate, brightly painted in red, green and blue picked out in gold, bearing on one side the characters for "water," on the other for "hills," as succinct a description of Cixi's Summer Palace as could be devised. "[F]rom here," wrote Der Ling, "we got our first view of the Palace gates, which were about 100 yards ahead." This was the East Palace Gate, measuring some sixty feet wide, with its three red-lacquered doors studded with golden bosses, arrayed in nine studs per row, nine rows from the top down — nine being auspicious in Chinese numerology.[4] Two bronze lions, dating from the time of the Old Summer Palace (they were too heavy to cart off to the British Museum), stood guard in front of the gate, set up high on marble bases. Another relic of the Old Summer Palace was the carved marble dragon panel set into the steps that led up to the central gate, over which only the emperor could be carried.

When the women came to the foot of the gate steps, as if by some unseen signal a contingent of palace eunuchs, dressed in the crystal hat buttons and silver pheasant *buzi* badges of the fifth rank,[5] appeared with large folding screens made of yellow silk. As soon as the bearers set the chairs down and the ladies emerged, the screens went up around them as shields. Even at this point in her limited experience Der Ling knew enough about court ritual to realize that Cixi had done her and her mother and sister "a great honor" thereby.[6]

Eunuchs had been *de rigueur* at Chinese royal courts since at least the Shang dynasty (ca. 1766–1122 B.C.E). They started out as castrated prisoners of war who were made to serve in the palaces, and early on gathered the power for which they became infamous. From the earliest records down to the Ming dynasty, when they are generally blamed for the governmental breakdown that paved the way for the conquering Manchus, eunuchs are made synonymous with all the varying levels of court intrigue. By then, castration for male servants working for the imperial family was received as necessary to preserve the purity of the dynasty — if eunuchs could get away with many other enormities, one thing they could not do was provide a warming pan baby. But there are many ways of giving and receiving pleasure, even for a eunuch, and indeed one of the accusations leveled by Prince Gong at the wastrel Emperor Tongzhi, Cixi's son, was that he was "always fooling around with eunuchs," the implication being that he was not always just engaging them in games of cards.[7]

In the late Qing period there were some two thousand eunuchs in the Forbidden City's employ, and all had had to endure the same process by which they got there: one went to a so-called "knifer" in the Imperial City (certified by the government), and after a brief bit of devil's advocate on part of the surgeon — which, considering this was his trade, usually was not too zealous — the patient was made to lie on a bed, with a man holding him from behind while two others parted his legs. He was given to drink a narcotic herbal tea (he might also be given opium), and his penis and testicles were numbed using a paste derived from hot chili peppers. Seizing the man's genitals, the "knifer" rapidly removed them using a curved blade, cutting as close to the body as possible, and as quickly placing a silver plug in the exposed urethra. Somewhat after the fashion of modern post-surgical practice, the patient was then made to walk around for a few hours, his wound salved and bandaged, and was not permitted any liquids for three days. After this period, the bandages were taken off and the plug taken out. It was because of this damage to the urethra that eunuchs had trouble retaining urine, and were referred to as "the foul-smelling brotherhood," whose approach could be detected even before they arrived. Unable to grow the beard that was the symbol of age and wisdom in China (and worse, unable to sire children to tend their graves after death), speaking in high, scratchy voices, with pockets of feminine fat that gave them a puffy appearance, eunuchs were also alleged to have a characteristic walk — hunched over, knees knocking as they took little steps. The psycho-physiological reason for this unconscious protective stance toward the genital region can only be described as obvious.[8]

Der Ling never liked eunuchs before she came to Cixi's court and would like them still less afterward. But the eunuchs who greeted her at the Great Eastern Gate were at least polite as they guided her, Louisa and Rong Ling into a courtyard beyond, which was bright with flowers and full of gnarled pine trees from the branches of which hung caged birds, twittering and fluttering, all kinds and colors. This courtyard was also populated by people wearing official robes, just as colorful. "[A]fter the Chinese fashion, all seemed to be very busy doing nothing," Der Ling observed, very much like an unthinking foreign tourist. "When they saw us they stood still and stared." Well might they have stared at these Asian women dressed in the latest Paris fashions: Louisa, plump but so tightly corseted she resembled an hour glass, in pale green chiffon and a black hat with long white plumes, and her two daughters in their flowing red velvet gowns from Stamler and Jeanne, feathered hats perched on their un-Chinese curls, at all of six o'clock in the morning.[9]

Through the quiet courtyard and its staring people, the trio was led to one of the waiting rooms that lined the north and south sides of the court. There was a scurry of feet, and a eunuch, dressed in court regalia, announced that by imperial order, *Yü tai tai* (as Der Ling renders the Empress Dowager's manner of addressing Louisa) and her daughters were to be conveyed into the Empress Dowager's presence. Der Ling noticed that immediately after this edict was recited, the eunuchs who had accompanied mother and daughters into the waiting room knelt down and said, *"shi"* ("Yes!") , as if the Empress Dowager had given the order in person.

Through the courtyard the women swept in their gowns, eunuchs at their sides and the silent but staring officials still standing among the pines and birdcages, to be conveyed through another courtyard, through which more bronze beasts ranged, among them phoenixes, dragons and a *qilin*, China's answer to the West's unicorn, with a dragon's head, deer's antlers, fish scales, and the tail of a lion. The eunuchs directed the women past the crimson-pillared Hall of Benevolence and Longevity, location of the "Nine Dragon Throne," from the yellow silk cushions of which

Cixi dispensed governance in the name of her sickly nephew, and into yet another waiting room on the east side of the courtyard. It was truly a waiting room. During the next two and a half hours, Der Ling had time to count and recount the fourteen foreign-made clocks, which ticked and chimed in a silence interrupted from time to time by servant girls announcing that Her Majesty was still dressing and would soon be ready, to eunuchs bringing refreshments and gifts of jewelry.

At one point Cixi's chief eunuch, Li Lianying, came into the room and all fell silent. "In person he is tall and thin," described a foreign witness who saw a lot of Li. "His head is, in type, like Savonarola's. He has a Roman nose, a massive lean jaw, a protruding lower lip, and very shrewd eyes, full of intelligence, that shine out of sunken orbits."[10] Li had come to reassure the ladies that the audience was not far off, and to bring them more presents. Der Ling thought Li very ugly, "but he had beautiful manners," she allowed.[11]

At his departure, a pair of court ladies ventured into the room, the two daughters of Prince Qing and therefore sisters to Prince Zaizhen. Holding their long silk handkerchiefs up to their faces, they "asked the eunuchs who were attending us if we could speak Chinese," Der Ling recalled, "which we thought a great joke." Piping up before her sister and her mother, Der Ling told the ladies in Chinese that they certainly could speak their own language, as well as several others. The ladies tittered: "Oh! How funny, they can talk the language as well as we do." The women exchanged worried glances, wondering, as Der Ling wrote, how "such ignorant people [could be found] in the Imperial Palace." Knowing that women who read and wrote Chinese were a rare commodity indeed at Cixi's court, Yu Keng had told his daughters not to make their literacy obvious. Der Ling would come to regret her sharp response: "After they found this out," she recalled, "some of the Court ladies were very disagreeable to me."[12]

The frosty atmosphere was not long-lasting, however; though behaving like sight-seers, Cixi's ladies-in-waiting were on a serious errand. Still tittering, the young women informed Louisa that Her Majesty was at last able to receive her and her daughters, and that they would escort the honored guests into the imperial presence. Louisa and the girls rose and left the pavilion, slowing their French heel-shod pace to that of clip-clopping Manchu court clogs as they passed through three more broad and shady courtyards. They arrived at "a magnificent building just one mass of exquisite carving," Der Ling remembered. "Large lanterns made of buffalo horns hung all over the veranda covered with red silk from which red silk tassels were hanging and from each of these tassels was suspended a beautiful piece of jade." This building answers to the description of the Hall of Happiness and Longevity, Cixi's favorite residence at the Summer Palace.

Waiting for them at the entrance was a princess who would only be described as "pretty" by the ever-optimistic American minister's wife, Sarah Conger. Der Ling was far more candid in her recollection of first meeting the so-called Young Empress, Longyu, wife of the Guangxu Emperor. The Young Empress was "very sweet and polite, and had beautiful manners," remembered Der Ling, "but was not very pretty." In fact, Longyu was quite homely: bone-thin, with a pronounced tendency to hunch forward, as if her chest were abnormally concave, with small, guarded eyes over a wide mouth full of buck-teeth that one observer described as "much decayed."[13] Longyu had been married to Cixi's nephew in 1889. Given Guangxu's many health problems, not to mention the fact that the one woman he is said to have loved, the Pearl Concubine, had been killed or had committed suicide after the Guangxu Emperor and the Empress Dowager fled to Xian in August 1900, Longyu's was a thankless union. But she was a kindly, intelligent young woman who had the misfortune of being Cixi's niece and, therefore, useful to the Empress Dowager in her effort to bind her own blood to that of the imperial house. Der Ling may not have thought her pretty, but she would find a sturdy friend in Longyu in time to come.

Der Ling was already impressed by the foreign-style handshakes the Young Empress had accorded her, her mother and sister. "Her Majesty has sent me to meet you," said Longyu in her soft voice. Der Ling then heard a woman bark from inside, "Tell them to come in at once." They hurried into the building, where Der Ling got her first glimpse of the Empress Dowager Cixi, whose person she had imagined and whose power she had envied. What she saw was "an old lady dressed in a beautiful yellow satin gown embroidered all over with pink peonies, and wearing [a] headdress with flowers on each side made of pearls and jade." A gorgeous carved jade phoenix was placed in the very center. But it was Cixi's cape that made Der Ling stare: it was "made of about three thousand five hundred pearls the size of a canary bird's egg, all exactly alike in color and perfectly round," with pendants of jade hanging down in a fringe and a jade clasp. Cixi wore more pearls and jade on her wrists and fingers; even her Manchu clogs were bejeweled, the pearl tassels hanging from the edge of the soles and colored glass designs appliquéd against the high white fabric instep. Even with all this heavy regalia, Cixi had a "carriage quick and graceful, and she lacked nothing physically to make her a splendid type of womanhood and ruler," reflected in her "vivacious and pleasing" features, as one foreign woman who knew her well described her.[14]

Cixi rose and gave the women the same brief foreign-style handshake as the Young Empress. "She had a most fascinating smile," Der Ling remembered, an assessment confirmed by many who saw Cixi in a good mood. (Der Ling is careful to avoid mentioning the missing teeth witnessed by foreigners who saw the Empress Dowager after the return from Xian.) The rough voice they had noticed on their arrival did not seem to match the gracious figure standing before them now. Indeed, the perceptive Sir Robert Hart, on first meeting Cixi a year before Der Ling's visit to the Summer Palace, admired what he called her "sweet feminine voice" and her ready laughter, and declared that "she must have been taking when in her teens!"[15] These feminine wiles notwithstanding, Der Ling would eventually gain all the evidence she needed to state just as perceptively: "Her Majesty always wanted to be a man."[16]

"Yu tai tai [Madame Yu]," said Cixi to Louisa, "you are a wonder the way you have brought your daughters up. They speak Chinese as well as I do, although I know they have been abroad for so many years, and how is it they have such beautiful manners?" Louisa explained that Yu Keng had always impressed on his children the necessity for learning their native language, leaving out the groans and moans the children — Der Ling especially — had made at the sight of their dry-veined Chinese tutor from Henan. Der Ling seemed to pose an especial attraction to Cixi, or so Der Ling tells us. Taking Der Ling's hands in hers, she gazed at the girl for a moment. She then, according to Der Ling, kissed her on the cheeks and turned to Louisa, saying, "I wish to have your daughters and hope they will stay with me."

Though she had seen many foreign women's clothing on several occasions, this was Cixi's first opportunity to really finger the fabric and ask questions about the structure of such garments, something she could not have brought herself to do with the ladies of the foreign legations. "Her Majesty asked all sorts of questions about our Paris gowns," Der Ling recalled, "and said we must wear them all the time . . . She was particularly in love with our Louis XV high heel shoes." She loved them to such a degree that she asked Der Ling if she could try hers on. Standing in her stockinged feet on the cool stone pavement, Der Ling watched as the old lady was helped off with her Manchu clogs and into the red velvet pumps. They fit her so well that later on Cixi gave Der Ling some of her fanciest court shoes.

While this scene of feminine fashion comparison was going on, the Empress Dowager remembered that the Guangxu Emperor was standing nearby, and she introduced the women to him, saying, "[Y]ou must call him Wan Sway Yeh (Master of 10,000 Years) and call me Lao Tsu Tsung (the Great Ancestor)."[17] Der Ling's description of the Guangxu Emperor fits neatly with Sir Robert Hart's later impression: of a slender, weakly man in his thirties, who looked half his age. "He was a man about five feet, seven inches in height," Der Ling wrote, "very thin, but with very strong features." His high nose and forehead set off his large, sparkling black eyes, praised unanimously by others who chanced to see him. Der Ling noticed they had a sad look in them, even when he smiled. "He was a lonely person," recalled another woman who saw Guangxu on many occasions, "with his delicate, well-bred features . . . no obsequious eunuchs knelt when coming into his presence; but on the contrary I have again and again seen him crowded against the wall by these cringing servants of Her Majesty."[18] Even Guangxu's cousins had no respect for him: one official reported that the emperor's brief heir prior to the Boxer troubles, the son of Prince Tuan, had once "struck the Emperor a heavy blow on the back so that he fell to the ground and could not get up."[19]

Der Ling was to come to know Guangxu well enough to describe him as "a fine, lovable character," whom she appreciated for "his kindliness, his breadth of knowledge and his understanding," and who she believed would have been able to save China from the 1911 revolution and much else besides had he been allowed to continue his reform policies of 1898. It was to Der Ling, if we are to believe her published recollections of almost thirty years later, that the emperor confessed his desire to become a Christian, telling her, "If I cannot go up to heaven, Yuan Shi-kai will be to blame."[20] For now, there was no time to say anything, because head eunuch Li Lianying appeared, kowtowed to Cixi, and announced that Her Majesty's chair was ready to bear her to the Audience Hall for a meeting with the directors of various government boards. Eight eunuchs stood near the waiting open sedan chair while servants followed them, carrying everything from clothes, shoes, combs, cosmetics, cigarettes, mirrors, and writing implements. The procession, observed an amused Der Ling, "made one think it a lady's dressing room on legs."

With Guangxu on the Empress Dowager's right and Longyu at her left, the chair was lifted and the march to the audience hall began, with Der Ling, her mother and sister following with the court ladies. They headed back in the direction of the red-pillared Hall of Benevolence and Longevity. Cixi stepped down from her chair and walked into the hall, where she climbed six steps up the dais and sat on the "Nine-Dragon Throne," with a table before her covered in yellow satin. Behind her stood a carved wooden screen, "the most beautiful thing I ever saw," recalled Der Ling, all of twenty feet long by ten feet high and covered with designs of flowers and phoenixes. Two ebony poles stood on either side of Cixi's yellow velvet-upholstered throne, with golden phoenix figures on top, from which curled green and purple mists of peacock feathers. Guangxu took a smaller throne on Cixi's left side. All the officials scheduled for the audience were kneeling on the floor, and while their heads were bowed the Empress Dowager ordered Louisa and the girls, along with the Young Empress and the other court ladies, to go behind the gorgeous screen, where they were to remain silent. "This we did," reported Der Ling, "and could hear the conversation between Her Majesty and the Ministers very plainly." She would put this access to good use.

Not that the ladies behind the screen, including Der Ling, had a chance to fully concentrate on the ministerial proceedings taking place at Cixi's pearly feet. "I was a great novelty among these exclusive

Court ladies," Der Ling recalled, "and I was subjected to a rapid fire of questions." If we can believe Der Ling, these whispered questions were as childish as they were naïve. One of Prince Zaizhen's sisters had the naiveté to ask Der Ling if she had acquired all the foreign languages she knew by virtue of drinking the water in the countries that spoke each language.

When Der Ling mentioned to the princess that she had met her brother in Paris, when Zaizhen was in Europe for the coronation of King Edward VII, Fourth Princess asked: "Is there a king in England? I had thought that our Empress Dowager was Queen of the world." The Young Empress knew better and chastised Fourth Princess for her ignorance. "I know that each country has its ruler," she lectured the court ladies, "and that some countries are republics." Longyu, it transpired, had taken up her husband's habit of reading translations of histories of countries outside China.[21]

Cixi, having concluded her audience and the ministers withdrew, called to the young women to come out again and follow her to the theatre; she dispensed with her sedan chair, declaring the day too fine to not walk. In a move that could not have endeared Louisa and the girls to the other court ladies, Cixi asked them to walk beside her, a rare act of condescension. "My reader may imagine how delighted I was to be treated in this way," Der Ling wrote. "In China the people think their sovereign is the supreme being and that her word is law . . . I thought these extreme favors must be most unusual." As the ladies proceeded toward the theatre, which lay north of the audience hall, Cixi made the small talk for which she was famous, chattering about her dog, her flowers, and her other interests, none of which was so different from that of many other elderly ladies of high and low station the world over. Seeing the Empress Dowager now, "so kind and motherly . . . I thought my informant must be wrong," recalled Der Ling, "and that she was the sweetest woman in the world."[22]

The three-story Great Stage stood in its own courtyard, facing a special temporary residence for the Empress Dowager that in position and creature comforts was not unlike a skybox in a modern sport stadium. Within this pavilion, called the Hall of Health and Happiness, Cixi could recline on a gilded throne-bed, covered in embroidered yellow silk and carved with her imperial symbol, the phoenix, within a kind of porch that looked out directly on the stage, between which and herself were placed framed sheets of glass or, in summer, screens of pale blue gauze, so that the actors might never be able to gaze upon her.

As Der Ling would discover, Cixi's wont was to watch the performances for a while, then sleep on this bed — which says something for her ability to nap through anything, as Der Ling points out: "If any of my readers have ever been to a Chinese theatre, they can well imagine how difficult it would be to woo the God of Sleep in such a pandemonium."[23] There were only two other stages as big as the Summer Palace's Great Stage, one being at the Forbidden City and the other at the Summer Hunting Villa at Jehol. Nearly seventy feet tall and over fifty feet wide, the Great Stage was open to the air, its lower story serving as the stage and the second story as a temple for performance of religious plays. Drops for scene changes, stored on the third story, were lowered from here, as were various mythical beings, appearing at critical points in the drama. The theatre also had a curtain that closed between acts, something of an innovation in China.

"[Cixi] was very fond of reading religious books and fairy tales," Der Ling wrote, and occasionally wrote operas herself. Today's show was of the type the Empress Dowager loved, a complex Buddhist melodrama: "The Empress of Heaven's Party, or Feast to All the Buddhist Priests to Eat Her Famous Peaches and Drink Her Best Wine." The scenario involved Buddhist priests descending in clouds, pagodas that opened to release more singing priests, a huge pink silk lotus blossom that unfurled its petals to reveal a white-costumed Guanyin (Goddess of Mercy), travels between heaven and earth and a troupe of renegade monkeys who must be taught a lesson. The visitors watched standing up, per court etiquette, while Cixi rested on her bed.[24]

Having seen some fine theatre productions in Paris, Der Ling had to admit that both performance standards and set décor of Cixi's Great Stage impressed her more than she expected. In turn, Cixi was impressed that Der Ling understood and liked the opera. Then she remembered that it was her lunchtime. "Are you hungry?" she asked Louisa and her daughters. "Could you get Chinese food when you were abroad," she questioned, "and were you homesick?"[25]

Even as the Empress Dowager mentioned food, it began to appear. Eunuchs laid tables and carried in wooden boxes, painted imperial yellow, which contained the various dishes that made up the afternoon meal. Bowl after bowl and plate after plate — the yellow imperial china with silver covers — were removed from the boxes, to the tune of some one hundred and fifty different kinds of food, per Der Ling, served with separate plates, Manchu style. Even if her estimate was off by as much as half — some sources indicate the dishes served amounted to close to fifty twice a day, rather than one hundred each meal — the amount of food was still gargantuan. Der Ling noted with dismay that as the crowd of eunuchs was setting up the plates and bowls in rows on the tables, court ladies she had met earlier appeared carrying a large yellow box. "I was very much surprised to see Court ladies doing this kind of work," Der Ling recalled, "and I said to myself, if I come here will I have to do this sort of thing?"

The box merely contained the Empress Dowager's favorite selections of pre-luncheon sweets, running the gamut from sugared lotus seeds and candied walnuts to fruits of the season, sliced and laid out in attractive patterns. Cixi offered her guests some of the "dainties" on the many little plates set before her, and when tea was brought, offered some of it to them, too, replete with honeysuckle blossoms to give the tea a faint floral sweetness that Der Ling enjoyed.

Yet the meal was not over. Cixi beckoned the women to follow her into an adjoining room, where the tables stood covered with more food. Der Ling describes it all in mouthwatering detail: "[P]ork cooked in ten different ways, such as meat balls, sliced cold in two different ways, red and white, the red being cooked with a special kind of sauce made of beans which gives it the red color and has a delicious taste. Chopped pork with bamboo shoots, pork cut in cubes and cooked with cherries and pork cooked with onions and sliced thin . . . there was a chicken, a duck and some shark fins in a clear soup . . . bread, made in a number of different ways, such as baked, steamed, fried, some with sugar and some with salt and pepper, cut in fancy shapes or made in fancy moulds such as dragons, butterflies, etc." [26]

"[G]enerally the Emperor takes lunch with me when we have the theatre," Cixi told them, "but he is shy to-day, as you are all new to him.

I hope he will get over it and not be so bashful. You three had better eat with me to-day." Even though the guests would have to stand through the meal, opposite where the Empress Dowager sat eating, this was a signal honor, and despite their feathered hats and stiff bodices, the women kowtowed. Cixi apologized for making them stand, "but I cannot break the law of our great ancestors. Even the Young Empress cannot sit in my presence." During the meal, the actors had launched into an opera based on another fairy tale, and their singing and the striking of cymbals and drums echoed through the empty courtyard.

When it came time for the guests to return to Beijing, the Empress Dowager ordered several boxes of fruit and cakes given to them to take back to Yu Keng. "Tell Yü Keng to get better soon," she told them, "and tell him to take the medicine I am sending by you and to rest well." The ladies had barely risen from their kowtows of thanks when the old lady added that she was quite fond of all three of them and wished them to return to the Summer Palace in three days to be her court ladies. This was another honor, requiring another kowtow, and yet Der Ling knew her mother was casting her mind to the house in Beijing, where Yu Keng lay recuperating — when would they ever be home to care for him? There was nothing to say but yes. The women accompanied Cixi for a tour of their future living quarters, a two-story building located on the west side of the Empress Dowager's private quarters, a sumptuous small palace called the Lodge of the Propriety of Weeding.[27] The compound was surrounded by a gallery which connected it to the three places where Cixi could most often be found: the Hall of Happiness and Longevity, which also contained living quarters, the Great Stage, and the path leading to Longevity Hill, where the Tower of the Fragrance of Buddha lifted its blue and yellow tiled eaves to the sky.

They were not done with kowtows. No sooner had Louisa and the girls arrived home but a small army of eunuchs scurried into the courtyard, bearing rolls of brocade from the imperial silk looms: a rich gift from the Empress Dowager. As the eunuchs watched, the entire family had to kowtow once more before the silken gifts, laid out gleaming on a table, and send their thanks back via the servants. It had been, remembered Der Ling, who had certainly experienced plenty of adventure, "the most eventful day of our lives."

15
Lady of the court

Though built near and in some cases on the ruins of the Old Summer Palace, destroyed by foreign troops in 1860, and then damaged again by same following the Boxer Uprising in 1900, Cixi's New Summer Palace was so literally new as to barely have had time for the paint to dry.

Situated on over seven hundred acres northwest of Beijing, three-quarters of the land being covered by Lake Kunming, the palace Cixi named *Yiheyuan* or "Garden of Nurtured Harmony" was the dowager's pet project from the late 1880s onward. She pursued the work with all the fury of a lover of beauty who has seen beautiful things destroyed — things which, even worse, were destroyed by the foreigners with whom she was to have an ambiguous relationship throughout her life. "If the palace had been destroyed by big guns during a battle," Cixi later told Der Ling, "I would not feel so bitter." Guns had no eyes, she pointed out. That men could see this beautiful place and still destroy it was a crime she could not forgive.

During the Second Opium War and the occupation of Beijing by the British and French, the Old Summer Palace, known as the Yuanmingyuan[1] [Garden of Perfect Brilliance] and considered one of the most exquisite royal retreats in the world, was so pilfered of its treasures and so thoroughly put to the torch that all that survived were a pavilion of bronze, dating from the reign of the Qianlong Emperor, the Yuanmingyuan's greatest patron, and a couple of buildings covered in heat-resistant tiles. The carved marble French style palace and fountains built according to the plans of the Jesuit priest Castiglione, in the grounds of which Cixi had known brief happiness as favorite of the Xianfeng Emperor, were shattered into a waste field of fancily carved rubble.

Cixi had no reason to love the West, but in reversing the damage Western powers had done to China's beauty she acted on impulses which did harm to China itself, by making it appear to both Chinese and the world at large that her real concern was not for her empire's welfare but for the beautification of her private pleasure haunts. She was not the only member of the imperial family to be obsessed with the remains of the Old Summer Palace. Her son, the briefly regnant Emperor Tongzhi, loved the ruins so much he staged lavish parties in their midst, and began to draw on the imperial exchequer to restore them as a country place for the two empresses dowager. Court ministers protested, as did the emperor's uncle, Prince Gong, but ultimately they raised the money to have the site cleared. Before any real work could be started, however, Tongzhi was dead. To what degree this young man's tragic demise further contributed to his mother's attachment to the ruined gardens is not known, but it must have been a factor.[2]

A classic accusation against the Empress Dowager, and one that continues to appear in modern histories of China and the Qing dynasty, is that she diverted funds meant for the imperial navy to pay for the extensive building and rebuilding projects required to restore the Summer Palace, and specifically to build the marble barge located at the western end of the Long Gallery. The irony of a stationary maritime playhouse being constructed for the pleasure of a wanton female ruler using money meant to be spent on real warships stuck to the popular imagination, much as gossip attributed to Queen Marie Antoinette not only the construction of the Petit Trianon (it dated from the previous reign) but also its walls paved with imagined gemstones. Calumny of this sort has always done females in power far more harm than males.[3]

Prince Chun (Yixuan), father of the Guangxu Emperor, was chairman of the Admiralty Board, and it was he who siphoned off money, which Viceroy Li Hongzhang had borrowed for improvement of the naval academy, and used it for luxurious toys in both Beijing and the Summer Palace as well as modern improvements — according to one source, Chun was responsible for bringing electric light to both Beijing and his own palace there.[4] To build a suitable residence at the Summer Palace for Cixi, as a way of gaining her favor and support for his policies, Prince Chun lobbied Viceroy Li for more cash; Li, in turn, floated a fund-raising campaign ostensibly for the navy, but in fact for Prince Chun's own nest-feathering redecoration purposes.

So the Summer Palace rose again beside Lake Kunming. "While the dowager was certainly aware that great sums were being lavished by Prince Chun and others on the restoration of the Summer Palace," writes one historian, "there is no evidence that she had any idea where the funds originated," or that she particularly cared to know. As with Guangxu's "Hundred Days" reforms, Cixi was obviously so focused on the minutiae of her responsibilities as dowager empress and of court life itself that she missed the big picture — it would not be the first or the last time. In any event, the marble barge had been built not by Cixi but in the reign of the eighteenth-century Qianlong Emperor; the only features added to it during Cixi's time were some adornments and the marble paddlewheels on either side — improvements that were taken on by Prince Chun, ever-fascinated with modern technology, not Cixi.[5]

By the time Der Ling saw it, the *Yiheyuan* had settled into the form we see today: Longevity Hill, with its more than one hundred shrines, sight-seeing belvederes, and pleasure-places, sites with poetic names like "Strolling Through a Picture Scroll," "Hall That Dispels the Clouds," and "Pavilion of Blessed Scenery;" Kunming Lake and its island pavilions and arching white marble bridges and shoreline heaving with the broad velvety green disks of lotuses with the pure pink and white blossoms nodding above; and the dowager's and emperor's lavish living quarters, centered around the Great Stage theatre. "We guess that many an intrigue has taken place amid the profusion and luxuriance of colorful nature," wrote one bedazzled foreign woman who visited the Summer Palace several years later, "in the blue and gold arbours that seem to play hide and seek among the trees; that tender words have been whispered and vengeful jealousies planned there."[6]

Der Ling will have us believe that her work as Cixi's newest court lady started the moment her sedan chair was set down inside the East Palace Gate. The Empress Dowager, surrounded by her fluttering women, announced to Der Ling, Rong Ling and Louisa that an important visitor, the wife of the Russian minister, was coming to the palace, and could Der Ling speak Russian? Der Ling admitted she could not, but relieved the old lady by telling her that since most cultured Russians spoke French, she could speak to the lady in that language. Turning slightly toward a court lady nearby, whom she seemed to intend to be part of the conversation, Cixi then said in a sarcastic voice, "Why don't you tell me you speak Russian, I won't know or be able to find out," leading Der Ling to conclude that the lady in question had been pretending to knowledge of foreign tongues, including Russian, when she knew none at all.

For the moment, Der Ling's primary concern was clothing. Madame de Plancon, the minister's wife, was arriving that day, which meant the summer court was already late in preparing for her reception. Louisa had dressed herself and her daughters in simple short gowns for their trip from Beijing. These dresses, they realized, would not do for receiving the Russian minister's wife. Cixi found their consternation amusing: "Why must you change your clothes? I see you look much better without that tail dragging behind you on the floor." Louisa prevailed, and soon she and her daughters were again in the imperial presence, gowned in lace and *crêpe de Chine* that would not have been out of place on a carriage ride through the Bois de Boulogne. The Empress Dowager admired their clothes — "I must say that no foreign ladies have yet been presented to me in such lovely gowns as you three have" — but she could not help quipping sarcastically, "Here are three fairies with long tails."

It was after the audience, with Der Ling translating, the luncheon that followed, and before Madame de Plancon had even departed for Beijing, that Der Ling discovered just how vulnerable to the itch of opinion the all-powerful Empress Dowager really was. "Her Majesty had a rule of custom that after all guests had departed, we must go to her and report everything," recalled Der Ling — undoubtedly, this "rule" had as much to do with Cixi's obsessive curiosity, particularly as regarded outside views of herself, as it did with the fact that she had spent so many years literally having to transact business behind a curtain. Cixi wanted to know everything: What had Madame de Plancon said about the audience, about the food, about herself? Did she care for the presents, and did her thanks seem sincere? "I suppose she was like all women," Der Ling reported of the dowager, "a bit of a gossip as well as the rest."

But Cixi had a point, as she explained later to Der Ling. When the foreign women came to court they brought their own interpreters, who tended as often as not to be non-Asian foreigners like themselves, with an imperfect grasp of the four toned complexities of Mandarin pronunciation, and the Empress Dowager frequently did not comprehend a single word. To have a Chinese interpreter fluent in the primary languages of the foreigners was a boon that moved the old lady to smile winkingly at Der Ling and say, "I am very happy to have you and I want you to stay with me as long as I live." Not only that, but Cixi intended to arrange a marriage for Der Ling, so Der Ling tells us, "but [I] won't tell you just now" who the groom would be.

While thrilled at the prospect of having pleased the Empress Dowager to such a happy degree, Der Ling was not happy at the mention of an arranged marriage. "[N]othing was farther from my mind than this," she remembered, and she spoke later to Louisa about it. Her mother reassured her, pointing out that it was her right to refuse even the Empress Dowager's choice of husband. Der Ling continued to worry about the topic — with good reason, as time would tell.[7]

1. Thomas Allom engraving of how a typical Chinese mandarin lived early in the reign of Queen Victoria, following the first "Opium War." It was images like this that fed occidental appetites for oriental plunder, not to mention romantic Western misconceptions of Chinese reality. Author's collection.

2. Rong Ling and sister Der Ling, dressed for Carneval in Paris, circa 1900, photographed by Charles Chusseau-Flaviens. This and the following two photographs have never been identified until now with Der Ling or her family. George Eastman House.

3. Xinling, one of two brothers of Der Ling, dressed for Carneval in Paris, circa 1900, photographed by Chusseau-Flaviens, circa 1900. George Eastman House.

4. Possible image of Yu Keng, Der Ling's father, in his office as Chinese minister to France, circa 1900, photographed in Paris by Chusseau-Flaviens. George Eastman House.

5. Li Hongzhang (1823–1901), statesman, friend and protector of Yu Keng. Author's collection.

6. Prince Qing (1836–1918), friend of Yu Keng and tutor to his daughters in the ways of the Manchu court. Author's collection.

7. Yuan Shikai (1859–1916), military official, political force through the late Qing and early Republic periods and, briefly, emperor. He was allegedly related to Yu Keng by marriage. Author's collection.

8. The Forbidden City photographed from Coal Hill, circa 1900. Author's collection.

9. Views of the Forbidden City, early 1920s. Author's collection.

SY-TAY-HEOU
Impératrice douairière de Chine

10. Imagined evil-visaged image of Empress Dowager Cixi on the cover of the French periodical *Le Petit Journal*, 1900, just before the explosion of the Boxer Uprising. Note the incorrect, possibly phonetic, spelling of "Cixi taiho." Author's collection.

11. Scroll painting by the Empress Dowager Cixi. Cixi's keen sense of humour, and of the absurd, are brilliantly on show here, as is her fluent technique. Originally collected by C. T. Loo (1880–1957) of Paris. The annotation on the right says "Painted in the Jia Chen year of the Guangxu era on our birthday, a work from the imperial brush," corresponding to 1904, during Der Ling's service at the palace. The verse reads: "Everyone is happy swimming in the pool together." Collection of Christopher Ives. Photographed by John Bonath, Denver.

大清國今慈禧端佑康頤昭豫莊誠壽恭欽獻崇熙皇太后聖母

12. Empress Dowager Cixi with handmirror — a woman fascinated by her own reflection. Photographed by Xunling, Der Ling's eldest brother. Author's collection.

13. A pailou gate at the Summer Palace, circa 1920, two foreign tourists standing to the left. Author's collection.

14. A view of the Tower of Buddha's Fragrance, Summer Palace, circa 1920, shot from a boat on Lake Kunming. Author's collection.

15. Der Ling garbed in the Empress Dowager's own gown, circa 1903. Author's collection.

16. The so-called Foreign Palaces at the Forbidden City, the interiors of which Der Ling claims she, her mother Louisa and sister redecorated for an unimpressed Cixi. Author's collection.

17. Louisa (back row, second from left) and her daughters Rong Ling and Der Ling (to Louisa's left) at a tea party at the home of the American minister Edwin H. Conger, 1903, as guests of the minister's Cixi-admiring wife, Sarah. Author's collection.

18. The Guangxu Emperor and his father Prince Chun. Guangxu was described as having a voice like the faint buzz of a mosquito. Author's collection.

19. Der Ling and Cixi, with eunuch Cui Yugui holding umbrella, standing on Peony Hill at the Summer Palace. Der Ling is visibly cold here, but the Empress Dowager was a great lover of outdoor activity in all weathers. Photographed by Xunling, circa 1904. Collection of Arthur M. Sackler Gallery/Freer Gallery, Washington, D.C.

20. Cixi with Rong Ling, Fourth Princess and eunuch attendants on the Lotus Lake at the Summer Palace. Photographed by Xunling. Author's collection.

21. Cixi and her female court, from left to right: Lustrous Concubine (sister of Guangxu's beloved the Pearl Concubine), Rong Ling, Empress Dowager Cixi, Der Ling, Louisa, and the Young Empress, consort of the Guangxu Emperor, by Xunling. Author's collection.

22. A rare image of Cixi showing the smile described by so many who met her. "She must have been taking in her teens!" exclaimed Sir Robert Hart, inspector general of customs. Photographed by Xunling. Collection of Arthur M. Sackler Gallery/Freer Gallery, Washington, D.C.

23. Cixi wearing her famous cape made of over 3,000 pearls. This photo was evidently taken after Cixi's stroke in 1903–04. Photographed by Xunling. Author's collection.

24. Cixi attended by eunuchs while Der Ling poses demurely to one side. Photographed by Xunling. Collection of Arthur M. Sackler Gallery/Freer Gallery, Washington, D.C.

25. Cixi, Rong Ling, Der Ling and Louisa on Peony Hill at the Summer Palace. Photographed by Xunling. Collection of Arthur M. Sackler Gallery/Freer Gallery, Washington, D.C.

26. Cixi, Fourth Princess and eunuchs in the snow at the Summer Palace, photographed by Xunling. Neither this nor the following photograph has ever been published before. Collection of Arthur M. Sackler Gallery/Freer Gallery, Washington, D.C.

27. Cixi, Fourth Princess and eunuchs in the snow at the Summer Palace, photographed by Xunling. This photograph has not been published till now. Collection of Arthur M. Sackler Gallery/Freer Gallery, Washington, D.C.

28. Silk calligraphic scroll brushed by the Empress Dowager with the character for long life and given to Der Ling on her departure from court in 1905. Der Ling's "title" is inscribed along the scroll's right edge. This image was included in Der Ling's Chautauqua lecture brochure, circa 1929. Redpath Chautauqua Bureau Collection, The University of Iowa Libraries, Iowa City, Iowa.

29. Katherine Carl (1865–1938), the American painter who was the first Western artist to paint the Empress Dowager's portrait. Author's collection.

30. Close-up of sketch by Katherine Carl, reproduced in *With the Empress Dowager of China*, showing the artist talking to two court ladies. Because only Der Ling and Rong Ling spoke English, and were detailed by Cixi to keep the other women away from Katherine, these girls must be Yu Keng's daughters. Author's collection.

31. Cixi standing alone in the snow — a poignant image often conjured in words by Katherine Carl and Der Ling. Photographed by Xunling. Collection of Arthur M. Sackler Gallery/Freer Gallery, Washington, D.C.

32. Katherine Carl's portrait of Cixi, in the camphor wood frame designed by the Empress Dowager, photographed by Xunling, ready for shipping to the St. Louis Exposition. The portrait occasioned much trouble in transport as it had to always be kept upright and covered with special imperial brocade. Author's collection.

33. The Empress Dowager's portrait, wrapped in imperial dragons for its long journey to St. Louis, attendant officials lined up beside the flatbed car. Author's collection.

La Générale Dan Pao Tchao
née Princesse Shou Shan Yü

34. Rong Ling (Madame Dan Paochao), from the frontispiece of her 1935 book on the Qianlong Emperor and his "fragrant" concubine, Xiangfei. Note the addition of her "title," Princess Shou Shan, which Sir Reginald Johnston claimed she never used. Author's collection.

35. Der Ling's English signature. Author's collection.

36. Der Ling in European finery with tiara. Curiously, this is the Europeanized image of Der Ling that was published in later editions of *Two Years in the Forbidden City*; she was shown wearing Manchu garb earlier. Author's collection.

37. Original painting by Bertha Lum (1869–1954) based on Xunling's famous photograph of the Empress Dowager, Der Ling and eunuch Cui at the Summer Palace. Private collection.

38. Der Ling as shown in the brochure for her lecture series on the Chautauqua circuit, circa 1929–30. Note the erroneous reference to "Her Imperial Highness." To what degree Der Ling actively participated in these overblown statements about her Manchu social status is not known, but we must assume she had to vet the lecture brochure from which this image derives and permitted this reference to a fantasy connection to the imperial house to remain. Redpath Chautauqua Bureau Collection, The University of Iowa Libraries, Iowa City, Iowa.

Her Imperial Highness
Princess Der Ling
of the Manchu Court of the Late
Empress Dowager Tzu Hsi of China

39. Der Ling at Bryn Mawr for a lecture, seated with chemistry major Vung-yuin Ting, the college's first Chinese student, in 1934. Collection of Christopher Ives.

40. Postcard image of the Princess Der Ling Pavilion at the 1939 World's Fair, Treasure Island, San Francisco, California. The roof was tiled in yellow — a reference to Der Ling's alleged imperial connections. Inside were manikins clothed in court robes seated on thrones and posing against embroidered hangings and screens. Author's collection.

To Mary Logoteta

Most sincerely
Princess Der Ling.

1939.

41. Der Ling in 1939. She inscribed this photo to her San Francisco hairdresser, Mary Logoteta. Collection of Mary Logoteta.

42. Der Ling and her American husband Thaddeus Cohu White, in what was said to be the first photograph ever taken of them together, in 1935. Author's collection.

43. Throne room scene showing thrones and robes belonging to Der Ling, auctioned after 1944, from the auction catalog created by her husband. Collection of Christopher Ives.

44. Bridal bed allegedly given by Cixi to Der Ling and her husband as a wedding gift, shown in the catalog of Der Ling's *objets d'art* sold after her death in 1944, from the auction catalog. Collection of Christopher Ives.

45. Beaded embroidered cloth-of-gold purse given to Der Ling by the Young Empress, Longyu, decorated with gourds (longevity) and crickets (luck) and tassels in the Young Empress' court colours (yellow, peach, green and blue) with cords of royal purple. Gift from Der Ling to her American friend, the Asian art collector Charlotte Hill-Grant (1894–1973). Photographed by John Bonath, Denver. Collection of Christopher Ives.

46. An unusual painted cut silk velvet vest (front), here depicting mandarin ducks, a symbol of happy marriage, a gift to Der Ling by the Empress Dowager (possibly at the time of Der Ling's marriage in 1907). Der Ling gave this vest to Charlotte Hill-Grant. Photographed by John Bonath, Denver. Collection of Christopher Ives.

47. Reverse of the same vest, showing cranes, symbol of longevity. Photographed by John Bonath, Denver. Collection of Christopher Ives.

48. The Hotel Carlton in Berkeley, Der Ling's last residence, a block from the south gate of the University of California. Poets Witter Bynner (who kept a "shrine to the mysterious Orient" in his rooms, in the words of UCB's William Benemann) and Rupert Brooke once lived there. Photographed by the author.

16
Eunuchs and jewels

Long after Der Ling and her sister got into their silk-hung beds they stayed up discussing everything that had happened during the day. One of the stranger occurrences was a confidence shared with the sisters by the eunuch who escorted them to their residence. Cixi had arranged for Louisa and her daughters to have four eunuch attendants, whose supervisor was their escort. Der Ling noticed that certain doorways had been walled over between where their pavilion was and where the emperor lived, and asked why this was.

"He smiled," she remembered, and said: " 'You will have to learn a lot before you find out this wicked place.' " The eunuch pointed out that the passageway between the emperor's and the Young Empress' residences had been blocked up, so that the only way they could see each other was to do so by first going through Cixi's own palace complex. In fact, within the emperor's residence, the Hall of Jade Billows, can still be seen a wall which was built on the pavilion's west side, blocking all exits — doors and windows — to the lake. By flickering lamplight in a dark courtyard, these stories gave Der Ling the shivers. When she told the eunuch she would like to rest, he bowed and disappeared.

Der Ling was awakened from a short sleep by a rapping on her window. It was another eunuch. He announced that it was five o'clock and time for her to rise for her duties. "[M]y thoughts wandered to Paris," she recalled, "and I thought how strange it was that I used to go to bed at 5 o'clock after the dances."[1] Then it swept over her just where she had spent the night, and "I immediately got up and opened my window and looked out," Der Ling wrote. "The day was just dawning and the sky was a beautiful deep red which was reflected in the lake, which was perfectly calm . . . I could see Her Majesty's peony mountain, which was literally covered with these beautiful flowers."[2]

It was a moment of calm before hours of flurry. On her way to Cixi's quarters Der Ling encountered a group of beautifully dressed young Manchu noblewomen, to whom the Young Empress introduced her, explaining that they were court ladies in training and thus were not allowed near the Empress Dowager till their grasp of etiquette was firm. Considering that Der Ling mentions having to undergo no training at all for her task of serving the Empress Dowager, save what she had learned at home, the comparative ease with which she had penetrated the court must have rankled in some of these young women as well as in the more seasoned ones. (Rong Ling's memoirs of many years later do point out that the girls and Louisa had a crash course in court etiquette from Prince Qing; why Der Ling did not mention this in *Two Years in the Forbidden City*, or whether Rong Ling was fabricating the lessons received, we cannot know.)

Der Ling says the Young Empress told them they would have to help Cixi dress for the day. On reaching her bedroom, they found the dowager still in her ornately carved bed, which like most traditional northern Chinese beds was built over a brick *kang*, a furnace that could be fired up to keep the occupant warm on cold winter nights. The dowager's bedding was just as eye-catching. She slept on three yellow brocade mattresses, Der Ling records, with several satin coverlets in various colors, over which was placed a yellow satin quilt embroidered with golden dragons. The bed was crowded with pillows of all shapes and sizes, and one that particularly drew Der Ling's attention: stuffed with flowers, this pillow had a square opening in the middle, into which Cixi could fit her ear and thus, theoretically, hear even in her sleep. This petal-filled pillow was just one of many fragrant objects strewn on or near the bed: its frame was strung with dozens of scent-saturated gauze sachets. "The odor from these bags was very strong," Der Ling recalled, "and made one feel sick until they became used to it."

To her surprise and apprehension, Der Ling was asked by Cixi if she would like to make her bed, a domestic chore Der Ling had never had to do for herself. With so many servants around to do this kind of work, was Cixi teasing Louisa when she told her "she could not bear to have the servant girls, eunuchs, or old women, touch her bed, that they were dirty, so the Court ladies must make it"? As Der Ling stood pondering this, Cixi then countered by telling Der Ling she was surprised "to see what a perfect little Manchu lady you are," and that if she did not make the bed properly she would be scolded and replaced by someone else. Never one to back down from a challenge, and wanting to please the old lady despite her sense of humour, Der Ling went to the bed and with help managed to make it. When she was finished, Cixi was already at her dressing table, washing her face and applying a scented pink powder to it — in full contravention of the rules prohibiting Manchu widows from wearing makeup — as well as fixing her long hair. Like the eccentric Empress Elisabeth of Austria, assassinated at Geneva a few years before, Cixi hated losing so much as a strand, and would frequently bring her eunuch hairdresser to tears if any hairs were found on floor or dressing table.

Given Cixi's age, Der Ling marveled at the hair's "raven black" color, but the reason for it lay on the dressing table: "several small pots of black, sticky looking stuff," Der Ling recalled. (It is possible this was not dye *per se* but the mixture developed by a palace doctor in 1880. Called *xiangfasan*, this quasi-conditioner used various herbs prescribed to deal not just with Cixi's graying strands but the fact that so many of them were falling out.) Using a small brush, the Empress Dowager would carefully paint the compound onto her hair, and while it did the job of darkening the gray hair, it also leaked through and stained her scalp. It was not exactly court protocol to suggest that the Empress Dowager was performing a less-than-perfect job of dying her hair to conceal her age, but Der Ling ventured to point this out gently by telling Cixi that she knew of a dye made in Paris that did not blacken the scalp, and that she could get some for her if she desired. When Cixi eagerly granted her permission, Der Ling posted a eunuch to her father in Beijing, asking him to send for the dyes immediately. It was the first of many triumphs Der Ling would experience, introducing the old lady to the accoutrements of modern womanhood.[3]

Though she was called "Old Buddha" because she preserved a countenance of watchful but unruffled serenity, Cixi was actually much given to impulsive actions, motivated by her taste for drama, which in turn was fueled by her strong-fibered emotions. No sooner had Der Ling sent away for the French hair dye, than the pleased old lady made an announcement. "Der Ling you are a great help to me in every way," Der Ling records the dowager saying to her, "and I make you my first lady-in-waiting. You must not work too much for you will have to make arrangements for the audiences for foreigners and you will have to interpret for me." Cixi added: "I also want you to look after my jewels and don't want you to have to do rough work at all." Unfortunately for Der Ling, this last statement was loud enough for all to hear. To the court ladies who had to do everything from carry luncheon boxes to fold the dowager's bed to trim away dead chrysanthemums, Der Ling's meteoric rise at court, responsible for nothing but speaking "foreign-devil" languages and seeing to the Empress Dowager's jewels, could scarcely have made them into her friends.

Some jealous woman at court had been at Cixi's ear already, because when the Empress Dowager took Der Ling into her jewel room, where shelves on three sides of the space were filled from floor to ceiling with ebony jewel boxes, each marked with a yellow label, Cixi said regretfully, "I am sorry you cannot read and write Chinese, otherwise I would give you a list of these things and you could keep a check on them." Der Ling, who wrote Chinese as easily as she wrote English and French, was taken aback. She insisted that though her Chinese was not of scholarly quality, she could read and write the language, and would have no trouble with the labels or the list. "That is funny," said the Empress Dowager, "someone told me the first day you were here, I forget now who it was, that you could not read or write your own language at all." As Cixi said this, she looked pointedly at the group of court ladies standing outside the room.

Meanwhile, there were walls of black boxes, each filled with treasures of personal ornament, each with its label to be memorized by kind and size of contents. "Her Majesty's greatest love was for her pearls," Der Ling recalled. Even as Cixi entrusted Der Ling with her lists of jewels, the latter claims she also gave her the job of assisting in the judging, weighing and counting of the pearls that came to the palace from all parts of China. One of the largest of the Empress Dowager's pearls was a drop-pearl the size of a hen's egg, called the "Eggplant Pearl," which Cixi wore as a pendant-brooch.

Cixi also owned some of the finest jade in the world, including a famous pendant known as the "Persian Pepper," which allegedly was fashioned for Xiangfei, the beautiful concubine of the Qianlong Emperor, in an unsuccessful effort to stem her homesickness for her Uighur birthplace, where such peppers formed a part of the diet. Der Ling describes the "Persian Pepper" as "gorgeous, flawless, and so clear one could see right through it." (The pendant later allegedly made its way, like so much imperial jewelry after the 1911 revolution, into the collection of the jewel-obsessed Madame Wellington Koo, wife of the Chinese ambassador to the United States, although there is some question as to whether her pendant was authentic.)[4]

Cixi's passion for jade at least matched her passion for pearls: she ate with jade chopsticks from jade plates, wore three sets of jade bracelets, as well as jade pendants and rings and hair ornaments, and revered a priceless jade sculpture of Guanyin, the Goddess of Mercy, with whom she so closely identified that she enjoyed dressing up as the goddess. Cixi also owned jewels typically more appreciated in the West than jade, such as diamonds, but according to Der Ling she held them in contempt as something approaching glass. Der Ling tells us that Li Hongzhang had given the Empress Dowager a crown set with a rare blue diamond, surrounded by a sea of white diamonds, but it languished unworn. Der Ling frequently saw it being pushed around as if it were simply "rubbish" in the way in the palace treasure-house.[5]

Cixi was back at her half moon-shaped dressing table, putting the finishing touches on her appearance as Der Ling hovered behind her, when the emperor walked into the room. He immediately knelt before the old lady, giving her his morning's greeting, and some conversation passed, which Der Ling spent in a quandary about how to acknowledge this man who was the emperor of China in nothing but name. Having been given no advice as to what to do about it, she fell back on her instincts, which were motivated in turn by the strong sympathy she felt for the fragile-looking Guangxu, and possibly also by her need to work her charms on the one intact male in the palace. When the emperor had passed from Cixi's room into a corridor, Der Ling followed him on some pretext, and when he looked back at her she knelt reverentially before him.

Der Ling's memoirs leave us overall a poignant portrait of the Guangxu Emperor, and they also make it plain that Der Ling was genuinely fond of him. Some of the conversations she reports they had during her two years at court imply that he felt the same. "He regarded me as a friend," she wrote — if this is true, Der Ling was one of the few the emperor had at the court.[6] A great deal of Der Ling's dislike for eunuchs revolved around their reputation — to a considerable degree an earned one — for carrying court gossip outside the palace walls, where it fell amid Beijing society and grew into weeds of gossip. But it was the treatment of Guangxu by the palace eunuchs that moved Der Ling to outrage, and not so much because he was their emperor as that he was a man who deserved more than his due of the kindness that had always been denied him, and which he himself was always able to show for others. "He loved his people," she recalled, "and would have done anything to help them whenever there was famine or flood."

Like Sarah Conger, Der Ling would witness eunuch insouciance and even abuse toward Guangxu. She had heard that the emperor could be cruel to his servants, but she soon saw this for the rumor it was. At any rate, she insisted, "I lived there long enough, and I know just what cruel people those eunuchs were. They had no respect for their master," undoubtedly taking their cue from the strict pecking order set up by the dowager herself: she made all the decisions and handed them to Guangxu only for his rubber stamped assent, and that meant he had very little value. For Guangxu, Der Ling may have reminded him of his beloved Pearl Concubine. Like the Pearl, she was sweetly pretty, she was graceful, yet she was an individualist and a bit of a troublemaker, all attributes which had categorized the Pearl Concubine as dangerous to Cixi. Also like the Pearl, Der Ling paid respectful attention to Guangxu, regardless of the customs of a court which largely ignored him. There were strong eunuchs at court, like Cui Yugui, who were far better specimens of strapping manhood than the Guangxu Emperor, but Der Ling thought him handsome and saw him as more masculine than other observers did: "I always felt he would have made a striking figure in military uniform," she wrote admiringly but not convincingly.[7]

Der Ling describes how she tutored the emperor in English, a language he had had a grasp of before her arrival, so that he often made her daily greetings in that language. She gave him lessons on one of the many pianos scattered about the palace and admired his musicality. "He loved the piano," she remembered. "I taught him some easy waltzes and he kept time beautifully."[8] She also enjoyed his sense of humor, which ran to the boyish practical joke variety — he loved to get the court in a dither by announcing that the dowager was shortly arriving in her chair, only to admit after everyone had knelt face to the floor that he must have misheard and she was not arriving after all. This was just the sort of French farce humor that gave Der Ling such pleasure.

Der Ling claims she and the emperor would even discuss freely the touchy subject of marriage, which to Cixi's face Der Ling professed was the farthest thing from her mind. "His Majesty Guangxu . . . told me," Der Ling wrote, "that it would have been an evil fortune indeed for me to have become his secondary wife, because he was the unhappiest of emperors, and life with him would have been a terrible thing." Had she been strong enough to withstand the challenges of Cixi's court and person, Der Ling might well have made Guangxu just the supportive, bright and sympathetic wife he needed. Considering how fond the Empress Dowager was of Der Ling, it is likely that life as Guangxu's wife would have rapidly descended into a tug-o'-war with Cixi, which might very well have ended up being as evil-fortuned as the Guangxu Emperor predicted.

Like J. R. Ackerley's eccentric Maharajah of Chhatarpur, Cixi just wanted someone to love her. Der Ling was happy to love the old lady, but she would soon find that with love for Cixi came chains broken only at one's peril.[9]

17
"A very precious child"

Der Ling's polite reverence to the Guangxu Emperor was her last, at least in the Empress Dowager's presence. As she rose, she looked up to see Cixi standing in the doorway. "She looked at me in a very peculiar way," Der Ling recalled, "as if she did not approve of what I had done, but said nothing."

Following Cixi back into the room, Der Ling stood behind her chair while the old lady vigorously sliced through envelopes with an ivory paper knife. Perhaps this vigor, and the scrutiny she applied to the memorial contained in each, pointedly ignoring the scene that had just taken place, was for Der Ling's edification — Cixi was a natural-born actress. Guangxu looked through each document in a glum, cowering and perfunctory silence.

The mail reviewed, part one of Cixi's morning's work was over; part two was announced by a eunuch, who had come to report that the Empress Dowager's chair was ready to carry her to the Audience Hall, where she was scheduled to meet with members of the Grand Council. The little train consisting of Cixi as engine, followed by the coal cars of the emperor and the Young Empress, and finally the court ladies as caboose, headed through the courtyards to the hall. The latter took their accustomed places behind the screen and listened while Cixi heard the Council ministers out, made decisions on the issues they raised, and turned to the emperor for his brief "Yes" that would seal each decision as final. Cixi, who was as good at remembering fancied slights as she was at recalling marks of loyalty and affection, was obviously still in a strange mood from seeing Der Ling kneel to the emperor. "[S]he said that she wanted to go for a walk to get some fresh air," Der Ling remembered.

Of course, this did not mean the dowager could simply walk out the door. First her servant girls had to take the wide Manchu headdress off of her head, leaving the knot of dark hair on top, which Cixi wished to adorn with simple jewels — a Manchu woman never adopted this informal headdress unless she was certain she would be receiving no visitors from outside her household. Der Ling was sent to fetch ornaments of jade and pearl from the black drawers in the jewel-room. After they had been tried and put back and tried again, finally placed as the dowager wished them, Der Ling was left carrying the jewels she had just removed, and found that she did not know what to do with them. Easy though it would have been to hand them to one of the several eunuchs standing nearby, and gaining no helpful glances from the other ladies, Der Ling decided the most logical course of action, though without the Empress Dowager's approval, was to take the jewels back to the treasure room herself.

She returned to find Cixi wearing another gown and chatting with Louisa in one of the shady courtyards. Already on edge from the incident earlier that morning, Der Ling was chilled by the questioning look directed at her as she approached the dowager. "Where have you been?" Cixi asked her. With her mother's concerned gaze upon her, Der Ling was flustered. But believing, as she would till her last day at court, that honesty (up to a point) was her best protection, she told the dowager that she had been to put her other jewels away herself, not wanting to entrust them to the eunuchs, and not having been told what to do by the other court ladies. The dowager's bright, hard stare softened: Der Ling had done just the right thing, Cixi assured her. "Anything you want to know," the old lady said, with what one can imagine was a stagy conspiratorial air, "you can ask me, but don't talk to these mean people here."

The technique was pure Cixi: she could not eradicate the sharks circling her court, but she could be trusted to warn Der Ling to avoid certain places where they were swimming. Control of this kind had always made Cixi happy, and so much improved was her mood that with a girlish laugh the dowager declared she not only wanted to take a walk, but to have lunch *alfresco*, atop temple-studded Longevity Hill. Like everything else this was no simple matter to arrange, but the court was so used to the dowager's impromptu declarations that soon the cavalcade of court ladies and eunuchs, carrying everything from lunch items to dressing table paraphernalia, along with the small dark waddling form of Cixi's dog "Sea Otter," began again. "Just see how many people are following us," Cixi smiled mischievously at Der Ling.

Cixi headed west, and she and her cavalcade entered the cool shade of the famous Long Gallery. Like so much else at the Summer Palace, the gracious ghost of an earlier structure haunted the foundations of the new one. Originally built in 1750, in the reign of the Qianlong Emperor, the Gallery, almost 2,400 feet in length and broken into quarters by four red-pillared pavilions bearing such names as "Living with the Ripples" and "Autumn Water," was rebuilt during Guangxu's reign. Not a square inch was left undecorated: the lacquered green pillars of the gallery contrasted with the crimson ones of the pavilions, and above every beam and joist was a kaleidoscope of color and whimsy reminiscent of *famille rose* porcelain, with some 14,000 scenic paintings lining lintels and ceilings, many inspired by famous Chinese novels and the lush garden landscapes of Qianlong's favorite southern China regions. Making the Gallery even more magical was the shimmer of Lake Kunming, the shoreline of which the structure followed closely, its bright colors and gilding separated from the water by strategically planted trees and a gleaming white marble balustrade.

Here, amid such overkill of loveliness that it was possible to imagine problems not just far away but solved through the distracting medium of sumptuous artistry, Der Ling would find herself a few years later weeping by herself in a pavilion, as she worried about her father and missed the freedoms of the life he had provided for her. For now, though, it was all she and the other members of the party could do to keep up with Cixi, who had donned flat slippers and was zipping along the Gallery like a speed-walker.

"We walked for quite a long while," Der Ling wrote, "and I began to feel tired, but Her Majesty, as old as she was, was still walking very fast and did not appear to be the least bit tired."[1] Cixi may have had another purpose in leaving the others behind, because as she strode along, Der Ling at her elbow, she began to pepper her with leading questions: Did Der Ling like the Summer Palace? Would she like to live there always?

But Cixi was not finished with her wooing of her 17-year-old lady-in-waiting. After showing Der Ling the infamous Marble Barge and pointing out the damage done to it by foreign troops in 1900 — damage which, she insisted to Der Ling, she intended to leave *in situ*, because it reminded her of the lesson she had learned (a remark which differs so greatly from the accepted portrait of the unrepentant Cixi that it is either a candid admission from the heart or a canny old woman's pandering to the sympathies of a gullible young one) — the dowager sat down on the yellow satin stool which a special eunuch carried behind her everywhere she went and watched the approach of two ornately carved boats, scudding over the lotus-choked waters of the lake. Der Ling describes the boats as "floating pagodas," curtained in red gauze trimmed in silk.

"We must go over to the west side of the lake," announced the dowager, "and have luncheon."

Der Ling accompanied Cixi into one of the boats, "very nicely furnished with carved ebony furniture with blue satin cushions" and potted flowers at the windows, with three cabins: a sitting room, dressing room and a regular bedroom, where the dowager could go for a floating siesta. Cixi seated herself on the throne in the sitting room and motioned for the ladies to sit on red silk cushions placed for them on the floor nearby — never must a subject of Her Majesty sit in the imperial presence except at her invitation and only at a lower level than that at which she herself reposed. The boat's eunuch rowers, elaborately costumed, of course stood, punting with long bamboo poles.

It was easy enough for a robe-clad Fourth Princess to gracefully seat herself this way, but Der Ling, Rong Ling and Louisa had to struggle with the trains of their gowns, the restrictions imposed by stiff corsets and by their foreign-style shoes, all of which caught the watchful dowager's eye. "You can stand up if you want to," Cixi told the women, with an amused smile, "and just watch those boats following us."

Der Ling put her head out a window and saw another craft just behind, bearing as passengers the Young Empress and various other ladies of the court; other boats followed, carrying the provisions and eunuchs to prepare and serve them at the imperial picnic. A few of the ladies waved to Der Ling, who laughingly waved back at them, at which point the mirthful dowager put an apple in Der Ling's hand, urging her to throw it to the ladies on the boat. Der Ling tried and failed twice, whereupon Cixi herself took an apple, aimed and threw. Not only did her apple reach the Young Empress' vessel but struck one of the court ladies squarely on the head (one envisions the headdress clattering like a disturbed chandelier). This had Der Ling and the other ladies collapsing in not the most tactful laughter.[2]

Der Ling would come to realize soon enough that "[i]t was a characteristic of Her Majesty to experience a keen sense of enjoyment at the troubles of other people." (On future boating trips, Der Ling would note how Cixi would deliberately direct her eunuch rowers to the muddy west side of the lake, where her launch would become stuck in the mire and have to be dragged out with great effort.) But for now, oblivious to the ramifications of the apple throwing incident and enchanted by her surroundings, she fell to musing. "The lake was beautiful and looked so green in the sun," Der Ling recalled. "I told Her Majesty that this color reminded me of the sea."

"You have traveled so much," the dowager chided, "and yet you have not had enough, but are still thinking of the sea. You must not go abroad any more, but stay with me."[3] Hearing this, Der Ling tells us, she could not help thinking: "Is it not too bad that one of the world's greatest rulers should be so circumscribed by custom that she must do all her water traveling on an artificial pond!" The palaces at the water's edge seemed like "the nurse which guarded Her Majesty, so that she was a child playing at boats — a very precious child who must have many teachers, tutors, and governesses to see that no harm came to her." She was to describe her in this way on a later occasion, too, when Louisa had arranged for members of a Russian circus visiting Beijing to come out to the Summer Palace for a command performance, and Cixi had clapped with glee at her first sight of men on flying trapezes and a baby elephant performing tricks. Cixi's habit of expressing pleasure frankly reminded

Der Ling of a child's honest emotions, and perhaps validated her own essential childishness.[4]

"We floated on a surface of gleaming silver," Der Ling recalled, "while all around the lake was a border of bright green lotus . . . [as] the broad leaves caught the water, they straightened in our wake, flirting off pearls of water that were like the tears of young girls who weep because they are happy." Der Ling herself was that happy girl, tasting lotus shoots that the dowager commanded the eunuchs to pull up from the shallows, and leaning over the side of the craft to watch red-tailed fish rise to pluck insects from the surface and dart back into the murk. Circling around the stationary Marble Barge and heading north, the pagoda boats were rowed through the narrow, willow-hung strait, overarched with delicate bridges, that led into the Back Lake. This artificial causeway, formed from excavations and dykes around the entire back of Longevity Hill, ended at the Garden of Harmonious Pleasures to the west of the palace complex, a south China-style garden complex of pools, pavilions and walkways built by the Qianlong Emperor, as a replica of the famed Jichang Garden of the scholarly Qin family of Wuxi. As the pagoda boats rowed on, servants sent ahead of the little flotilla could be seen between the trees, hurrying along pathways beside the shore, each carrying boxes for the luncheon feast.

By the time the boats had reached their mooring place, Der Ling saw awaiting them Cixi's yellow chair and red ones for her, Louisa and Rong Ling: a signal mark of the Empress Dowager's favor, for which the women kowtowed their thanks. Once all were seated and lifted up by the bearers, the procession of chairs began to head straight uphill, the bearers behind lifting the poles high to keep the passengers level. The harrowing climb proved worthwhile, because Der Ling was set down outside the one building among the dozens dotting the acreage of the Summer Palace which she felt deserved the superlative of most beautiful — the Pavilion of Blessed Scenery. With its slender red pillars and delicate railing surrounding a broad, south-facing hall, the pavilion opened on to as gorgeous a view of Kunming Lake and its distant islands and arching white marble bridges as could be found anywhere in the palace precincts. Cixi, who loved such natural phenomena as the light of the full moon, falling snow and driving rain, would often be carried to the pavilion just to sit and silently soak in the sights.[5]

Another reason for Der Ling's love of the Pavilion of Blessed Scenery was that on the slope below it boasted two tiny Chinese villages, built entirely of clay, similar to the miniature town Der Ling had enjoyed in childhood in the garden at the Chinese legation in Tokyo.[6] Der Ling had no chance to explore the little houses, however: responsible for setting out Cixi's pre-luncheon sweetmeats and then hovering near the dowager's table to answer any wants she might have, Der Ling was fairly dizzy from hunger and from what was already feeling like a long day. The dowager offered her some welcome pieces of candy, for which the weary girl gave a grateful if painful kowtow, only to be kindly but firmly pulled up short — "Whenever I give you small things," Cixi said, "you need not kowtow. Just say 'Xie Lao Zu Zong Shang' (Thank the old ancestor), that is enough."[7]

Der Ling still had a lot to learn besides restricting her kowtows to gifts of appropriate munificence. When the dowager gave her sweets to give the eunuchs for transporting home, Der Ling instead took them outside to the veranda and offered them to the Young Empress, who reacted with some surprise. Der Ling had taken a candy herself when the dowager called her urgently from the hall. Expecting a reprimand, Der Ling found the old lady placidly eating lunch and once again obsessing on the Russian minister's wife. Had Madame de Plancon said anything that Der Ling had omitted? Was she truly happy with her audience and luncheon, or just pretending? Out of left field, Cixi then asked: "Do you think they, the foreigners, really like me?"

"I was very much surprised that [Cixi] should call me in and ask me such questions during her meal," recalled Der Ling, and reflexively "I assured her that no one ever said anything about Her Majesty but nice things." Though Der Ling would not have known some of the crudely pornographic stories that were circulated about the dowager, and only later heard some of the accounts of Cixi's supposed relations with so-called "false eunuchs" and a myriad of lovers, she knew her words were not the least bit true: few foreigners in Beijing or elsewhere would ever forget or forgive the Boxer Uprising and Cixi's real or imagined role behind it, nor would the heads of most European nations ever see her as anything but a reactionary conservative, willing to pit her own people against what the Europeans viewed as the manifest destiny of commercial progress.[8]

Cixi herself had her doubts, despite Der Ling's assurances. "I can't worry too much," she mused, "but I hate to see China in such a poor condition. Although the people around me seem to comfort me by telling that almost every nation feels very friendly towards China, I don't think that is true." Der Ling murmured a few comforting words, but in fact she sensed that this moment, with the dowager all to herself and in a rueful mood, might be just the one in which she could "advise her on some points" of reform. "I felt sorry for her," she recalled, "and would have given anything in the world to help her by telling what the general opinion of her was so as to let her know the truth, which no one dared to tell her. Something told me to be silent." That something was part fear and part strategy: not wanting to offend the old lady, Der Ling also felt that the right time for her counsels (such as they were, coming from a girl of seventeen) had not arrived yet. "I wanted to study her first thoroughly," she wrote confidently, "and then try to influence her to reform China."[9]

Proof that reform was needed not just throughout the empire but within the dowager's own household seemed to confirm that now was not the time for this type of conversation. Cixi harangued some of the eunuch gardeners about unattractive branches which had not been trimmed back. The dowager was especially solicitous of the health of flowers she or others had planted many years before — as she once told one of her gardeners, "You know, trees and flowers always become more charming when they are old. If you treat them well they will never die."[10] To mistreat them was to fail to reverence the same things the dowager did: what the dowager admired, so should everyone else. There was also in Cixi a paranoia about proper care for things of beauty which, as we have seen, dated back to her horror over the destruction of the Old Summer Palace.

As the eunuchs whom Cixi had accused of neglecting her flowers cowered before her on the floor she turned to Der Ling and said, "You see, I have to look after everything myself, if not, my flowers would be ruined." Her eunuchs were due for punishment anyway, she laughed, adding, "I will not disappoint them, but give them all they wish to have." No doubt prodded by Der Ling's silent reaction, the dowager asked her if she had ever seen servants being whipped. Der Ling had indeed once seen convicted men flogged in a magistrate's courtyard in Shashi, but the

Empress Dowager was not impressed: "That is nothing. The convicts are not half so wicked as these eunuchs."[11]

She then ordered the eunuchs out of her sight, changed to yet another gown, and sat down to play a game with Der Ling called *Eight Fairies Travel Across the Sea*. Not surprisingly, after a two-hour round, Cixi "won."

18
Rumblings in paradise

On her return to the palace, which took place over land rather than backtracking through the lake, Cixi announced she needed a nap. For Louisa and the girls, the break came just in time.

"My legs were very stiff and my back was tired," Der Ling remembered. "Foreign attire is out of the question for the Imperial Palace of Peking" — not to mention the fact that she had been up since 5 a.m. and on her feet most of the time. Just as she was preparing to change her gown and lie down on her bed, her eunuch came to the door to tell her that she had visitors. Rising to her aching feet, Der Ling found herself facing two court ladies and a thin, sickly, cold-eyed servant girl of about her own age, whose name, Graceful Long Life, seemed to Der Ling an irony on all points. "We have come to see you," the older ladies told Der Ling, "and also to find out if you are comfortable."

For the wives of foreign ministers who had met them, the ladies of Cixi's court were an attractive if naïve group of people. Living in rarified circumstances since birth, most of them illiterate, these Manchu noblewomen with their rainbow-colored silks and doll-like painted faces would giggle over their reflections in a silver teaspoon and ask ingenuous questions about the world outside China as might interplanetary visitors who had alighted on the Earth. They enchanted people like Sarah Conger, wife of the American minister, whose kindly heart saw nothing but good. "The Chinese are taught etiquette from their earliest childhood," she wrote her daughter, after a tea party she had given at the American Legation for princesses of the court in March 1902. "Their grace of manner, gentleness, politeness, and respect are most beautiful and attractive."[1]

What most foreigners could not know was that these same ladies, exemplars all of exquisite behavior in the public realm, could be as back-biting as the women of any royal court once ensconced in their own element. For Der Ling, what bothered her most was the strange impression that Graceful Long Life, though no court lady but something of a glorified chambermaid, seemed to be calling all the shots of the peculiar interview. The ladies began by asking Der Ling increasingly leading questions, starting with how she felt about the Empress Dowager. Der Ling answered truthfully, glad of an opportunity to air her views. "I told them that Her Majesty was the most lovely lady I had ever seen, and that I already loved her very much, although I had only been [at court] for a few days."[2]

The women glanced at each other knowingly, and then at Graceful Long Life, who was smiling in a way that gave Der Ling a chill. Well then, they went on, did Der Ling plan to remain for some time at court, and for how long? Der Ling again gave a candid response. "I said I would love to stay long, and would do my best to wait on Her Majesty," she recalled, "for she had been so kind towards us in the short time we had been here." It was also, she pointed out, "my duty to serve my sovereign and country."[3]

This statement provoked laughter from the court ladies and even from the taciturn Graceful Long Life, though she had a strange way of showing mirth. "When she laughed," Der Ling recalled, "one could only hear the noise she made; no expression was on her face at all."[4]

"We pity you," the ladies said, "and are sorry for you. You must not expect any appreciation here, no matter how hard you work. If you are really going to do as you have said just now, you will be disliked by everybody."[5]

By now, Der Ling knew she was being guided into treacherous waters, and tried to change the subject by asking the women about their clothing and hair. The court ladies fell silent. "Tell her everything about this Palace," Graceful Long Life muttered to them, "and I am sure she will change her mind when she actually sees things for herself." The court ladies nodded, their headdress ornaments jingling in the quiet room. "Now let us tell you everything," they said conspiratorially. "No one else will know . . . so as to be able to protect yourself whenever you are in trouble . . . You don't know, and have no idea how wicked this place is; such torture and suffering one could not imagine." They then launched into a full-scale indictment against the Empress Dowager — how she and the palaces were actually ruled by the evil eunuch Li Lianying, of whom everyone at court was terrified. Not only were the eunuchs afraid of him, but they transferred their fears to their treatment of the court ladies, to whom they could be as rude as they wished, knowing Li would never call them to account. But Old Buddha was even worse, they added. Because while the women generally knew what to expect from Li and his eunuch minions, Cixi's mind and actions could not be predicted from one moment to the next.

"She may like one person to-day, to-morrow she hates this same person worse than poison," Der Ling was told. "She has moods, and has no appreciation whatsoever." Even the Young Empress, who never put a foot wrong, was frightened of head eunuch Li, and in turn of the dowager, who followed Li's advice slavishly. This catalog of Cixi's sins might have gone on longer had the women not been cut short by a eunuch's cry echoing through the courtyard outside: "Lao fo ye xing le!" ("The Great Buddha wakes up!"). The court ladies and Graceful Long Life gestured their respect and withdrew from Der Ling's room, leaving her unrested, still clad in her uncomfortable French heels and corseted gown and worried about what they had said to her and why they had said it.[6]

Her apprehension and, indeed, her guilt at having listened to the women without shutting them up, was not alleviated by going to greet the dowager in her room. She found Cixi sitting cross-legged on her bed, refreshed from her rest and smiling at seeing Der Ling enter. "Have you had a good rest?" Cixi asked her. Der Ling pretended otherwise, but the perceptive old lady was not fooled. "I think you must have been on the hills to gather flowers," she suggested, "or walked too much, for you look tired."[7]

The dowager must have known very well that after the busy day they all had just had, the last place Der Ling would have been was hiking over the hills. Just then, in came the court ladies who had been gossiping in Der Ling's room. Both looked straight into Der Ling's face as if nothing untoward had occurred, a *sang froid* she found alarming. Watching them help the dowager prepare her hair and clothing, Der Ling could hardly return their glances. "[I] felt ashamed for them to face her," she recalled, "after having said so many disagreeable things."[8]

Cixi appeared to be none the wiser, as the women assisted her with her preparations. But as she sat playing solitaire dominoes, she suddenly looked up at Der Ling and asked: "How do you like this kind of life?" Automatically, Der Ling told her that she loved being with Old Buddha at her beautiful palace. The old woman knew better; she began to probe. "What kind of a place is this wonderful Paris I have heard so much about?" Cixi asked. It must have been difficult, she added, for Chinese people to leave their homeland for several years. "I suppose you were all pleased when you received the order to come back," Cixi finished, watching the young girl all the while she turned her dominoes.[9]

"The only thing I could say was 'Yes,'" Der Ling recalled, "because it wouldn't be nice to tell her that I was awfully sorry to leave Paris."[10]

"What is dancing?" enquired the dowager suddenly. "Someone told me that two people hold hands and jump all over the room. If that is the case I don't see any pleasure in it at all. Do you have to jump up and down with men?" She had heard that even old white-haired women occupied themselves in public with this inexplicable and undignified activity. Was this a veiled reference to the dancing Der Ling had done in Paris with Prince Zaizhen and to the rumors of her misbehavior?[11]

The way she put her question and her concept of dancing would have made Der Ling laugh at any other time. She seems to have realized she was explaining dancing as well as defending herself; she carefully explained the dances she had attended in Paris, the balls given by dignitaries and the amusing sort of dance known as the masquerade ball, all of which were considered perfectly suitable for old and young. Cixi objected most vociferously to the latter entertainment. How could a person know with whom she was dancing, if his identity was concealed! It was bad enough to be "jumping" together at all, but to not know one's jumping partner, this was potentially scandalous. Der Ling patiently clarified the process whereby hostesses issued invitations only to people they knew personally or knew could be counted on to know how to behave in good society, which mollified the dowager's Confucian principles to some degree. She also told Cixi about her studies with Isadora Duncan, and gave her some of the broad outlines of Duncan's philosophy of movement.

"I should like very much to see her," Cixi commented. Perhaps Miss Duncan could be coaxed into coming to China for a command performance? Though if she did, the dowager added with a shudder, "I hope she hasn't any hair on her upper lip, like all the other foreign ladies!" For now, Cixi was keen on a demonstration. "I would like to see you jump," she said, "can you show me a little?"[12]

Der Ling went in search of her sister, and bringing her back to the dowager's room, told her they must demonstrate dancing for Her Majesty. This in turn brought all the other court ladies in tow, with the Young Empress heading the pack. The one thing they needed was music. According to the painter Katherine Carl, there were two upright pianos and one grand piano at the back of the Audience Hall, which she was invited by Cixi to play, even though the dowager found the piano *per se* "lacking in volume and tone for so large an instrument."[13] But there was no piano in Cixi's room, and the other pianos in the palace were too far away.

Rong Ling remembered seeing a gramophone and records somewhere in a palace room. This machine was probably a relic of Guangxu's early obsessive interest in foreign gadgetry, ranging from simple foreign wind-up toys in childhood to Edison phonograph machines, operated by a pedal-pumped mechanism similar to an old-fashioned sewing machine (leading one to imagine that there may be wax cylinders buried somewhere in a Chinese vault, carrying the only known recording of the Guangxu Emperor's "mosquito-like" voice), to clocks that rang tunes every hour or made enameled shepherds and shepherdesses dance atop the dial.[14]

The gramophone and some records were duly brought by some eunuchs. Among all the Chinese songs and opera arias Der Ling found a waltz. The needle was lowered, and from the fluted bell came a jaunty tune in three-four time. Der Ling and her sister clasped hands, lifted their trains, and waltzed around the room, surrounded on all sides by court personnel in their bright Chinese silks and satins, silently looking on. When the dance ended, Der Ling records that Cixi laughed and declared that "jumping" was something she could never do. "I don't think it would look nice to see a man dancing with a girl like that," she pronounced. But perhaps, she conceded, foreigners had broader minds about such matters. Cixi was to ask Katherine Carl to play on a future occasion so that Der Ling and Rong Ling could waltz for her, and Western dance continued to fascinate her.[15]

Dinner followed, per the pattern Der Ling had come to expect, and then came another walk along the Long Gallery. It was early evening, but the electric lights strung along the Gallery had not yet been switched on, so that the women could look past the leafy shield of trees on the Gallery's south side and see the purpling sky glimmering in the lake. Cixi led the way to a small, unornamented bamboo kiosk, in which all the furniture and fittings were also made of bamboo, all carved with auspicious symbols. Der Ling would later discover that court ladies like herself were expected to provide these carved decorations.

The dowager sat down and ordered tea, gazing out at the twilit scenery with frank satisfaction. Here was a Cixi, Empress Dowager of China, who would have startled the many foreigners who held her to be nothing but a red-clawed tyrant. "This is my simple way of enjoying life," she told Der Ling as she looked wistfully out the tea-house window at the lake, its marble bridge, and the pavilion-crowned islets. "I love to see the country scenery." Only when the electricity came on, turning the Long Gallery into a winding snake of light, did Cixi rise to go back to the palace, now walking more slowly. She asked Der Ling to play dice with her before bedtime, and probably with some effort on Der Ling's part she lost to the dowager, who showed no surprise at having won. The old woman's nightly milk was brought, and then, when Der Ling had been lulled by the busy day and its calm ending into a sort of unguarded reverie, the dowager spoke words that chilled Der Ling's blood more than anything the trouble-making court ladies had said or done. "I want you to burn incense sticks and bow to the ground every night to the Buddha in the next room before I go to bed," Cixi ordered. "I hope you are not a Christian, for if you are I can never feel as if you are mine at all. Do tell me that you are not." There was no question about it: Der Ling *was* a Christian, baptized by the Bishop of Beijing himself and blessed by the hand of Pope Leo XIII. It was through suspecting her father's Christian faith that Prince Tuan had ordered his Beijing mansion burned to the ground and declared himself disappointed that Yu Keng and his family were not in it at the time.

One of the strongest tenets of Christianity was that one should not deny one's faith — Christian martyrs had suffered the ultimate penalty for their beliefs, unwilling to re-enact St. Peter's trio of denials. Yet Der Ling had been brought up in a Christian household that knew how to compromise in order to protect itself. "I knew I had to answer her question at once," Der Ling wrote later. "For my own protection I had to say I had nothing to do with the Christians ... Although my face showed nothing, my heart stopped beating for while." More than fear, Der Ling was ashamed at lying to a woman of whom she had grown fond. To her relief, Cixi chose to believe her. "I admire you," she said, "although you have had so much to do with foreigners, yet you did not adopt their religion ... You have no idea how glad I am now, for I suspected you must believe in the foreign God."[16]

Whether this suspicion had been planted by one of the court ladies, of whose negative attitude toward her she could no longer have any doubts, or arisen of its own accord (and the rumors of Yu Keng's secret Christianity must have reached Cixi long years before), Der Ling now knew she would be under even tighter scrutiny than she suspected — not just by the court personnel, but by the dowager herself.

19
The Forbidden City

"I began to take great interest in the Court life," Der Ling wrote, "and liked it better every day."

With a pride in the Summer Palace's beauty that was as much that of the artist as the empress, the dowager showed Der Ling all over the estate — one of the abiding images in Der Ling's court memoirs is that of Cixi, sitting on her little yellow satin stool, at the apex of the white marble Jade Girdle Bridge, sipping tea as she gazed out over the lake and the palaces and pavilions that made a splash of color along the greenery-choked northern shore. She took Der Ling, Rong Ling and Louisa to her working farm, which she visited every week. "[I]t always pleased her if she could take some vegetables and rice or corn from her own farm," Der Ling records.

But this was no Manchu Marie Antoinette. According to Der Ling, Cixi would actually do some cooking of her own, using movable brass stoves lined with brick, which were set up in an open courtyard. It was the dowager who taught Der Ling how to cook fresh eggs from the farm in her own special way: one hard-boiled them, then gently cracked but did not split the shells, added black tea, salt and spices to the water, and cooked the eggs in the liquid till the flavors had soaked in. "I thought that was good fun," Der Ling recalled, "and also turned up my sleeves to help her cook." The court ladies would then gather to partake of the food, which Cixi always tasted for quality before letting them begin. "Do you not think this food has more flavor than that prepared by the cooks?" the dowager queried her captive diners. In fact, according to Der Ling, the dowager was an excellent cook. She seemed to derive happiness from the informality of it all. "I am always glad to see young people having fun," she said, "and not such grand dames when we are by ourselves. Although I am not young any more, I am still very fond of play."[1]

Der Ling's impression of the Empress Dowager as a charming infant spoiled by endless but circumscribed luxury was still holding strong, and so solicitous were the old lady's attentions toward her that she began to fall into the trap of teacher's pet. Part of this was because Der Ling sincerely wished to serve the Empress Dowager as perfectly as she could manage. But at least as much of it was her studied response to the envious glares and double-edged advice being proffered by the other court ladies. They were watching and waiting for her to fail the dowager, proving that they had been correct to paint the court as a terrible, thankless place, the dowager herself as just as terrible and thankless, and Der Ling the interloper they clearly believed her to be. This, perhaps, is why Der Ling listened so attentively when a court lady came to her one evening and told her that as the ladies took turns waking up the dowager in the morning, the next day's duty was Der Ling's.

"While she said this she smiled in a most peculiar way," Der Ling recalled. The lady went on to describe in detail the correct procedure by which to awaken the old lady, who could be testy in the morning and would scold at the drop of a hat, particularly if she were awakened later than she had asked. The proper time to wake the dowager, said the lady, was 5:30 a.m. and no later. "What this Court lady said to me worried me quite considerably," wrote Der Ling, "but from what I had seen of Her Majesty so far, I could not believe that she would be angry with anyone who was doing her duty properly."

The following morning, Der Ling got up earlier than usual, frightened that she would be late, and hurried to the dowager's palace. She found several court ladies and the Young Empress standing in the porch of the building. The Young Empress did not seem to know whose duty it was to do the awakening, but accepted Der Ling's assertion that it was her turn and that this was the proper time to do it.

For an empress of China, there was no chance to ever be alone, even in sleep. Outside the dowager's room Der Ling found some maidservants as well as a court lady sitting on the floor. According to Der Ling's account, inside the room was a pair of eunuchs, whose sole job was to mind the actions of two older women servants, who in turn watched over two young girl servants whose primary purpose in life was to massage the Empress Dowager's legs and feet every night. Der Ling walked past these numerous personages to the yellow silk bed where the dowager lay, her face turned to the wall. "Old Ancestor," she whispered, "it is half-past five." From the dragon-embroidered quilt came an annoyed voice. "Go away and leave me alone," muttered the dowager. "I did not tell you to call me at half-past five. Call me again at six."

Der Ling withdrew, too frightened to ask anyone what to do next. After a shivering half-hour, she leaned over the dowager's sleeping form again. Cixi was now angry. "This is dreadful. What a nuisance you are," she growled. Only then did she turn over and see that her dreadful nuisance was her favorite Der Ling. "Oh! It is you, is it? Who told you to come and wake me?" Der Ling replied that one of the court ladies had done so. "That is funny," said the dowager. "How dare they give orders without receiving instructions from me first?" It soon became clear what had happened: it was not Der Ling's job to wake Cixi at all. Because the court ladies whose responsibility it was disliked doing it, they had palmed the task off on Der Ling.[2]

The court was not such a nice place after all. Along with the dowager's unpredictable moods and the bitterness of her court women, Der Ling began to see that a certain amount of physical violence, not to mention animal cruelty, was normal at the Summer Palace. One day some of the younger eunuchs captured a crow, which was not only considered an unlucky bird by the Chinese but was also an animal to which eunuchs were often compared (perhaps because of its mincing walk). A eunuch tied live fireworks to the bird's leg and it flapped away, trailing a stream of sparks. The bird managed to reach the courtyard of Cixi's residence before it exploded in a noisy hail of feathers, blood and flame. The dowager was furious on two counts — as a lover of birds, she often purchased large numbers of them in cages and then released them to gain points in the Buddhist Heaven; she was also a master of the art of charming wild birds to perch on her finger. (Both Katherine Carl and Lady Townley witnessed this gift.) And she had been startled out of her nap by the explosion. On hearing that the culprit was nearby, the dowager commanded all her ladies-in-waiting, including Der Ling, to seize rods she kept in a special yellow silk bag, and go down to the courtyard to beat the eunuchs with them while she watched.

As if in a trance, Der Ling carried her stick with the others and like them began to rap the eunuchs with it. The scene was so strange to her and her sister that they could hardly keep from bursting into nervous laughter; yet an order from the dowager was an order, and Cixi was looking on from the terrace, her eyes squinting angrily, so the women had to obey. By the time chief eunuch Li appeared, Der Ling and the others "were laughing so much that we did not have enough strength to hurt [the eunuchs]." They sobered up at the sight of Li's grim, pockmarked face. It turned out that Li's nap had been interrupted by the firecrackers, too. He glowered as the perpetrator was delivered up and observed while he was beaten on the back and legs with bamboo rods.

Eunuchs were not the only servants who bore the marks of punishment at Cixi's court, and for less troublous transgressions. On another occasion, Der Ling was present when a maidservant who had accidentally brought Cixi two stockings for the same foot was ordered by the dowager to be slapped on the face, ten times per cheek. The punishment was to be meted out by another maidservant. But because the girls were friends, the slapper did not strike the other hard enough, so Cixi sadistically ordered the one who had started the slapping to be slapped by the girl of the mismatched stockings. As with the young eunuch's punishment, had the scene not been so strange, Der Ling recalled, it would have been very funny. As befitted a court where incidents like these were commonplace, the girls themselves told Der Ling later that they had found the whole thing amusing.[3]

When the fourth moon came around, Cixi's mood focused less on human than on celestial targets. There had been no rain for several weeks — as Der Ling was unhelpfully reminded by a eunuch, none had fallen since she and her mother and sister had arrived at court. The dowager was a highly emotional woman, given to a self-centered view of the world, and when the weather did not obey her will it was as if some part of her power were being denied her. It was the throne's job to protect the empire's husbandmen, who were after all ranked just below scholars in the Confucian hierarchy of society. Not only that, but it was well known, undoubtedly to Cixi as much as to government officials, that prolonged periods of drought had often led to uprisings in China.

After ten straight days of no rain, storm clouds instead began to gather around the dowager; she became mute and worried, pacing her rooms and lighting incense and partaking of little food. It is a measure of Der Ling's Europeanized perspective that she at first could not understand what the dowager was upset about: "[W]e were having lovely weather then, day after day," she recalled. Her eunuch Wang explained: "He told me that Old Buddha was worried for the poor farmers, as all their crops were dead without rain for so long."

The Young Empress also filled Der Ling in. She told her that Cixi would stop eating meat for a period of several days, and it appeared no one else would have the pleasure of eating it either, because the dowager put an official stop to all slaughtering of swine within the walls of Beijing. "The reason of this," wrote Der Ling, "was that by sacrificing ourselves by not eating meat the Gods would have pity on us and send rain." The Qing dynasty had had a tradition, activated by drought and famine, of emulating the Buddha's selfless concern for mankind, in an effort to reverse oppressive circumstances. In 1807, the Jiaqing Emperor punished his officials and members of his family for coming to the Yuanmingyuan to greet him for the Mid-Autumn Festival, his reason being that when the farmers had had to do without rain for so long, neither he nor they must be seen to indulge in celebrations, as if they were unaware of the people's sufferings.[4]

Cixi further commanded that everyone should cleanse their bodies and wash out their mouths to prepare for a period of fasting and prayer. The most important ritual lay ahead: Guangxu's journey to the Tiantan or Temple of Heaven in Beijing, to pray to the Jade Emperor, the ninth-century Daoist-Buddhist deity who as the highest heavenly ruler held ultimate power over Earth, Man and Heaven. As Nature God, the Jade Emperor controlled such life-giving phenomena as rainfall, so that when drought seemed to threaten his temple, located in the northwest corner of the Imperial City, was the first place China's ruler would head for, to pray to the image with pearl-hung hat and jade tablet at his lips. However low an opinion the eunuchs and Cixi herself had of the Guangxu Emperor, and however slight his role at a court overdecorated with images of the phoenix, the symbol of the Chinese empress, there were some matters of ultimate concern where Guangxu was the only authority who could negotiate with the divine.

It was thus because of what Der Ling saw as heavenly sunny weather, and the emperor's responsibility for praying at the Hall of High Heaven for it to end, that Der Ling would visit the shadowy Forbidden City for the first time.

Before the court transferred to Beijing, a number of rituals had to be enacted, most of which puzzled Der Ling, who as a Christian had not been brought up to know all the byways of Buddhist belief. Guangxu began the process by donning a small jade tablet carved with an admonishment in Manchu and Chinese to pray for heavenly mercy. Cixi, who for reasons genuine or political seems to have desired that her court resemble a Buddhist convent as much as possible, did her part by giving up all personal adornment whatsoever, requiring the same sacrifices from her women. "Her Majesty wore a pale gray gown, made very plain, with no embroidery or trimmings of any kind," Der Ling wrote. Cixi then presided over a ceremony by which members of the court, including herself, plucked leaves from a branch of willow carried in by eunuchs and placed the sprigs in their hair or, for the men, on their hats. Vases stood about filled with more drooping willow branches.

The dowager prayed in a small pavilion near her residence, with all her court ladies lined up behind her, burning sandalwood in a censer with Der Ling's assistance. Because Der Ling did not know the prayer, the

Young Empress kindly taught it to her: "We worship the Heavens, and beg all the Buddhas to take pity on us and save the poor farmers from starving. We are willing to sacrifice for them. Pray Heaven send us rain."[5] There was no question of letting Guangxu travel by himself to Beijing to pray at the shrine of the Jade Emperor, so the dowager asked her court ladies to prepare for a stay in the Forbidden City. She would need no jewels or other ornament, but she would require a few gowns to wear — to the tune of some fifty of them, of all styles and colors. Der Ling asked the lady in charge of the wardrobe why she was bringing so many for a stay of just a few days. "She said it was safer to bring many," Der Ling recalled, "for one was not sure what would be Her Majesty's idea for the day." Given the temperamental manner in which Cixi had been behaving lately, Der Ling had to agree that to provoke her further was the last thing anyone would want to do.[6]

First in the train of carts heading east toward Beijing were the eunuchs, bearing luggage. The dowager, stiff and dour, was next, carried past her entire court, including the emperor and the Young Empress, kneeling on either side of the route. Then Guangxu and Longyu followed in their yellow chairs, with the red chairs of the court ladies bringing up the rear, accompanied by more eunuchs on horseback.

This traveling snake with yellow head and long red body reached Cixi's customary stopping place before entering Beijing, a temple called the Wan Shou Si or Temple of Long Life. Built in 1577 by a favorite eunuch of the Ming emperor Wanli, and restored by Cixi and Guangxu, the temple boasted an artificial rock hill in its eastern courtyard that was high enough for the dowager and Guangxu to sit atop it and enjoy the scenery, which included a view of distant Beijing.[7] The dowager seemed in a better mood at the temple. Der Ling found her walking in the courtyard. "My legs are so stiff, riding in the chair. I must walk a little before we leave here." She asked Der Ling and the other court ladies to walk with her, which they did, around and around the perimeter of the courtyard. At one point Cixi looked back and said with a smile, "We are just like horses taking their rounds at a stable," something the bannerman captain's daughter must have seen often enough in her Beijing girlhood.[8] The cavalcade could only depart at the auspicious hour the dowager had chosen, but once the court was on the road they reached Beijing within an hour, with the emperor, the Young Empress and the rest of the court taking a shorter route, so that all could satisfy convention by kneeling in a row for the dowager's later arrival.

The title of Der Ling's first and most famous volume of memoirs, *Two Years in the Forbidden City*, is strongly ironic: in fact, she spent at most a total of a few months within the winter palace's walls, most of her time being passed at the Summer Palace. She shared Cixi's dislike of the winter palace, which would account for her peevish remark on first seeing one of the world's masterpieces of architecture: "The Palace in the Forbidden City was so old, and built in such a queer way." Old the palace certainly was, dating from the fourth reign year (1410) of the great Ming emperor Yongle. Unlike the Summer Palace, which had suffered destruction at the hands of foreign invaders again and again, and apart from a few lucky pavilions and gardens, dated from no earlier than the late nineteenth century, virtually everything the Yongle Emperor had built at the Forbidden City — despite the conquests and mayhem which had occurred in the interim — was still standing.

Weeds and peeling paint aside, the Forbidden City was the very center not only of the Chinese world, but of the universe itself, with only the emperor as intermediary between men and the gods. "What poetic suggestion in the very name — a Forbidden City of palaces reserved for a Son of Heaven!" wrote one foreign visitor. "What dignity in the conception of a sovereign hidden away in a secret place from the people of a vast empire whose profound reverence willingly accepted his seclusion!" The writer went on to say:

> A foreigner visiting the Forbidden City for the first time is surprised and overwhelmed . . . [He] is prepared to see a palace in the western sense of the word — one large building with perhaps a few dependencies, like Fontainebleau or Windsor. But instead he enters the mazes of a city within a city and is conducted up and down a network of streets to groups of throne halls or living quarters, each group separately surrounded by walls, and giving the impression of a nest of square boxes fitting one within the other.[9]

Where the Summer Palace was built to absorb as much light as possible, even in the winter, when the window casements were covered with obscuring white rice paper, the palaces of the Forbidden City obeyed a steadfast rule: imperial power, like the ocean-dwelling, crag-scaling dragon that protected it, must function far from the eyes of mortals if it is to preserve the secrets of its magic. "The courtyards were small," Der Ling noted, yet the porches surrounding each building were broad, pushing the apartments well back from the yellow-tiled eaves. There were few windows. "All the rooms were dark. No electric light. We had to use candlelight. One could not see the sky except by going into the courtyard and looking up." The Forbidden City was also in much poorer condition than the Summer Palace. Photographs taken of it by foreign visitors at the time of the Boxer Uprising show marble paving stones choked with weeds, grass growing from the gold-tiled roofs, peeling paint everywhere. Even the Altar of Heaven, one of the most sacred places in China, suffered from lack of care, its marble platform furred with brambles. Cixi seems to have told Der Ling that she hated the place, with which Der Ling heartily agreed.[10]

The dowager may have had deeper reasons than interior décor for her hatred of the Winter Palace, stretching all the way back to her first introduction there, as a Manchu maiden fresh from the crowded alleyways of Beijing, with years of stiff court training, the heartbreak of the Xianfeng Emperor's brief affections, and the short, fevered life of her imperial son ahead of her. In the Forbidden City, Cixi had had to toe the line in her powerless youth, bow and kowtow to people she did not respect and to people who were cruel to her. It was from this palace that she and Guangxu had had to flee, in August 1900, through the same Shen Wu Men, the northernmost gate ironically named for military prowess, through which Der Ling and the other ladies in waiting now entered the Forbidden City. (The Shen Wu Men was the same gate through which the last Chinese emperor, Puyi, and his wives would depart the palace forever some twenty years later.) Perhaps, too, being within the Forbidden City was too close for comfort for her. Cixi was fascinated by her reflection (she was photographed by Der Ling's brother gazing intently at her reflection in hand mirrors; Der Ling saw her studying her own photographs for hours), and if her past lived in the Forbidden City so did her present power — the palace was the *ne plus ultra* seat of Chinese imperial power. Life at the Summer Palace allowed her just enough distance from the Forbidden City for Cixi to enjoy that symbol of what had given her her power, much as she might study herself in a looking-glass after donning another gown or set of jewels.

The somnolent spell of the Forbidden City and its aura of ancient Chinese customs preserved like dodo birds under glass seem to have also irritated the normally tactful Louisa. Shortly after the court's removal to the Winter Palace, she remarked caustically to the dowager, "The bound feet of the Chinese woman make us the laughing-stock of the world." No defender of foot-binding, Cixi was still very much aware that Western women also put up with painful customs in the name of high fashion. "I have heard that the foreigners have a custom which is not above reproach," she replied tartly, "and . . . I should like to see what the foreign ladies use in binding their waists." Louisa asked Rong Ling to show the dowager just what a corset looked like. Cixi frowningly examined the contraption of whale-bone, steel grommets and tight laces. "It is truly pathetic what foreign women have to endure," she exclaimed. "They are bound up with steel bars until they can scarcely breathe. Pitiable! Pitiable!" Der Ling says Cixi could hardly believe it when she was told that foreign women did not wear their "bandages" to bed — how was this better than bound feet?[11]

Even if they had given up their corsets (something the plump Louisa was not about to do), the women's European clothes were a decided liability at the cramped, inconveniently laid out palace. When rain fortuitously came, after Guangxu had passed through the great triple *pailou* outside the Tiantan and prayed at the altar, and the court had worn a whole forest of willow leaves, Der Ling got caught in the downpour in one of the courtyards, clad in a heavy wool dress. Unable to change before presenting herself to the dowager, she arrived soaked to the skin. Cixi again clucked at the hampering yardage of foreign clothes, and said, "I think you will look much prettier in our Manchu gown. I want you to change and put away your Parisian clothes as souvenirs." She had wanted to see how such clothes were worn, and for her foreign lady guests at court to see that she knew a thing or two about them. Now the experiment was over, and of the three Der Ling could not have been happier about the order to switch her wardrobe — Der Ling believed her clothes had set up a gulf between her and the other court ladies, which had helped lead to rifts and jealousies. It was, however, not yet possible for Louisa and her daughters to simply put on Manchu clothes. Consulting her calendar book of auspicious days, the dowager picked out a date mid-month that would be luckiest for the switch. In the meantime, orders went out to the imperial weavers and shoe shops that complete outfits were to be made for all three women.[12]

With the coming of rain, and the passing of Cixi's dark mood, the court returned to the Summer Palace just in time for the sort of "foreign-devil" entertainment for which Der Ling, her sister and mother were originally brought to the court.

20
Cat's eyes and big feet

Clothes were still very much on Cixi's mind when she presided over the first garden party of the year at the Summer Palace, and the clothes that most obsessed her were, as usual, those of the foreign women who made up the majority of the guests. The list of those attending the dowager's spring *fête* gleamed with the cream of both Chinese and foreign Beijing society. Besides such court grandees as Prince Qing and other members of the imperial government, Cixi had invited all the foreign ministers' wives, including her favorite among them, the sympathetic Sarah Conger, and one who was only sympathetic when in her presence, Lady Susan Townley, wife of the British Legation's First Secretary.

Lady Townley was flighty but was an amusing writer with as keen an eye for the absurd as Der Ling. Lady Townley also made what she may not have realized at the time was a certain contribution to the *Times'* reportage on China, by frequently sharing her catty observations while at court functions with George Morrison, the fabled *Times* correspondent who never learned a word of Chinese. In her 1922 memoir, *The Indiscretions of Lady Susan*, the author echoed some scuttlebutt she told Morrison, that Guangxu had "glazed eyes and a fixed expression" due to presumed opium addiction encouraged by Cixi herself. She also described Cixi as "a funny old lady," with the face of "a kindly Italian peasant" (Lady MacDonald, wife of the British minister, described her the same way — perhaps the ladies spoke on the matter in the garden), who gave the impression of being a woman of younger years, despite a disfiguring goiter. By this time, Der Ling had received the hair dye from Paris and had showed Cixi how to use it, with much more natural-looking results than the painted-on variety she had used for years.

Lady Townley had the tactlessness to ask the dowager for one of her own dinner plates as a souvenir, though knowing that these things were forbidden to anyone but the imperial user (and that a few years before, soldiers had made off with such items in their knapsacks). On the other hand, Lady Townley also claims to have given many foreign items to Cixi who, she claims, in an impression of Cixi not given by anyone else, would become obsessed with some item belonging to someone else and admire it until the only thing to do was give it to her. Lady Townley certainly did not approve of the quality of what she believed were gifts from foreign rulers: "I don't know why it is," sniffed this daughter of an English earl, "that European potentates always show such a preference for blue Sèvres when selecting presents for an Eastern ruler."[1]

Conspicuous for her absence from the guest list was Madame von Rosthorn, wife of the Austro-Hungarian minister and proud daughter of a Viennese dentist, who refused to participate in Cixi's garden parties because she felt them "common." But everyone else of consequence was there, including Der Ling's friends from Tokyo, Madame and Mademoiselle de Carcer, wife and daughter of the Spanish Minister.[2] Madame von Rosthorn missed seeing one of the more spectacular gowns in Cixi's collection, described by Der Ling as "a most beautiful gown of peacock blue, embroidered all over with phoenix. The embroidery was raised and each phoenix had a string of pearls two inches long sewed into its mouth. Whenever Her Majesty stirred, these strings of tiny pearls moved backwards and forwards and it made a very pretty effect." Louisa outfitted herself and her daughters in foreign-style gowns, in which the East of Chinese silk was united to the West of Irish lace trim. Cixi had decided to try a foreign concept for her party, that of having stalls set up in the garden, after the fashion of a charity bazaar, in which were displayed embroideries and curios which later were given to the guests as gifts. As was often done in the warmer months, mats were stretched over the courtyards to make a cool and shady outdoor living space, where ladies could sit with their tea without being cooked by the hot Chinese sun.[3]

Along with her dazzling gown, Cixi put her charm on full display, enthusiastically showing her guests around the gardens and explaining the curios in the stalls. Sarah Conger had heard that the dowager was studying English, but Cixi never made enough progress to say more than a few words; and in any case, for this occasion Der Ling was principal translator, standing beside the seated dowager as guests were presented to her. Cixi had provided knives, forks and spoons for her guests, and even had a brass band to play foreign tunes (perhaps an idea taken from Sir Robert Hart's private garden orchestra). Tea was served in a building specially constructed for the occasion.

Der Ling was later grilled by the dowager in the expected way. According to Der Ling, Cixi could not resist making comments on the foreign ladies who had been present, which showed that Lady Townley had nothing on her for caustic barbs. "How is it that these foreign ladies have such large feet?" Cixi wanted to know. "Their shoes are like boats and the funny way they walk. I haven't yet seen one foreigner with pretty hands." And the worst of it: "Although they have white skins, their faces are covered with white hair." She asked Der Ling whether she thought such women were at all attractive, and sniffed at her response that she had seen some lovely American ladies in her foreign travels. "No matter how beautiful they are they have ugly eyes," the dowager shuddered. "I can't bear that blue color, they remind me of a cat." Given that Lady Townley's eyes were of an especially plangent blue, it is conceivable the dowager had her in mind. Seeing how graciously she made her guests welcome, hairy faces, scary eyes, big feet and all, it was just as well that none guessed the savage commentary going through her mind.[4]

Preparations were under way for Louisa, Der Ling and Rong Ling to commence wearing Manchu costume, and Cixi had no end of fun taunting Der Ling with the sight of the beautiful gowns, handkerchiefs, headdresses, and jewelry that she had chosen for her. She even teased her about her curly hair. Der Ling explained that she made the curls herself, using hair papers that she rolled up before she went to sleep at night. "[Cixi] said that I could not pull my hair straight in time to wear Manchu clothes," Der Ling wrote, "and that everyone would laugh at me, and how ugly I would look."

This was affectionate raillery, but not so the brief conversation Der Ling had with a court lady not long afterward. Der Ling had been sitting on the veranda, enjoying the flower-scented twilight (perhaps unaware that in the China of the period, a young unmarried woman who watched the sunset from her porch was advertising the fact she was in love),[5] when she was joined by the court lady, who asked her bluntly whether she thought she would look presentable in the Manchu court dress. Der Ling bristled: "I told her I only wanted to look natural." The lady replied that she did not see how that could be possible, as Der Ling had lived out of China for so long she would be like a foreigner dressing up in Chinese clothes — a clever and discerning comment. As Der Ling would demonstrate in later years, when traveling the Chautauqua lecture circuit, she did regard court clothes as more exotic costume than "natural" wear. But she was so incensed by the court lady's smiling rudeness, and perhaps by the truth of her words, she abruptly left the veranda.

When Der Ling had finally dressed herself in her new gown and had pinned on her new flower-decked headdress, she gazed in the mirror. "I could not believe my own eyes," she recalled, "and asked several times whether that was myself or not." When Louisa and her daughters appeared in their new Manchu dress among the other court ladies, they caused quite a stir, with everyone except the emperor declaring that they looked much more attractive in Manchu clothing. Guangxu turned to Der Ling among all the smiling admiration and said, perhaps with irony, "I think your Parisian gowns are far prettier than this." Cixi was certainly pleased, though afterward she criticized Der Ling for a pardonable offense. "You never put enough paint on your face," she admonished. "People might take you for a widow."[6]

The dowager also gave Der Ling pieces of jewelry from her own younger days, including a pair of earrings. She teasingly handed the jewels to Der Ling in Louisa's presence, saying that it was clear that *Yu tai tai* cared more for her younger daughter than the elder, as Rong Ling had pretty earrings and Der Ling none. "You are mine now," Cixi said, smiling at Der Ling. To Louisa she said airily: "You have nothing to do with her."

If kowtowing in train and feathered or flowered hats had been a challenge, the heavy Manchu headdress caused its own problems, but Der Ling adjusted. As if Cixi's beneficence thus far were not sufficient, she made another pronouncement: that Der Ling, her mother and sister were dressed as full court princesses because they were to be ranked as such, and that on the dowager's seventieth birthday, in November 1905, she would make their rank official. If this is in fact what Cixi promised, she could have no idea what trouble her gift would cause Der Ling in years to come.[7]

21
A portrait for the Empress

For all her plain appearance and sober ways, Sarah Pike Conger was a woman of warm and appreciative affections, who said of herself "I am a seeker in China, and am interested in Chinese [things]. I recognize their beauty, then I wish to know something of the people who produced them."[1]

This pleasant combination of kindness and open-mindedness no doubt helped endear her to Cixi, who was curious enough about the American woman to find out from Louisa that she had become a grandmother in June 1903. Sarah was almost as overjoyed at receiving the dowager's congratulations on the birth of little Sarah Buchan as she was at the telegram announcing it. This was the turning point — she began to think in earnest of ways to make it clear to the world at large that far from being a cruel termagant, the Empress Dowager was actually a sensitive woman and a thoughtful ruler. Sarah was convinced that world opinion would not change until the "horrible, unjust caricatures of Her Majesty in the illustrated papers" were supplanted, literally, by a true portrait — in paint rather than words — of the dowager. She now proposed to convince Cixi to have such a portrait painted.

"I had written to the artist, Miss Carl," Sarah wrote her daughter Laura, "and found that she was willing to cooperate with me."[2] As was written in Wang Kai's seventeenth-century manual of painting, "It is better to be audacious than commonplace," a painterly admonition that Sarah clearly took to heart in all matters.[3]

Sarah wrote to Katherine Carl, an American-born painter living in Shanghai, as early as April; such was her enthusiasm for the project, and her certainty that Cixi would assent to it, that she made it sound almost as if the negotiations were a done deal when they were not yet even off the ground.[4] Sarah saw herself as an ambassador for her entire sex. "With intense love for womankind, and in justice to this Imperial woman," Sarah intoned, "I presented my subject without doubt or fear . . . As the result of this conversation, the Empress Dowager gave consent to allow her Imperial portrait to be painted by an American lady artist for the St. Louis Exposition."[5]

Agreeing to the portrait had not been as easy as Cixi led Sarah to believe. As the dowager greeted Sarah, Der Ling took note: "[I] saw that she was very nice and amiable, with such a pleasant smile — so different from her everyday manner." (So was Cixi pleasant to be with or not? Did she habitually pull a frown until a foreigner hove into view? Der Ling drops this hint without further explanation.)[6]

In Sarah's presence, Cixi was in very different form from the white-knuckle discussions she had had with Der Ling when the request for the audience had first been broached. Der Ling endeavored to calm her about what the audience might be about by saying that she knew Sarah had a very good grasp of court etiquette and would never approach her with an over-reaching request (little did she know), but there remained many other difficulties to thrash out, the most pressing of which was that visiting foreigners should never see just what Cixi's living quarters really looked like. This meant that furniture and décor in the dowager's bedroom, including curtains and upholstery, had to be changed. Der Ling got to see just what this entailed a few days before the audience. Cixi's favorite pink silk curtains were replaced by blue (which, per Der Ling, was her least favorite color), and all her jade Buddhas were replaced with foreign-made timepieces, of which armies seemed to exist at both the Summer and Winter Palaces. Even the bed had to be covered up, as its component parts had been sanctified in temples and foreign eyes were not fit to see it. In a moment of prescience (and perhaps because Der Ling had shared her interest in writing about her experiences?), the dowager said to Der Ling: "You must tell [about the preparations for the visit] some day, otherwise no one will know it at all, and the trouble would not be worthwhile."[7]

After they had finished moving the furniture, the dowager harangued her court ladies on the proper behavior before foreign guests: they must not wear fresh flowers but leave them for the Empress Dowager to wear; they must be polite and well-bred, and not hesitate to show them any place they wanted to see.[8]

As it happened, Cixi was such a commanding presence the day of the audience that there was little her court ladies could do but stay out of the way. After the first meeting, a matter of exchanging formal greetings, was over, followed by a luncheon for Sarah Conger and the nine foreign ladies who had come with her, the dowager descended on the group to see whether they were being properly entertained. She even went so far as to coyly declare that "[O]ur country, although very old, has not such fine buildings as there are in America," adding that if only she were not so old herself, and China so dependent on her physical presence, she would enjoy taking a trip around the world.[9]

This friendliness evidently gave Sarah hope. Before addressing the dowager about the portrait project directly, however, she talked it over with a Mrs. Evans, a missionary who spoke Chinese. As she listened to the ladies, unable to understand a word, Cixi was driven to distraction. "Her Majesty became rather impatient as she wanted to know what they were talking about," recalled Der Ling, and asked Der Ling to tell her what was being said. Mrs. Evans then turned to the dowager and explained in Chinese that Sarah wanted her to sit for a portrait by Miss Katherine Carl, with the object of displaying the finished painting at the St. Louis Exposition, "that the American people may form some idea of what a beautiful lady the Empress Dowager of China is." The request surprised Cixi for a reason that seems not have occurred even to the China-savvy Sarah Conger.

Der Ling knew why the old lady drew back in astonishment. "[I]n China, a portrait is only painted after death," Der Ling wrote, "in memoriam of the deceased, in order that the following generations may worship the deceased," rather than as a piece of portrait art *per se.* Asking Cixi to sit for her portrait was like voicing the strange desire to see what an elderly person, though still very much alive, might look like as memorialized after death. There was also the touchy issue of such a picture being displayed before unknown thousands in that mysterious city of St. Louis — Confucian regulations on feminine modesty dictated that no woman should present herself in this manner, least of all a semi-divine one like an empress dowager. "I did not want Her Majesty to appear ignorant before these foreign ladies," Der Ling recalled, like a hip teenager embarrassed by her grandmother's old-fashioned ways, "so I pulled her sleeve and told her that I would explain everything to her later."[10]

Cixi graciously thanked Sarah and Mrs. Evans for their thoughtful request, adding that she could not make such a decision without consultation with her ministers (in reality, this meant her one and only minister on this topic, Der Ling). So ended the interview, and Der Ling and the other ladies escorted the foreign visitors on a tour of the Summer Palace's islands. In the dowager's rooms, Der Ling was assailed by the usual hail of questions, not least of which was: What *was* portrait painting? When Der Ling described the process of how one sat for an artist for a few hours each day, Cixi became agitated, "afraid she would never have the patience to see it through." "I shall be an old woman," groaned the 67-year-old dowager, "by the time the portrait is finished." It helped for Der Ling to point out that while she was in Paris, she had sat for a portrait by Katherine Carl, who had become a friend, and had been extremely happy with the results. Immediately the dowager wanted to see what the portrait looked like, so Der Ling sent a eunuch to Beijing to fetch it from her father's house.[11]

One thing Cixi could not comprehend was why an artist should need to have the subject of her painting in view so much of the time, when Chinese painters required only one session to take a likeness. She might have added that the sort of portrait she had in mind, the posthumous ancestral variety, was by definition not sketched from the life but was invariably built up from a book of common facial features. Meeting with the artist who would be depicting their deceased family member, the family would select Nose #5, Eyes #13, Mouth #9, and the painter would use these to create the likeness. "Of course," Der Ling recalled, "I explained the difference between foreign portrait painting and Chinese, and told her that when she had seen it she would see the difference and understand the reason for so many sittings."[12]

Cixi then took another tack: Who was Miss Carl? Der Ling told her all she knew. Katherine, or Kate, Carl was a young American woman whose brother, Francis, was in the customs service at Yantai. She was distantly related to Hester Bredon, Sir Robert Hart's absentee wife — a connection that Cixi, with her fondness for Sir Robert, could not but have approved. In her forties at the time of Sarah Conger's broaching of the imperial portrait project, Kate had studied at the Académie Julian in Paris, where young women were permitted to sketch from nude male models, during Der Ling's residence in the city. The Académie was *alma mater* of such widely diverse talents as Marie Bashkirtseff, Marcel Duchamp, Henri Matisse and Beatrice Wood.

Kate was in China at this time because her mother, fearing she would not live long, insisted on seeing her son Francis before she expired. Accordingly, Kate brought Mrs. Carl east on the Trans-Siberian Railroad, reaching China in 1902, and as she had predicted, Mrs. Carl had died shortly after being reunited with her son, and Kate had remained in China. A short but stocky woman, with freckles on her cheeks and hair so blond it looked white, Kate had a pixie smile and a no-nonsense manner. Her artistic abilities were somewhat less forthright, not quite artfully emulating Renoir's milky impressionism. Kate's gift to the future was not so much the portrait, which ended up forgotten in a dark exhibit room in the National Museum at Taipei, but her acutely observant pen. *With the Empress Dowager of China*, her piquant and tender account of her time at court, published in 1905, stands as the earliest favorable account of the dowager to reach print, drowned though it was in the sea of anti-Cixi propaganda.[13]

The dowager's most pressing concern turned out to be more politically than artistically related. She was relieved to discover from Der Ling that Kate did not understand Chinese. Having a foreigner in the palace, for who knew how long, was one thing, but a foreigner in the palace who also understood Chinese was another. "With my own people gossiping," she told Der Ling, "they might tell her things which I don't want anyone to know." Not even Der Ling's reassurances could quell Cixi's paranoia — even if no one at court but Louisa or her daughters could communicate with Kate, there would be courtiers, the dowager was sure, who would find other than linguistic ways of giving her information. "Someone will have to watch her all the time," she mused. Then she had an idea: Der Ling could be Kate's ever watchful guide. "Do you think you could manage it in such a way that no one at the Palace will have a chance to talk with her during the daytime[?]" she asked. Cixi included Guangxu in the list of off-limits interlocutors.

As Der Ling stood thinking this over, the old lady had another brainstorm. "I have it," she said. "We can treat her as a prisoner without her knowing it." She would order servants to air out the nearby palace of Prince Chun, father of Guangxu, for Kate to live in. If the irony of Cixi's notion of keeping Kate Carl "prisoner," in the paternal home of the emperor whom Cixi was actually rumored to keep prisoner, made an impression on Der Ling, she left no record of it.[14]

In any case, Cixi's interest in the portrait project was only heightened by the sight of Kate's painting of Der Ling, which arrived at the Summer Palace the next day. Der Ling had the portrait brought to the dowager's bedroom. "She scrutinized it very carefully for a while," Der Ling remembered, "even touching the painting in her curiosity. Finally she burst out laughing and said: 'What a funny painting this is, it looks as though it had been painted with oil,'" oil paint being a medium not used in China. She also seems to have objected to the European use of texture and shading to achieve maximum realistic effect, which she described as "rough work." Above all, she decried Der Ling's revealing apparel in the portrait. Kate had painted Der Ling in typical European evening wear, a sleeveless green gown with low décolletage, but to Cixi this outfit seemed the height of immodesty. "I have heard that foreign ladies wear their dresses without sleeves and without collars," said the dowager, astonished, "but I had no idea that it was so bad and ugly as the dress you are wearing here . . . Don't wear any more such dresses, please. It quite shocked me."[15]

Around this time, a letter had reached Cixi from her minister to the Austro-Hungarian Empire, curiously a friend of Yu Keng's, begging to be relieved of his position among the "insufferable barbarians." The women in Vienna, claimed the shocked Sang Chi, "go naked, not entirely naked, but naked from the shoulders entirely too far down, and smoke in public . . . They have public gatherings, where they have what they call music, and men and women put their arms around each other and jump around like monkeys. They call it dancing, but it isn't that. They tell me this barbarous custom has no immoral meaning, but I am no fool; I know better."[16] Kate's portrait of Der Ling in European evening wear was proof that Sang Chi was right and that Yu Keng had allowed his daughters to fall in with these "barbarous customs." "This is getting worse and worse," Cixi told Der Ling. "Everything seems to go backwards in foreign countries" — an amusing reversal of what the West had been saying about China for centuries.[17]

What most confounded the dowager about Western portrait painting was Kate Carl's use of light and shade. "Why is it that one side of your face is painted white and the other black?" she queried. "I explained that it was simply the shading," Der Ling wrote, "and was painted exactly as the artist saw me from the position in which she was sitting." Cixi would have none of it. The finished painting was to travel to America, to show that country's people just what the fabled Empress Dowager looked like, and "I don't want people over there to imagine that half of my face is white and half black," she complained. All Der Ling could do to calm her was to tell her that she would make it crystal clear to Kate just how the portrait was to be painted, obeying any and all of the dowager's wishes in the matter.

One supremely foreign artistic medium with which the Empress Dowager had no trouble dealing at all was photography. While waiting for an auspicious day for Kate Carl to come to the Summer Palace, Cixi discovered several photographs in Der Ling's room (most of them, Der Ling tells us, of herself), and expressed delight with the likeness captured in them, which she declared were far better than Kate's or any other portrait. She instantly wanted to have her own photograph taken. Luckily, one of Der Ling's brothers employed at the palace, Xunling, was a trained photographer, with all his equipment handy. It is thanks to his efforts that we have the first posed photographic images ever made of the Empress Dowager Cixi.[18]

This was Cixi's first time to go before a camera, but where photographed Asian monarchs were concerned she was a latecomer. Der Ling's beloved Meiji Emperor and wife Empress Haruko had posed for photographers as early as 1872, while Siamese King Rama IV (who employed a certain English governess named Anna Leonowens) apparently holds the earliest record for an adult Asian ruler's photograph — he and his wife were photographed in 1856. (Child prince Maharajah Duleep Singh of the Punjab was photographed at age ten in 1848, a year before his deposition.) While Louis-Philippe King of the French, photographed in about 1842, holds what may be the European record for earliest photographed royal, Queen Victoria, Cixi's hero, comes in a close second. She also understood the camera in a way no other royal did until well into her lengthy reign. Victoria sat for a camera, her doll-clutching daughter Vicky (the future Empress Frederick) at her side, in 1844. Called by some the first true "Media Monarch," Victoria deliberately used the new technology to her and her family's advantage, providing hundreds of examples of what we would today call photo ops for the press. People could look at these photographs and ponder happily how warm and cosy family life was for their dear queen. Victoria handed her photomania down to her descendants — her granddaughter, Tsaritsa Alexandra of Russia, in turn handed the habit down to her son and daughters, none of whom went for long without a Kodak Brownie in their hands. With her knowledge and admiration of Queen Victoria as queen and woman (and perhaps, deliberate emulation of her), it is not impossible that Cixi saw herself following Victoria's proud tradition of being photographed for the public view. Whether Cixi saw her photographed image in terms of public relations is debatable, though as Der Ling tells us, Cixi was very intrigued and interested in the uses of regular court news reported to the public through newspapers as a way of downplaying gossip.[19]

Before Xunling had even set up his camera, the dowager had devised a number of settings in which she wanted to be captured: as she looked when being taken in her chair to audiences or the theatre (one of which photos shows what must be the only picture of Chief Eunuch Li smiling), or when dressed up as Guanyin, Goddess of Mercy, flanked by her two chief eunuchs Li Lianying and Cui Yugui, costumed as fairies-in-waiting, against a backdrop of painted bamboo, sometimes with court ladies posing nearby. Cixi not only wanted to be photographed sitting in high state on her throne in the Audience Hall, but also outdoors, walking amid her beloved flowers, in all kinds of weather. Xunling photographed her in broad daylight, as in the image of her being rowed on a pagoda boat on Lake Kunming, beside her an incense burner from which Xunling painted trailing smoke formed into the shape of the Endless Knot, a Buddhist symbol of which Cixi was fond. He also photographed her in snow, both alone and with Der Ling holding her arm to steady her on the slippery path leading down from Peony Hill, her giant second head eunuch Cui Yugui holding an umbrella over both. There was something about the spontaneity of photography, not to mention its economic use of her time, that appealed both to Cixi's strong dramatic instincts and her distaste for any activity that bound her to a certain pattern or locale for long periods.

Cixi did not know enough about the rest of the world to realize it, but with Xunling's efforts she, like her first lady-in-waiting, was entering the age of the photographed celebrity, so soon to become the era of motion pictures. In her excitement to be depicted in all these costumes and settings, Cixi was blazing a path for Der Ling, who in the near future would also not flinch from a camera lens, especially when wearing her "court robes" — if anything, this fascination with studying herself from a distance, as audience to actress, court to queen, preening in full enjoyment of her Otherness, was one that made Cixi a soul sister to Der Ling.

The equipment used was of great fascination to a woman who kept an enormous collection of foreign-made gadgets about her palaces. On the sunny day chosen for the photo taking, Cixi looked over Xunling's cameras with great interest. "How funny it is that you can take a person's picture with a thing like that," she remarked of the bulky, boxy cameras lined up in the courtyard. (Guangxu was to make a similar remark about Der Ling's Kodak Brownie.) The dowager ordered a eunuch to stand in front of one of the cameras so that she could peruse him through the focusing lens, only to exclaim that she saw him upside down. She ordered Der Ling to stand in the same place, to see if she got the same result. Then the dowager positioned herself at a distance from the camera and had Der Ling focus on her. "She waved her hand in front of the camera," Der Ling records, "and on my telling her of it, she was pleased." But just getting the photographs made required an unheard-of supervening of imperial court etiquette. As Xunling's niece, Lydia Dan, would later recall, before Cixi entered the courtyard Xunling measured his distance and selected a camera. On her arrival, he fell to his knees along with everyone else, holding his spectacles in his hand as these were forbidden in the dowager's presence.

"In such a position, he certainly could not reach the camera lens [and] he looked abjectly up at the camera . . . By now, the Empress-Dowager was tired of waiting, grasping the problem, she said: "Hsün-ling is permitted not to kneel when taking our picture."

Cixi also gave her photographer permission to put his glasses back on.[20]

With an almost childish glee, and rather like the fashion-mad silent screen goddesses so soon to supplant royals in the popular press, the dowager ordered Der Ling to prepare several sets of jewelry for her to wear, and had her wardrobe ladies bring out a number of gowns to try on for a succession of different "looks." She was so impatient with the results of the sittings, and so basically curious about the workings of the process, that she even asked Der Ling's brother to show her how he developed the photos — surely the first time an empress dowager of China had ever been in a darkroom. This led Cixi to pelt Xunling as well as his sister with more questions. Why, on the plates that Xunling was developing, did her hands and face come out dark? How did the chemicals make the image appear on the paper? She stopped asking questions when the photographs were printed and ready for her to examine. Astonished by this first glimpse of her exact likeness, the dowager took all of the prints to her bedroom, where Der Ling saw her sitting with them on her bed, quietly looking at them for hours. "She even took her mirror," recalled Der Ling, "in order to compare her reflection with the photographs just taken." If Cixi was surprised, pleased or dismayed by what she saw, she never shared her impressions with Der Ling. The elderly woman sitting on her bed staring at photographs of herself nonetheless remains a poignant image.[21]

22
Hungry ghosts

As Kate Carl's arrival date approached, Cixi returned to the business at hand with a vengeance. Because Kate would be staying in Prince Chun's palace, the dowager sent Der Ling to the estate to oversee preparations for her stay there. She was also to select rooms for herself, her mother and her sister.

"I want you all to be very careful not to let this lady know that you are watching her," Cixi advised Der Ling. It must have been all Der Ling could do not to roll her eyes at the inconvenience. Considering the fact that Kate knew no Chinese, and no one but Louisa and the girls knew English, there was zero chance that anyone at court would try to gossip with her. But as with all else, the dowager's wish was Der Ling's command. The one pleasure of serving as Kate's chaperone at Prince Chun's palace was that Yu Keng had been permitted to come from Beijing to stay with his wife and daughters.[1]

On August 5, Kate set out for the Summer Palace from Beijing, accompanied by Sarah Conger, an interpreter and a large number of painting supplies, the better part of which consisted of the big canvas (measuring six by four feet, according to Der Ling) on which the dowager's portrait was to be painted. Kate's happiness at being chosen for the portrait project was reflected in everything she saw that day:

> It had rained the night before and everything was beautifully fresh. The wet, stone-paved road stretched ahead like a shining stream; the wheat and corn fields along the road were of a brilliant green, with here and there the somber note of a clump of arborvitae, out of which rose the walls of a temple! The distant hills, where lay the Summer Palace, were delicately limned against the soft blue-gray sky.[2]

Red chairs awaited the women when they arrived at the Eastern Gate — Cixi was sparing no honors in greeting her guests — and they were carried to the plate glass doors of the Audience Hall, each "blazing with the huge red character 'Sho' [*sic*] (longevity)," remembered Kate. She and Sarah greeted Louisa and her daughters, and Kate was already glad to see familiar faces. "[Louisa, Der Ling and Rong Ling] seemed a link between the real, every-day world," she recalled, "and this Arabian Nights Palace into which we had been wafted."[3] In a letter written later to her daughter, Sarah gushed over Yu Keng's wife and daughters: "Lady Yü and her daughters in their midsummer dress were truly attractive," adding that she was glad they were there to interpret: "[Y]ou know they speak English most fluently."[4] After the audience, when Cixi had Der Ling to herself, she remarked on Kate's manifest gladness to see her old friend from Paris, and said airily: "We will handle her pretty easily, I think."[5]

Kate and Sarah had only just arrived when Cixi and Guangxu made their sudden entrance into the Audience Hall. "One of the Ladies Yu-Keng whispered, 'Her Majesty,'" recalled Kate, "but even after this it seemed almost impossible for me to realize that this kindly looking lady, so remarkably young-looking, with so winning a smile, could be the so-called cruel, implacable tyrant, the redoubtable 'old' Empress Dowager, whose name had been on the lips of the world since 1900!" She was also amazed, as many were, at the youthful appearance of the almost 32-year-old Guangxu. When it was time for Kate to approach the dowager, she did so reverentially, though breaths were taken throughout the room when she took the hand extended to her for a handshake and kissed it. Cixi was not all that taken aback, for she would later remark on the genuflection to Der Ling, more out of interest than mortification. Cixi kept up her gracious smile throughout the ensuing conversation, turning to Der Ling and watching her as she interpreted for Kate and Sarah Conger, then asked that Kate's painting materials be brought into the hall. Cixi left to get into one of the gowns she had chosen to be painted in. While the dowager was away, Kate surveyed the throne room's available light and found it disappointingly wanting: "When I thought I must paint here, and begin at once upon the canvas which was to be the final picture, my heart fell," she wrote. Meanwhile, in the bedroom, Der Ling was helping Cixi dress and listening to her comments upon Kate Carl: "The first question Her Majesty asked was how old I thought Miss Carl was, as she herself could not guess her age, her hair being extremely light, in fact almost white. I could hardly refrain from laughing outright on hearing this, and told Her Majesty that Miss Carl's hair was naturally of a light color."[6]

When Cixi reappeared, all-American Kate could not restrain herself from blurting, "How beautiful Her Majesty looks in this dress!" The gown was one of Cixi's most gorgeous, with purple wisteria vines and blossoms embroidered thickly on a ground of imperial yellow silk gauze. (Kate also painted another portrait of Cixi, in a different position and wearing a gown with a design of bulb flowers interspersed with the "shou" symbol, with her cape of pearls arranged over this.) "Her Majesty advanced with animation," recalled Kate, "and asked me where the Double Dragon Throne was to be placed. After the eunuchs had put it where I said, she took her seat" and the session began, heralded in unnerving fashion by what Kate remembered as eighty-five clocks, all chiming the hour of eleven in eighty-five different ways.[7]

"When Miss Carl commenced to make the rough sketch of Her Majesty," Der Ling remembered, "everyone watched with open mouth, as they had never seen anything done so easily and so naturally." Kate was under more pressure than she let on. Between the ticking clocks and the court personnel standing around staring at her, commenting in their unintelligible language, she felt besieged by distraction. But she managed to outline the figure on the canvas and fill in some of the details before Cixi abruptly declared the sitting finished for the day — an early sign of things to come. Stepping down off her throne, the dowager approached to inspect the sketch herself. "After looking critically at it for a few moments, she expressed herself as well pleased with what had been done," recalled Kate. Cixi then told Kate that she very much wanted to continue with the project, though as she was always busy she could only spare a few minutes' sitting each day, and invited her to stay at the palace for the duration of the work.[8]

Like any serious artist, Kate was champing at the bit to continue uninterrupted (she planned two portraits of Cixi, and was sketching court ladies and the dowager in action besides), but Der Ling succeeded in convincing her that the best thing to do, in modern parlance, was go with the flow — the Empress Dowager had to have her afternoon naps, and when the dowager was napping the entire palace snoozed. Controlling as ever, Cixi had instructed Der Ling to tell Kate not to work while she was resting. Cixi would eventually begin to use Der Ling to stand in for her occasionally when she was not able to be present for sittings, which soon turned into a chronic absence. Though thrilled to wear Cixi's robes and jewels — the famous pearl cape especially — Der Ling ultimately would give up several hours of each day to posing in the dowager's place. This may well explain why Kate's oil portraits of Cixi have a cartoonish, unrealistic quality as compared to the excellent pencil sketches she made of court ladies willing to give her all the time she needed.

In any event, Kate was happy with her new lodgings at Prince Chun's palace. The scars of 1900 were still to be seen — "many of the pavilions and summer-houses in the grounds were in ruins," she recalled — but the palace was beautiful even in its disrepair, with its lotus lake, bridges curving delicately over artificial streams, scholars' stones on which were carved poems by members of the imperial family, which Der Ling and Rong Ling translated for her, and even a theater that had, like Cixi's Great Stage, a special viewing box for the prince and his family. From one of the summer houses in the garden, Kate could see the paved road leading to the Summer Palace from Beijing, and would go there to watch the passing traffic:

> "[C]hairs" of the officials, with their outriders, going to and from
> the Palace; messengers galloping past, bearing dispatches; all sorts
> of itinerant vendors, with their wares; heavily laden wagons, with

small yellow banners flying, which showed they carried supplies to the Palace. Sometimes a group of horsemen would dash gaily past, the retainers of some splendidly attired young Prince, who rode in their midst on a red-saddled, handsomely caparisoned horse with silver trappings [along with] the cumbersome, red, fringe-bedecked cart of some Princess . . . the black carts of her women bringing up the rear.

Kate would become such a fixture at Prince Chun's palace that the pavilion in which she was housed came to be called, in her romanization, the "Ker-Gunia Fu" or "House of Miss Carl."[9]

Kate was soon favored with invitations to accompany Cixi on her long walks, which were as apt to end with a boating trip around to the Back Lake and a hike to one of the dowager's favorite pavilions (where Cixi called Kate to her side and "made a graceful, sweeping gesture of the hand that said, 'This is all mine, but you may share it with me')[10] or a detailed survey of the Great Stage, as include a tour of the imperial kennels. Der Ling had already visited the latter. Cages of bamboo were set around the edges of a courtyard, each pen containing a prized Pekingese dog. So prized were these animals that when British troops stormed the Summer Palace in 1860 they made off with not just jade and gold but Pekingeses: one, given the tactless name Looty, was gifted to Queen Victoria, who pampered it for years. As Der Ling recalled, the moment the eunuch in charge announced that Old Buddha had arrived, the dogs ran around their cages, yipping and yapping at the sight of the dowager. The cages were opened, and the dogs all rushed out, only to be caught short by an order from the eunuch — "Zhan zhu!" — which Der Ling likens to the military order "Fall in!" "All the dogs lined up before the court retinue," she remembered, "their bulging eyes, full of intelligence, peering out at Her Majesty." Cixi's favorite dog, Sea Otter, merely sat and stared, occasionally ringing his neck bell with a shake of his ears. From one of the prize bitches, Black Jade (the same name as the spirited heroine of the eighteenth-century novel by Tsao Hsueh-chin (Cao Xueqin), *A Dream of Red Mansions*), Der Ling received a puppy of her own.[11]

Kate's experience was somewhat less sunny. On her visit to the kennels, she watched the dogs bound across the courtyard to the dowager, "not paying the slightest attention to anyone else. She patted their heads and caressed and spoke to her favorites." Then the dogs noticed that Kate was standing nearby and ran over to investigate her. "I bent down to caress them, and forgot my surroundings, in my pleasure at seeing and fondling these beautiful creatures," Kate recalled. "I glanced up, presently, never dreaming that Her Majesty had been paying any attention to me, as I was standing a little distance behind her, and I saw on her face the first sign of displeasure I had noticed there." Cixi, it appeared, could be as jealous of canine as of human affections. Kate tactfully backed away from the romping Pekingeses: "One does not like to see one's pets too friendly with strangers," she remarked, giving the dowager the benefit of the doubt. Despite Cixi's obvious disapproval of Kate's all-too-American familiarity with her animals, she gave one of them to her, telling her to call it Golden Amber. "From that day, he became my constant companion and faithful friend," Kate wrote.[12]

Still, these outings and adventures were not sufficient to relieve Kate of the frustrations of not being able to get on with her work. "I was living through a unique experience, seeing what I could never hope to see again," she wrote. She had quickly recognized in the Empress Dowager "a psychological study full of ever-varying and constant interest." Her efforts at painting, however, were always being curtailed. "Could I but have had permission to work more, I should have been very happy," she recalled. For a portrait painter to do his or her sitter full justice, Kate pointed out, a degree of intimacy had to be built between artist and subject. Given the fact that when she did see Cixi outside the occasional sitting — Der Ling having to stand in for the dowager more often than not — she was surrounded by her retinue, and moving about quickly from one activity to another, Kate felt that she was missing that vis-à-vis experience that would have enabled her to breathe the dowager's spirit into the flat canvas. Kate persisted to the end in believing that Cixi was a prisoner of her own rank: "Had Her Majesty been alone to be considered," Kate insisted, "she was artistic and progressive enough to have, in the end, allowed me more liberty." As we know from Der Ling's account, however, Cixi had grown bored with the sittings almost from the beginning, and the many outings on which she took Kate may well have been her own oblique way of salving her guilty conscience. The fact that she asked the trusty Der Ling to be her substitute for the sittings (and, according to Rong Ling's later memoirs, herself as well) is one indication of just how important it was that Kate not know how she really felt.[13]

Few courts are friendly to artists or their needs, even the court of such a great patroness and amateur painter like Cixi, and Kate had to resign herself to snatching what painting time she could manage, the rest of her sojourn being taken up with amusements arranged by the dowager. She would soon, however, see that all was not fun and games with the woman whom Der Ling once described as a "child" at play among her toy boats. Toward the latter part of summer, Kate noticed, Cixi began to look "tired and anxious," and would walk by herself in the gardens for long periods of time. "One day when we were out," recalled Kate, "after days of this anxiety, and she was sitting alone in front of the 'Peony Mountain,' the Empress and Princesses standing in a group at a little distance, she looked a pathetic figure. Her strong face looked tired and worn. Her arms hung listlessly by her sides and she seemed almost to have given up." Kate thought she saw the dowager wipe away a tear. The source of this unease was soon determined to be the rumors now penetrating even the idyllic setting of the Summer Palace, that war between Japan and Russia was inevitable (war did break out between the two empires the following February).[14]

Der Ling had another idea of what was causing Cixi such barely hidden unhappiness. Her husband, the late Xianfeng Emperor, was born in July and had died in August, roughly corresponding to the seventh moon during Der Ling's first summer at court. Two more important dates occurred in the seventh moon. First was the Double Seventh, the seventh day of the seventh moon, when the Cowherd and the Weaving Maid, both symbolized by stars and separated by the flowing waters of the Milky Way, were reunited on the backs of sympathetic magpies, who formed a bridge for the lovers to cross to one another, that they might meet just once a year. It was commonly believed that during the night of the Double Seventh, anyone sitting in a grape arbor between the hours of midnight and dawn could hear the lovers' cries.[15]

The second significant date was a festival approximating the Western holiday of All Hallows Eve. "The fifteenth day of the seventh moon each year is the day of the festival of the dead," Der Ling wrote. Known as the Festival of Hungry Ghosts, the fifteenth of the seventh moon was believed to be a time when the ghosts of the unhappy dead roamed the land of the living, offering a chance for the living to show by word or deed — ceremonies, festive theatricals, the burning of everything from paper money to paper houses and servants — that they cared for and reverenced their dead, thereby avoiding the bad luck that unhappy spirits were said to bring. The coincidental proximity of the feast of the separated lovers and the Festival of Hungry Ghosts to the birth and death dates of Xianfeng seems to have worked on Cixi's emotions to a degree that Der Ling, being young, found excessive.

"I could hardly understand the reason for such grief," she noted, observing Cixi's tears, "seeing that the Emperor had died so many years previously" — a heartless but pragmatic remark with which many critics of the constantly mourning Queen Victoria would have concurred. In a later memoir Der Ling would reveal that she had been with Cixi when the death of her great friend, and possible former suitor, Ronglu, was announced in spring 1903, and was not so adolescent that she did not notice that "she was never the same after his passing. Something of her soul, of her stout old heart, went to the grave with her staunch favorite — and something of her mind, too."[16]

While the dowager sat silent and solemn, Der Ling and the other court ladies followed the festival custom by launching floating candles onto Kunming Lake, where they sparkled as they bobbed out into the darkness. Cixi showed she had some sympathy for her young court women by excusing them from wearing black — that was for Cixi to do, while Der Ling and the others wore garments of blue, the mourning color worn in summer.[17]

In the days leading up to the date of Xianfeng's death, the dowager wept into her black handkerchiefs; when the day itself arrived she knelt before his spirit tablet to pray, crying quietly. After all the playful activity of the spring and summer, this dark period gave Der Ling pause, and she may have kept her distance from the inconsolable old woman. But the Young Empress, always thoughtful, advised her to stay close to the dowager in her grief. Der Ling obeyed; in fact, so close did she stay that she began to share Cixi's tears, prompting the dowager to regain some of her iron authority. "[Her Majesty] would tell me that I was too young to cry," Der Ling recalled, "and that in any case I did not know what real sorrow was yet."

Cixi trusted the young girl's sympathies sufficiently to confide to her some of her own hard personal history. She began with her childhood in Beijing, as daughter of Huizheng, an obscure captain of the Bordered Blue banner.[18] She claimed she was the least favorite of her parents' children, and much of her later behavior — her willfulness and extravagance as well as her indomitable fortitude and her obsessive need to please — tends to support her account. Because the handed-down stories of Cixi's early life have become so muddied over time, we have only her own story of this (via the sensationalizing given it by Der Ling) to go on, but her character would indeed seem the result of a childhood deprived of the warmth of affection and the pleasure of attention. Cixi also described to Der Ling how, from the day she first came to the court of the Xianfeng Emperor, in 1851, her longing for attention was resolved in a way she could not have expected, in the form of bitter rivalries. "[A] lot of people were jealous of me because I was considered to be a beautiful woman at that time," the dowager explained to Der Ling. "I must say myself that I was a clever one, for I fought my own battles, and won them, too."

The basis for this jealousy was not just Cixi's beauty and her brains, but also the emperor's decided preference for his young concubine's company, which resulted in her pregnancy and the birth of the son whose appearance guaranteed her overnight rise up the palace and dynastic ladder. With that brief glory would come lasting misery. Not long after the birth of Tongzhi in 1856, Xianfeng took another concubine, called Li Fei, who dominated the emperor in what was probably largely a sexual way. That the emperor would push Cixi aside for a woman who could provide him none of the intellectual stability or force of will that she offered hurt her to the quick.

What was worse, all she had gained had almost been torn from her just as quickly as it had been given. Cixi ably summed up her grievous situation when describing the foreign invasion of Beijing in 1860, during the second Opium War, and the court's flight north to the hunting villa at Jehol.[19] "I was still a young woman," she said, "with a dying husband and a young son" — the two pillars which held up a woman's worth in

China, neither of which she could lean on in the traditional way. She had literally had to think on her feet, she who had only recently been allowed into the inner sanctum of the court and its tangled web of alliances, grudges, plots and counterplots. Discovering that her dying husband's board of eight handpicked regents was scheming a coup to wrest from her and the Empress Cian all control over the new heir, Cixi had rushed to Xianfeng's deathbed with the little boy in her arms. "I said to him 'Here is your son,'" she recalled, "on hearing which he immediately opened his eyes and said: 'Of course he will succeed to the throne.'"[20]

That, however, had not been enough to master the Gang of Eight. Xianfeng finally died, "mounting the dragon to become a guest on high," as court euphemism had it, and the Gang got down to the business of securing their stake in the planned coup while undermining the authority of the emperor's widows. Despite her grief, Cixi was still a match for any scheming mandarin. Through the offices of their brother-in-law Prince Gong, Cixi and Cian mounted a lightning-fast counter-coup, the result of which was that all the conspirators were jailed, tried and executed, their families scattered and their goods confiscated. Cixi's son, that one piece of fleshly evidence that Xianfeng had once loved her, was now safe and his future mapped out with vigor.

There had then followed the years of sitting behind the curtain, first with Cian at her side and then, after her death, alone, guiding the unmanageable Tongzhi until losing all control of him, and living to see him die in the agonies of smallpox, even younger than his father. Yet through all of this, through attempted poisonings, a succession crisis, the "Hundred Days" and the Boxer mayhem, all Cixi could still remember with crystal clarity, almost without being able to help it, was the sight of her once-handsome, now wasted husband, bloated with dropsy on his bed. It was, she sighed to Der Ling, "just as though it all happened only yesterday," adding, "I would not wish anyone to experience what I myself passed through at that time." She spoke even more candidly when she said, weeping, "I am disappointed with everything, as nothing has turned out as I had expected."[21]

This was the woman at whose mercy lived some four hundred million subjects, who had at her disposal an endless source of wealth, palaces filled with treasures silted up over centuries of imperial rule — the woman whose position Der Ling, as a girl, had once envied. What had started out as a fairy tale had ended in flame and destruction, death and despair. Yu Keng had been right to discourage his daughter's fantasy.

This was a very different side to a woman who had once said to Der Ling, "Although I have heard much about Queen Victoria and read a part of her life which someone has translated into Chinese, still I don't think her life was half so interesting and eventful as mine." (According to the surprised Katherine Carl, Cixi also had engravings of Victoria, Prince Albert and their children in her living quarters.) But both women, similar in certain features of character and even of physique and the same girlish, "silvery" speaking voice, knew the high price of a throne, not to mention the dangers of placing the weight of all their love on the fragile flesh of one man. No wonder, as Cixi pointed out to Kate Carl, that her face and Victoria's bore the same longevity lines. They had earned them.[22]

23
Imperial birthday

"When [Cixi] was sick she was ill humored," Der Ling recalled, "and none of us could forget that we lived, breathed and had our being subject to her slightest whim. I am afraid that all of us thought of her then as a grim old ogre threatening our safety."[1] The magistrate Wu Yung, whose portrait of Cixi is flagrantly admiring, once saw her in a rage at an audience. "Her eyes poured out straight rays," he remembered, "her cheek bones were sharp and the veins on her forehead projected. She showed her teeth as if she were suffering from lockjaw."[2] If this is how the dowager could behave in formal circumstances, Der Ling must have witnessed far worse behavior when the old lady was sick.

Despite her many bouts of ill health and considering she was approaching her sixty-eighth birthday (on November 29), Cixi was in what seemed to most people a surprisingly youthful condition. As Der Ling records in a frank description of the dowager's unclothed body, this youthfulness was no illusion. Early in her court service, Der Ling was deputed to be present for Cixi's bath, which like her sleeping arrangements seemed to require an army of servants and onlookers. Before she was disrobed, the dowager was seated in a special chair with a removable back and open sides. Eunuchs brought in a silver basin filled with hot water, along with loads of dragon-embroidered towels. "I gasped in amazement when I saw her [naked]," Der Ling recalled. "Knowing her age, I expected to see the body of a wrinkled old woman. But it was not so. Her body was really beautiful, the flesh very white and utterly smooth. It was a body that any young girl might have envied."[3]

Oddly, it was the dowager's face that seemed to most show her age, according to Der Ling (though this was possibly due to the high lead content of the white face paint she had had to wear as a concubine). The dowager had a vast arsenal of facial unguents, starting with simple white of egg and followed up by a complicated astringent lotion she had invented, the primary ingredients of which were glycerin, alcohol and honeysuckle blossom. Of a morning, before putting on her makeup (which, though forbidden to widows, was evidently permitted to an empress dowager of China), the dowager placed a warm cloth saturated with mutton fat against her face, using the same process on her famously white, soft hands. Less efficacious but undoubtedly helpful from a psychological point of view were the doses she took every ten days of ground pearls and the therapeutic qualities of the gold-mounted jade roller she used to smooth her cheeks, a dressing-table tool which she later gave to Der Ling.[4]

Cixi was still alive and attractive as much due to luck as to any cosmetic reasons. Court life in China had always been dangerous to the health of both emperors and courtiers, and Cixi discovered just how dangerous in the mid-1870s. During the succession crisis following the death of her son Tongzhi, the dowager and her family fell within the sights of some still unknown person or persons intent on removing all of them at once. Her sickness was generally believed to be caused by a liver ailment, the liver being one of the first organs to be affected by toxins or poisoning by heavy metals (gold leaf was a favored method of killing oneself or someone else). Whatever it was that made her sick, Cixi felt the after effects until 1883.[5]

To have overcome all of this the dowager had to have a strong constitution, but it was fading with age. Soon after Der Ling came to court Cixi experienced a minor but debilitating stroke. "One day, during the eighth moon," records Der Ling, "Her Majesty was taken slightly ill, and complained of suffering from severe headaches." Cixi still managed to get up and attend her morning audience, but the strain was obviously too much for her; she had a relapse at lunch time. "I could, sometimes, soothe her," Der Ling recalled, "make her forget her worst moods," and so had been asked to come to the dowager's side. "I was vain enough to think that I could manage her," she added. There she found the dowager sitting on one of her smaller throne chairs, surrounded by court doctors writing prescriptions and taking the dowager's pulse. "In spite of the fact that they must examine and prescribe for the Old Buddha," she remembered, "the doctors dared not look at her!" Making the process all the more difficult was the fact that since no man could touch her, Cixi's wrists were covered with thin silk kerchiefs — how the physicians could determine the old woman's state of cardiac health from this method, wrote Der Ling, was a mystery, "unless they had some means of mental telepathy." They knelt around the throne, gingerly touching the imperial wrists, their heads turned to the side. It was, recalled Der Ling, "an odd tableau," the old woman on her golden throne, four brilliantly robed doctors at her feet.[6]

When the doctors had completed the procedure, they got up, backed away, and set to mixing medicines. Cixi tersely ordered Der Ling to follow them, as if the doctors needed supervision — had Der Ling had her way, they would all have been fired and a Western-educated doctor brought in; but she knew that even to suggest such an alternative was to court trouble. Der Ling and the other court ladies first had to give the medicines to Cixi to look over, then for the doctors to try. As fascinated by others' discomfiture as ever, even when ill, Cixi turned slyly to Der Ling and said, "They drink as though it were not bitter, but we know that it is very bitter." She then only took the medicine she preferred.

Cixi was not a good patient, according to Der Ling. Eunuchs had to be stationed at all doors and windows of her room, armed with horsehair flyswatters to discourage any insects from entering. If a fly happened to land on the dowager or her food, she shrieked — possibly a complex from a girlhood spent in the fly-ridden hutongs of Beijing. Der Ling says she was sent chasing flies on one occasion. When the dowager's fever rose, she demanded that her ladies stay with her, especially at night. It was at this time that Der Ling made the discovery that the eccentric old grandmother, with her dogs, flowers and tears for her dead husband, could change overnight into an impossibly demanding "ogre," whom even she, the alleged favorite, had reason to fear.[7]

Eventually, Cixi regained enough strength to leave her bed, but no move was made without her doctors observing her. It is this stroke that makes for photographs of a very different Cixi from the ones Der Ling's brother had first taken. The right side of her face drooped down noticeably, and she began to show her age almost overnight.[8] Perhaps as a consequence of her illness, Cixi's possessive comment to Louisa about her daughter — "She is mine now" — began to take on more weight. The dowager leaned more heavily on her young lady-in-waiting, particularly during audiences. One of these, requested by Sarah Conger, had turned into a logistics nightmare for Der Ling. For her late August visit to the Summer Palace, Sarah brought with her a couple of relatives she wished to be presented to the emperor and Empress Dowager, along with a friend named Miss Campbell and another female missionary (probably to translate). Sarah's ultimate purpose for the visit, however, was not to placate relatives but to see how Kate's portrait, which she regarded as a personal diplomatic triumph, was coming along. It was well that she did not really know how Cixi felt about the whole project (or that she had snapped at Kate on at least one occasion, when the artist innocently asked her to shift her hand position). "Her Majesty was out of patience with the portrait painting," Der Ling recalled. When she greeted Sarah and the other ladies, "she was extremely polite and told them that the portrait was going to be a masterpiece." Already it was treated as an extension of Cixi's self, covered with imperial yellow silk gauze when Kate was not painting it and treated by the servants with all the same reverence they would show toward the flesh and blood dowager. But Cixi, from boredom and possibly from guilt, stayed away from the picture as much as possible.[9]

Because Der Ling was her primary interpreter, she had to follow the dowager everywhere for the duration of her audiences. Given Cixi's propensity for taking her guests on tours of the palace and grounds, all at breakneck speed, and the stresses of having to not only interpret for the dowager but make guests comfortable, Der Ling frequently found herself pulled in several directions at once. Her duties increased when, during the tour of Sarah's relatives and Miss Campbell, Cixi ordered ordinary guest's chairs brought into her bedroom. There were plenty of what Der Ling describes as "small thrones of Her Majesty's" throughout the room, but etiquette proscribed the guests or anyone else from sitting in them — any chair, once sat in by the Empress Dowager, became a throne unto itself, and was kept apart only for her own use. An exception could be made only if she gave the order to do so.

This imperious regulation would not have been known even to the etiquette-savvy Sarah Conger, and certainly not to her guests, one of whom promptly seated herself on a throne. Cixi noticed the infraction immediately and flashed a glance at Der Ling, who had to leave her translating and gingerly make her way over to the lady in question. By asking her to come with her to see some curio, Der Ling managed to get the woman off the throne until the eunuchs could bring in the ordinary chairs. The lady, however, perhaps fatigued by Cixi's rapid pace and Der Ling's frenzied show-and-tell among the curios, found another, even less acceptable place to take her ease. "There she is again," Cixi murmured to Der Ling, "sitting on my bed. We had better leave this room." This is probably the same occasion on which Der Ling recalled how a foreign woman "rushed up to a gorgeous Manchu lady who stood aloofly apart from the rest of us [and said to her friends], 'Oh, come and look at this one! Isn't she cute?'" fingering the astonished court lady's silken robes as if they were on display in a dress shop.[10]

All in all, Sarah Conger left her second audience on a cloud. But later on, during the usual debriefing session, Cixi railed against the cheek of the woman she had brought with her. "Perhaps she does not know what a throne is when she sees one," she scoffed, "and yet foreigners laugh at us. I am sure that our manners are far superior to theirs." She was also upset by a mysterious package which she had seen being passed from Sarah Conger to Kate Carl, and asked Der Ling to go in search of it. Though tired, Der Ling did as commanded, but after looking everywhere for it found nothing. Just before one of her sessions with Kate, Der Ling was relieved when Kate told her she was working on the background of the painting and would not need a model for that day, and even more so when she handed her an American magazine to pass the time in the makeshift studio. This magazine turned out to be the parcel which had so exercised Cixi's imagination. Finding that the dowager had gone out boating, Der Ling took a chair down to the lake shore at the double-quick, had herself rowed out to the boat, and pantingly presented the magazine to the old lady. Cixi only smiled. She already knew what it was; her eunuchs had been watching, as usual.[11]

Der Ling was also kept busy with a new translating job. As matters began to heat up between Japan and Russia, Cixi became concerned that the information she received on the situation was not always correct or up to date. When Der Ling mentioned that she could easily find out the tenor of events from foreign newspapers, the dowager leapt at the opportunity and asked that several papers be subscribed to in Yu Keng's name and delivered from his house to the palace. It then became Der Ling's job to translate whatever she thought relevant for the dowager's perusal, which often ran into hundreds of lines of newsprint. "Each morning during the audience I translated into Chinese all the war news," Der Ling claimed. This also included all news of whatever the various European potentates were doing. The fact that people completely unconnected with a royal court could find out through news services what everyone there was doing, from the ceremonial to the personal, astonished the privacy-loving Cixi. However, it also made her think about how her own situation compared unfavorably with the ways of Europe. As she admitted to Der Ling, "It would be a good thing if [people outside the court] knew a little more, then perhaps all these rumors about the Palace would stop."[12]

Der Ling would soon add the translation of telegrams to her workload, a task she lightened to a degree by reading instead of writing out the articles and memos for the dowager's morning audiences. As if these and all of Der Ling's duties as court lady were not enough to keep her busy, she, Louisa and Rong Ling were also called on to do duty as interior decorators, or so Der Ling's account will have us believe. The Yu Keng women had already given Cixi some French furniture in the Empire style, the brocade upholstery of which they had chosen themselves, as well as perfumes and other lady's boudoir staples, all of which Der Ling tells us Cixi was delighted with. While the court was at the Sea Palaces in the Imperial city in Beijing, Der Ling recalls being shown by Cixi the plot of ground where the old Audience Hall had stood before being burned down in the Boxer Uprising. "Her Majesty pointed out that this had been purely an accident," says Der Ling, "and not deliberately destroyed by foreign troops." Now she had ordered the Board of Works to build not another Chinese pavilion on the site but a European-style structure that would serve as a hall for foreign audiences. Der Ling calls this building the "Sea Coast Audience Hall"; after the fall of the Manchu dynasty the government of the Chinese republic would take the building over and make it into the president's reception hall (where Rong Ling, as mistress of ceremonies in the presidential suite, would one day serve the president's wife). In her 1931 book on Peking, Juliet Bredon described the "Sea Coast Audience Hall" as an "ugly, red, foreign-style" building, and the picture of it reproduced in Fei Shi's *Guide to Peking* seems to confirm this assessment. A strange mixture of Dutch gambrel roofs, French Renaissance façade decoration, urns and balustrades and quasi-European carved details, the audience hall came nowhere near matching the haunting marble beauty of the destroyed European-style palaces of the Old Summer Palace.

Perhaps Cixi realized this as the buildings rose, because Der Ling describes her critiquing everything severely. "Her Majesty compared the different styles of furniture with the catalogues we had brought with us from France," writes Der Ling, "and finally decided on the Louis Fifteenth style, but everything was to be covered with Imperial Yellow, with curtains and carpets to match." Once the selection had been made, Louisa asked to be allowed to pay for the order herself — she had ordered from the firm before, when redecorating the Chinese legation in the Avenue Hoche. Perhaps Cixi was hedging her bets more than being a gracious ruler when she accepted Louisa's offer: if the project went wrong, it would not be her fault. "By the time the building was completed the furniture had arrived," Der Ling recalled, "and was quickly installed," probably with Louisa directing the installers. Then they unveiled their work for the dowager, who promptly "[found fault] as usual." She liked nothing about what Louisa had done, "and said that after all a Chinese building would have been the best as it would have had a more dignified appearance." Was Cixi, as seems to be the case, pushed into this project to placate foreign interests and balking when she got fed up with the pressure? Or was it just a matter of trying to be as up to date and cosmopolitan as Louisa and her daughters, and seeing, with the irony she never failed to appreciate, that "Imperial Yellow" Louis XV furniture in a bastardized French audience hall would upstage her? In the end, "the thing was finished," she told Der Ling, "and it was no use finding fault now, as it could not be changed."[13] Nobody could accuse Cixi of not being a realist.

Plans were already underway for the dowager's 68th birthday (69 *sui*) celebrations in November. Cixi insisted she did not want a big celebration. Per the Chinese custom, the emperor indulged in some purely ceremonial pleading that the dowager allow a celebration worthy of her, telling her he wanted to add more titles to the sixteen already connected to her name. As Kate soon determined, however, "the adding of a new title would necessitate an annual grant of twelve thousand dollars in gold," an emolument Cixi knew the imperial exchequer could ill afford.[14]

While this could be considered another piece of evidence that, despite the stories of her extravagance, the dowager was well aware that her treasury could only bear so much expenditure, Cixi saw no reason why she should stint in her latest round of gifts to Der Ling. Most of these were made in form of clothing, occasioned by the coming of cold weather. Der Ling and Rong Ling spent over a week choosing rich materials for their winter clothes, along with the fabrics to be used in the making of the robes they would wear for the dowager's birthday festivities. "These dresses were full winter Court dresses," Der Ling remembered, "of red satin embroidered with golden dragons and blue clouds, and were trimmed with gold braid and lined with grey squirrel." Most exciting of all, however, was Cixi's granting of the right to wear sable at cuffs and collar, a perquisite normally reserved only for princesses (*gong zhu*). Der Ling did not realize what an honor had been shown her until the Young Empress advised her to immediately kowtow to the dowager. Hurrying to Cixi's rooms, Der Ling knelt before her in thanks, only to be ordered to stand up. "You deserve it," the old lady told her. "You are certainly entitled to be ranked as a Princess, and in fact I never treat you different from the Princesses, but rather better in some ways."[15] If the Qianlong Emperor, Cixi's hero, could ennoble elephants and a tree, surely the dowager could make Der Ling a princess.

The clothes the dowager showered on Der Ling were certainly fit less for a princess than for a queen. Among the many other garments Cixi gave was a pink satin informal robe embroidered with one hundred butterflies, in colored silk and gold thread, now in the Asian collection of the Metropolitan Museum of Art in New York City.[16] Generous Cixi was, but she was not sensitive to the ill effect her gifts would have on the other ladies of the court. One of the more embittered women waited for Der Ling outside the door of the dowager's rooms. As she backed out of Cixi's presence, Der Ling found herself face to face with the court lady, who made a few sharp comments about how lucky Der Ling was to be given so many gifts by Her Majesty, many more than even a ten-year court veteran like herself ever received. The Young Empress, standing nearby, came to Der Ling's rescue. "[She] told her that when I arrived at the Palace I had nothing but foreign clothes," Der Ling reported, "and how was I to manage if Her Majesty did not get me the proper dresses." At Cixi's court, Der Ling just could not win — if she wore her foreign clothes, she was a Chinese posing as a European; if she wore, as now, Manchu clothes, she was a foreigner strutting in costumes that had no cultural relevance for her.

Possibly Longyu, well aware of the animosity toward the "foreign" interlopers and toward Der Ling in particular, made it her business to remain close by when Der Ling was within proximity of the other court ladies — she certainly always seemed to be at hand when Der Ling required a champion. She had also rushed to Der Ling's defense when another of the court ladies, a younger woman who claimed to have been Cixi's favorite prior to Der Ling's arrival, made cutting remarks about the dowager's largesse to such a rank newcomer. The Young Empress had no power at the dowager's court, but she did have one trump card: the authority that comes from plain speaking. She told the offending court lady "that some fine day I would be telling Her Majesty about [what she had said]," Der Ling recalled. "This seemed to have a good effect for they never troubled me much afterwards with their talk."[17]

The Empress Dowager was born at 2 a.m. (Hour of the Ox) and that was the hour scheduled for the celebration of her birthday on November

16. (She was actually born on November 29, Year of the artistic but hard-to-please Sheep.) Kate Carl was present for the occasion, and her painter's eye missed nothing:

> Her Majesty was to receive the prostrations of the Emperor and Empress, Princesses, and members of the Imperial Family, on a Throne in the Palace, that was built half-way up the terraced hill crowned by the Temple of Ten Thousand Buddhas [corresponding to the Hall of Glorious Virtue, which stands on the hill overlooking the Hall That Dispels Clouds] . . . The elevation of this Palace permitted all who were allowed to enter the Precincts to offer their congratulations, to get a glimpse of Her Majesty . . . There were three pairs of huge silver candelabra standing on either side of the Throne to hold enormous wax candles of Imperial yellow, entwined with golden dragons, which weighed fifty pounds each . . . The whole terrace below, all the temples and buildings in the grounds, were brilliantly illuminated with splendid lanterns, elaborately ornamented with tassels of red silk, with the characters for longevity emblazoned thereon in vermilion.[18]

The palace grounds swarmed with invited noblewomen from all parts of the Chinese empire, gowned in brilliant embroidered satins lined with fur and fur hats encrusted with gems, going up and down the crimson-carpeted marble stairs to wish the dowager long life. Some ladies had even traveled from as far afield as Manchuria, over which region fears of war between Japan and Russia were drifting like so much acrid smoke. Between Der Ling and Kate, only the latter seems to have been aware of the dowager's worries amid all the fanfare of what she describes as a "forced celebration." In Kate's view, the dowager clearly found the occasion "far from happy": the nation she ruled was "in so perilous a position — war threatening on its confines, foreign complications of all kinds to deal with, and rebellion within," referring to an uprising in Guangxi that had threatened to blow into a larger conflagration and had only been put down with difficulty, that there was little in the way of birthday celebrations that could take her mind off the problems. But to most of those present Cixi, with her long practice at Buddha-like waiting and watching, allowed none of her concerns to show.[19]

So soon after the whirlwind of the birthday party, it was necessary to start making ready for transferring the court to the dowager's residence among the Sea Palaces in Beijing. Cixi's court was used to having to pack up at a moment's notice, and less than a week after the birthday celebrations the imperial machinery was on the move, setting forth for the Forbidden City in a 6 a.m. snowstorm. As the drifts piled up, even eunuchs on horseback had trouble navigating, with several horses slipping on the icy paving stones of the road. Fatigued, chilled and barely able to see through the blowing snow, the bearers whose job it was to carry the imperial pair and the court ladies in their closed sedan chairs were at a decided disadvantage. Just outside Beijing's western gate, Der Ling heard cries of "Stop!" from the head of the train. The chairs were set down, and a eunuch ran past, saying, "See if she is still alive." Der Ling scrambled to where the Empress Dowager's chair sat in the middle of the road. Her elegant chair was surrounded by chair-bearers quivering face down in the slush; chief eunuch Li was berating them mercilessly. To everyone's relief, especially that of the chair-bearers, it turned out that Cixi was not hurt by the sudden fall. Der Ling saw her sitting quietly, "composedly giving orders to the chief eunuch not to punish this chair-bearer" — she had probably enjoyed the excitement. But Li insisted on giving the man eighty lashes with a bamboo cane.[20]

Cixi's residence, the Palace Steeped in Compassion (*Huairentang*), lay on the west side of the Zhonghai or Central Sea, to the west of the Forbidden City compound. The spreading compound of interlocking courtyards, pavilions and galleries was broken up in places by private gardens full of vine-entwined rockeries, serene pools and waterways spanned by delicate arching bridges. One of the most striking buildings, the carved and painted two-story Tower of Prolonged Prosperity, had been built especially for the dowager. Much in the layout of the palace and its garden setting, with the nearby Central Sea for boating excursions, would have reminded Cixi of the Summer Palace, and helped her take her mind off the Forbidden City that rose up indomitably in the east.[21]

Like her summer residence, Cixi's Sea Palace was built more for enjoyment of the warmer months. By the time the dowager's chair was set down in the courtyard and all could retire with her indoors, everyone was shivering. "Her Majesty complained of the cold," Der Ling recalled, "and ordered that fires should be brought into the hall." These fires consisted of the sort of brass stoves lined with clay that Cixi used to make her black tea eggs in the Summer Palace courtyards. While the imperial party remained in their fur-lined coats, teeth chattering, eunuchs hurriedly lit four of the brazier-stoves (each filled with the round coal briquettes habitually used in Beijing) in the courtyard, waited till they stopped smoking, then brought them into Cixi's rooms. Here they proceeded to warm up the space and also to fill it with carbon monoxide — a mild annoyance to those used to it, a source of respiratory distress for those who were not. Der Ling, brought up with well-ventilated Western heating, was among the latter. "All the windows and doors were closed, there being no ventilation of any description," Der Ling remembered, "and very soon I began to feel sick." She continued putting the dowager's many belongings in order, overseeing the unpacking of her boxes and trunks. Then "the next thing I remember was waking up in a strange bed and inquiring where I was." She was awake long enough to sip a cup of pungent turnip juice (a Chinese remedy for everything from abdominal distension to coughs), which the court lady who gave it to her insisted was on the dowager's orders. Before she slipped away again, Der Ling could hear the dowager's robust voice in the next room. "When I awoke," she recalled, "Her Majesty was standing by my bedside. I tried to get up, but found that I was too weak, so Her Majesty told me to lie still and keep quiet and I would soon be all right again." Curiously, Der Ling does not report the whereabouts of her own mother.

As Der Ling lay helpless, unable even to make a show of rising at the dowager's entrance, Cixi ordered the eunuchs to move Der Ling to the room next to her own, so that she could keep watch over her while she recovered. Here was a scene of maternal concern of which few in the West, or in China, would have believed the dowager capable. It also shows something of Cixi's possessiveness — as she had once told Louisa, Der Ling belonged to her.[22]

By the time Der Ling began to assume her usual duties a few days later, tensions over the war rumors increased, to the point where each new day revealed the absence of another handful of eunuchs. Cixi knew the reason why: the eunuchs had heard her speak of the coming war, and fearing a repeat of the Boxer disasters, or a Japanese invasion from

Manchuria, they had taken the risk of fleeing the palace. Customarily search parties were sent to find AWOL eunuchs, but not on this occasion. "Her Majesty gave instructions that nothing was to be done about recapturing them," Der Ling remembered. It was as if the aging dowager could not summon up the fire which had once made men tremble. Yet when one of her own personal eunuchs disappeared, she was infuriated. Der Ling's eunuch, who evidently relished any opportunity of telling his mistress about the hidden side of eunuch life, claimed that the chief eunuch Li was just as capable of fleeing the palace as any of his underlings, just as he had pretended to be ill when Cixi and Guangxu had fled to Xian, preferring to bring up the cavalcade's rear in case he needed to hotfoot it out of the region entirely.[23] "These disappearances continued from day to day," noted Der Ling, "until Her Majesty decided that it would be safer for us to remain in the Forbidden City until the following spring at any rate." After hearing her eunuch's ghastly tales, Der Ling could be pardoned for feeling that no palace staffed by eunuchs could be any less dangerous than rumored battles in distant Manchuria or invading Japanese soldiers.[24]

Perhaps to take her court women's minds off these unsettling circumstances, Cixi played den mother as zealously as she was wont to do at the Summer Palace, and offered to give them a tour of the Forbidden City. Like any guide, Cixi exaggerated the palace's attributes to a sometimes comical degree, as when she told Der Ling that the brown bricks that made up the floor of the audience hall known as the Hall of Supreme Harmony were in fact solid gold beneath the layers of paint. Der Ling also seems to have been told that no foreigner had ever been in the Hall of Supreme Harmony when in truth several had not only penetrated the inner sanctum, following the flight of the emperor and the Empress Dowager in August 1900, but were even photographed sitting on the throne. There were other parts of the palace complex that Cixi did not seem to know enough about to describe. Many of the pavilions Der Ling saw had not been used for years — "nobody seemed to know what they contained," Der Ling wrote, "or whether they contained anything at all." She even got a glimpse of Guangxu's musty unused rooms, the same ones Pierre Loti had seen when he stayed in the Forbidden City in late summer of 1900. "The immense setting in which former emperors lived frightens him and he abandons it all," Loti wrote presciently of Guangxu; "grass and brushwood grow on the majestic marble railings and in the grand courtyards; crows and pigeons by the hundreds make their nests in the gilded vaults of the throne room, covering with dirt and dung the rich and curious rugs left there to be ruined." Everything was dark: furniture, shadows, "even the mournful bouquets under their glass cases." In the emperor's room, Loti found one of the many foreign-made gadgets Guangxu seemed to need to cheer himself; but far from inspiring merriment, this particular gadget, "a big music-box that gives Chinese airs" played its tunes with a haunting sound "that seems to come from beneath the waters of a lake."[25]

In a room of Cixi's own palace, the Qianlong Emperor's old residence in the northeastern corner of the palace complex, Der Ling claims she and and the others watched while Cixi commanded a eunuch to remove two false walls in a passageway. Beyond lay "a kind of grotto," Der Ling recalled. "There were no windows, but in the roof was a skylight. At the end of this room or grotto was a large rock, on the top of which was a seat with a yellow cushion, and beside the cushion an incense burner." Cixi told her that the room had been built as a meditation chamber by one of the Ming emperors. She had put it to less spiritual uses: it was here she had hidden her valuables when she and the emperor had fled Beijing. While the old lady seemed to enjoy the stares she provoked by showing off her secret room, it dawned on Der Ling that it was precisely these secrets of the Forbidden City that made Cixi so dislike it.[26]

On her own, Der Ling sought out a few of the secrets Cixi least wished to be reminded of, namely the three secondary wives of the Tongzhi Emperor, the dowager's late son, women who were technically something like her daughters-in-law. Amazingly, all three ladies were still living out their days in the northwest corner of the Forbidden City, as if invading foreign troops had not passed through the palace a mere three years earlier. One of these ladies, named Yü T'ai, was of especial interest to Der Ling. Yü T'ai had been Tongzhi's principal concubine, and as such she lived in a fine pavilion of her own, which Der Ling calls the T'i Yüan Tien or Hall of the Basis of Propriety. In 1924, when the Xuantong Emperor, Puyi, and all his retinue were forced to leave the Forbidden City for good, this woman would still be living there. The wives and concubines of a deceased emperor who had not managed to bear him a son were to all intents and purposes dead to the world, and had to drag out their lives within the same four courtyard walls, doing nothing more productive than making false flowers to attach to the branches of winter trees. By reason of her long seclusion, Yü T'ai fascinated Der Ling, because even though cut off from most other human beings, and from art and literature and music, "She could write poetry and play many musical instruments," she recalled, "and was considered the best educated lady in the Empire of China. Her knowledge of Western countries and their customs surprised me very much."[27]

It was difficult to grasp that this articulate woman should have to remain hidden away like a piece of broken pottery. Yü T'ai told Der Ling that unless the dowager called for her and the other ex-concubines to appear, they had to stay where they always were, in their rooms, busied with embroidery or flowers. Der Ling admired Yü T'ai's hunger for literature, which she slaked on a large private library. Happy to have someone to show them to, especially this young girl who had lived so much of her life in the world outside China, Yü T'ai let Der Ling read some of her poems. Der Ling found them "of a melancholy character, plainly showing the trend of her thoughts."[28]

Most astonishing of all, Yü T'ai turned out to be every bit as much a progressive as Der Ling's own father. "She was in favor of establishing schools for the education of young girls," she remembered, "as only very few could even read or write their own language." She asked Der Ling to press Cixi to spearhead reforms like these, being forbidden to make such suggestions herself. It must have been obvious even to Yü T'ai that her own predicament was the best argument for emancipation of the minds and the bodies of all Chinese women, the sooner the better.[29]

24
War clouds

Moved to a makeshift studio at the Forbidden City, Katherine Carl continued to work, while Der Ling continued to pose and listen to Cixi grumble. The dowager even suggested sarcastically, when Kate asked for a room with more light, that to satisfy the artist's whims she would have to order that the roof be taken off for her. When Kate was not working Der Ling was free to be present at the dowager's morning audiences, which were still held with the same clockwork regularity as at the Summer Palace; and it was here she came face to face with Yuan Shikai, Viceroy of Zhili and future short-lived emperor of China. Yuan also may have been a relative by marriage: one of his wives was said to have been a cousin of Yu Keng's.[1]

He had been summoned by Cixi to give his opinion of what was happening between Japan and Russia, and advise her as to whether China had anything to fear. Yuan had certainly come through for the dowager before, alerting her to the cabal formed by the reformers surrounding Guangxu, which resulted in Cixi's resumption of power and the pre-emptive blighting of any further modernizing policy-making on the part of the emperor. It was for his contribution to Guangxu's permanent retirement from the scene of affairs that Der Ling disliked Yuan, as well as for what seem to have been more subjective reasons. The sight of his short, plump figure waddling up to kneel at the throne made her think of a strutting rooster. "[A] cheap showman," was Der Ling's sharp verdict. "He was the sort of man who, by the mere gesture of brushing his sleeve, could get someone in trouble," she recalled, blaming him — as many did, though it took more than Yuan Shikai to create it — for his part in the eruption of war between Japan and China in 1895.[2]

Though not from the same background, the Han Chinese Yuan shared some important similarities with Li Hongzhang. Circumstances forced both to abandon scholarly pursuits for military ones. Like Li, Yuan was extremely adaptable, and as his betrayal of the reformers of 1898 demonstrates, well able to hold his own as an *agent provocateur*. Yuan had served as a puppet for Li Hongzhang's own political ends. After Li's death, his baton of office slipped without interruption into Yuan's sweaty hand, where it was not grasped as firmly. His three wives evidently knew they had nothing to fear from him: during a rehearsal for his coronation as the Hongxian Emperor in January 1916, they got into a catfight over precedence that Yuan had to step down from his brand new throne to break up. (Besides these wives there were several concubines, with a grand total of some thirty children.)[3]

Probably the strongest reason for Der Ling's dislike may have been Yuan's slick way with Cixi. Knowing her appetite for power was not far from resembling his own, he poured her great drafts of money raised not unreluctantly from business and official interests. Everyday with Yuan was like Christmas. He had a twenty-five-mile railroad laid just for Cixi's trip to the Western Tombs in April 1903, and gave her an automobile which contained a specially built throne. Kate Carl, who saw this car, described it as "gorgeously fitted up in the Imperial yellow and gold lacquer, with the Double Dragon," and according to what she had heard, Cixi was all for trying out the car, but was dissuaded by her ministers — no one could remain seated in her presence, even her chauffeur.[4] Characteristically, one of Yuan's most expensive gifts, what Der Ling describes as a satin robe appliquéd with precious stones and jade in designs of peonies, was too heavy for the old lady to wear. Cixi had been surrounded by shysters for years before Der Ling's birth, but after almost a year at court Der

Ling felt about the dowager as granddaughter for old grandmother; the blandishments of Yuan and his ilk brought out all her protective inclinations.[5]

When Cixi asked Yuan for his take on the brewing troubles between Japan and Russia he responded that "these two countries might make war against each other, [but] China would not be implicated in any way." He was, however, certain there would be trouble in Manchuria afterward. Cixi told Yuan she knew that was the case, and that in her view the best position to take was a neutral one. She then asked him who he thought would win the war. Japan, of course, Yuan replied. According to Der Ling, the dowager thought this better than a Russian victory — as time would tell, having Russian troops on Chinese soil would have been far better in the long run than Japanese. But she did show concern for China's readiness for military eventualities. "We [have] nothing ready," Der Ling reported the dowager saying to Yuan, "no navy and no trained army, in fact nothing to enable us to protect ourselves," adding that memorials urging various reforms poured across her desk all the time, yet nothing ever seemed to get done about them. Yuan assured her, as well he might. Like others who alternately flattered and hoodwinked the dowager, he was just stringing her along.[6]

Chinese military brass came for daily audiences, during which Der Ling had a hard time not laughing. "Many foolish suggestions were made by these generals," she recalled. "During one of the conversations Her Majesty referred to the fact that we had no trained naval officers. One of the generals replied that we had more men in China than in any other country." Where ships were concerned, there was even less to worry about: "we had dozens of river boats and Chinese merchant boats, which could be used in case of war." This assertion tipped Cixi's typical audience hall equanimity. "Her Majesty ordered him to retire," Der Ling wrote, "saying that it was perfectly true that we had plenty of men in China, but that the majority of them were like himself, of very little use to the country." The general bowed out of the hall to general laughter, but Cixi found nothing funny about it: "she was too angry to think that such men held positions as officers in the army and navy," Der Ling recalled.[7]

Far more worthy of Cixi's time, and more interesting for Der Ling, was an audience the dowager held with Zhang Zhidong, Yu Keng's old boss. It had been over ten years since Der Ling had admired the jade collection in Zhang's Wuchang house, and just as long since Zhang had come to Yu Keng's house to criticize his provision of Western-style education to his daughters. It was thanks to that education that Der Ling had been called to Cixi's court, but Der Ling mentions no recognition of her or of the irony of the situation on the part of the now aged Zhang. As no doubt she knew he would, Zhang gave Cixi his frank opinion of just what the coming war might spell for China. He had often pointed to the handwriting on the wall. In 1902, with his fellow viceroy Liu Kunyi, Zhang had presented three memorials on reform to Cixi, who had requested them. These memorials outlined a structure for reforming China's outmoded educational, administrative and military functions; one of the suggested changes, the elimination of the examination system, would not be acted upon until 1905. Even so, Zhang was China's elder statesman, and Cixi knew she could trust him to tell her the truth.

"He answered that no matter what the result of the war might be," Der Ling wrote, "China would in all probability have to make certain concessions to the Powers with regard to Manchuria for trade purposes, but that we should not otherwise be interfered with." He also pointed out that while reform was long overdue, to rush things would be to court disaster. After the events of 1898 nobody needed to tell Cixi that, but as Der Ling reports, "Her Majesty was delighted with the interview, for Chang Chih Tung's opinions coincided exactly with her own."[8]

What he told her did not fail to hit home. Der Ling saw the old lady sitting by herself later on, much as Kate Carl had seen her, "in silence, unblinking, her eyes staring at nothingness . . . My heart went out to her in pity . . . Here before me, a very old lady sat on a yellow upholstered throne — and on her shoulders might well rest the fate of an Empire."[9] In the end, Zhang's prediction would be correct to the degree that Manchuria would indeed become a vast gaming table of warring nations. When Russia lost the war, her troops were obliged by treaty to clear out of Manchuria. Yet the Japanese were ceded Southern Sakhalin Island and the Liaodong Peninsula, which Russia had forced the Japanese to return to China after the Sino-Japanese War — footholds on Chinese soil that were to briefly soothe Japan's itch for imperial aggrandizement. Even more grievous to China was the fact that Korea, long affiliated with the Middle Kingdom, was now firmly under the control of the Japanese, a goal of the Meiji government since the 1890s.[10]

During the discussions and audiences dealing with the coming war, Der Ling remembered how Guangxu sat on his throne and made no response other than to agree with the dowager's decisions. With Zhang Zhidong, the emperor seemed relaxed. When Yuan Shikai entered the audience hall, Der Ling noticed how Guangxu's lips compressed and his face went pale. Had he the opportunity, she believed, Guangxu would have ordered Yuan's smiling, ever-nodding head lopped off instantly. But it was he who, as emperor only in name, was truly headless. All he could do was doodle maps of Manchuria, the Great Wall and notes on imagined battle plans on the backs of imperial theatre programs, using the same Vermilion Brush which for his ancestors had dictated the laws and lives of a nation.[11]

Roused by politics, Cixi now turned her eye on Kate Carl's portrait. Kate was invited to the Sea Palaces to show Cixi her progress on the portrait and give her some idea how long it would take before it was finished. Far more at ease with the old lady now than she had been when the portrait project was begun, Der Ling frankly told Cixi that "unless she gave a little more of her time to posing it might not be finished for quite a long time." This information was sufficient to galvanize the dowager into presenting herself for Kate's brush for a few minutes each day; but after the second day she declared she felt ill and could not continue. When Der Ling pointed out that she had to give Kate more time, the old lady swallowed her anger and sat until the face was completed. Then that was it: she was through. "She absolutely refused to sit again whether it was finished or not," Der Ling remembered, "saying that she would have nothing more to do with the portrait."[12]

Cixi remained a very good actress, doing her best to charm Kate into ignorance of her backstage grousing. Cixi told Kate she hoped she could complete the portrait before four o'clock in the afternoon of April 19, 1904, as this was a date and time that her augury book had indicated would be most auspicious. "She would sometimes say, 'I am giving you a great deal of trouble, and you are very kind,'" recalled Kate. Honest as ever, though, Cixi certainly did give Kate much to gnash her teeth over. If on a certain day Cixi did not care for a jewel Kate had painted into the portrait, she asked her to paint it out and put in another. "She seemed to think it was as easy to take it from the picture as to remove it from her person," recorded the amused artist. When the picture was finished, the dowager ordered a camphor-wood frame built for it based on her own design. "The Double Dragon at the top struggled for the 'flaming pearl' with the character 'Sho' [*sic*] on it," Kate wrote. The sides of the frame were carved with the symbols for ten thousand years, and the whole frame (shaped like a foreshortened throne) was set into a pedestal that writhed with more carving. Kate was thrilled to discover that the frame had been carved by the dowager's own imperial artisans.[13]

Once the frame was finished and the canvas set in it, Cixi commanded Der Ling's brother to officially photograph it.[14] What was now referred to as the "Sacred Picture" was sent to Beijing to be viewed by officials in full court dress — for the portrait of Cixi, so unusual for being visible during the dowager's own lifetime, was considered no step removed from her real person. "[I]t was enclosed in a satin-lined camphor-wood box, covered with satin of Imperial yellow, and the box was closed with great solemnity," wrote Kate. Placed within two other boxes, the portrait was then covered with a satin tarpaulin covered on each side with five-clawed dragons, and was placed with great ceremony on a flatcar for the trip to Tianjin and thence to Shanghai and America. So great was the respect for the portrait that it was never laid flat during its entire journey but stood upright (so as not to be in the unauspicious position of a deceased person), causing much trouble during transport.[15]

The picture was received in St. Louis on June 19 by Prince Pulun, the emperor's and Empress Dowager's representative at the Exposition. "Then, for the first time, it could be seen by the ordinary individual — then only it became the subject of comment as any other picture at the Fair," noted Kate. "Then it was open to the gaze of the vulgar and the comment of the scoffer," but she clearly did not reveal this possibility to Cixi, who did not reveal to her that she felt it unnecessary to pay her for her work. Der Ling was Kate's champion in the matter. "I told [Cixi] that as painting was Miss Carl's profession, if she had not been engaged on painting Her Majesty's portrait she would most probably have been engaged on other similar work for which she would have received compensation," Der Ling recalled. "It was difficult to make Her Majesty understand this." Der

Ling explained that many women in Europe and America made their own living, which mystified Cixi: could Miss Carl's brother at Yantai not afford to support her? "I told Her Majesty that Miss Carl did not desire him to provide for her," and that he had a family of his own to support. "Her Majesty gave it as her opinion that this was a funny kind of civilization," which, compared to the family-centered structure of China, individual-centered Western customs would certainly seem.[16] In the end, Kate Carl was paid, and was also given a wardrobe of elegant court clothing, including a sable hat with a pearl "princess button" on the front — another sign, as with Der Ling, her sister and her mother, of Cixi's casual habit of handing out to her favorites what appeared to be genuine titular honors.[17]

After Kate left, Der Ling began to mourn the loss of this English-speaking, up-to-date American friend. "I had found her a genial companion," she recalled, "and we had many things in common to talk about." This was probably one of the times when, after the court moved back to the Summer Palace, Der Ling wandered off by herself down the Long Gallery and wept for loneliness in the little pavilions facing the lake. Cixi, who would have also noticed that Der Ling made very few friends among the court personnel, became aware of Der Ling's sadness at the departure of Kate. "Her Majesty was very nice about it," Der Ling remembered, "and said she wished that she was a little more sentimental over such small things, but that when I got to her age I should be able to take things more philosophically."[18]

This was the same woman who moved heaven to assure the health of her prized peonies and chrysanthemums and would have her gardeners whipped if so much as a petal was bruised. Evidently Cixi's "small things" and those of the rest of the world belonged to separate orders.

25
"First-class female official"

It was likely Der Ling's melancholy following the departure of Kate Carl that brought on what was to become the basis of her one significant argument with the dowager: that of marriage.

The subject had come up already, when Der Ling had first come to the Summer Palace, and she had shyly evaded it then. On the anniversary of Der Ling's first year at court, Cixi brought up the topic again. "She said that the only way to make sure of me" — in other words, to keep Der Ling at court and under her control — "was to marry me off," she recalled. "Last year when this marriage question came up I was willing to make allowances," the dowager told Der Ling sternly, in spring 1904, "as you had been brought up somewhat differently from the rest of my Court ladies, but do not run away with the idea that I have forgotten all about it. I am still on the lookout for a suitable husband for you."

As she had done before, Der Ling responded that while she wanted nothing more than to remain at court to serve the dowager as long as she wished her to be there, "I had absolutely no desire to marry." According to Der Ling, Cixi was miffed. "She made some remark about my being stubborn," Der Ling recalled, "and said that I should probably change my mind before long." In effect, by not immediately acquiescing to the dowager's plans, Der Ling was flouting the imperial will.[1]

Yu Keng was not surprised by his daughter's intransigence, but he was concerned about where it would lead her. "I am worried about you," he had repeatedly told Der Ling, "because you are different from other Chinese girls . . . The Chinese will never understand you, and if you marry among your own kind you will be unhappy." He added, "I fear you will never be happy with any man!" He may have guessed — and guessed correctly — that for Der Ling to be happy with a husband, that man would have to be as much like her father as possible, and that she would have no easy time finding that perfect fit. Indeed, might never find it within China or with a Chinese.

Der Ling is the only source for the information that there had been many requests from fathers, mothers, marriage brokers and young men for her hand. Yu Keng had put a stop to all of it. Further lionizing her father's protectiveness and ambition for her, when told that he could not keep his daughter to himself forever, Der Ling proudly records Yu Keng's retort: "I shall allow her to choose for herself!" Neither power nor fame made the least difference to him, per his adoring daughter, though all indications from her own portrait of him are that they had always made a difference to him indeed. Citing example of Yu Keng's own independence of judgment, Der Ling describes how a viceroy once asked him to marry Der Ling off to his son. That the viceroy asked by telegram would have infuriated any father, but Yu Keng made a response that brooked no discussion: "Ten thousand times no!" "What sacrilege this," Der Ling observed amusedly, "in a country where for thousands of years parents had arranged marriages!" But she also confessed that without her father to back her up, she might not have had the courage (or the protection) to refuse.[2]

As Der Ling approached her second autumn in the Empress Dowager's service, news of another betrothal effort on Cixi's part came not via the dowager herself but through a servant. Der Ling ignored the story at first, believing it below-stairs gossip. But when the dowager summoned her and abruptly announced that she had found her the perfect husband, she saw that the tale was all too true. "Her Majesty informed me that everything was arranged," she recalled, "and that I was to be married to a certain Prince whom she had chosen."[3] It was high time, too, remarked the dowager. "You are old enough to marry," she said, "and I have just the man in mind for you!" He was titled, "worth millions." And he came from that magic circle of Cixi's rapid rise to power in the 1860s: he was a son of her tireless supporter, the late Ronglu.

Perhaps in trying to mate Der Ling, whom Der Ling claims she loved like a daughter, to a son of a man she had loved but could not have, Cixi hoped to tie up some of the many loose emotional threads that trailed throughout her life. There was much to recommend the marriage socially and financially. Had she married this young man, Der Ling would have become an aunt to the Xuantong emperor, Puyi, and relation to the greatest Manchus in the land. "But I don't wish to marry," Der Ling told the old lady.[4] Already on edge from prior refusals — and probably expecting one on this occasion — Cixi was furious. "[S]he told me that she considered me very ungrateful after all she had done for me."[5]

The dowager had never been so angry with Der Ling, and she tells us that the battle the situation set up between her for the old woman and protecting her own interests made her ill. Perhaps hoping that contact with the sensible Yu Keng would make Der Ling see what a treasure she was throwing away, Cixi granted her court lady a few days' reprieve. (Louisa and Rong Ling, to whom Der Ling never seems to have applied for advice or comfort, remained at court.) No sooner had she reached her father's house than Der Ling broke down, telling him about the dowager's marriage plans for her and the argument they had had when Der Ling had baulked. Yu Keng was a sick man, not fated to survive more than another year, but he was clearly inspired by his daughter's bravado. Instead of agreeing with her immediately, however, he played devil's advocate.

"Do you care for him?" he asked her. Did his title or millions interest her? Der Ling says she sobbed that she cared for nothing whatever to do with Cixi's choice of husband — that she would never marry a Manchu, never be able to abide by Confucian rules of wifely conduct that she had not been obliged to follow at any time during her life and could not be expected to abide by now. "This is a bad marriage," Yu Keng said finally. He would not tell her how to prevent the marriage, as whatever idea he had in mind would, he felt, get her into more trouble. "You are clever," he told her. "I leave it to you to find a way out." Der Ling only cried more. She could not refuse — Cixi might cut off her head. Yu Keng must have smiled a little at this. "I had rather see you decapitated," he told her, "than see you married to this man!" Yu Keng suggested to Der Ling that she go back to the palace and find Li Lianying, tell him the whole story and ask for his help in influencing the dowager. (Perhaps Yu Keng sent a quantity of money back with his daughter. Li was not known for doing something for nothing.)[6]

Yu Keng's advice was easier given than acted upon. While she needed Li in this instance, he being the one member of her staff that Cixi trusted, or at least depended on, implicitly, and whose counsel she respected, Der Ling had also heard enough horror stories about him to dislike and fear him. Needless to say, because of these stories she had formed no sort of close friendship with him during her service in the palace. But she did go to Li in the end, and as Yu Keng correctly surmised, the old eunuch proved surprisingly helpful. Indeed there was probably more than a little self-interest involved in Li's efforts on Der Ling's behalf, because if marrying Der Ling off to a Manchu prince meant keeping her indefinitely at court, where she would continue to influence the dowager in all things suspiciously foreign, it would behoove Li to prevent such a marriage at all costs, and keep the brash young "foreign" woman away from the throne, while preserving his influence over the dowager intact.

"[H]e promised to do his best for me," Der Ling remembered. He clearly did as he promised: after Li communicated to Cixi whatever version of Der Ling's dilemma it pleased him to share, nothing more ever came from the dowager about marriageable princes and their millions. In effect, Der Ling, who always let the dowager beat her at *Eight Fairies Travel Across the Sea*, had won a game of far higher stakes. If Cixi admired her *savoir faire* in doing so, she never let on. After all, she had not reached her own place in history by being the traditional acquiescent Asian female.[7]

Soon Cixi was able to forget her altercation with the stubborn Der Ling: her 69th birthday celebrations (70 *sui*) were approaching, which for this year would be more complex than any before in that not only was she receiving gifts but handing some out, primarily promotions and increases in salary to her court personnel. She would, Der Ling assures us, also confer titles on those of her court women eligible for them; Guangxu would do the same for the male officials with whom he dealt on a regular basis. Further complicating matters was that for these important ceremonies, Cixi agreed that the Forbidden City was the proper place for them to be convened, yet because she refused to leave the Summer Palace until a few days before her birthday it was necessary for both the Summer Palace and the Forbidden City palaces to be decorated for the celebrations. Of all the dubious accusations of waste flung at the dowager, recurrent thoughtlessness of this nature is the most provable.

"Everything was hurry and bustle," remembered Der Ling of the days leading up to the ceremonies. Yet busy as she herself was, with her audiences and reviews of memorials as well as involving herself with all the party preparations, the dowager found time to enjoy the heavy snowfall which had blanketed the Summer Palace grounds in powdery white drifts. Cixi loved to walk in snow as much as she did in rain, scorning umbrellas and those who used them, and for this occasion she wished to be photographed on Peony Hill, where her treasured flowers were now so many black sticks frosted with snow. Der Ling's brother hauled his equipment up the hill, somehow positioned his camera from various picturesque locations on the slope, and captured the dowager in a flowered satin cloak, clinging to a branch as she paused on one of the stone steps leading down from the crest of the hill. Along with her she took Louisa, visible at a discreet distance in the background, and her two daughters — Rong Ling reserved and willowy to the dowager's left and sturdy Der Ling always at her right side, assisting her down the path, and eunuch Cui Yugui, holding aloft a large umbrella to protect the old lady and Der Ling from the falling flakes.[8]

When all was ready, the court moved to the Forbidden City. The centuries old palaces, now decorated with tasseled horn lanterns and brightly colored silk banners painted and embroidered with the character for long life, rang with music and laughter as they had not done for years. As a modern touch, says Der Ling, the courtyards were roofed in glass. "The theatres were in full swing each day," Der Ling remembered, both with Cixi's favorite Buddhist religious plays and the fairy tales she so enjoyed. It was here in the Forbidden City, among the other titles and gifts dispensed by the dowager and the emperor, that Der Ling claims she and her sister were granted the court titles of *jun zhu xian yi deng nü guan*. This title, translated as "princess, first class female official," was interpreted by Der Ling to emphasize the rank of "court princess." In fact, the Chinese title carries a great deal more weight than the rather fluffy "princess," which implies royal connection and which in any case would be written as *gong zhu* rather than *jun zhu*. (*Jun zhu* was a courtesy title usually accorded unmarried female cousins of the emperor.) Chinese historian Zhu Jiajing states that "Deling casually called herself a lady-in-waiting" when she and her sister were merely "nu kwan" (*nü guan*) a temporary honorary title associated only with certain ceremonies. Once the ceremony had ended, the title elapsed. The sisters, per Zhu, were merely at court to entertain the dowager, and whatever honors they held when they served her were not transferable to the world outside the court. Whatever the origin of the title that would help her sell books and lectures and undermine her authority as an expert on the court that was her specialty, Der Ling reports that after the ceremony at the Forbidden City her name, title and the date were brushed on the sides of a silk calligraphic scroll painted for Der Ling by the Empress Dowager with the character "shou." The scroll was later reproduced in a publicity brochure for Der Ling's Chautauqua lecture series in the late 1920s, and offered for sale by Der Ling's husband after her death. She evidently considered the scroll something of a patent of nobility, whether or not that is what it was, or was meant to be.[9]

Shortly after the ceremonial on the dowager's birthday, the entire court removed to Cixi's favorite Sea Palace, west of the Forbidden City. Amid the gaiety and exhaustion, Der Ling received word that Yu Keng's health had taken a turn for the worse, as a consequence of which he had sent in yet another resignation. This time the dowager had some of her servants visit Yu Keng at home, and their report confirming his poor health moved her to at last release him from her service. She also did something else, per Der Ling, that broke the pattern of her past dealings with Yu Keng. Repeatedly Yu Keng had requested the dowager's permission to seek help from his doctor in Shanghai, a foreign physician in whom he had great trust. The dowager had always responded with the advice that Yu Keng should have more faith in Chinese doctors, several of whom she would send to bother him. Now, it was obvious that Yu Keng needed care beyond that offered by traditional homeopathy, so she agreed to let him go.

Cixi also agreed to let Louisa accompany her husband on the long trip south. "I begged Her Majesty to let me go," Der Ling remembered, arguing that her father might worsen and die before she could get to him. The dowager "offered all kinds of objections" — she had not seen her own father again after entering the palace at fourteen, so what may seem coldness was more a lack of the practice of any sort of family feeling. The dowager finally relented, then like a fond but annoying grandmother clucking over her grandchildren, she held up the women's journey and Yu Keng's treatment by arranging to have the palace tailors make up several sets of new clothes for them. Thus they did not get away to join Yu Keng and begin the trip to Shanghai until some time in December 1904.

"We kowtowed and said good-bye to Her Majesty," Der Ling remembered, "thanking her for her many kindnesses during our stay with her. Everybody cried, even Her Majesty." Guangxu shook Der Ling's hand and said in English: "Good luck." Based on their behavior as described by Der Ling over her year and a half at the palace, it is likely that at least a few court ladies were glad to witness the departure of the "foreign devils" with the Asian faces.[10]

Shanghai of 1904–1905 was a city of sparkle and spending, though hardly to the degree it would lavishly exhibit during and after the First World War, when fortunes made through munitions and wartime supplies enabled millionaires to literally roll in an effulgence of cash.

"To adherents of the old order," writes Stella Dong, "Shanghai was heresy incarnate,"[11] but this heresy existed mostly in the eyes of respectable Confucian Chinese, who looked askance at the antics of "foreign devils" who made millions overnight and kept beautiful Chinese mistresses in their new mansions in Bubbling Well Road. While Shanghai had been settled as early as the tenth century — not exactly ancient by Chinese standards but aged enough to rank among the empire's older towns — it did not burgeon into the bustling port of legend until the 1600s, and by the eighteenth century had burst its four miles of encircling walls. The city could not have avoided commercial success had it tried — to the east lay its port, less than twenty miles from where the Yangzi River emptied its yellow waters into the coastal shallows, which served the merchant junk trade that plied the Chinese coast; while to the west lay some of the most fertile land in China.

The foreign element that was to characterize the city for a century and a half had, like many of the first foreigners in Chinese ports, gained a foothold through the sale of opium, which well before the mid-nineteenth century became a stranglehold on an estimated one out of every ten Chinese, and would lead to the first and second Opium Wars, the destruction of the Summer Palace and continual loss of Chinese land and cash through ceaseless indemnifications, not to mention the downfall of the Qing dynasty itself. Had the Qianlong Emperor been more interested in purchasing the goods of foreign lands, when approached by England in the eighteenth century, however right he was to declare his empire self-sufficient and European goods useless to him, the imbalance caused by the heavy flow of British money for Chinese tea might not have been redressed quite so drastically with a drug that came to be pandered in every Chinese port, to become the ruin of Chinese families and the Chinese state. But Shanghai's location on the Huangpu River, along with a generally more tolerable climate compared to the older southern port city of Guangzhou, worked to make the city a true metropolis of foreign commerce, particularly when the international settlements had effectively pushed the native Chinese back from the profitable waterfront.

The city's very name is synonymous with lawless behavior: to shanghai someone, according to one dictionary definition, is to "drug or render unconscious or kidnap for service aboard a ship . . . To cause to do something by force or deception."[12] Even so, Shanghai held beauties for some. Enid Candlin, a tea merchant's daughter who grew up in the city's International Settlement, recalled her birthplace in a reverie:

> When I look back at Shanghai, I always feel that the sky was our
> luxury. That, and the light which always pervades deltas, where the

great arc of the heavens is uninterrupted ... In default of anything
else, at Shanghai we had these skies, soft, open and luminous,
pouring out penetrating light, enriching everything we saw.[13]

It must have seemed to Der Ling as if the skies, so constricted by the
overhanging eaves of the Forbidden City's palaces, had suddenly opened
"a great arc of the heavens" for her. The Yu Keng family had been in
Shanghai only a short time, Der Ling tells us, before invitations addressed
to Louisa and her daughters began to pour in — for balls, dinners, the
theatre, and all the other European-style amusements that had made it
so hard for Der Ling to leave Paris. Shanghai had always been for her the
ugly stepping-stone set amid ugly yellow waters, from which she had set
forth for the precise, formal beauties of Japan and the whirl of elegance
and modernity that was Paris. Now she had left the fantasy of Cixi's
court, replete with her new "title," and Shanghai held nothing for her.
Concern for her father took precedence, even over a certain American
who was paying her court.

Despite his improvement on the trip south from Beijing, and the
progress under the care of his foreign doctor, Yu Keng was still sick.
Yet he was, as ever, sensitive to the moods of his most emotional child.
Yu Keng must have noticed Der Ling's misery, because it was he who
suggested to her that as he was doing so much better, she should return
to the Empress Dowager's service. Whether Yu Keng really felt up to
letting Der Ling go, or covered for the truth of his condition, Der Ling
does not say; but she did not take much convincing that matters were
stable enough for her to return to the palace.

Der Ling left Shanghai for Beijing soon after New Year 1905. This
time, after an exhausting journey up the coast and then by slow-moving
train to Beijing, she arrived at the palace alone — Louisa and Rong Ling
had stayed behind to look after Yu Keng — and almost as soon as she
reached the court she regretted having come there. Though she describes
being met by a tearful Cixi, life at the palace turned out not to be the same
as when she left, perhaps the dowdier for having lived in sparkling new
Shanghai. What had been a series of daily adventures had become settled
and routine; perhaps, too, Der Ling's star as Cixi's favorite was waning, a
detail of court life she would not likely have shared with her readers. It is

also possible that Yu Keng's absence from Beijing significantly reduced his daughter's confidence and, certainly, her sense of security. Now that she was back among the splendors of the dowager's country court, assisting her with her jewels and interpreting for her morning audiences and afternoon teas, Der Ling began to miss Shanghai. It is easy to surmise that she missed her parents and sister, not to mention the dances and parties, where she could now be announced (perhaps spuriously) as a princess. How long Der Ling could have endured the deepening disappointment we may only speculate — certainly, at some point Cixi must have been aware of the young woman's tearful wanderings along the Grand Gallery, where even when she thought herself alone there would have been a quiet eunuch or two watching and listening from the shrubbery.

Der Ling's court service was not to last much beyond March, 1905, the anniversary of her second year at court. "I received a telegram summoning me to Shanghai as my father had become worse," she remembered. Yu Keng's condition was indeed serious, a measure of which was clear from his request that Der Ling leave the palace to come to him. This was something Yu Keng would not have done had he not felt that time was of the essence. Perhaps, too, he had had letters from Der Ling and realized that his daughter was no more cut out for the life of the court than he had been for the life of a conservative Manchu mandarin, and that in summoning her home he was throwing her a rope back to the Western, modern life she was meant to live. Cixi took her time granting Der Ling's request to go to her father's bedside, but when she finally gave her assent there were no delays over clothing to be made or delicacies packed for the journey. Maybe the dowager was thinking of a long-ago father who had died without seeing his daughter again. The tears Der Ling describes at her leave-taking sound genuine enough.

On her arrival in Shanghai, "I found my father in a very dangerous condition," Der Ling wrote. As with the trip from Beijing to Shanghai, Yu Keng seems to have improved somewhat with his daughter nearby, and lingered on through the spring and summer and into the first part of winter 1905. Now living in her parents' Western-style, permissive household, for Der Ling Shanghai's distractions proved a way to forget her father's impending death. "I made many new friends and acquaintances," she remembered. Not surprisingly, amid the European-style architecture, lifestyle and culture of Shanghai, Der Ling also came to meet her true self for the first time. "At heart I was a foreigner," she would admit. The girl who had studied dance with Isadora Duncan, who had partaken of tea and theatricality with Sarah Bernhardt, emerged from her Chinese court robes like a butterfly from a second chrysalis. She again wore the French heels and *décolleté* Paris gowns she loved and danced with young men at public balls and parties. She says she also arranged at least one public performance of dances Duncan had taught her and her sister, which they performed dressed in thin silk chemises which would have shocked the Empress Dowager but which were *de rigueur* for Shanghai's foreign-born, foreign-friendly audiences.

During the social rounds that went with Shanghai like the soda with whiskey dispensed at the exclusive Shanghai Club, Der Ling met an American, a New Yorker by birth named Thaddeus Cohu White. A marshal of the American Court, White would later serve in the United States consular service in Shanghai and in Beijing. Six years older than Der Ling, son of a seaman and tall and handsome in a professorial way, White hailed from Long Island, and before coming to China had fought as a private in the Spanish-American War.[14] An engineer by profession, like many other foreigners who came to China (and like his future wife), White would find himself capable of playing as many different roles as circumstances required, some of them more dubious than others — according to the editor of George Morrison's letters, White later "undertook many shady dealings as a commercial agent," and would come to the attention of the sardonic and suspicious Morrison himself in 1916.[15]

Der Ling stayed as close to Yu Keng's sickbed as the proud old man would permit. A passage from one of her later short stories, *Golden Phoenix*, could describe her own emotions at the time: "She had loved her kindly father with a love beyond words." As his strength ebbed, the tall, broad-shouldered Yu Keng was reduced to a withered old man, lying helpless in his bed. Der Ling often climbed up to lie beside him, and they would talk — about the past and its happy times, and about the future, which Yu Keng envisioned as a very different place from the China in which even his children had grown up. "The day is coming soon when there will be no Manchu court in China," Der Ling reports her father telling her, "when there will no longer be Manchus and Chinese, but when all of us will be Chinese. I shall not live to see that day, but it is very near."

Soon the old man grew too weak to talk. On a cold day in mid-December, the family was told by Yu Keng's doctor that he was dying, that nothing more could be done for him. Der Ling stood in her father's darkened room. "I had never looked upon death," she wrote, "and could not believe that Father was actually going." Der Ling did as she had been doing over the past several months and crept up onto Yu Keng's bed to lie beside him. "But with his last feeble strength he waved me away," she recalled. "Go away! Go away!" said her father. "I don't wish you to see!"

Der Ling writes that Yu Keng had never spoken to her in this manner and he increased her grief with his outburst. But Der Ling came to understand what he meant. "Father's last thoughts were of me," she wrote, "and when he did not wish me to come near unto him, he motioned me away, because he wished to spare me as he had always spared me pain." Looking into his haggard face, Der Ling pretended she had not heard and drew close, holding his hands, "which had done so much for me." She was witnessing, as she would later describe it in her memoirs, the passing of "the greatest man I ever knew." Yu Keng had been her guide as well as defender. After his death, she would have to embark on the odyssey of the rest of her life without his steadying hand. It would be rough seas for her from here onward.[16]

PART III

Westerners are hustlers.

— Princess Der Ling

26
East is West, West is East

China and Russia, those massive cultures precariously balanced at either end of a massive continent, have always shared certain intriguing similarities.

Not only have both Chinese and Russian cultures had a legacy of hiding away their women, in an effort to preserve chastity — in Russia's case, a practice of the royal court, whereas in China any woman above the field-laboring peasant class, where women perforce had to show themselves, was to be concealed from the sight of men, within separate female quarters in the family compound. They shared a similar style of bed, built over a furnace to heat the sleeper through cold northern winter nights — the *kang*, in China, seen in imperial bedrooms in the Forbidden City, and the homely Russian version, which doubled as a cooking stove in many peasant cottages. China and Russia share legends about magical birds (the Chinese phoenix, the Russian firebird), even a reverence for the color red, which in Russian also means "beautiful," and to a Chinese is the color of happiness and good luck (and the hue worn by a bride for her wedding gown). And they had versions of the same folk saying: "Heaven is high, and the Emperor is far away."

These nations — one European with Asian undertones, the other Asian with European veneer — also shared something else very similar: two revolutionary leaders, one a dyed in the wool Communist, the other more than just open-minded on the subject, who took credit for revolutions at the beginning of the twentieth century which, on closer examination, prove activated more by accident than action, and in fact took place when either leader was out of the country undergoing the upheavals each professed to have created. These men, Dr. Sun Yat-sen and Vladimir Lenin, lived short lives — they died a year apart, in 1924 and 1925 — but survived long enough to witness the parlous state in which their revolutions had left their respective nations. Lenin himself had once pegged Dr. Sun as a personality of "inimitable — one might say virginal — naiveté," one of the few but significant areas where the two men were not cut from the same cloth. Both, perhaps not surprisingly, were accorded similar funerary rites and temple-like entombments, and are revered today, with various strengths of patriotism and *Realpolitik*, as the fathers of their nations.

Der Ling's father was one of many men courageous, scheming or a combination of both, who, according to Der Ling, had literally helped save the life of Sun Yat-sen, a well-meaning reformer who but for constant assistance might well have ended up suffering the traitor's death of a thousand cuts in a market square in Beijing. When Dr. Sun had come to see Yu Keng at the Chinese legation in Paris, he was putting Yu Keng in danger, not a situation likely to earn Yu Keng's friendship; and he was also trusting that Yu Keng was a man of his word and not just a conniving opportunist, who would entrap the fugitive revolutionary and ship him off to Beijing to earn points with the dowager. As we have seen, according to Der Ling Yu Keng was up to the challenge.

Like Lenin, who would arrive at St. Petersburg's Finland Station from exile abroad only after the March 1917 revolution, Dr. Sun was also abroad, in Denver, Colorado, on a trip through America to drum up financial support, when an act more accidental than intended toppled Qing rule and laid the way clear for the founding of the Chinese republic. In early October 1911, in a garrison at Wuhan on the Yangzi River, a homemade bomb stored by a group of dissenting army officers exploded, literally blowing the cover for their anti-Qing plot. When arriving authorities discovered evidence to that effect, including the location of the dissenters' headquarters, they put the conspirators under arrest. This event might well have ended as most anti-Manchu conspiracies had done over the past couple of generations, had it not been that the shock discovery galvanized the conspirators into courage: the officers mutinied, and before long Wuhan was theirs. In the days that followed, the imperial army and navy fought a losing battle against the revolt. Yuan Shikai was called out of retirement, and though he acquitted himself well, it was not Yuan's style to play only one side of any game. Events proved helpful to him in this respect, as the amazing momentum of the October 10 revolt spread down the Yangzi River and from there to the rest of China, igniting long-standing Han Chinese hatred of Manchus.

"The 1911 Revolution, after a slow start, gathered strength so rapidly that it is easy to overlook the violence it unleashed," writes Manchu-Han historian Edward Rhoads. "Popular as it may have been, it was by no means bloodless."[1] All Manchus, or suspected Manchus, were fair game. Enraged vigilantes began to seek out Manchus, looking not just in the banner-held sections of towns and cities but everywhere for Chinese who bore all the signs of being Manchu: women with natural feet, people with flat cranial configuration at the back of their skulls (Manchus were popularly supposed to have flattened heads due to being strapped in infancy into the suspended cradles used by some Manchurian people), and tell-tale mispronunciation of tongue-twisting Chinese words and phrases. Neither women nor children were spared the massacres.

Wuchang was where the revolution had begun, and it was also the first scene of Manchu slaughter. The beautiful city where Der Ling had lived when her father was provincial treasurer back in 1895 had become a death trap to Manchus and those who defended them. When it was clear what their fate would be if they remained, Manchus of rank, such as Yu Keng's successor in office, Lian Jia, escaped Wuchang in droves, along with scores of ordinary banner people. The banner people of Xian, the Manchu garrison town which had been the place of Cixi's exile in 1900, were not so lucky. After the Manchu City had put up a courageous fight, the revolutionaries overwhelmed the city, and on October 24 began to murder every Manchu they could find. "Old and young, men and women, little children, were alike butchered," reported the British missionary

J. C. Keyte. He was told that many bodies of Manchu dead were found in kneeling position, shot in the act of begging for mercy. While some Manchus fled, disguising themselves as Chinese, others sought escape in suicide. One banner officer actually killed himself and his family by burning them all alive.

Even in the more orderly precincts of Nanjing, no Manchu was safe. Along with mass murder the revolutionaries who took the city in early November also subjected the Manchu quarters to plunder, burning and destruction. And quiet, backward little Shashi, setting of Der Ling's childhood, had fallen under the revolutionaries' control. Accounts survive of Manchus pleading for their lives by pointing out that their family had started out Han and was only Manchu by adoption. The *Eastern Times*, late in October 1911, published several crude cartoons showing a banner-woman trying to hastily remake herself as a Han by having her feet (belatedly) bound and altering her hairstyle and dress, as if her desperate efforts were amusing.

By February 1912, it was over: the revolution had succeeded, and the boy emperor, Puyi, had abdicated. Dr. Sun Yat-sen had finally attained his dream of becoming president of a Chinese republic. The trouble was, China had no idea how to run such a government, any more than it was able to start building the massive system of rails that Dr. Sun naively sketched across a map of the nation (blithely sending his imaginary locomotives over 15,000-feet peaks). The other trouble was new prime minister Yuan Shikai, who clearly had his cap set for the presidency, and on that other thing that lay beyond, just barely visible to his squinting middle-aged eyes: the restored throne of a new Han dynasty.[2]

In late December, Dr. Sun came back to China from his latest exile — a fly in the ointment Yuan was so carefully brewing. In Nanjing, Dr. Sun was acknowledged Provisional President, but like so many of his other forays into politics, the office was of short duration: in February, following the abdication of the Xuantong Emperor, Dr. Sun resigned in favor of Yuan Shikai, who then gave China's greatest hero a high-paying but obscure job as director of the national railroad system. Sun made another tactical error by falling in love with the intense Ching-ling Soong, daughter of the wealthy, meddlesome Christian Chinese publisher Charlie Soong, whose daughter Ai-ling had already served as Dr. Sun's secretary and to whose children Sun had always played an avuncular role. When Soong forbade the engagement the couple eloped — preceded, of course, by Sun's divorce from his extant wife. In hindsight, this marriage only redounded to the greater glory of the Soong dynasty, but the complications it wrought on Sun at the time of the fledging republic were the last thing he needed.

Part of the reason Provisional President Yuan and the Shanghai and Guangzhou gangs that backed him wanted to keep Dr. Sun safely in a cage was his increasing interest in Communism, of the Russian variety, which culminated in the early 1920s with the visit to China of Mikhail Borodin, sent by Lenin to be head Comintern agent in China. Cixi's fear during the Russo-Japanese War, that Russia would use the opportunity to seize land in Manchuria, would play out in reality soon enough. But for the moment Russia was gently palpating the fractured surface of Chinese republican politics, seeking a hole to get a finger through. Interestingly, the Guangzhou apartment which Borodin, his wife and sons were given had in its waiting room two telling photographs facing each other from opposite walls: one of Lenin, the other of Dr. Sun.[3]

Like many Chinese who had studied outside China, Sun was not so much intrigued by Communism's philosophy as about its (alleged) efficiency; Borodin had greatly impressed him with his defense of Guangzhou during a November uprising. That naiveté so apparent to Lenin prevented Sun from seeing just what sort of game the Russians were playing. Even on his deathbed, in March 1925, Sun (or Borodin) composed a valetudinarian farewell to his "Dear Comrades" in the U.S.S.R., adjuring the ever-slippery bureaucrats in Moscow to assist China's Kuomintang party to throw off the imperialist yoke and breathe free. Shortly before his death, Sun allegedly whispered to his brother-in-law H. H. Kung, a descendant of Confucius who had married another of Charlie Soong's remarkable daughters: "Just as Christ was sent by God to the world, so also did God send me."[4]

Significantly, the Russian legation in Beijing forwarded a Russian-style coffin, replete with viewing window, similar to the kind in which the mummified Lenin had been ensconced the year before. Instead, Sun's widow wisely insisted on a traditional Chinese coffin. After lying in state for two weeks, "The Father of Modern China" was taken in his enormous casket to a temple in the Western Hills. In June 1929, two days after Der

Ling's 44th birthday, and after five years of waiting in the Western Hills, Sun was finally buried in the mausoleum he had desired, located near the tomb of the first Ming emperor, Hongwu, who had also risen from the bottom to the top. Atop a hill and reached by a vast staircase 320 meters long, the blue-tiled, white-walled tomb boasted ceilings of gilt and crimson, with a white marble statue of Dr. Sun and at the back, where the great man's body lay, another likeness in white marble, a recumbent effigy lying with hands crossed. Even Lenin, in his boxy red granite tomb in Red Square, could not boast of burial in anything quite so incongruously grandiose.

Through this monument, Sun was still as passive a witness to the passage of time as ever, but he had never remained in any one place for so long. And as one pithy American observer pointed out, "The death of Dr. Sun Yat-sen probably did more to unite the Kuomintang Party than anything he had done in his lifetime. As long as Dr. Sun was alive, his mistakes and his lack of political acumen divided his party." Death bequeathed to him a sagely wisdom: "[H]e became the embodiment of all the ideals of the Nationalist movement . . . in a few centuries Sun Yat-sen will be a worthy rival of Confucius."[5]

27
Flapper "princess"

As Dr. Sun was being laid to rest outside Nanjing, in a China which seemed to have finally been brought under control by Chiang Kai-shek, Der Ling was preparing to pull up her Chinese roots and embark for the country she had always wanted to visit, America. She would be doing so as the wife of an American and the mother of a seventeen-year-old son, Thaddeus Raymond White. And she would also be doing so as the author of two memoirs and a biography of the Empress Dowager Cixi which had already brought her both renown and criticism, in and outside of China.

In the two decades between her 1907 marriage to Thaddeus White and their removal to America at the end of the 1920s, Der Ling had watched China pass through not one major upheaval but several, including not only the overthrow of the Manchu dynasty but the establishment of China's ill-fitting republican government and the chaos of the warlord takeover preceding Chiang Kai-shek's seizing of control. But for Der Ling, life had already made an abrupt change with her father's death. He had been her supporter in all the ideas and actions that put her outside the rules and regulations of conservative upper-class Chinese society. Without him, she understandably felt lost, but the loss was even greater than this, because with Yu Keng went one of the few Chinese who understood and sympathized with Der Ling. Even in death she obeyed him, keeping her promise to him that she would never marry a Manchu. In the Yu Keng household, things American would have ranked as the most modern of all, and thus an American husband would seem to satisfy all criteria. Der Ling clearly believed she had found the perfect catch when, at one of Shanghai's glittering foreign social entertainments, she met the American to whose fate, for better or worse, she would tie her own destiny. According to one source, Der Ling first encountered Thaddeus while dancing at a benefit for a singer friend who had fetched up penniless in the city. That this was within the lifetime of the Empress Dowager Cixi demonstrates further that Der Ling's nerve was, if anything, strengthened by her time at court. If Cixi was shocked that her former court lady was dancing in Shanghai in Isadoran shifts, neither Der Ling nor any other source informs us, nor does Der Ling seem to have cared. In his preface to Der Ling's 1911 book, *Two Years in the Forbidden City*, Shanghai newspaper publisher Thomas F. Millard noted that with her engagement to White, who was called T.C. by Der Ling, some time in late 1905 (and therefore prior to the death of Yu Keng), Der Ling "took a step which terminated connexion with the Chinese court." As with her parents' marriage, Der Ling's union with T.C. broke one of the cardinal rules of a young Chinese woman: she did not accept a man chosen for her by her parents — or recommended by the Empress Dowager — but instead fell in love with a man on her own, and that man was not even Chinese. But according to text Thaddeus wrote for the catalog of items to be auctioned after Der Ling's death (in 1944), he refers to Cixi not only approving the match but giving the young couple elegant bedchamber accoutrements and a pair of pearl-studded *ruyis* (good-luck scepters). Probably Cixi took her maternal feelings for Der Ling to their natural conclusion and, like her mother, acceded to what was best for her "daughter." "She is mine," the dowager had told Louisa. Now Der Ling belonged to her husband, and Cixi would have respected that. (Interestingly, however, given the fact that they claim Cixi gave her permission for the marriage to take place, Der Ling and T.C. only returned to Beijing to live on a permanent basis after Cixi's death.)

Marriage took place on May 21, 1907. Despite the disapproval this union may have raised in conventional quarters, in and out of Der Ling's family, she had made a good move in allying herself with a foreign national and setting up housekeeping in foreign-controlled Shanghai: with her father dead and no longer able to protect her, she must have seen that marriage to an American would give her a certain armor against most Chinese governmental vicissitudes.

As Der Ling would racily tell a reporter in 1930, by comparison with Chinese males, "American men are better lovers," and clearly this was a quality T.C. brought to their relationship — a photo taken of the two in 1935, said to be the first ever shot of them together, shows a middle-aged couple not just loving but playful. It was clearly not just T.C.'s own American taste for adventure and bucking of the established rules that attracted Der Ling to him. Like many foreigners in general and Americans in particular in Shanghai, T.C. came of a vaguely unstable past, with a decidedly unstable future ahead of him. In her own world of shifting identities and allegiances, this may well have made Der Ling feel right at home. Alternately described over the years as a marshal of the American Court in Shanghai, a vice-consul at the American ministry in Beijing, and a commercial agent alleged to have been involved in the pilfering of the overstuffed imperial warehouses at Mukden, T.C. was a New Yorker by birth, the son of a sailor named William White and wife Ada Moore. After he and his wife moved to the United States, T.C. would continue to pursue romantic adventures, including the expensively elusive one of speculating in gold mine leases in the California desert.

Though Der Ling makes it clear that she and T.C. met during her father's last illness, in 1905, they waited nearly two years before marrying. The mores of the Victorian age still obtained in the decade after Victoria's death, particularly in a far flung quasi-British colony like Shanghai, but the long engagement may well be chalked up not so much to old-fashioned rules as to Louisa's habitual protectiveness. On few pages of her memoirs does Der Ling not sniff at her mother's strict notions of proper behavior, while celebrating her father's joy in breaking hidebound rules. On the other hand, it is possible Louisa was waiting and watching to see whether T.C. could provide for her daughter in the manner to which she had been long accustomed; and given Der Ling's willfulness, it is also quite possible she refused to give in until she got her way. Rong Ling, on the other hand — she who had obediently remained in Shanghai with her parents when Der Ling returned to Cixi's court — married the wealthy Chinese General Dan Paochao and lived in China all of her life. The fact that Der Ling does not refer to her family at all in her later books (only her father, whom she considered her soul mate) seems to point to difficulties around her marriage to T.C. and her subsequent move to the United States, with only brief journeys back to China, to gather information for her books or to secure belongings left behind for shipping to America.

From the start, the myths of just who "the Princess Der Ling" was and was not were balanced between these two nations. There were the naysayers in China — like Reginald Johnston, Puyi's tutor, and the brilliant forger, Sir Edmund Backhouse — doubting Der Ling's right to even use her title, not to mention the veracity of her published accounts of her experiences at court. And there were the goggle-eyed fans in America, who could address Der Ling as "Her Imperial Highness" without batting an eyelash, and do as much to overly humanize her by interviewing her in her kitchen, trading secrets in the basting of turkeys, as to overly romanticize her brief two years at the court of Cixi. (Aided, in turn, by Der Ling's own penchant for romanticizing China, once she had got away from its unromantic realities.)

Der Ling's *Two Years in the Forbidden City* was published by Dodd, Mead and Co. of New York City the summer prior to the October 1911 revolution. This might be seen as the worst possible timing for a book describing the Manchu imperial court and the intimate life of its oft-demonized empress dowager, but the book was a success. Written in a dry, sometimes frothy and even girlish style appropriate to the age of the writer when at court, but not at all impressive to such old China hands as J. O. P. Bland and Reginald Johnston, *Two Years* was a sort of sequel to Katherine Carl's 1905 memoir of her experience at Cixi's court, *With the Empress Dowager of China*. It may have been a corrective, too, not just of some of Kate's mistakes or misconceptions but also to show that though Der Ling, Rong Ling and their mother Louisa play but a small part in Kate's narrative, they had had a much more important role in reality. Where Kate relegates Der Ling to the position of "translator," rather than lady-in-waiting, Der Ling seems to answer back with an almost page-by-page reiteration in *Two Years* that she was "Her Majesty's First Lady in Waiting," even at the expense of her sister and mother, who also served these roles (her sister served at court until Cixi's death in 1908). And she also makes pointed reference to such details as the fact that Cixi's least favorite color was blue, where Kate describes Cixi as preferring it.

One thing both women were agreed on: though both had heard their share of horror stories about the old dowager, and both had seen many of the dowager's least favorable characteristics during their time at court, they had come away from her not just believing the stories exaggerated but, for the most part, untrue. As one modern historian has put it, "Behind the trappings of an Oriental potentate how could there be only a dowdy matriarch, a Jewish mother, a bridge-club granny who liked flowers, lapdogs and overelaborate clothing and of late had been inclined to weep?"[1]

Rather than asking questions of the press from which their skewed picture of Cixi had been unquestioningly painted over the years, those who preferred to see her as the secret murderess of her son Tongzhi and co-empress Cian, the string-puller behind a thousand plots and the instigator of the Boxer Uprising, could not dislodge her from their minds as the focus of blame. Nor could some, like J. O. P. Bland and Edmund Backhouse, authors of the forgery- and gossip-based *China Under the Empress Dowager*, take lightly the fact that first-hand accounts of the dowager, not just by young women they could dismiss like Kate Carl and Der Ling, but by the older, respected Sarah Conger and the Headlands, tended not to support their image of a scheming, thieving witch on a throne but of a tired old woman trying to hold together a country flying apart at the seams, who was not always nice (few potentates are), but was not unlikable and certainly no red-fanged harpy.

Of the women who wrote of the Cixi they had personally known, it was easiest to target Der Ling, who perhaps unwisely chose to use her court title of "Princess" as author. From ridicule, Der Ling's critics passed to deliberate avoidance of her works as being "tainted" by rumors of falsehood, if not forgery, and their commercial success only seemed to taint her credibility further. This, perhaps, as much as the political upheavals smashing China like so much crockery, may have been one of the primary reasons why she and T.C. decided to make America their home. Where better to go, where face value would remain the standard for reality long after Der Ling's and T.C.'s lifetimes. Yet by doing so, they were to find it all too easy to fall into the sort of hyperbole about both their pasts, the sort that does not begin as a lie but ends as something just as bad: fantasy accepted as truth.

28
"To others she may have been cruel . . ."

After Der Ling left the Summer Palace for good, in autumn 1905, life went on for Cixi: the picnics at the Summer Palace and the review and approval of memorials and other business, the audiences with foreigners, opera performances and games of *Eight Fairies*.

She would also sit for another foreign artist. In June 1905, before Der Ling had left the court for good but was still in Shanghai with her dying father, the Dutch painter Hubert Vos arrived in Beijing to paint a portrait of the dowager. A native of Maastricht, Vos was a hale and hearty fifty, a master of what was then termed "ethnic types": he had painted Plains Indians, South American aboriginals, Hawaiians, Japanese and Koreans, and lived his life just as exotically as he painted, marrying (bigamously) a Hawaiian woman of royal island ancestry. A late bloomer constrained to make a living before he could formally study art, Vos made up for lost time at the Académie Royal de l'Art in Brussels and academies in Paris and Rome. It was his portrait of the aged Prince Qing, once seen by Cixi (and perhaps her dissatisfaction with Kate Carl's portrait), that moved the dowager to ask Vos to paint her. Luckily for Vos, his habit was to take photographs of his subjects so that he could study them later at his leisure and work without tiring his sitter. In the dowager's case this technique would prove handy, as Kate Carl's portrait clearly suffers from its impatient sitter having made herself scarce. Cixi was no more generous where Vos was concerned, and in fact less than she had been toward Kate Carl, granting him only up to ten minutes of sitting at a time.[1]

The first sitting took place at an ungodly 5 a.m. — Cixi's working hour — and Vos nearly missed reaching the palace in time. Prince Zaizhen, Der Ling's old friend from Paris, met the panting and nervous artist and guided him into the imperial presence. "I had seen the picture [by Kate Carl] in St. Louis," Vos recalled, "which told me nothing," and had been studying photographs of the dowager (probably Xunling's). But as with so many who met Cixi in person, Vos was immediately struck by the charisma of her presence, full of "a tremendous will power . . . hard firm will and thinking lines, and with all that a bow of kindness and love for the beautiful." Cixi had conquered at first sight: "I fell straight in love with her," Vos recorded, echoing Der Ling's reaction on first meeting the dowager. Cixi seems to have fallen for Vos, too. On leaving the room one day after a sitting, which included the dowager's painterly advice about adjusting the features in her face (and giving Cixi a chance to scribble a little with a foreign pencil, a writing implement she had never before used), the old lady "turned round and smiled to me," remembered Vos. "The first smile I got, I will get more!"[2]

Later on, a member of the court told Vos that Cixi liked him very much. Vos repaid her confidence in him by concealing from her the "as is" portrait he was sketching and instead painting her as she would have appeared in her heyday thirties, the mother of the young Tongzhi emperor and bright-eyed student of every wayward twist of court politics. Significantly, considering how the shadows of her own towering but fading life were lengthening, Cixi's most oft-repeated request to Vos was "No shadows, no shadows!" And she kept her painter well-stocked with champagne. When Vos took his leave of her, Cixi, heavily coached by an English-speaking mandarin, managed to mumble smilingly, "Very good." That was more English than Der Ling ever got from her.[3]

Regardless of the time-warping magic of paint on canvas, and no matter her temporal powers, Cixi could not command that age and ill-health keep their distance from her. It is doubtful that she had ever completely recovered from the stroke she suffered while Der Ling was at court in 1904, and the fact that the emperor was in even poorer health meant that she had to carry part of his weight along with all of her own in the running of China. Guangxu's health, never very good, was becoming more and more a grave concern. In none of her published recollections does Der Ling refer to witnessing examples of Guangxu's debilitation, but it is clear from other sources that they were obvious. The fact that Der Ling was so often in Cixi's company, which naturally precluded that of the emperor, may explain why readers of her memoirs gain a picture of a sardonic but sad and pale-faced man, who was both old before his time and kept perpetually immature by the ineluctable presence of his imperial aunt. To Der Ling, Guangxu's enforced indolence seemed far worse than the effects of any physiological problems.

Some Western observers, like the ever acerbic George Morrison, had already heard in November 1908 that neither Cixi nor Guangxu were doing very well. "The Emperor is suffering from constipation and the Empress Dowager from diarrhea," noted Morrison in his diary. "Through the Empress dowager the Emperor even defecates vicariously."[4] The situation was hardly funny. Guangxu was not just the victim of the circumstances of being the empress dowager's choice for emperor after the death of her son Tongzhi, but was also the victim of a weak father and a neurotic mother (Cixi's sister), which must have made the transfer to the weird world of the Forbidden City look like a picnic compared to home. The primary irony of Cixi's selection of Guangxu was the fact that he would never be able to father children. According to the data compiled from the accounts of Chinese doctors, some of them schooled outside China, by the British doctor Douglas Gray, Guangxu suffered from

> a congenital condition in which there is absence of some part of the floor of the urethra. It is a surgical fact that in almost all these cases there is some degree of arrested development of the testicles and scrotum [which would affect his] ability to procreate. The local irritation caused by this is capable of setting up the spermatorrhea, or rather a false spermatorrhea in which there is a discharge of seminal like fluid, destitute of spermatozoa. The presence of this

complaint would serve to keep him in a more or less debilitated
condition — a lack of virility — all his life.

Dr. Gray went on to point out that if anything was responsible for the
death of so stricken a young man, it was his heavy court duties, worsened
by chronic malaise (to which Der Ling does attest, though ascribing it
to causes more emotional than physical, in which she was probably not
entirely in the wrong).[5]

George Morrison filed reports to the *Times* of London, or rather put
his name to "reports" concocted by Edmund Backhouse, purporting to
be privy to all manner of intimate court details about the emperor and
the Empress Dowager — shocking emotional outbursts on the part of
Cixi shortly before her death (all part of the spin making all her actions
agree with the reprehensible dragon-lady caricature), Guangxu drooping
about the palace in a fainting condition, suffering under the thumb of
his evil aunt, and so forth. What is known for certain is that Guangxu
became very ill in mid-October, and ominously did not perform the
Winter Sacrifices, which only he as emperor could carry out, scheduled
for later that month. He grew weaker. Several hours before his death, on
November 14, Guangxu is said to have received word from Cixi that she
had chosen his successor, Puyi, son of Prince Chun (whether this relieved
or grieved him it is hard to say, as the dowager's selection again broke the
regulations for succession). He is also said to have refused to be shrouded
in the robes customarily wrapped around a dying emperor, possibly again
because in a life of never having his way, this was his last chance to assert
himself.

In her biography of Cixi, Der Ling tells a curious story she had heard
about the illness and death of Guangxu. According to this account, the
chief eunuch Li Lianying found a diary of Guangxu's in which the emperor
frankly delighted in the idea of outliving the empress dowager and taking
revenge on his enemies — Yuan Shikai being chief among them. Li told
Cixi, who then gave him the subtle nod to "[take] charge of the ailing
monarch, of his diet and of his medicinal care. Shortly thereafter," she
wrote, "Kwang Hsu took to his bed," from which he never rose.[6] But we
know from the abundant medical evidence now available that Li would
not have had to work very hard to do Guangxu to death — nor is it clear

why this particular time, rather than during some other health crisis, was optimal for giving the emperor the *coup de grâce*. In fact, if anything contributed to the unease that was already attending the Empress Dowager at the news of her nephew's illness (she herself was ill with some malady which was believed by Dr. Gray to have been a flu bug going the rounds of Beijing at the time), it was the death of Guangxu; because now, as she had had to do in the case of Guangxu, she had again to choose an heir. And she must have known that, as before, nothing she did in the matter would make everyone, or anyone, happy.

In his busy collecting of data, Dr. Gray had heard an earful about the dowager's failing health in the last weeks of her life. At an audience at which the doctor had been present, Cixi presented the contradictory appearance of seeming to be well but looking considerably older than anyone who saw her thought normal. Cixi had shown in the past that appearances mattered almost more than life itself, and the effort it must have cost her to conceal her illness would have worn her down further. Just being empress dowager may have proved her undoing. In October 1908, Dr. Gray reports, influenza was felling people in Beijing, and it was his impression that Cixi had possibly been exposed to the virus from someone from outside the court. The supreme isolation of a woman in her position, for the better part of her life, would have rendered her immune system weaker than most. It was her seventy-third birthday that proved the final straw, or in her case, the final rich meal of the many Der Ling had seen her work her way through. On that day, wrote Dr. Gray, "[Cixi] ate more than usual and took some fruit which was over ripe. By the next day she was suffering from dysenteric symptoms, and the acute diarrhea with loss of blood very soon brought her into a debilitated state." It is quite possible that she contracted food poisoning; it is also possible she had a bleeding ulcer exacerbated by the meal.[7]

Her past serious illnesses (whether by causes natural or planned) proved that she took a long time getting her famous strength back. Cixi had just barely survived an attempt on her life some thirty years before, and despite her stamina of will and body was laid up for a year recovering. She was younger then, and had only endured some of the many blows life at the top of China's imperial heap had sent her way. Now she was too old, too sick, to rebound. The only thing keeping her going now was "her determination to keep her promise to order the succession of [Guangxu's] nephew Puyi. She could not leave such important things to ministers or to quarreling princes." She had never been able to leave anything to other people.

Many, even among her servants, disagreed with her choice. Der Ling claims to have met an elderly eunuch in Tianjin who was present at the hastily arranged coronation for the toddler. According to this eunuch, Puyi cried when placed into a miniature version of the coronation robes and resisted being seated on his throne. "The eunuchs felt that this coronation was not a real coronation," the aged servant told Der Ling, "but a ghastly jest . . . Many of the eunuchs were old — so old that they had witnessed the life of the Empress Dowager almost since the passing of Hsien Feng — and they knew that this coronation was wrong." Der Ling's informant added that "he knew this coronation was the last he would ever witness, that it was the last coronation of a Manchu . . . He knew, moreover, and cannot explain how he knew, that the days of Tzu Hsi, who still would rule because Puyi was but a child, were numbered."[8]

On November 15, an edict was issued from the palace, supposedly dictated by the infant Puyi but in reality proceeding from Prince Qing, which informed the foreign diplomats, all waiting for news with bated breath, of the death of Guangxu: "I have the honour to inform Your Excellency that on the 21st day of the 10th moon [November 14, 1908] at the yu-ké [5.17 p.m., Hour of the Rooster] the late Emperor ascended the dragon to be a guest on high. We have received the command of Tze-hsi etc., the Great Empress Dowager to enter on the succession as Emperor. We lamented to Earth and Heaven. We stretched out our hands, wailing our insufficiency."[9]

That insufficiency was to dog Puyi for the rest of his official life, as on-again off-again emperor of China and during his messy rulership, in name only, of the "empire" called Manchukuo. The process of the transfer of power, however, was remarkably clean-cut. "The world looked on in awe," wrote the Headlands, who knew all about the sort of chaos that could happen in China. "It expected a demonstration if not a revolution but nothing of the kind happened . . . China once more had upon her throne an emperor, though only a child, about whose succession there was no question. And all this was done with less commotion than is caused by the election of a mayor in New York or Chicago." Yet of stormy commotion there was indeed enough to topple the gnarled old pine that was the Empress Dowager. When she died in the afternoon of the day after the death of Guangxu, properly robed for her dragon ascent on high and with her face turned to the lucky south, a weeping little boy, almost a baby, was on the throne of a dynasty already in the twilight of its last few years.[10]

"The Tianjin eunuch was at her bedside when she passed," recalled Der Ling, "and from him I got a picture of a subdued chamber where few lights were, where words that were spoken were whispered, where candles flickered softly in such breezes as there were, where the wrinkled face of Her Majesty, calm now in the greater majesty of death, awaited the day when she would be carried forth to her last resting place in Hsi Ling." Following her death, Cixi, Great Empress Dowager for a day, was given the posthumous name celebrating that status, and her spirit tablet was set up in the Imperial Ancestral Hall, among the other Qing rulers.[11]

The morning of the funeral, scheduled for the auspicious hour of five o'clock, "the Empress' coffin, covered with a pall of dragon-embroidered yellow silk, left the Palace under a huge catafalque carried by eighty-four bearers, and moved solemnly toward the North-eastern gate of the Tartar City. The streets had all been strewn with yellow sand ... The procession was led by Prince Chun, the Imperial Princes, and all the members of the Grand Council and Grand Secretariat," backed up by the foreign diplomatic corps and Lamaist dignitaries. Prior to this procession, a 180-foot paper barge, staffed with oar-bearing paper attendants and floating on paper waves, was burned before the hall in which Cixi's remains lay in state, "the object being to provide the Empress Dowager in the next world with the means of gratifying that passion for boating which she had indulged so freely in this life." In addition to the boat, an army of paper cavalry and infantry, musicians, officials, and servants of various grades, was also sent up in flames.[12]

Writer Moore Bennet, in an article published in the *Illustrated London News* in 1928, after the looting of the Eastern Qing Tombs, described the items said to have been buried with Cixi as having been "tabulated at the time [of Cixi's death] by the notorious eunuch Li Lien-ying," as including a pearl-embroidered mattress some seven inches in thickness, covered with a cloth studded with more pearls, with the dowager's body lying on a cloth on which the image of the Buddha was worked in pearls. The body was decked in cloth of gold, with pearl ropes and loose pearls scattered scattered over it, and 108 small Buddhas made of all manner of precious materials lodged in beside. "On each of her feet were placed one watermelon and two sweet melons of jade, and 200 gems made in the shape of peaches, pears, apricots and dates," Bennet finished in mouthwatering detail.[13]

"There is something harrowing in the profanation of a sepulcher," wrote Daniele Varè, ten years after Cixi's coffin was split open, its pearls and jade scavenged, and her corpse left face down on the floor. "But when a tomb is supposed to contain untold wealth its desecration becomes inevitable, in a country impoverished and brutalized by civil wars." Poverty and wars for which, no matter the real story and the many hands that went into their making, Cixi alone would be, and still is, blamed.

"To others she may have been cruel," Der Ling admitted. "To me she was a kind old lady who needed understanding."[14]

29
On the defense

In *Two Years in the Forbidden City*, Der Ling is at her most business-like and unspeculative; the book reads in places like the dry entries in a daily appointment diary, in others with an eye-witness immediacy that conveys the comedy of Cixi's court as well as the minor teacup tempests and the mild infiltration of major political events outside the cocooned halls and courtyards of the Summer Palace and the Forbidden City. Intriguingly, in the book's several editions over a period of almost twenty years, the image it offered of Der Ling changed, too: the first edition, from 1911, features a frontispiece photograph of Der Ling in a brocade décolleté evening gown, upswept hair and tiara, a conventional image of a graceful seated woman who could belong to any particular ethnicity, and is clearly, as Der Ling was fond of pointing out, much more European than Asian. The 1924 edition, however, brought out a few years before Der Ling and T.C. moved to America, shows Der Ling dressed in a silk court robe decorated with all of Cixi's favorite images — chrysanthemums, birds and bamboo — with full headdress, fingernail protectors, and the spot of crimson on the lower lip proper for an imperial court lady. Another early edition featured a photo of Der Ling looking coyly into the camera from under a feathered hat, her hands buried in an astrakhan muff. It was as if the author were deliberately refusing to be categorized or stereotyped, changing her clothing and setting with each new edition, leaving her readers tantalized as they tried to guess who the real Princess Der Ling was.

The book would prove itself a divider where Der Ling's family was concerned. "Her family was very upset by her writings," noted Der Ling's niece, Lydia Dan. Dan adds that though Rong Ling always received Der Ling on her return visits to China, their brothers would not speak to her. "Their Manchu friends looked upon her behaviour as 'bad taste and cheap.' The feeling was that Der-ling lacked respect for her former mistress Empress-Dowager Tze-hsi by using the latter as a subject to entertain the *foreign devils*." And the books Der Ling wrote were no doubt not the only matter that cut her off from her family and Manchu society — her lectures and the accompanying brochures lavishly illustrated with photographs of Der Ling posing in Chinese court dress and other clothing, and her claims to belong to the Manchu dynasty, could only have done her harm in these conservatives' eyes. Der Ling would not have helped raise her stock with her disapproving relatives very much in the 1930s when she lent her name to a fortune-telling game produced and marketed in Hollywood. *Fu Lu Sho* [Happiness, Wealth, Longevity] *Forecasts Your Future* was a board game based on the temple oracle exercise of shaking sticks out of a cup, that Der Ling claimed dated back to the Five Kingdoms period (early to mid-tenth century CE). Boxed in imperial yellow with crimson lettering, the game was emblazoned with Der Ling's own signature (in English) with her Chinese seal and an explanation of the game's history. (Also interesting is T.C.'s description of his occupation in the 1930 Census as "marketing novelties," among which the *Fu Lu Sho* game must have figured to some degree.) The game itself was harmless, but Der Ling's endorsement of a piece of parlor entertainment that smacked of that lowest of commoner pastimes, fortune-telling, would not have sat well with either her relatives in China or many of her American society friends.[1]

Two Years' sympathetic image of Cixi — grandmotherly rather than raddled, cantankerous rather than dangerous, a woman who had feelings like other women — was hardly a sole cry in the tangled wilderness of anti-dowager propaganda. Katherine Carl's *With the Empress Dowager of China*, from 1905, the Headlands' *Court Life in China* and Sarah Pike Conger's *Letters from China*, from 1909, and Philip Sergeant's *The Great Empress Dowager of China*, from 1910, all presented a similar, even exaggeratedly positive, perspective on the ex-concubine who had ruled China for over forty years.

Unfortunately, the books that gave a negative picture of Cixi also echoed the image of her rampant in the popular press. Some of these authors committed to paper information not just mean-spirited but ignorant; and some writers had started the caricature, of both dowager and the nation she ruled, well before her death. Eliza Scidmore, for example, in her pre-Boxer Uprising travel-book *China: The Long Lived Empire*, sneers at Cixi's nation in general and at Cixi in particular, inaccurately naming her "Tsze Hsi An," an obvious confusion of the two empresses dowager that would remain a problem in the press for years to come (in its obituary for Cixi the *New York Times* published a photograph of neither co-empress but of one of the surviving concubines of the Tongzhi Emperor). Scidmore also gave a totally inaccurate physical description of Cixi.[2]

The most damaging book, however, was *China Under the Empress Dowager*, from 1910, for reasons that, under any other circumstances, should have made it a classic (and in some ways, despite all, has): its authors had both lived in China for years, knew many Chinese people close to the centers of powers, and read Chinese; and together, they crafted fluid prose of entertaining and detailed piquancy. In Edmund Backhouse's case, linguistic ability rose to the Everestian heights of genius, where the thin air does strange things to a scholar's mind. This genius was sufficiently impressive to give him a reputation for scholarship before he had earned it. J. O. P. Bland, whose name is listed first on the title page, was perceived by most as the co-writer who had both feet solidly on Chinese soil, with his long-time alliance with the *Times* and his own writings on China to lean on. Bland's trouble was that he took too much of Backhouse at face value, including the fantastically useful diary of the fantastically imaginary Ching-shan, whom Backhouse described as a comptroller of the imperial household and holder of that office during the Boxer Uprising in 1900, on whose account rests much of Cixi's evil reputation.

According to Backhouse, he had found this diary in Ching-shan's house, where he claimed he had been permitted to live by the Allies after they took control of Beijing on August 14, 1900. This Ching-shan, said Backhouse, died during the uprising, not at the hands of Boxers but of his son, a Boxer enthusiast. The diaries go into great detail on the matter. Ching-shan had confided to its pages candid criticism of the Empress Dowager Cixi, assigning her a fundamentally evil nature which had, after half a lifetime of leading China down the path of perdition, now moved her to turn the Boxers' hatred on the foreign legations like a rattling Gatling gun. Maddeningly for the fact-checkers but ideal for Backhouse, Ching-shan's son could not be contacted for confirmation of the details because, per Backhouse, he had been court-martialed and executed after the fall of Beijing to the Allies. Backhouse claimed that he had told Sir Ernest Satow, the foreign minister Der Ling had so admired in Tokyo, about his discovery and had been advised by him to hold tight to the diaries until Cixi was safely dead. In what must be one of the few instances of Backhouse actually doing what he was told, he concealed the diaries until they were unveiled in extract in his joint effort with Bland. (Satow, a smart man and one who had actually met the Empress Dowager, may also have sensed that the diaries were fakes and had the kindness to talk Backhouse into keeping them under wraps.)

What would not be known for years afterward was that very little of what Backhouse had to say or write about the Ching-shan diaries, Ching-shan's son, Sir Ernest Satow or much of anything else about the subject was capable of holding water. There is no mention in Satow's own detailed diaries of such a conversation with Backhouse. We know that Ching-shan was not a household comptroller but merely an assistant secretary, who died not in 1900 but in 1902, and no proof has ever been found that he had left such a diary as Backhouse claimed to have found.

Backhouse seems to have deliberately chosen to "reveal" his discovery when he did, after a decade of turmoil which had marred memories and destroyed papers — he would later claim he had had to sell off sections of the diary, in one case to a dealer who had subsequently fallen afoul of a knife (just how was never clarified), and so no longer had the originals. It was the sort of dust he was good at raising, and the timing meant that few could follow his meandering trails back to their source.

George Morrison was one of the early doubters that the Ching-shan diary was genuine; but the word of a non-Chinese speaking foreign journalist counted for little against that of the confirmation of linguists like the Dutch J. J. L. Duyvendak and of Reginald Johnston himself, who pronounced the diary authentic. In his 1938 biography of Cixi, Daniele Varè cast doubt on the diary, but added with equanimity that it was on deposit in the British Museum and those interested in testing the text's authenticity were free to examine it there.

China under the Empress Dowager did incalculable damage not just to Cixi's posthumous image, but has run tarnished yarn through the otherwise sound material of many biographies and other works about the dowager's reign, simply because those who used Bland and Backhouse's book and its sequel, *Annals and Memoirs of the Court of Peking*, did not know — or did not want to know — that said annals and memoirs were based on at least one major forgery, and probably many more, twisted together and made "substantive" with a few real facts. For example, the authors claimed that "Europeans . . . have usually emphasized and denounced [Cixi's] cold-blooded ferocity and homicidal rage." But beyond the pornographic screeds published against the dowager by the exiled Kang Youwei, no Westerner had promoted this portrait of Cixi until after Kang's version became common currency.[3]

What made this concoction believable was the way in which the authors seemed to defend the dowager against fantastical charges of corruption, greed, murder and sexual license, yet introduced hints along the way that if these were her true traits, well, who could blame a woman who had spent most of her life in the enervated, immoral atmosphere of the Manchu court — who, being female and Asian, was naturally lacking in the fortitude and judgment to steer clear of the Chinese court's ancient catalog of evils. Bland and Backhouse also made sure they inserted a clause roundly condemning accounts of the dowager written by "those Europeans (especially the ladies of the Diplomatic Body and their friends) who saw her personality and purposes reflected in the false light which beats upon the Dragon Throne on ceremonial occasions, or who came under the influence of the deliberate artifices and charm of manner which she assumed so well . . ."[4] This was a blow not against Der Ling, whose *Two Years in the Forbidden City* had yet to appear, but against the candid and often fascinating memoirs of women like Sarah Pike Conger, Kate Carl and Dr. Headland — ironically, in light of Backhouse's "Ching-shan" source, these women could at least produce their original documentation and prove that they had actually known Cixi and her court. It was after 1911, after the ousting of the Qing dynasty and the publication of Der Ling's book, that Der Ling would find herself added to the spotlight trained on her by Bland, Backhouse and others. These men had a vested interest in proving that their published version of Cixi and her court was the only reality anyone should know, and that Der Ling's recollections of Old Buddha, and Old Buddha herself, were rank fakes at best.

A year after the publication of Der Ling's first book in 1912, she gave birth to her only child, a son named Thaddeus Raymond who, thanks to his American-Chinese parentage, would be known as "the International Baby" in the U.S. press. By the entry of China a few years later, in 1917, into the effort of supporting the Allies in the First World War, the Whites had left Shanghai and were living in Beijing, where T.C. took a position with the American consulate. Though prepared to fight morally if not materially, China was only permitted to contribute workers rather than soldiers to the war effort, most of whom were sent to the French front to serve as coolie labor. This cheap method of getting supplies delivered and trenches dug would accomplish more than what the Allies had in mind, since many of the Chinese sent to France became acquainted with Socialist thought and Socialist thinkers, ideas which they brought back to China as fertilizer for the future Communist Party.

Like many of her American women friends in the city, Der Ling immediately signed up with the Beijing Red Cross, and was photographed posing on the front steps of the headquarters wearing her svelte white uniform, her waved hair pinned in a bun. She was also photographed, probably for publicity purposes, directing gaunt and puzzled looking Chinese men in the operation of a sock-weaving machine, which had been set up in the middle of a cluttered courtyard.[5]

"Life pressed around us in Peking," recalled Lady Hosie of the capital of those days, "[P]overty, patience, injustice, agony of heart, death, jostling intellectual debatings, old-fashioned courtesy and occasional new-fangled abruptness."[6] It was the same Beijing Der Ling had left years before, yet different characters inhabited the stage, and the dramas they acted out made the most implausible antics of Beijing opera's Monkey King seem reasonable by comparison. Yuan Shikai, after his brief flirtation with his Hongxian reign, the fitting remnants of which would be scads of fragile porcelain created (without the usual Chinese sense of superstition) to celebrate his reign's first year of glory, had died in early June 1916; and with his death all the porcelain, figurative and literal, would be shattered for the next ten years by warlords in the china shop. Out went his constitution, in favor of the instrument formed by the provisional government four years earlier, and in, too, came parliament. In Shanghai, Dr. Sun began to take up the reins of government again, despite the fact that much of his power was in his head and nowhere else. Provincial militarists began to pound their various tabletops, so that by a month after Yuan's death the government in Beijing had recast these men as *tuchun* (*dujun*) or semi-independent military governors, a move that was to do everything to fragment the nation just when it needed to pull together.

Though they parted company on the character of the Empress Dowager, one of the areas in which Der Ling and Kang Youwei shared full conviction was feminism, which with the changes sweeping over China was awakening young Chinese women to a fuller sense of their rights as citizens and human beings. Throughout the 1920s, the feminist movement which had begun to gain concessions and rights in other nations was just beginning to kick up its heels in China, where it girded itself in the characteristically Chinese armor of outspoken literature. "Love, marriage, sexual relations, and the emotional states these engendered, all explored from the woman's point of view, for a substantial part of women's writings from the 1920's," writes Yi-tsi Feuerwerker, "in proclaiming their right to love freely, even their right to suffer for love, they were repudiating the traditional treatment of women as depersonalized objects, whether contemplated with desire or with a combination of fascination and horror . . ."[7]

While writers like Ding Ling, Ping Hsin (Bing Xin) and Su Hsüeh-lin (Su Xuelin) explored depths of personal pleasure and torment quite foreign to Der Ling's literary and family experience, including the whole gamut of suffering related to arranged marriage, threats of imprisonment, poverty and banishment from their family homes, Der Ling and these "new" women shared one very important trait: "In the works of their youth they wrote to keep up with their own lives; they wrote, over and over again the story of their own lives."[8]

It is against this ferment of feminism that Der Ling's pretty, perfect sister Rong Ling proved unable to climb those hard hills that kept most Asian women mere vessels of motherhood and social ornament. We do not know as much about this sister who was always considered prettier, more graceful and more ladylike than Der Ling, but we have a glimpse of her in her chosen domestic setting courtesy of a Chinese woman writer who was to become famous for her radical beliefs. Han Suyin had an opportunity of meeting Rong Ling, now Madame Dan Paochao, whose daughter Suchen (also known as Lydia Dan) she had befriended at school, and left a detailed recollection of her first visit to the Dan household. The child of a marriage that brought East and West together in an unhappy union, the half-Chinese, half-Belgian Han Suyin sympathized with people who had to dwell between two often disparate worlds. Suchen was definitely one of these. Both girls attended Chinese and European schools, but Suchen was brought up in a style as foreign to Han Suyin as the etiquette of the Forbidden City. Dan Suchen was taught at home by five tutors — one for flute, a pair for the Chinese classics, another one for poetry and the art of calligraphy, and one for German language and mathematics. Suchen was multilingual, having learned English and French. What made her brilliance poignant was the fact that she was a cripple, a victim of polio, with a twisted hip and one leg shorter than the other. One of her shoes was a kind of boot with a high instep, which helped her just approximate a balanced mode of walking. None of this had made the girl bitter or despondent, but charming, witty and bright.

"She spoke the most wonderful Peking Chinese," remembered Han Suyin. This, too, she would have heard in her home which, however, was not a particularly happy place for a girl like her. "Suchen wanted to be a politician and a revolutionary," Han Suyin recalled. "If it had not been for her leg and for her mother the princess, she probably would have become famous."

Madame Dan was almost frighteningly perfect, according to Han Suyin's recollections.[9] But that was fitting, considering she had been lady-in-waiting to the old Empress Dowager, and now lived in surroundings that harked back to that splendor she had known at the Summer Palace so many years ago. The Dan palace was a museum of Ming porcelains, jade and agate and crystal snuff-bottles, brush-stands, lacquered furniture and thick carpets, all washed over by the scent of incense and nasturtium. Not that Rong Ling had always held to traditional srurroundings or dress. When American travel writer Grace Thompson Seton met Madame Dan while the latter was serving as Mistress of Ceremonies for the wife of the Chinese president Li Yuanhung (Li Yuanhong), she remembered being introduced to Der Ling's sister in a room "where Chinese pictures, embroideries and tapestries were conspicuously absent," Rong Ling being dressed in a sleek white satin gown. But with her Chinese marriage Rong Ling had become more comfortable in, or resigned to, Chinese robes and a traditional Chinese way of life.

Suchen had a library to gorge on, as well as such modern conveniences as a camera and a phonograph machine, but much about the Dan palace threw the visitor back to an earlier era, when servants scurried silently and one did not bound up to the mother of one's best friend but came to her in stages, via a succession of beautiful apartments. This was how Han Suyin came to meet Der Ling's sister. When Han Suyin first saw Rong Ling, the latter was sitting on a sofa of contemporary make, and after bidding the girls sit with a gesture, she wordlessly picked up a flute and began to play it. "Princess Dan was lovely, a delicate oval face like a melon seed," Han Suyin remembered. She had a small, thin nose with the "Manchu hook" in it, and swooping black brows. Rong Ling also made herself up in the Manchu fashion, with pink and white powder, but she had used her rouge discreetly.

When Han Suyin had her mouth full of cake, Rong Ling turned to her and said, "My daughter tells me that you are intelligent." Han Suyin could only nod, further embarrassing herself; but she found her voice when Rong Ling asked her what she planned to do after she finished school. "I want to be a boy," announced Han Suyin. Rong Ling's mask of pink and white powder broke into laughter; it was as if she were both surprised and thrilled to discuss a subject forbidden to her. Most women *did* want to be men, she agreed. She herself, she added, had wanted to be a man. This admission helped humanize Rong Ling for Han Suyin, as did another revelation. Suchen told her one day that she was not Madame Dan's daughter at all, but adopted by her and her husband out of a peasant family, with hopes that by virtue of the same process that turned Eliza Doolittle into a lady the Dans could have a daughter who would be eligible for marriage into the highest Manchu nobility. Suchen had become ill, and then lame, and her mother turned against her. Hints of beatings, of being forced to kneel in courtyards with a heavy stone on her back, infiltrated the girls' conversations. Few who revered Dan Rong Ling as the introducer to China of modern European dance techniques, sanctified by her training under Isadora Duncan, would have believed this side to her gracious personality. But then who, seeing Rong Ling waltzing in Paris and daringly wearing men's breeches at Carneval, would have believed her capable of becoming so severe and uncompromising a Chinese housewife?[10]

30
Scheherazade of the Hotel Wagons-Lits

Der Ling, in the meantime, was doing very different things with her life — most of them unacceptable to the women of Rong Ling's circle. While Rong Ling was playing the part of decorative general's wife in her red-columned palace, Der Ling was taking on a more active role in Beijing society — not her sister's high society milieu but in the company of foreigners, European and American, who had come to Beijing to see the sights and have a good time. For this, most Pekingese native and foreign-born congregated at the Hotel des Wagons-Lits, Der Ling's home until she moved to America.

Writer Fei Shi, in his 1924 book on Beijing, commented that "Any visitor to Peking who loses his way should say to a ricksha coolie 'Liu Kwo Fan Tien,' whereupon he will take him at once to the centre of Legation Quarter, in other words to the Hotel des Wagons-Lits." The hotel's Chinese name meant "The Hotel of the Six Nations," and such the Wagons-Lits was, being "a meeting place of Princes of the Blood and of the highest mandarins of the Empire." The Grand Hotel de Pékin, lavishly monikered "The Ritz of the Far East," was newer and fancier than the Wagons-Lits, but the latter had the cachet of being the "only

Hotel inside Legation Quarter and in the Centre of Legation Street, since early days the "Rendez-Vous of Diplomats, of Hommes de Lettres, the Military, Concessioneers, Business-Men, Globe-Trotters, Tourists, etc.," as a Wagons-Lits advertisement from the 1920s blaringly described it.[1]

American writer Ellen LaMotte, freshly arrived in Beijing around the time Der Ling first lived there, stayed at the Wagons-Lits, which she claimed was called by local marines the "Wagon-Slits." "It is the most interesting hotel in the world, too," she wrote,

> where all the nations of the world meet, rub elbows, consult together, and plan to "do" one another and China, too. It is entertaining to sit in the dark, shabby lounge and watch the passers-by, or to dine in the big, shabby, gilded dining room, and see the various types gathered there, talking together over big events, or over little events that have big consequences.

In the lounge it was possible to see, all at one time, British advisors to the Chinese government, marching portentously to and fro among the palm fronds, "concession-hunters and businessmen," from the small fry adventurers out to make a quick buck to "representatives of great commercial and banking firms from all over the world," antiques buyers from Europe and ministers wandering in from the nearby foreign legations, along with tired and sallow tourists.[2]

LaMotte also saw in the lounge a most unusual woman, "a so-called princess, a Chinese lady, very modern, very chic, very European as to clothes, who was formerly one of the ladies-in-waiting to the old empress dowager . . . Next to her sits a young Chinese gentleman, said to be a grandson of one of the old prime ministers, a slim, dapper youth, spectacled and intelligent." LaMotte must have done more than give Der Ling a glance in the rich gloom of the lounge, as she remarked on how intimately connected the two seemed to be. Newcomers like herself found this display unusual, she pointed out, but not the old hands in the lounge: they had seen it all before. Given the fact that Der Ling was the wife of a consular official and mother of a seven-year-old boy, LaMotte's remark says more about Beijing gossip, which had always cast Yu Keng's daughter in a jaundiced light, than it does about Der Ling's private life — Der Ling would later hint that people who saw her with her teenaged son, Thaddeus

Raymond, would tattle similar opinions about her relations with young men, not realizing that the young man in question was her own boy.[3]

Living at the Wagons-Lits, which was around the corner from T.C.'s office at the American embassy, probably served as the most secure place to live in the turmoil caused by the warlords. It seems to have only added to Der Ling's sense of herself as being above the fray. American Mrs. Gertrude Bass Warner, who later left her collection of Manchu antiques and textiles to the University of Oregon, was staying at the Wagons-Lits and knew Der Ling at this time. Both were on their way to an errand outside the walls of the Imperial City in November 1924 when missionary Dr. John Calvin Ferguson (also an art collector) warned both women to stay at the hotel. General Feng Yuxiang, called "the Christian general" after his conversion to Methodism in 1914, had taken the city. There was no railroad or telegraph service, and Beijing had already been sectioned off, each section guarded by troops. No one was allowed to leave the city. Mrs. Warner was intent on retrieving a court robe she had left with a tailor outside the wall (foreigners often had robes and jackets of court officials retailored to Western styles), but obeyed Dr. Ferguson's advice. Der Ling, however, could not be held back. "Mrs. White felt that she, as a Manchu princess, would go where she liked." None of this washed with the guards a block away; they stopped her car and made her turn back.[4]

While at the Wagons-Lits, Der Ling seems to have taken this opportunity to exploit her fame, and assure her notoriety, as former court lady by arranging for lectures in the hotel, in which she told stories of her life at court, supplementing her published account with greater detail and, we may assume, racier topics than were permitted in most mainstream books of the day. The motley crowd in the lobby and lounge of the Wagons-Lits described by Ellen LaMotte would have been a tailor-made audience: mostly foreign, mostly from out of town, mostly ignorant of China under the Manchus and mostly curious not only about what that nation had been like before 1912 but curious, too, about what was going on in it at the present time, when the winds of political change swept through the old Chinese capital city with greater force than the gales from north of the Great Wall. And, of course, eager to hear all about it from a genuine "Manchu princess."

Citing one of the reasons why serious historians of Manchu China did not take Der Ling's writings seriously, historian Wu Hsiang-hsiang asserted that Der Ling gave her lectures and told her stories at the hotel to make a living, and in the words of one commentator "there were obvious gaps to fill in her knowledge and memory of imperial affairs and personalities; artistic and literary license came in handy." Reticence to take Der Ling's recollections seriously had less to do with the usual shadow of doubt that lies over any work of subjective memory and interpretation, but "because of their mixed bag of contemporary gossip and fabrications."[5] Considering how well Der Ling's first book had done financially (by the late 1920s it had gone through several editions), and the fact that she had a gainfully employed husband, it is unlikely she needed to make a living telling stories at the Wagons-Lits. But this in itself shows the trend of gossip about her: Manchus impoverished by the fall of the dynasty and unfit for any other employment, thanks to the defunct dynasty's restrictions on bannerman commercial activity, frequently told stories about the *ancien régime* in the streets of Beijing for paying customers. Given the rumours that circulated, it was easy enough to paint Der Ling with the same brush as was used on these street entertainers. That this gossip was known to her is shown in her angry reactions on the few occasions when some unthinking American hostess chanced to use "entertainer" in tandem with her name.

Another reason for the scholars' chary treatment of Der Ling's account of life within the Forbidden City and the Summer Palace may have been rumors that the tours she conducted through these places, which after Yuan Shikai's death and the beginning of the warlord period were open to the paying public, were another money-making scheme for her. There is no evidence of this, either in Der Ling's own published account of such a tour, in her 1932 fantasy satire of Beijing society, *Jades and Dragons*, or in the account left by writer Arthur Burks, a friend of Der Ling's who was taken through the palace complex by her in the late 1920s. That does not mean the rumour was not in some part true. In the preface to Der Ling's biography of Cixi, *Old Buddha*, Burks wrote,

> I close my eyes, and my fancy goes back to an unforgettable
> afternoon when, with Princess Der Ling and a small party of

friends, I paid a visit to the Summer Palace, toward the Western Hills.

Every building in the Summer Palace, every courtyard, every winding pathway, every cobblestone, almost, had a story to tell the Princess, and each of the stories she told me. For me she peopled the Summer Palace with living, breathing human beings, instead of ghosts without substance or shadow.

Der Ling also told him of the times she had wandered out to the Long Gallery and wept by herself, lonely for her father and for the life she had had before being subsumed again in a China that was, for her, far more foreign than Paris. Der Ling's evocation of that loneliness was so vivid that at the Beijing banquet held later, after the tour, in Der Ling's honor, Burks could not enjoy his food. "I was thinking . . . of the little lady-in-waiting, who had sat in the shadows under the famous Colonnade, and wept because she was lonely!"[6]

Der Ling had very little to weep over when taking like-minded friends like Burks through the settings of her happy past. Based on her description of an outing she arranged for her friend's friends, however, it is hard to imagine that the small fees she might have received for leading such tours would have counterbalanced the challenge of tolerating the sort of ignorant and rude tourists these friends proved to be. "I Take Some Tourists Through the Forbidden City and the Summer Palace," from *Jades and Dragons*, is a little masterpiece of farce, tinged with the anger of a Chinese woman who has been taken at face value by foreigners, an anger which would characterize most of Der Ling's writings after her move to America.

"One day," she began, "a friend of mine had friends coming out from the 'Old Country,' whom she wished fittingly to entertain. Since I was equally at home among foreigners, Chinese and Manchus, it was not unusual for my foreign friends to call upon me to assist in such cases." But nothing prepared Der Ling for the numbers of tourists she would be leading through the palaces. "There were twenty odd cars of us, not including my own two cars," she recalled. In her own car she took an elderly colonel, his wife and their unmarried daughter. The daughter fancied herself an expert on China, and frankly "marveled at my English, the fact that my feet were not bound, my knowledge of foreign customs, my clothes . . . [She] asked . . . if I could eat with anything besides chopsticks." As they drove over the road which Der Ling had traversed in Cixi's imperial crimson sedan chairs, the old colonel proved almost as annoying as his daughter. Because Der Ling wore a green dress, he asked her what she knew about St. Patrick's Day, then insisted on lecturing her in all aspects of of the holiday's customs, like a pushy missionary dispensing Christian homilies to ignorant natives.

Arrival at the Summer Palace fully opened the Pandora's box of tourist mayhem. One woman wrongly insisted on calling the gate lions "dogs," while another, spying Peony Hill, loudly announced to the other tourists that Cixi used to send her eunuchs to Beijing to sell the flowers for her in the public markets. In an effort to escape this, Der Ling took the crowd through the courtyards she herself had entered for the first time some twenty years before, pausing before the two-story building near the Lodge of the Propriety of Weeding where she, her sister and mother had lived when at court. "I used to live in this house," she began, only to be interrupted by a young woman who pointed out that as the building was clearly the office of the palace commandant, Der Ling's memory must have failed her. As they moved on, a woman crept up beside Der Ling and said, "pleasantly," that among all the Chinese servants she had at home, there was none who resembled Der Ling. Drily, Der Ling assured her, "[They] must be far better looking."

Der Ling had now guided her charges into the courtyard before the Hall of Benevolence and Longevity, the dowager's favorite residence at the Summer Palace, their camera shutters snapping in the echoing spaces. Then she noticed that two of the younger tourists, a boy and girl, began to take full advantage of having the courtyard to themselves: he jumped on the back of a bronze phoenix, where he was photographed in a Tom Mix pose, while the girl stood in the Empress Dowager's doorway flapping a French tricolor. The young woman who had protested that Der Ling had forgotten where she had lived at the palace now posed in the courtyard with a friend, who pulled her blonde braid straight over her head while another girl held an unfurled parasol, sword-like, over the grinning condemned's bared neck. The scene made Der Ling wonder just what kind of corporal punishments might have been meted out had Old Buddha walked around the corner and caught them.

She was hard put, remembering her happy days spent in this same courtyard, "not to compare the glorious past with the inglorious present." But worse was to come. After taking the same group through the Forbidden City, Der Ling was approached by a woman with a $5 bill, which she proffered as cumsha. "We can all go home and tell people we've been taken through the Forbidden City and the Summer Palace by a real Chinese Princess!" the woman cooed.[7]

Stupid, racist, bed-hopping foreigners were not the only constituency that Der Ling took on in her *mémoir à clef* — plenty of Chinese and Manchus were skewered on her sharp pen. When the "Christian General" Feng Yuxiang first swooped down on Beijing in 1919, Der Ling was staying in the Wagons-Lits and saw both terrified Chinese and foreigners come rushing the doors of the hotel, bearing wives, concubines, assorted children, and household furnishings. The queue of refugees reached from the clerk's desk all the way down and around to Hatamen Street almost a mile away. With each successive wave of frightened guests, she says, the hotel charged higher rates.

One of the more prominent personages who came flying through the doors of the Wagons-Lits was a new official in the government whose clarion call was "China for the Chinese," and ousting the "autocrat foreigners," yet who sought to protect himself from harm by flying the U.S. flag on his new American car, and consoling himself with American appliances and furniture ordered from Sears Roebuck and Company. But another, whom she names "William Kong," is clearly Wellington Koo, the foreign minister and future foreign ambassador. Another proponent of "China for the Chinese," Koo, claimed Der Ling, also had no qualms about hiding from the Christian General's depredations by purchasing a safe house in Shanghai, conveniently (and only with lots of arguing with the property owner) located within the protected foreign concessions, literally leaving "China for the Chinese" — a sticky subject that would have gained Der Ling no friends within the Republican government, and may explain why she did not publish her thoughts on same until moving to New York in the late 1920s.

Der Ling took on Manchu high society and its mores, or what passed for same in those post-1911 days of penniless princes and crumbling mansions, on the skeletons of which she claimed much in the way of inside knowledge. She also attacked Chinese male chauvinism. Der Ling was infuriated by rules and regulations that kept talented Chinese women locked away, all in the name of virtue. "I'm terribly sick of hearing about Chinese virtue," Der Ling begins one chapter. "I never liked it, and have been told many times that a foreign education had spoiled me." One Chinese scholar, educated in the classics, accosted her with the worst epithet he could summon: "you are just like a foreign flapper!" She greeted a dozen men she did not even know, behavior that should earn a horsewhipping from her outraged husband! Chinese women were virtuous, Der Ling insisted, because they knew no other way to be, and dared never reveal any questions on the subject; "but if, in some dread delirium, she should suddenly break into speech, and tell the exact truth without fear or favor," Der Ling noted, "I'll wager that the code of Chinese virtue would have to be pretty thoroughly revised . . ."[8] As a consequence of this, Der Ling would tell an American reporter a few years later, "Chinese men are good husbands because their wives force them to be."[9]

In 1929, she would write of these young Chinese women breaking free of the restraints imposed on their mothers, grandmothers and for generations into the mists of time: "Feminine China is in explosive revolt today, and the high-heeled slipper is the symbol of that revolution." The woman who had been a free-wheeling Parisian debutante, only to return to China again and step back centuries, speaks for herself as much as for the next generation: "In youth, I was considered in China a wild harum-scarum radical . . . If the Chinese women 'go Hollywood' for a time, well and good. They'll get over it, and what's more, they'll undoubtedly benefit from the experience."[10]

Old-fashioned Chinese notions of social class were also caught in Der Ling's sights. Perhaps her own parents' equivocal position in society, noted by Sir Robert Hart years earlier, and her father's unpopularity among not just conservative Chinese but his own Manchu social milieu, inspired Der Ling to question the social segregations that went into the makeup of Chinese and Manchu society; clearly, her own marriage to an American and the controversy over her modern ways formed part of her mindset as well. But what obviously frustrated her as much as the everyday prejudices based on class and ethnic origins was the dubious place set aside in Chinese society for the creative artist — even if she still had some prejudices of her own toward "entertainers."

She became involved in planning a charity bazaar in Beijing to benefit Chinese famine victims. "Americans, Britons, Germans and Chinese were all enthusiastic, save as regarded the actual work connected with the affair," she added. She noted that it was the women of the foreign legations who actually got the work done.[11] The big draw for the event was the Beijing Opera star, Mei Lanfang, whom Der Ling pseudonyms as "Mr. Blue Plum." Already considered one of China's greatest actors, Mei offered his services free of charge, an altruism he was to show on many future occasions down the years. Nine years Der Ling's junior, Mei was the son and grandson of renowned opera actors, and began his studies early, debuting at age twelve. His grandfather was famous for playing the roles of empresses and grand courtesans, and Mei followed in his steps, gaining fame in China and abroad for his female impersonations and the great depth he brought to roles well known and those he had rediscovered in forgotten operas. He played the whole variety of female characters with endless subtle shades of color, so that in later years, when women were allowed to take the stage, they came to Mei for coachings.

Fame did not bring Mei as much respect off stage as on it. "An occasional remarkably gifted player attached to a permanent theatre in Peking or Canton — and who makes a great deal of money — may end by receiving a degree of deference but he is the rara avis of his profession," wrote one commentator of the 1920s. Because women were forbidden to act on stage, men took female roles; and while many actors, like Mei, became celebrated for their work, gossip intimated that these men could be had for homosexual sex, and were in any case of not very high morals if they could appear on the stage in the first place. Time would show that Mei's morals were very high indeed (during the Japanese occupation of China in the late 1930s to the early 1940s, he grew a mustache so he would not have to perform his famous roles for the Japanese commanders.) "The Chinese say of Mei Lan-fang that not only is he unusually gifted, but that he is a student, pleasing of voice and face, careful of his civilian position, and unwilling to play an immoral role," noted the commentator quoted above, "and that by force of these qualities he is influencing the general public to regard the actor with less disfavour."[12] But in Beijing society of the 1920s he was an outcast.[13]

Der Ling first encountered trouble with her Chinese society friends when she offered to sell boxes at the event, at $100 apiece. Der Ling well knew that most of the people she approached were able to give far more than the amount she was asking, and they knew she knew it, but each had his reasons for why now was not the time to spend money, even on charity. Eventually she sold some boxes to a few government officials she knew, who may have bought them as much for the public relations angle as to save the starving country folk. Der Ling chastises herself for accommodating her highly-placed friends by not associating openly with Mei. "It is probable," she quipped later, "that Blue Plum did not feel he was being especially injured in that none of the aristocrats spoke to him, even through their servants — for they would probably have tried to borrow money from him if they had!"[14]

In the end, Der Ling tells us, Mei's free performance was the success of the event, and one of the American women present was so impressed by him that she scheduled a banquet in his honor. Having set the date, the lady began contacting all the Chinese officials to whom Der Ling had sold boxes for the bazaar, only to receive regrets from every one of them. The only guests who attended her dinner party were foreigners — even Der Ling had to turn her down. One of the officials who thought himself above consorting with Mei Lanfang at a dinner table had not been above paying for his box with bills from the Bank of China, which had a value of only sixty cents on the dollar, the balance of which Der Ling had to make up for out of her own funds, and for which she was never redressed by the said official. Another official paid for his box properly, but then sold places in it to a number of friends, enough to reimburse himself for the amount he had laid out for charitable purposes. Another aristocratic family watched three of Mei's performance before deciding they were displeased and demanding their money back.

In the meantime, wrote Der Ling, "Had it not been for Mr. Blue Plum . . . the carnival would have closed with liabilities far in excess of their assets."[15] She might have added that in siding with her friends and not speaking to Mei she was showing her own ambivalence not just toward him but not living up to her oft-repeated insistence that she was a foreigner at heart and far more comfortable with Western customs than Asian. In at least once piece of correspondence, a letter from the early 1930s canceling an engagement to speak to the Los Angeles Business Professional Women's Club, Der Ling herself haughtily pointed out to her hapless recipient that to describe her as an "entertainer" in the booking agreement was the worst possible insult. People of her class in China were disgraced forever, she added, just for speaking to entertainers in the public streets. This is so curiously out of character for a woman who prided herself on her European attitude to the mores of old China that there must be some deeper reason for it. Perhaps, in her heart of hearts, Der Ling could see that there was a great difference between the artistry of Mei Lanfang's performance of "The Drunken Concubine" and her own heavily publicized self, costumed as a Manchu princess and posing as the ultimate insider at the ultimate of royal courts, a sort of female Figaro to the Empress Dowager Cixi — may have seen, indeed, that if either was truly an "entertainer," and less in touch with who they really were under costume and makeup, it was not Mei but Der Ling.[15]

31
"...she means to educate Americans..."

No doubt the parlous state of political affairs in late 1920s China, in which a nation already fragmented by impending civil war had to also watch the back door lest the Japanese stream suddenly in (something the battles between Communists and Nationalists eventually allowed to happen), a well as her burgeoning career as writer and public speaker, had a certain bearing on Der Ling's decision to explore the comparative security of the United States.

Mid-decade, the Kuomintang Nationalists in southern China, led by Chiang Kai-shek, began to make their move on the northern warlords, assisted by planners from the Soviet Union. The latter were allowed to get comfortable in their new Chinese bed, only to be turned out of it again when, in 1926 and 1927, Chiang brought down thirty-four warlords and then pulled the rug out from under the Communists, Russian and Chinese, charging them with plotting against him and arresting those organizers and leaders who were unable to flee into the countryside. Capturing provinces and cities like Wuhan, Shanghai and Nanjing, Chiang set up Nationalist headquarters in the latter city and himself was set up as Nationalist Chairman, an office he held, in various strengths and permutations, until his death in Taipei, Republic of China, in 1975, having ultimately lost China to the Communists in 1949. After leaving China in 1928, Der Ling would only return for brief visits, to gather materials for her writing and to gather up her belongings to ship out of the country when it became clear that Chiang's obsession with Mao Zedong and the Communists was leaving the door open to a Japanese takeover.

New York would be the initial stop for Der Ling, T.C. and their son (who had already been there, at age four, in 1917, and told his mother that he liked the city very much "because it had such nice big holes [subway entrances] in the ground"). But one of the first times Der Ling appeared in the American press was in a February 9, 1928 *Los Angeles Times* article, describing a "delayed Chinese New Year's" banquet given in her and T.C.'s honor in Los Angeles; and it was T.C. who was quoted, not his wife. "For many years," he announced to the party, consisting of guests both Asian and American (including Julius Mittwer, credited with having introduced the films of Charlie Chaplin to the young emperor of Japan; Der Ling was seen conversing with Mittwer in Japanese), "Americans and Europeans have been presuming to educate China. Now the Princess intends to turn the tables — she means to educate Americans."[1]

Part of this education process, according to the article, would take the form of a grandiose architectural project, designed by the Chinese architect S. S. Kwan: building a reproduction of the Forbidden City, on land outside Los Angeles (property that may have formed part of T.C.'s mining claims on the outskirts of the city), which would "contain art exhibits, a theater and other attractions." This replica of the Chinese Winter Palace, the original of which had now been a museum for several years, would serve as a kind of Chinese cultural center. While this stands as the first and last mention of the proposed center — presumably quashed by the Great Depression a year and a half later — Der Ling's idea was an intriguing concept, several years before the official formation of L.A.'s Chinatown and very much before the idea of a center celebrating Chinese culture seemed plausible anywhere in California, where there were still laws on the books preventing Chinese ownership of land.[2]

America's early history vis-à-vis the Chinese was one fraught with racist abuse. A century before Der Ling's Forbidden City idea, the first recorded Chinese woman in America, Afong Moy, was displayed like a circus freak in New York City museums, as spectators oohed and aahed over her wielding of chopsticks and her tottering about on bound feet, against the backdrop of an "authentic" Chinese diorama.[3] But nowhere did the maltreatment and racism take so virulent a form as in California; and to no other state, known to the native Chinese as "Gold Mountain," did so many Chinese risk everything to go to seek their fortunes, starting with, for many of them, their recruitment — and abduction — in port cities like Guangzhou by a Chinese underworld that trafficked in human flesh as much as native slave traders had done in Africa. Exploitation was something that did not just take place on American soil (and continues to take place courtesy of "snakehead" smugglers), but it certainly continued once a Chinese immigrant, having evaded the crimps in Guangzhou, Hong Kong or Macao, stepped off the steamer after several weeks of exhausting travel to cross the Pacific Ocean and touched the shores of "Gold Mountain."

In the decade after the discovery of gold in California in 1848, the majority of Chinese living and working there were engaged in mining, working harder than many whites who held more profitable claims. They came to the towns that sprouted overnight in the golden foothills and valleys, mining for gold, building the rock fences that can still be seen crisscrossing the spare lowlands of the Sierras or, when the Chinese populations in these places grew sufficient to support specialized commerce, setting up markets and stores where both Asians and Caucasians could purchase necessities, whether bolts of calico or a handful of ginseng root. Many of these town Chinese became servants and laundrymen to white families; few gold-rush town newspapers in the mid- to late nineteenth century refrained from sometimes overtly racist commentary on the local "Celestials," as the Chinese were called. It is no surprise that after some of the fires that raged through these mostly wood-frame municipalities, a tipped joss-stick of some heathen "Celestial" was often fingered as the cause.

As early as 1852, the California legislature levied heavy taxes on the cheap "coolie" labor provided by Chinese, who were blamed for taking jobs from whites in the mines and elsewhere and meant to serve as a disincentive to Chinese immigration. One San Francisco daily joined the growing racist chorus throughout the state by describing the Chinese as "a morally far worse class to have among us than the Negro," citing non-Christian religious practices as proof positive of moral and racial degradation.[4] In antebellum California, the buying and selling of Chinese women was conveniently overlooked,[5] while in 1875 a "doctor" published a study purporting to prove that Chinese immigration and concomitant prostitution had fueled a syphilis outbreak in the United States, threatening the health and welfare of clean-living whites. Two years later, a riot broke out in San Francisco, in protest against both Chinese and the shipping companies that brought them to U.S. shores; and in 1882, the Chinese Exclusion Act was signed into law by President Chester R. Arthur, who despite his misgivings bowed to overwhelming pressure. The Act barred Chinese laborers from immigrating to the United States for ten years after its signing into law, and meanwhile did nothing good for the Chinese already in the country: there were outbreaks of violence against Chinese, both in urban and rural areas, in the years after the Act went into effect. Twenty-three years later, another roadblock was put in place when the Supreme Court ruled against the plaintiff in the 1905 case, United States v. Ju Toy, the outcome of which determined that even Chinese who claimed American citizenship were forbidden to take to any American court their protests at being denied entry to the country.[6]

The image Der Ling presented to Americans on her arrival in their country matched her reputation as a "harum-scarum radical" in China, but it also struck even sophisticated people with a strange sense of vertigo. Looking at this Asian woman who clearly had some Caucasian blood in her veins, with her marcelled short-cropped hair and the men's suits and ties she sometimes favored, people with rigid ideas of what an Asian and a woman was supposed to be, found themselves unable to pin Der Ling down. In the lavish brochure printed for Der Ling's Chautauqua lectures around this time, she is shown wearing a sumptuous sampling of the gowns, headdresses, jewels and court clogs given to her by Cixi, but on the page describing her three hefty lecture topics — "The Modern Woman of China," "At the Manchu Court" and "Chinese Politics of Today" — Der Ling is shown as she appeared most of the time in the new Republic, garbed in jodhpurs and high boots, riding-crop in hand, for camel rides to the Great Wall and the Ming Tombs, or draped in bright Chanelesque silks on the beach at Qingdao or guiding foreigners through the courtyards of the Summer Palace. This is a woman one can expect to find just about everywhere, and fitting right in.

Now, almost a century after Afong Moy was stared at in her *chinoiserie* diorama in New York, another curiosity-provoking Chinese woman had arrived who was more American than anyone expected, who even "uses American slang," as one reporter noted, "which she considers a whole language of its own." Der Ling told a New York reporter that her plan on reaching America was "to write books, to be near her American husband, and to rear her half-American son as a 'genuine little roughneck,'" who insisted he wanted to be a bell-boy, like the ones he had seen and admired in New York City, when he grew up.[7]

From the start, Der Ling was a puzzle. Was she Eastern, or Western? Was she a princess of an ancient imperial court or a slang-using modern woman? A flapper or the mother of a 17-year-old son? Her arrival in the U.S. was her best opportunity to tell the same reporters dogging her about her days as Manchu court lady that she was in fact one-quarter American herself; why she let the chance pass remains a mystery. (Her sister Rong Ling freely told American writer Grace Thompson Seton in the early 1920s that she was the "daughter of an American woman, a Miss Louise Pearson [*sic*], of Boston.") Yet without hesitation she could allow herself to be photographed in a manner the complete reverse of that expected of the high-born Manchu princess she claimed to be: slouching nonchalantly in one of Cixi's imperial chairs, wearing her dragon-covered court robe like a Maggie Rouf cocktail gown, holding a Chinese book but grinning over its gravely aligned characters like a friendly Western woman poking her head through a painted scene at a carnival. "Look at me!" she seems to say in a photograph she later gave to her Berkeley hairdresser. "Don't I look just like the Empress of China?"

This strange yet familiar mystique surrounded Der Ling soon after she touched down in the United States, and never really went away, in part because she seemed to prefer it that way, even deriving perverse amusement from the discomfiture of a New York saleswoman who presumed an Asian would have few ideas about how to wear Western clothing or know what she wanted. "You certainly know something about clothing," the woman told her as she wrapped up the knee-length sport suit Der Ling had purchased. "Why should I not have known?" Der Ling wrote later, remembering the Paris gowns she and her sister had worn in the most fashionable and fashion-conscious of societies before the Great War, and noting with pleasure the looks both approving and curious that she received when she wore to the Metropolitan Opera an ermine wrap she claimed was given her by Cixi.[8]

Der Ling seems to have spent much of her time in New York on her own, but she had plenty enough to do: in late November 1929, over 1,500 people showed up for a lecture Der Ling gave for the League of Political Education (LPE), in which she paid tribute to Georges Clemenceau in childhood memories of his visits to the Chinese legation in Paris. "He and my father were great friends," Der Ling told the crowd, and one can well see the two men, so alike in their humorous approach to life and their rock-hard attachment to principle, enjoying one another's company. Over the coming years, Der Ling would appear again at the LPE, in league with such luminaries as Pearl S. Buck, Fannie Hurst, Ida Tarbell, and other influential women, as well as speaking for the first show of the Geographic Theatre, in an evening at the Waldorf-Astoria that combined all the best things she loved of past and present: films of archaeological explorations in the Gobi Desert, lantern slides of famous Asian gardens, and examples of ancient Chinese dance and music.

T.C., now described as an engineer with "mining interests in the Mojave," was in the Los Angeles area; whether Thaddeus Raymond was with him or with his mother is not known. In an article written around this time, "The Forbidden City and Broadway," Der Ling made it clear that however much culture shock her very presence inspired in those who met her, she herself could not walk down a street in skyscrapered New York City without being reminded, paradoxically, of her Chinese past. Though an avid supporter of the China of the Republic and the modernization creeping over the Celestial Empire, like many of her mind in Asia and outside it, Der Ling saw railroads and air travel among the surest means to knit China together into a stronger unity. In 1934 she attended the Washington congress of the Federation Aeronautique Internationale, at which Postmaster General James A. Farley predicted the advent of regular air service connecting Europe and the U.S., in such august company as Igor Sikorsky, Louis Bleriot and Paul Tissandier.

At the same time, Der Ling also expressed concern that Chiang Kai-shek and the modernizers might toss infant China out with the old bath water. "China is philosophical, harboring the belief that what is to be will be," Der Ling commented. "Personally I think that China enjoys life the more, because she takes it up in her hands, regards it thoughtfully, accepts it, and lives it in luxurious ease."[9]

Her fears that China's culture — that quality of mind and of art, of birth and death — was losing its respect within China itself, to be replaced by a harsh materialism, came to her at this most critical point in her life, when she walked the fine line between what was considered most Western and what most Eastern, in a nation like America, where the melting pot was the ideal but misunderstanding of other cultures than the predominant Anglo-Saxon one was the reality. Even among some of the friends Der Ling made in New York City, friends who loved China and things Chinese, she was confronted with ignorance and prejudice. One upsetting incident occurred at a friend's apartment, "twenty-odd stories above Broadway."

"We were all seated about the table, and the talk was general," Der Ling recalled. "Absently I fingered the cloth which covered the table, and something in the feel of the ribbon which bordered the cloth caused me to study it for a moment." She had to conceal her shock: the tablecloth was edged with the Chinese ribbon called "the ribbon of the endless knot," the design of which referred to the six-looped woven knot of that name, one of the Eight Auspicious Symbols of Buddhism, symbolizing eternity and the ultimate unity of all things. Before Der Ling had left the dowager's court in 1905, Cixi had given her a gown made for a woman much older than the 19-year-old court lady, which nevertheless was of marvelous workmanship. When Der Ling was living in Beijing years later, she was befriended by an American woman who had a fascination for items from the imperial court. Der Ling gave her the gown, and the lady brought it back with her to the United States where, as Der Ling discovered, it caught the eye of a friend. From the gown Der Ling's friend removed the "ribbon of the endless knot," gave it to the importuning friend, and now Der Ling sat at the latter's table, running fingers over the braid. "From the gown of an empress to a tablecloth upon which men and women who talked of horse racing dropped the ash from their cigarettes,"

Der Ling mused. "A strange, even weird, cycle; oddly, I thought, like my own." What Der Ling does not ponder is how responsible she was for allowing this piece of her imperial past to make its way to crass Broadway in the first place.[10]

32
Squeeze money

Der Ling's first book since the 1911 publication of *Two Years in the Forbidden City* was *Old Buddha*, her 1929 biography of the Empress Dowager Cixi. While the book presents a picture of a woman both ambitious and querulous, it does not veer to any great degree from the portrait Der Ling painted of Cixi in *Two Years*: of a woman who loved power yet sat uneasily on her throne, who lived in circumstances far removed from all other women's reality yet still was a woman like other women. Yet on the other hand, it is obvious Der Ling still had scores to settle, and she used this book, as she did *Jades and Dragons*, to do so. Unfortunately, she does this at the expense not of pseudonymous Beijingers but of the woman she professed to love, the Empress Dowager.

Old Buddha carries an edge of anger that *Two Years* does not, directed toward unnamed "writers" whose accounts of the dowager "emanate from tea houses in Beijing and other cities, where folk who knew nothing whatever about her gathered and gossiped," while trying to pass their work off as history — clearly a blow at people like J.O.P. Bland and Edmund Backhouse, whose massive 1910 biography of Cixi, *China Under the Empress Dowager*, had made both men famous and respected overnight as experts on the dowager's reign and the inner secrets of her court. Der Ling's competitiveness with these men and what she considered their uninformed portrait of the dowager led her to try to outdo them with her own "insider information." "I knew and spoke with most of the characters mentioned in this story," Der Ling wrote pointedly in *Old Buddha*'s preface. Bland and Backhouse could not say, as Der Ling could, that they had known Li Lianying, the Guangxu Emperor, pockmarked Prince Tuan of the Boxers, the cold but kindly Young Empress Longyu, or Prince Gong, long-time friend and supporter of Yu Keng, to name a few. On the other hand, as Der Ling confesses, "I am not unmindful that . . . I myself may have been too close" to the dowager to do her justice.[1]

Der Ling met Bland in Shanghai some time before 1910. John Otway Percy Bland was part-time Shanghai correspondent of the *Times* and a self-styled China historian (he had come over from England), partner to the translator and Sinophile Edmund Backhouse. He approached Der Ling with the manuscript of a book he and Backhouse had written on the reign of the Empress Dowager Cixi, asking her opinion of some documents he planned to use in facsimile in the book. He would leave the meeting angrily insistent on the authenticity of the documents in question, which he used despite her doubts. It is here that the real battle between Der Ling and her foreign-born naysayers, and her plans for a tell-all Cixi biography, can be said to have begun.[2]

An anti-imperialist convinced that constitutional government would have a hard time taking root in the brittle shale of Chinese politics, Bland had served as secretary to Sir Robert Hart (from whom he may well have picked up early gossip about the family of Yu Keng), then moved on to the Municipal Council of Shanghai. Described by one historian as a "genial extrovert, of sporting tastes and some literary interests, a fluent, prolific and elegant writer, expansive and sociable," Bland, who looked like a handsome greyhound, was a better-than-average Chinese scholar, but he depended — unfortunately for future scholars — on the superior linguistic abilities of (the future Sir) Edmund Trelawny Backhouse. Sweet-faced scion of a Quaker banking family, Backhouse had an almost supernatural genius for languages European and Asian and a criminal yen for forgery and falsification. "All his life," wrote his biographer,

Hugh Trevor-Roper, "Backhouse would strike all observers as a perfect gentleman," which was one of his greatest tools in concealing from most of his victims and admirers the imperfect underpinnings of that outward persona.[3] Though a scholar of high ability at Oxford, Backhouse suffered a nervous breakdown around age twenty and went down in 1895 without his degree. His finances also suffered a breakdown while at Oxford: Backhouse emerged with enormous debts for a man so young (up to £23,000, per one account). By 1899, he was in Beijing, for reasons which have never been satisfactorily explained, his creditors far behind and further adventures ahead of him. He sought a position with the Imperial Customs, run by Sir Robert Hart, but failed to gain a place. Trevor-Roper assumes that Backhouse worked as a student-interpreter for the legations. It was also during this time that he met both J. O. P. Bland and George Morrison, the Australian-born *Times* correspondent for whose dispatches from Beijing Backhouse would soon become an *éminence grise* unawares, feeding Morrison what were purported to be translations of Chinese court rescripts and announcements which were then fueled into reports to the outside world that painted a polite portrait of Cixi as a harridan and Guangxu as her hapless victim.

When the Boxer Uprising smashed into Beijing in summer 1900, Backhouse found himself in his element; no longer just constrained to filch materials out of thin air, he could now join the countless other foreign and native looters who, from the high-level robbery of the Hanlin Academy's priceless volumes to the low-level grabbing of vases and silks from abandoned households, swarmed over the stricken city. Not that Backhouse's activities went unnoticed: according to Morrison, Backhouse and a companion named Peachey were put under arrest by Russian soldiers "on a charge of blackmailing, looting and robbery." Trevor-Roper suggests that the blackmail charge arose from evidence that Backhouse and Peachey had threatened to denounce innocent Chinese to the allied troops as Boxers or Boxer sympathizers unless they handed over what the two men desired from them, a scenario which, given Backhouse's history past and future, sounds all too plausible.[4]

It was also during the mayhem of 1900–01 Beijing that Backhouse laid claim to another man's property by characterizing his theft as an act of virtue: his "discovery" and appropriation of the diaries of the Manchu official, Ching-shan. After finding his former place of residence, in Wang Fu Jing, a little too unprotected for his liking, Backhouse switched to the British section of the Imperial City, where he was granted permission to live in a portion of the "deceased" Ching-shan's house. It was here, "on August 18th," a mere few days after Ching-shan had been killed by his pro-Boxer son, that Backhouse claimed he found the old man's diary, which was about to be "burnt by a party of Sikhs," though considering, by Bland and Backhouse's own admission, the fact that "Ching Shan . . . was personally quite unknown to foreigners," it is not clear why foreign troops were interested in burning his scrolled diaries.[5] Not a few of the foreigners who had been trapped in the besieged legation quarter had been keeping diaries which, in various forms of veracity, would be published over the next several years, but there were as yet no Chinese accounts of the events following the Uprising, including the flight of the court to Xian, the Allied invasion of the city, and the mayhem that befell a Chinese home like Ching-shan's, most members of which committed suicide before he himself was forced down a well by his son, En Chun. The diary ends on August 15, late at night, with the old man's piteous comment that there is no one left to make him dinner.

The diary's bombshell was the information that Cixi's Grand Secretary, Ronglu, had been eager to protect the foreigners in the legations and had taken steps to ensure their safety, often at his own personal risk — information that we now know has some basis in fact. But the diary also included what seemed like intimate glimpses of the court from a true insider (Ching-shan allegedly being a favorite of the Empress Dowager's), with plenty of character sketches of the dowager acting out in high-opera mode. For nine years, Backhouse kept his discovery to himself, only revealing it to Bland after the death of the dowager in 1908, when they decided to write a full account of her long reign, using the sensational Ching-shan document as a selling point. To further bolster the document's authenticity, Backhouse sent the manuscript of the portions he had translated to Bland, who deposited them in the British Museum, for scholars to review at their leisure.

This they would do over the next several decades, each time with increasing doubts as to the document's true origin. Meanwhile, *China Under the Empress Dowager* appeared in late 1910, and made an immediate splash, to such a degree that the current empress dowager, Longyu, was said to have had it translated (per Backhouse) and was so enraged to find herself described as "unattractive" that she ordered the book banished from the palace. Most who read the scholarly yet engaging 525-page book, with its photograph illustrations and pages choked with Backhouse's translations of official court documents, found the book as fascinating reading as most do who pick it up today. Today, however, we know that the Ching-shan diary, the book's primary selling point and the basis of another writer's work on the China of Cixi's reign, is a total forgery.

Considering the fact that a photograph of Der Ling, Rong Ling and Louisa, posed with Cixi, was used in Bland and Backhouse's book (ironically amid the very pages of the Ching-shan diary translation), it makes sense that Bland — whom Der Ling tellingly calls "Mr. Blank" — had been in touch with Der Ling, as a former member of the dowager's court, and that he would ask her for her opinion of his research. He was not, however, prepared to take her advice; he "argued with me endlessly over every objection I made and made few changes," she recalled. "His material had been secured from the bazaars and market-places, from people who had learned to recognize, after a lot of similar experiences, so-called writers when they saw them coming, and had gathered information — of a kind — to be sold at a profit to those who sought 'inside information.'"[6]

The crux of the argument came when Der Ling was shown a letter, "purporting to be a receipt signed by Li Lien Ying, Chief Eunuch to Old Buddha [for] 'squeeze money' or *cumsha*, given him for favors procured at court." Der Ling asked for proof that the receipt was signed by Li Lianying, only to be assured that the receipt's seller, "a shopkeeper in Lantern Street [in Beijing]," had sworn it came directly from the family of the man to whom the receipt was written. If Bland knew China well at all, Der Ling replied, "you would know that 'squeeze' is never even admitted, much less does a man sign a receipt to the man who pays him 'squeeze.'" She pointed out that she had known Li Lianying well enough to make that comment. She also noted that the amount mentioned in the receipt was laughably small for the grasping Li, who regularly charged "from fifty thousand to a hundred thousand taels for procuring a one-minute interview for anyone with the Empress Dowager." Interestingly, Mrs. Archibald Little seems to have heard that Li Lianying charged "about £1,000 for an interview" with the dowager, which is close to what Bland's alleged receipt is for, suggesting that her information was based on the same hearsay as his.[7]

Given how Backhouse had duped him, Bland's retort, via Der Ling, is rich with irony: "According to you, and figuring in proportion — if what you tell me is true — if you are not a liar — if you are not prevaricating, equivocating, telling fibs, falsifying or simply twisting facts, he probably wouldn't sign his name for [the small] amount!" Der Ling noted that she had been saying that all the time, and the interview ended on that sour note. "[T]he writer must have gone back to the shopkeeper on Lantern Street and been convinced," she wrote, "for the book carried a full-page facsimile of a receipt from Li Lien Ying to Mr. Somebody-or-other . . . admittedly [for] *cumsha* or 'squeeze money'!"[8] In fact, between pages 98 and 99, in *China Under the Empress Dowager*, such a receipt is reproduced, with a telling comment from one of the authors on the facing page: "The paper on which [the receipt] is written is of the commonest," perhaps more of a clue to the receipt's real origins than Bland was willing to admit.[9]

Thus began a systematic derogation of Der Ling's contribution to the corpus of work dealing with Cixi and her court, for reasons which, on the surface, look to have been activated primarily in order to protect the image of the dowager as presented in Bland and Backhouse's successful book (an image built up, in turn, on Ching-shan's diary entries). That Der Ling struck back only in 1929, and then through the medium of pseudonyms, not all of which are as opaque as she may have hoped, seems to indicate that she feared a more direct attack, but indicates as well that the battle of innuendo had been raging for some time. Beyond Bland, who had now taken upon himself the task of "exposing" Der Ling and her memoirs of the court as a fraud, a task that would still be going strong well into the 1930s, a new character was added to the ranks of male, foreign-born and self-styled China experts who ranged themselves against her: Reginald Johnston, tutor to the Xuantong Emperor, better known as Puyi.

In *Twilight in the Forbidden City*, his 1934 account of his time spent as tutor to Puyi and as an official in the deposed emperor's "government," Johnston had risen quite high — after his name come several ringing post-nominals, including the C.B.E. which entitled him to preface his name with "Sir," and a list of his academic and literary credentials. Sterling Seagrave notes that Johnston, who examined the Ching-shan diary and, like the Dutch sinologist J. J. L. Duyvendak, in 1924, proclaimed it authentic, "pretended to dislike Edmund Backhouse, but during his years as British magistrate in Weihaiwei had made trips into Beijing where he and Backhouse were commonly seen together making the rounds of popular theaters on the back streets of the city" — despite the fact that Johnston declared he had never met Backhouse until 1914. Interestingly, both Johnston and Backhouse worked as interpreters at one of the parties given in 1903, at the British legation, for ladies of the Manchu court; it is possible both men met Der Ling at that time.[10]

It was in 1924, the year he passed the Ching-shan diary as genuine, that Johnston was appointed overseer of the Summer Palace complex, which, as we have seen from Der Ling's account of giving tours at this time, had been opened to the public. Perhaps now, too, he came face to face again with Der Ling, by this time known as "Princess," from her successful 1911 book and by word of mouth in chattering Beijing. Certainly Shao-ying, head of the *Nuweifu* or Household Department and colleague of Johnston's, knew of her, because on being asked about her by Johnston, he replied that Der Ling was in no way a real princess. "She held no high position at court," Johnston wrote Bland in 1935, echoing Shao-ying, "but was brought in to help to interpret when foreigners were present. She never appeared at court functions during the years I was attached to the court [*sic*: Johnston was at court for only five years, all post-Der Ling]." Johnston finished by saying that while he knew Der Ling had been in Beijing during the time, he was absolutely certain that she had never entered the Forbidden City. Even to experienced scholars, this absolute certainty would translate to "Der Ling was a liar."[11]

In his letter, which was written in response to one from Bland, who was about to review Der Ling's last book, *Son of Heaven*, and wanted

Johnston's opinion of her, Johnston urged Bland "to do all you can to give that 'princess' and her book a good trouncing," adding that "I remember making enquiries about the 'princess' when I was in the Forbidden City. The Emperor himself denied that she was a princess." Johnston's reliance on Shao-ying's negative opinion of Der Ling makes for questionable reading not only when, throughout the rest of *Twilight in the Forbidden City*, he paints a picture of a strained relationship between himself and Shao-ying's Household Department, faith in which he demonstrates at no point. But when he gives Puyi as a source for information on Der Ling, he is skating on even thinner ice. Der Ling and Puyi had only "met" once, when the future last emperor of China was a two-month-old infant in swaddling clothes and Der Ling in her late teens;[12] and by the time Johnston came to court, in March 1919, to serve as the emperor's English tutor, Der Ling had been separated from the imperial court for a full thirteen years, and had only recently moved back to Beijing. The emperor was only parroting what he had heard from officials like Shao-ying, who in tandem with eunuchs surviving from Cixi's reign would have had no love for a woman whose account of court life had cast all of them in such a poor light.

It is also possible there was another reason for animosity toward Der Ling on part of the little court of Puyi. In "Pu-Yi, the Puppet of Japan," an article written for the *Saturday Evening Post* following Puyi's 1932 accession to the "throne" of Manchukuo, Der Ling described being approached by the boy-emperor's Grand Guardian, a year or so after the 1912 abdication. "The new republic, although importuned many times by the head of the imperial household to pay the four million dollars a year [stipulated in the Articles of Favorable Treatment that were part of Puyi's abdication instrument], never paid it, and the ex-emperor and his retinue were soon in dire straits." The wealth extant in the imperial treasury, according to Der Ling, took the form of gold and silver bars, and could not be used to pay expenses. By means that Der Ling does not explain, the Grand Guardian, Puyi's governor, visited her, explaining that he knew she had friends among foreigners and foreign banks in Beijing. He asked her if she would serve as go-between in a deal to sell the bullion to foreign banks in return for cash to pay the court's bills, all without letting on to Yuan Shikai's government. "I went to the American bank in

Peking," wrote Der Ling, "[but the manager] said he was afraid to handle the transaction for fear of diplomatic complications."[13]

The following year, Der Ling says, she was again approached by the Grand Guardian: this time, the household was interested in selling items of great value stored in the imperial palaces at Mukden, antiques which the court regarded as the boy-emperor's personal property. The only person she could think of who had the money to buy such treasures, and was a collector of Asian art, was J. P. Morgan Sr. A Morgan representative, whom Der Ling knew, was in Beijing, and she laid the matter before him. This time, the project was showing a great deal more success, with Morgan himself cabling his interest, and negotiations began between him and the Grand Guardian. According to Der Ling, an expert in London had assigned a value of several million dollars to the items offered for sale. Then, when details were leaked to Yuan Shikai, the proceedings came to an abrupt halt. Yuan "again . . . prevented the imperial family from obtaining money," Der Ling wrote, claiming the collection belonged to the nation and should be placed in a museum.[14]

The collection was indeed brought to Beijing, and was placed in a museum, though only, as Der Ling points out, after Yuan had removed items from it for his own collections. If this story is true, Der Ling's inability to be of use to the ex-emperor's household may have rubbed more salt into the wounds precisely because Der Ling claimed to have powerful friends in the foreign community and may have assured the Grand Guardian that she could carry the money-making projects through to success. Clearly, there was no more to be gained from dealing with foreigners in 1914–15 than there had been over fifty years earlier. That Der Ling had been asked to do something that came dangerously close to breaking the law, and that she had been willing to do it, seems not to have bothered either the Grand Guardian or her.[15]

Easy it was for Johnston and Bland both to snort over "the extremely ignorant inhabitants" of the United States, who could be expected to believe anything Der Ling or other "frauds" fed them; yet one of Johnston's most glaring errors in his letter to Bland is to claim that "Der Ling's sister . . . never claimed to be a princess or used any such title." But as we have seen, in her 1930 account of the Fragrant Concubine and the Qianlong Emperor, Rong Ling indeed used the title "Princess Shou

Shan," evidently believing, as Der Ling did, that the honorary titles given to her and her sister had all the bona fides of public usage.[16]

Bland and Johnston were on firmer ground when criticizing Der Ling's literary style, which is at a particular disadvantage in the book they so loathed, *Son of Heaven*. This highly imagined account of Guangxu's life would have worked better marketed as a novel (and was described as one in newspaper accounts of Der Ling's trips to China to gather information for it). Future historians worked off of Bland's and Backhouse's opinion of Der Ling and perpetuated it based not on examination of Der Ling's work and personal history but on the opinions of these men. As Hugh Trevor-Roper, biographer of Backhouse, wrote to me shortly before his death: "In view of Johnston's position at the Chinese court, [Johnston's and Puyi's testimony] was good enough for me," despite the fact that Johnston was not at court during Der Ling's 1903–05 service there and Puyi was only an infant then.[17]

The ignoring of Der Ling's writings continued till just a few years before her death: in *The Last Empress*, his 1938 biography of Cixi, Daniele Varè goes so far as to give the long-forgotten Katherine Carl acknowledgement in the foreword, as well as Der Ling's sister, "Mme Dàn," still living in Beijing, who had yet to write a line about her court experiences, and virtually everyone else who had published some recollection of the dowager — but not a word about Der Ling. In ways she may never have expected, Der Ling's light-hearted treatment of events and people she had actually known, as against the writings of people with nothing to go on except theory and hearsay, and her inability to withstand what were clearly her publisher's efforts to increase sensationalism and sales by framing her recollections as insider biography and by making the most out of her "title," would work not for but against her. This was true not just in China but — contrary to Bland's assertions — in the United States as well.[18]

33
China reborn

While the Whites were absent from China in the last two years of the 1920s and the first few of the 1930s, events destructive but in themselves small were beginning to add up to the greater cataclysm of invasion by the Japanese. As the ex-Xuantong Emperor, Puyi, put it in his memoirs, "1928 was for me a year of excitement and shocks."[1] For him, the decision to throw his lot in with the Japanese eager to seize Manchuria from China had its birth in the ransacked chambers of the tombs of the Qianlong Emperor and the nearby one of Cixi, at the hands of soldiers under army commander Sun Tien-ying (Sun Dianying) in July of that year, when the chaos surrounding Chiang Kai-shek's taking of Beijing gave easy cover.

The symbolism of desecrating these last private spaces of two of China's most enigmatic and luxury-loving monarchs could not have been more obvious, but when the white marble-lined passageways were broken into and the treasures heaped about the deceased monarchs' coffins were seen flickering in the gloom, sheer greed took over, and in the scramble and, probably, fight to seize the most jade, gold, pearls and countless other priceless funerary objects, the bodies of both the

Qianlong Emperor and of Cixi were desecrated as well, disinterred and stripped in the search for valuables. Because so many of the objects stolen were immediately put on the twilit Beijing antiques and jewel market, we will never know exactly what was buried with either ruler; hyperbolic accounts of the grave goods transmitted later to the *Times* turn out to have a connection with Edmund Backhouse, which does not permit of their being taken very seriously. Puyi claimed to have heard that Cixi was buried with dozens of "pearls, gems, emeralds and diamonds," the latter a curious adornment for a woman who looked askance at them, with jewelry and other ornaments in the shape of her favorite flower, the chrysanthemum — but a more reasonable account compared to the Ali Baba's treasure-cave description proffered by Backhouse.

The news of the tombs' robbery struck the entire Aisin-Gioro family with anger and mortification, but none more so than Puyi, for whom the incident "gave me a shock worse than the one I had received when I was expelled from the palace."[2] Between the events of summer 1928 and those of March 1, 1931, when the Japanese-backed Manchukuo was called into being, there was not much of a leap for Puyi to make to go from unemployed ex-emperor dwelling in the cramped quarters of the Japanese concession in Tianjin to chief executive of the new northern nation, particularly as it was a position that paid a hefty salary, with promise of greater things to come.

To describe Puyi's reaction, at his first glimpse of his bleak Manchuokuoan "palace," as one of disillusionment barely touches how he felt, which comprised a composite of culture shock and dawning realization. After his eviction from the northern palaces of the Forbidden City in 1924, Puyi and his retinue had moved to the gloomy elegance of the Chang Villa in Tianjin, where the little "court" — his principal wife, Empress Wan Rong, secondary wife, brother Pujie and assorted officials and eunuchs from the old court — subsisted in a degree of curtailed splendor. As Puyi describes in his self-denigrating (and questionably authored) memoir, *From Emperor to Citizen*, "I made the most of the clothes and diamonds of the foreign stores . . . to dress myself up like a foreign gentleman from the pages of *Esquire* . . . My body would be fragrant with the combined odours of Max Factor lotions, eau-de-

Cologne and mothballs, and I would be accompanied by two or three Alsatian dogs and a strangely dressed wife and concubine."[3]

The ex-emperor would later claim, unsuccessfully, that the Japanese had kidnapped him away to Manchuria in 1931, but as Reginald Johnston himself would point out in *Twilight in the Forbidden City*, Puyi went to the Japanese of his own free will. He was disgusted with Tianjin and, most of all, with his own impotence — the Chang Villa's owner had begun to ask for rent, which Puyi could not (or would not) pay, resulting in the transference of the ever-shrinking "court" to a house ominously near the Japanese barracks, called the "Quiet Garden." In the waning weeks of 1931, discord erupted openly between the Japanese in Manchuria and Nationalist troops in Mukden, the old Manchu power center: an intelligence official in the pay of Japan was executed by the Nationalists as a spy, a bomb exploded on the South Manchuria Railway, a line owned by Japan.

Both events were enough to trip the Japanese hair-trigger. The Japanese captured Mukden and the rest of southern Manchuria; and Colonel Doihara, string-puller behind most of the action, came to visit Puyi in the Quiet Garden, where the ex-emperor was holed up, fearing for his life under accusations from the Nationalists that he was involved with the Japanese marauders. It was at this point that the colonel with the deceptively cheerful smile of a laughing Buddha and empty implications that the chief executive of today would be the emperor of tomorrow, laid the cards on Puyi's table and set him on the path that led to Manchukuo and what he described in his memoirs as being " 'Emperor' for the Third Time." Johnston, based on what he wrote of Manchukuo later on in *Twilight*, was in the city at the time and could conceivably have talked some sense into Puyi. He refused, assigning the ex-Lord of a Thousand Years far more autonomy and good judgment than he had ever possessed (a situation Johnston was in a position to know better than most of the people who surrounded Puyi); and the day after he left Tianjin, on November 10, Doihara staged another coup.

Under cover of gunfire and spilled blood, Puyi was taken away to a Japanese steamer, clutching his jewel bag and leaving his bewildered empress standing in the Quiet Garden's doorway, to be taken in hand later — and ushered into opium addiction — by the Japanese spy, Eastern

Jewel, through whose father, "Mad" Prince Su, she was a cousin of both Wan Rong and Puyi. Later, Wan Rong (Puyi's Secondary Consort, Wen Xiu, had divorced herself from the ex-emperor in Tianjin) joined her husband in the bleak cement box with its corrugated iron roof, located in Changchun, which was to be the new chief executive's Manchukuoan "palace." There, bowing to his Japanese sponsors three times, Puyi was handed his "seal of office," wrapped in imperial yellow silk.

Thus the strangest of his strange reigns began, of which Der Ling would presciently write one month after the Manchukuoan emperor's ascension to his throne, "What a pathetic figure the last of the Manchu emperors is today. He is a man without a country, and should the plans of the Japanese in Manchuria for any reason fail, his life may well be forfeit."[4] As an emperor who would not be allowed to escape into the death which had saved the dignity of so many other Chinese sons of heaven, but to live on far past his conceivable usefulness in a world that no longer cared for his kind, Puyi was unluckier than Der Ling knew.

As the Japanese threat grew to the north like one of the huge sandstorms that spilled over the Great Wall in autumn and spring, Der Ling was in China again, gathering more material for what was to be her final book, *Son of Heaven*. And while in Beijing, at the beginning of 1934, she entered the eccentric orbit of the second most misunderstood woman of her life, the American millionairess Barbara Hutton.

Born in New York City on November 14, 1912, ten-year-old Barbara fell heiress to the modern equivalent of over a half-billion dollars. An isolated upbringing in her grandparents' shadowy mansion, with a mad grandmother upstairs and a grandfather fond of playing his eerie pipe organ, and in her aunt's walled estate outside San Francisco, gave Barbara a taste of the loneliness that would haunt her for all of her life, as well as a yen for the strange. European titles, exotic locales, music of the Chinese and Japanese imperial courts, all would figure prominently during her lifetime, with or without (as at the end) the money to pay for it all.[5] Given the later events of her life, it is highly possible that when "Prince" Alexis Mdivani crossed the stage of Barbara's experience, the Georgian adventurer with the fleshy face of a depraved cherub seemed an ideal life preserver for an heiress lost at sea and desirous of nothing better than escaping her controlling father and vaguely vulgar stepmother. Mdivani, known as Alec to his friends, was so little a real prince that his father, a Georgian colonel, claimed to be the only parent to have inherited a title from his children.[6]

It was negative publicity arising from the latest of Alec's family travails — namely, a lawsuit hanging over the heads of Serge and David, filed by their ruined ex-wives, actress Mae Murray and opera singer Mary McCormick, whose funds had soaked like oil into sand in the founding and management of the Pacific Oil Company — that drove Barbara and her husband to leave the U.S. for a second honeymoon in January 1934.

That same month, according to a lavish article in the January 20, 1934 *New York Times*, Der Ling was back in New York City with Thaddeus, dressing up in Cixi's imperial regalia for the Beaux-Arts Ball at the Waldorf-Astoria; she played a character named "Empress Karachin"; one of the other four empresses of the event was Mrs. Kermit Roosevelt. Der Ling was cited by the writer as wearing "one of the most gorgeous costumes" of the evening, of yellow satin embroidered with the phoenix and peony blossoms and adorned with pearls and kingfisher feathers. A photo of Der Ling was run showing her in this outfit, between two New York debutantes gowned as ladies were imagined to be garbed in the thirteenth-century Venice of Marco Polo (in which Der Ling's Manchu gown and headdress were several centuries ahead of time). Before spring, Der Ling was back in China, where in Beijing she and "Princess" Mdivani crossed paths and became fast friends.[7]

"Word had spread quickly," writes Philip Van Rensselaer, "about the heiress's generosity so everybody from the highest to the lowest was trying to sell her something."[8] Whether Der Ling offered Barbara items from her own collection of imperial items, most of which were still stored in China, is unknown; Der Ling still had enough to fill over two dozen packing crates when she finally had her belongings shipped from China to the U.S. just before the Japanese invasion of 1937, and Barbara was known for buying in bulk. What Barbara seemed to value most in Der Ling was something less tangible: her mind and her feelings. Barbara had read Der Ling's books and had been clearly intrigued by her experiences at the court of Cixi and the whirl of her girlhood spent in the capitals of Europe and Asia, perhaps seeing in the life of this woman who seemed to belong to no world in particular an echo on her own. Whether she had ever heard criticism of Der Ling's title is not known — her own being questionable, it seems reasonable to assume she did not think much about the subject.

As she would do with the languages of other cultures that caught her fancy, Barbara yearned to learn Chinese, and hired Der Ling to teach her. She also leaned on Der Ling's knowledge of Qing antiques to make informed purchases, and walked with her through the Forbidden City and the Summer Palace, her large blue eyes glowing as Der Ling described life as a lady-in-waiting, the scurrying of eunuchs, the boat rides on the lotus-covered lake and the indomitable presence of the imperial old lady whom Der Ling had loved. It was not to last. During these tours, Alec pulled his hat over his face and napped on a bench; back home at the palace, he indulged in temper tantrums, screaming as he lay on the floor. After two months in Beijing, Barbara could see it was time to move on to the *louche* maharajas of India, where perhaps Alec could feel more at home.[9]

But Barbara, who for all her other failings made up for them by being the sort of friend who never forgot a kindness or a friend, would not forget Der Ling. Late in 1934, when T.C. and Der Ling were in New York, Barbara threw a Chinese banquet in their honor, replete with antique porcelains and chopsticks and a Mandarin chef imported from the Hotel Pierre and dinner guests of the ilk of famed Metropolitan Opera baritone Lawrence Tibbett (who would perform several of Barbara's Beijing poems, set to music by Noël Coward and, of all people, Elsa Maxwell), all of which was tailored to give Der Ling pleasure while honoring her culture and background as few in the U.S. knew how to do.[10]

By March 1935, when Barbara packed her bags and walked out on the pouting Alec, Der Ling and T.C. had returned to Los Angeles, where they stayed with heiress and aviation pioneer Elizabeth McQueen at her home on North Doheny Drive in Beverly Hills, and where Der Ling was interviewed at the *Los Angeles Examiner* studios for broadcast over KFWB. "Air-minded Young China," declared an accompanying article, "speeding the wheels of industry, building the highways of commerce and erecting democratic structure of government, is out to set the pace of progress for the rest of the world!" Der Ling gave Chinese progress a feminist spin: "Count on China's youth, particularly the young women, to finish the job," she told her interviewer.[11] Where both feminism and airplanes were concerned, Der Ling knew something of what she spoke; she had been writing articles on aviation in China for *Flyers* magazine since the late 1920s, and her feminist ideology (which was always triggered by examples of Asian machismo) had been in place for some time.

By May, Der Ling and T.C. were in Reno, Nevada, standing as witnesses to the marriage of Barbara Hutton to Count Court Reventlow-Hardenberg-Haugwitz, a handsome Austro-Danish nobleman with the lean, hard body of a leisured sportsman and the lean, hard face of a man who knew how to get exactly what he wanted out of life. Divorced from her questionable Russian prince only a few hours, in the presence of Der Ling and T.C., Jimmy Donohue, the bride's parents, and a few close friends, Barbara became a real countess.[12] Soon after, Der Ling was back in Los Angeles, where she spoke to two hundred Chinese and American students at a Cosmopolitan Club luncheon at the University of California-Los Angeles. She again defended Cixi against accusations that she had loathed all foreigners, pointing out that the dowager was particularly drawn to Americans and adding that because of this favor, "Americans still hold an advantageous position" in the eyes of modern Chinese.[13]

Now that the Whites had purchased a house in the Monte Vista Del Mar neighborhood of West Los Angeles, Der Ling was beginning to settle in. (The Whites had earlier indicated to the press that they intended to live in Beverly Hills; perhaps the prices, or the fact that Chinese residents, even the likes of actress Anna May Wong, were not welcome there, may have been factors in choosing to live elsewhere.) "California is a real place to write," Der Ling told a reporter, adding that she planned to give up the lecture platform to write full time.[14] She was also beginning to think of her treasures left boxed up in Beijing, and what might happen to them if the Japanese did, as everyone now feared, sweep down from their stronghold in Manchuria. By early September, she was sailing across the Pacific on the Dollar liner *President Coolidge*, "to pass three months in Peiping obtaining material for another novel." Whether mistake or Freudian slip, the reporter's characterization of Der Ling's planned biography of the Guangxu Emperor as fiction was one that would be echoed for real among several prominent China scholars and critics following its 1935 publication.

Wrote one reporter who talked to her when she disembarked at San Francisco in November, "Princess Derr [*sic*] Ling declared she felt a growing tension in China at the time of her departure." Besides gathering information for *Son of Heaven*, which included seeking out old court eunuchs in hovels in Tianjin and Beijing and tapping their fading memories for details of a past so distant it might have been the court of the Mings instead of the Qings, Der Ling made an effort to gather up the remains of her own past, remains which at this stage were virtually written out. More practically, in the two months she remained in northern China, she would see that her belongings were crated up and ready to be shipped out of harm's way — the last of the old China she loved and the last of it whose fate she could control.[15]

34
Princess of patriots

Cixi may have entertained a benevolent attitude toward the United States (or flattered the American women at her tea parties that such was her feeling), believing the United States had cut a more honorable figure in Chinese affairs than any of the other nations which had put their hands in the pie. But in reality, the U.S. had not done much, besides its honorable posings, to deserve Old Buddha's praise during her lifetime or for a long time after it.

Even at the time of the Japanese invasion of Manchuria in 1931, the U.S. had not shown itself disposed toward intervening in the situation despite calls to do so. When Japanese bombers strafed Shanghai in 1932, allegedly to protect their own civilians from harm (no evidence that such was the case has ever been uncovered; if anything, the bombs were a response to the national boycott of Japanese goods), the U.S. similarly stayed out of the fray. The U.S. Neutrality Acts of 1935 and 1937 made it easy to duck any subsequent opportunities to check the Japanese advance, and when Japan launched war against China in summer 1937, the United States offered no aid to the Chinese; American ships running scrap steel to Japan did not cease their coming and going, lining the pockets of scrap corporations and the families that owned them.[1]

As in the "Manchurian incident" of 1931, Japan proved it knew not just when the iron was hot enough to strike but how to keep it at highest temperature until the optimal moment. When Chiang Kai-shek was arrested at Xian in December 1936 by officers critical of his obsessive focus on fighting the Communists instead of warding off Japan, it took Communist intervention, in form of future premier Zhou Enlai, to negotiate Chiang's release. It was hoped that a Nationalist-Communist alliance could be parlayed into just the sort of united front needed to fight the Japanese threat, which was growing more ominous by the day. For Chiang, it was a hated marriage arranged by ineluctable forces with a bride he had already seen and found wanting, but the efforts made to make the best of the situation were counteracted by a new Japanese scheme. For now Japan saw the attempted alliance as proof positive that China would never agree to a pact whereby China and Japan banded together to fight the very Communists who were now seeking to bind themselves to the Nationalists and block the Japanese.

Based on China's unwillingness and inability to subscribe to such a pact, Japan took the step it had been waiting for: causing a war, which was done one July night in 1937, when shots were fired at Chinese guards at the Marco Polo Bridge near Beijing by Japanese soldiers ostensibly searching for a lost comrade. When the Chinese fired back, the second Sino-Japanese War began in everything but name. Thirty-five thousand Japanese troops poured into the region around the city and soon took Beijing.

Significantly, and perhaps predictably, considering what it had lost in Manchuria to the Japanese, the Soviet Union was first to see that a war had actually begun and signed a non-aggression pact with China; most nations with a right to be concerned, including China itself, persisted in seeing the hostile actions as something containable. The Japanese had clearly planned their thrust into China at a number of tables on a number of late nights, because the process of invading and consolidating their spoils functioned like clockwork. This included their knee-jerk response, reminiscent of the bombing of Shanghai in 1932, when a Japanese officer in that city was shot as he tried to make his way into the Chinese airdrome outside Shanghai. Over thirty warships were sent steaming toward Shanghai, which their troops captured at huge cost in men and matériel. They then turned their sights on Nanjing, locale of the Nationalist government.

Chiang Kai-shek was all for defending the capital, despite being advised against it by German military aides — had their quasi-Daoist advice to let what must happen happen been followed, instead of resisting the Japanese and whipping their commanders into a froth of racist rage, what occurred next in Nanjing might have turned out differently. When the Japanese took the city, in December 1937, one of the most barbarous acts against a civilian population, hideous even by the extremes of the Hitlerian and Stalinist mid-twentieth century, took place over the course of several weeks, as men, women and children were tortured, raped and murdered. Had a few technology-enthused Japanese, happy to handle a camera no matter what they were pointing it at, not taken photographs of the beheadings, burnings and burials of living beings, raped and eviscerated women and bayonet-punctured babies (and then been unwise enough to have them developed at a public photography shop in Korea), it would be as hard to believe the "Rape of Nanjing" had occurred as to conceive of the mounds of heads and right hands described in ancient battle chronicles throughout world history.

"When one looks back on it," wrote Harry Hussey, who was present in China and sidestepped his own share of raining Japanese bombs, "it is now evident that the attacks on Shanghai and Nanjing were but steps toward Pearl Harbor and the complete control of China and Asia."

"The Japanese are very poor propagandists," added Hussey.[2] After the fall of Nanjing, neither the Japanese nor the world cared why they were doing what they were doing — the horrors the Chinese people were enduring and the rapidity with which the invaders did their work seemed to obviate all ability to think on part of all who looked on. The Japanese then proceeded to gather up several other major cities and ports, including the most crucial, Guangzhou — without this port, China had no way of supplying itself. Thanks to the kidnapping of Chiang Kai-shek and his subsequent rescue by a Communist knight on a white horse, Nationalist and Communist military cooperation was at least not folding completely under the Japanese assault, but territory was slipping away like sand in the tide.

By October 1938, the Chinese government removed to distant Chongqing, in the wilds of western China, burning and destroying everything they left behind lest the Japanese capture goods as well as cities. Chiang Kai-shek established himself there in January 1939, by which time it was clear to everyone that another world war was on its way, far outside the boundaries of ruined China. Not long after the outbreak of the 1937 hostilities, Americans began to mobilize to aid the Chinese, and newspapers from New York to California filled with articles and announcements of charity benefits organized by newly founded relief agencies. One of the last articles about Der Ling just before the Japanese invasion, in the April 30, 1937 *Los Angeles Times*, is a model of the sort of fluff published about her: set in the kitchen of her "ultramodern Southern California home," the interviewer chatters about soggy cakes and tasteless salads, segueing abruptly to Der Ling's memories of the vast meals served from Cixi's imperial kitchens and an explanation of the origins of the kitchen god, pinned up on Der Ling's kitchen wall (it should have been under the oven), which is cautiously referred to as the "kitchen guardian," lest the *Times'* readers imagine the Americanized Der Ling clung to some unsavory pagan practices. The only serious note is the interviewer's reference to the "twenty-five packing cases of belongings [Der Ling] had stored in the northern capital," which she had gone back to China to fetch the previous year, doing so at what was described later on as serious peril to her safety. "[She] succeeded in getting her treasures out of Peking just forty-eight hours ahead of the Japs," wrote the author (probably T.C.) of the *Princess Der Ling Chinese Art Collection* catalog.

By October, Der Ling's role in the press had made a 180-degree turn. No more such silly kitchen interviews with Prudence Penny: "Princess Aids China Relief," blares the headline in the October 20, 1937 issue of the *Los Angeles Times*:

Tons of Articles to Leave This Week for War-Torn Country

Princess Der Ling, author; T. K. Chang, Consul from China to Los Angeles, and Soo Yong, actress, yesterday joined the forces at Chinese Relief Headquarters, 225 North Los Angeles street, assisting the 100 Chinese there to sort clothing and other supplies to be sent to stricken China.

A few days earlier, Der Ling had hosted a Chinese buffet supper at the Ambassador Hotel. "Princess Der Ling will present a pageant of Chinese court life as she knew it during the reign of the late Empress Dowager Tzu Hsi," noted the *Los Angeles Times* article announcing the event.

In June 1938, Der Ling was one of the dignitaries assembled to dedicate Los Angeles Chinatown's Central Plaza. California Governor Frank F. Merriam and his wife, actress Anna May Wong, Consul T. K. Chang and other guests watched while four hundred Chinese boys and girls paraded in native costumes. Governor Merriam dedicated a plaque fixed to the West Gate (*pailou*), "Dedicated to the Chinese Pioneers Who Participated in the Constructive History of California."[3] Der Ling had also stepped up her role in the relief effort, serving as chairperson of the Los Angeles observance of the "Rice Bowl" evenings that were occurring across the nation. These "Rice Bowl" evenings had started, as most benevolent movements do, with an act of rebellious violence. In January 1938, just as a cargo ship loaded with scrap metal bound for Japan was about to leave port, the ship's Chinese crew refused to let it sail. There were picket lines, riots, fights. Support came gradually but powerfully from the International Longshoremen and the Warehousemen's Union, and grew to embrace the notion of an embargo on all goods that Japan might be able to use for armaments.

That same year, San Francisco's Chinatown started what came to be known as "Rice Bowl" parties, gatherings that filled streets and hotel reception rooms with supporters of the beleaguered Chinese. "Like Mardi Gras celebrations," writes Iris Chang, "they were boisterous, noisy affairs, lavish in scale and lasting for days." There were dragon dances, fireworks, mock air raids and hawkers of "humanity" buttons. Participants filled rice bowls and Chinese flags with money. When the fundraising came to an end several years later, some $20 million was donated by twenty American cities for the Chinese War Relief Association; Chinese Americans on their own gave $25 million. While there are well-founded doubts that all of this cash and donated goods actually reached the people they were meant for, the effort to band together and help the suffering Chinese brought ordinary Americans together with their Asian neighbors, engendering a sense of community that had not existed before.[4]

As Der Ling wrote, "I feel assured that the West will come in time to understand the East, and that of all the Western nations, the United States will be the first to make that understanding mutual. She is too good a salesman to allow others to out-sell her . . . When the United States realizes more fully the need of mutual understanding . . . she will waken to find it already attained."[5] The gap between this feet-on-the-ground commentary and the wispy imaginings of *Son of Heaven* could not be greater, and one is tempted to believe it signaled a change of direction for Der Ling, as writer and thinker on her favorite subject, China's role in the greater world.

As chairperson of the Rice Bowl festivities, Der Ling ensured that Los Angeles Chinatown's party was an experience meaningful for both West and East, calling on her memories of entertainments at the dowager's court — the jugglers, dragon dancers, musicians, singers — as well as her experience, whether genuine or not, helping to manage the court's large imperial galas, to encourage partygoers to give to their utmost to preserve the culture from which those entertainments sprang. She pointed out to one reporter that the ceremony of the wedding shared one important similarity, whether in Philadelphia or Beijing: with a shower of rice, well wishers called out "Plentiful harvest and prosperity" to the newly married pair. It was a touch she must have known would appeal to men and women, mothers and fathers, wives and husbands, whatever their race or creed.[6]

She went on to volunteer for positions of greater responsibility. When a Chinese branch of the American Women's Voluntary Services (only the third in the country) was opened in Los Angeles in November 1942, at the sponsorship of Der Ling, she was made senior chairperson, and was joined in the opening ceremonies by Los Angeles mayor Fletcher Bowron and other officials at the North Spring Street headquarters. Colonel Theodore Roosevelt Jr., son of the United States president and a war hero in his own right, named Der Ling head of the United Council for Civilian Relief in China. Along with this, she took on the chairmanship of the Chinese Service Men's Center in Los Angeles.[7]

Der Ling even turned the treasures she had rescued from China over to the cause, though her earlier efforts at displaying her *objets d'art* smacked more of show and tell on a grand scale. One of the first times

Der Ling had put her items before the public was at the San Francisco World's Fair of 1939, when a complete throne room scene was arranged with manikins wearing costumes from Der Ling's collection, including what was described as her own court clothing, in a yellow-roofed building in the three-acre Chinese Village called The Princess Der Ling Pavilion. It could be no accident that the pavilion, though tiny, bore a striking resemblance to Cixi's favorite residence at the Summer Palace, or that the yellow tiles signified resident royalty. But was it an accident that the printer of souvenir postcards commemorating the Fair should list Der Ling, on the verso of a view of her pavilion, as "the last surviving member of the Chinese royal family"? Printer's error or intentional, it serves as a good example of the kind of hyperbole which increasingly surrounded everything Der Ling did, which it would also appear she did nothing to contradict, and in the creation of which she or T.C. probably played some significant role.

A less glitzy but no less public opportunity to show off her imperial collection came in August 1941. As part of United China Relief Week, Der Ling arranged for Barker Brothers furniture store in downtown Los Angeles to display a number of items from the gifts given to her by Cixi: "The carved teakwood bed used by the Princess Der Ling will be on display," reads the announcement, "accompanied by an imperial bedspread once owned by the Dowager Empress. It is the only one in existence and occupied the entire time of two seamstresses for five years," dealing out the same sheaves of superlatives as the auction catalog of these same items would do after her death.[8]

Four months after "the Princess Der Ling collection" filled Barker Brothers' plate glass display windows with color and carving and a faint whiff of the world that had created them, the Japanese bombed Pearl Harbor, destroying the American fleet and bringing not just the United States into the Second World War but China as well. For the time being, at least, China would no longer be fighting for her very existence entirely alone. Der Ling could feel, as many Chinese Americans did, that she had fought the battle along with her adopted country, and would see it through till the end. It is a pity she did not live to see the war to its conclusion. The enormity of the cataclysm overtaking the world had silenced her stories about imperial Beijing and its semi-mythical court, but had opened up her energies and compassion for the new China in ways she had only lectured about. Now she could really serve a purpose, not as commemorator of a dead world and a flashpoint for gossip, but as a Chinese woman intent on the survival of her homeland and her people. Perhaps now Der Ling was mature enough to really write about the times she lived in, when so much more was at stake than at any time during her brief service to an aged empress dowager in a decaying empire. But the real world caught up with Der Ling in the worst possible way. A grocery truck on a November morning in 1944 silenced whatever new voice Der Ling might have been ready to speak.

Legacy

Der Ling would not see the unfolding of one of the United States' least appetizing wartime acts — the forced internment of thousands of Japanese Americans, most from the West Coast, in camps located inland — as well as one of its greatest: the landings on the Normandy coast which came to be known as D-Day, signaling the beginning of the end for Adolf Hitler.

Nor would she have to watch her homeland endure greater sufferings than when she was alive. China faced harder times than ever. At the time of Der Ling's death in late 1944, Chinese were calling the past twelve months their "disaster year," only because there was no worse adjective to use to describe it. "China entered 1945 an exhausted nation," writes Harry Hussey. The Burma campaign had cost the nation dearly, with little to show for it, while weakening defenses to such degree that the Japanese were able to make sallies into fresh territories, including Henan, formerly known as the "rice bowl of China."[1]

American support continued, and it is likely that Der Ling's move to the San Francisco Bay area in 1942 was as much motivated by a desire to ally herself with the steadying structure of academic life as her ongoing Chinese relief work. Her death certificate lists her last occupation as teacher of Chinese at the University of California-Berkeley, but no record exists of Der Ling having ever been part of the regular faculty. It is possible she was a lecturer in languages or Chinese history, a tenuous position which would account for no trace of her work at the university. A more likely scenario, however, is that Der Ling worked on the U.C. Berkeley campus for the displaced California College. Founded in 1910 in Beijing, the California College served English-speaking clientele, among them missionaries as well as members of the business and diplomatic communities. In 1930, missionary William B. Pettus incorporated the institution as the California College in China Foundation, its primary goal being to educate Americans in all things Chinese, including language, history, customs and politics — a desideratum of Der Ling's life from the start of her writing career. With the Japanese invasion of China and the outbreak of the Second World War, Pettus ironically moved the College *to* California, settling it into temporary quarters on the campus of U.C. Berkeley. While a search of the Pettus Papers, now at Claremont College, unearthed no mention of Der Ling, the same reason may apply as that which may explain why there is no trace of her at U.C. Berkeley: as a lecturer, it is not likely her presence at California College would become part of the long-term record. If nothing else, her work for California College would clarify why she was on the campus of U.C. Berkeley; the temporary nature of the work itself would also account for why she and T.C. rented rooms at the Hotel Carlton, a hostel for students, faculty and guests of the University at Telegraph and Durant, for two years, rather than selling their Los Angeles properties and taking a house in the Bay Area.[2]

After 1942, Der Ling no longer appears in the *Los Angeles Times*, the paper that had featured her regularly, whether in New York, Chicago, or San Francisco, for the past thirteen years. It was as if, through the Sino-Japanese War and the world war that followed, she had found her voice as teacher, spokesperson and defender of the tortured country of her birth and upbringing — as if she, after almost twenty years of living as an American, with her modern house and modern ways, had rediscovered herself as Chinese.

Following Der Ling's death, T.C. moved back to Los Angeles, where he lived until 1953, offering pieces of Der Ling's imperial collection for sale. The glass negatives for Der Ling's brother's photographs of Cixi and life at court, for example, were sold to a private collector, who then sold them to the Smithsonian Institute in Washington D.C. When he died, at the Veterans Administration hospital in Los Angeles, T.C.s' last will shows he did well enough for a "soldier of fortune," bequeathing thousands of dollars in property and cash to friends and a sister; but the many disinherited heirs listed in the codicil seem to point to an old man embittered rather than mellowed by the years. The Chinese antiques described as being stored in two Southern California warehouses were auctioned off by the Citizens National Bank and a few pieces have been traced to museums and private collections across the United States.[3]

Der Ling's books had been popular since her first published work in 1911, but by her death she was forgotten. Even without the controversy surrounding some of her claims, including the troubling business of her title, as a historian and biographer Der Ling's appeal was always limited to the unusual and the anecdotal rather than the broadening and the abstract. Her recollections of life at court do focus, as duly criticized, on small daily details to the exclusion of the bigger picture of imperial high politics, of which she only claims to have become aware to a moderate degree yet for the pageant of which she had an enviable front row seat. But most damning to her reputation was the questioning of her veracity, which began early and continues to this day.

Der Ling's subjective, dramatically enhanced style of writing biography, along with her books' popularity (especially in America), instantly relegated her to the dust-bin in the minds of men like J. O. P. Bland and Sir Reginald Johnston, who held themselves as "China experts" and saw anecdotal memoirs such as Der Ling's the flimsy product of gossip from the women's quarters. The pervading sense that Der Ling's recollections were more fantasy than fact was only assisted by her use of illustrations rather than photographs, even for her memoirs, as well as by the mixing of these recollections with her melodramatic re-tellings of Chinese fairy tales and ghost stories. Much worse, her use of the title she believed Cixi had bequeathed to her in 1905 was to further place her in disrepute in China, even as it enhanced her reputation once she came to America. But popular acclaim did not equal being seen as she wished to be seen, a witness to historical events and friend of historical personages.

Der Ling had an unforgettable charm, as many of her friends remembered. "As a lady of quality in the true sense of the word," wrote actor James Zee-min Lee, "Princess Der Ling was democratic, philanthropic, altruistic and a charming personality."[4] But a part of that charm was a desperate need to be at the epicenter of everything exciting, glamorous and important, along with which went an equally powerful need to please. Her writings and their deterioration from plausible eyewitness accounts to sensationalist "insider information" describe something that was happening to the woman as well as to the writer. While sophisticated, Der Ling was also gullible. She may have seen things at court which her Western-oriented mind read as one thing when in fact they were quite another. As scholar Zhu Jiajing has pointed out, Der Ling and her sister both committed inaccuracies in their memoirs of Cixi's court. They were teenagers when they first went to court, impressionable young women when they left (Rong Ling having stayed till the Empress Dowager's death in 1908); they were inclined to please the old lady because she liked their father and was kind to them, if fascination with things foreign — the girls' main draw for Cixi — ranks as kindness. One thing Der Ling never points out, though bright enough to have done so, is that while she and her sister were awed by the strange glamor of Cixi's court, the old lady herself was equally awed by the girls' strange French shoes and hats, their ability to speak foreign languages and play foreign instruments, the different way in which they moved and reacted to her, so at variance with the Chinese surrounding her up to the girls' arrival on the scene.

At heart Cixi was a foreigner, too, but if Der Ling thought so she never noted it. *Two Years in the Forbidden City* comes as close to how one would like to see Der Ling interpret her weird new world, at once the court life she loved to be a part of but as foreign to her as if she were a Westerner thrown into an alien culture. But like the spoiled and somewhat supercilious adolescent she never really stopped being, she loses herself in a welter of details about jade pendants and pearls and lapdogs and patterns on china, and in perorations on how beloved Cixi was to her and vice versa, rarely approaching the heart of her and Cixi's shared dilemma: defining their identities against the backdrop of a rapidly changing world.

When she embarked on *Old Buddha*, published in 1928 as a tell-all biography of the Empress Dowager, Der Ling was moving in a different milieu from when her first book appeared. She was living in the late 1920s' United States, dizzily dancing the Charleston on the decks of a doomed ocean liner. If Der Ling's first book, appearing after the disintegration of the Manchu dynasty, glitters with the torn glamor of ruined Eastern kingdoms, her second takes even more advantage of a fascination with lost empires and disenfranchised princes brought to birth by the First World War and the fall of European thrones. This was a time when princes and countesses, real and imagined, were seen on the streets and in the cafés of New York, Paris, Berlin and Istanbul, waiting tables, driving cabs, walking the lapdogs of the nouveaux riches. This was also the age during which the long degradation of Puyi, the last emperor of China, unfolded miserably, allowing Der Ling to follow him in her books and articles like a dogged reporter, describing her first sight of him in diapers at the imperial court and lamenting his tragic end as a puppet of the Japanese. A culture of displaced celebrity, rife as weeds in pre- and post-Depression American society, launched this self-promoting Asian woman with the tissue-thin title (and an unacknowledged American grandfather) on a flood of public fascination with throneless royalty and exotic pretenders. Not only were princesses like herself fawned over, they were rarely authenticated and their recollections of once glorious pasts were actively promoted. The Jazz Age had died out, but the Age of the Impostor lived on. It cannot be argued successfully that Der Ling did not take advantage of its longevity.

The novelistic tone of *Old Buddha*, suspect today, was acceptable in 1928, as apparently was Der Ling's irresistible need to tease her readers with an omniscience which claimed to reveal the truth about Cixi at last and at the same time carelessly recounted some of the worst of the gossip about her — her alleged murders of Cian, her son Tongzhi, the Guangxu Emperor. At least this book included genuine photographs, again those taken by Xunling. When a prequel to *Two Years* appeared, an account of Der Ling's childhood and life up to the death of her father in 1905 which she called, oddly, *Kow Tow*, an illustrator was hired to create images throughout the book, none of which reassures the reader that what he is reading is 100 percent true. And the book's cover, embossed in gold with an Asiatic stereotype — a cross-legged male with pigtail, sparse mustache and beard, sharp fingernails on fingers spread in a gesture like a hawker in a bazaar — does not inspire a sense that Der Ling valued her Chinese heritage as much as that elusive Europeanness which was part education, part put on, and part wishful thinking.

Taking her view of herself as cosmopolitan to what is perhaps its natural goal, yet doing so via the fantasy world of pseudonyms and innuendo, Der Ling brought out another book, in 1932, *Jades and Dragons*, which I have called her *memoir à clef*. Having left Beijing and the gossiping denizens of the diplomatic quarter, Der Ling evidently felt she could let fly at them with both barrels, skewering the pidgin English of hotel clerks and merchants and the comical genteel-poverty of ruined Manchu aristocrats, not forgetting to send up unfaithful foreign wives and their philandering foreign husbands, with much wit and much malice. *Jades and Dragons* is a pointed effort blunted by pseudonyms, which leave an uncomfortable aftertaste: Has Der Ling used phoney names the better to shoot at her prey from convenient cover, or used them the better to fool her American readers into believing she had any real prey to shoot at? Even with this growing instability in Der Ling's literary output, *Jades and Dragons* does give tantalizing glimpses of the real Der Ling, the hardened, worldly, well-traveled ex-court lady who has seen it all, has nothing to fear, and nothing to hide — or rather, no compunction about hiding some things and revealing others. The Omar Khayyam quote she chose for the frontispiece, topped by an illustration of Thai shadow puppets, says much about her life at the time: "We are no other than a moving row / Of Magic Shadow-shapes that come and go ..."

While democratic and philanthropic, Der Ling was also mesmerized by the trappings of courts and the rulers who formed their mysterious center, which overwhelmed and subjugated her inborn democratic credo. Thanks to her brief foray into the last days of a once-great court, Der Ling had, or thought she had, material to keep her busy for the next thirty years. But her crop came up thinner and thinner with each book, to the point where by her fourth, fifth and sixth books, loose collections of memoir-essays and short stories called, respectively, *Lotos Petals, Imperial Incense*, and *Golden Phoenix*, she fell back on such non-Chinese recollections as her meetings with Sarah Bernhardt and her lessons with

Isadora Duncan in Paris, or stories she wanted her readers to believe were based on ancient Chinese legends — Der Ling as a Manchu Scheherazade. Some of the chapters in these collections had originally been published in article form in the monthly women's magazines that were helping worried housewives through the Depression, much as movie spectacles churned out by Hollywood were doing for the same reason.

It is in *Imperial Incense* that Der Ling recounts a story of taking a train trip with Cixi, in which she traveled with the Empress Dowager to Tianjin and then on to the old royal palace at Mukden, that Chinese scholar Zhu Jiajing has called into question, since it figures nowhere in the Empress Dowager's surviving court itineraries. Indeed, Der Ling herself makes no mention in *Two Years in the Forbidden City* of this trip or another with which she must have been involved, that Cixi made to the Western Tombs in April 1903, only a month after Der Ling, her sister and her mother came to court. Her detailed description of Cixi's imperial train carriage, with its throne and its shelves for jades and porcelains, could as easily come from going with other curious Beijingers to see the car, as it was on public display after the 1911 revolution. It is possible that this whole trip was constructed as elaborate wish-fulfillment, because it culminates in a scene that could only have been written by Der Ling after the death of her own son, Thaddeus Raymond, who succumbed to pneumonia at age twenty in New York City in April 1933.[5] *Imperial Incense*, which appeared shortly after his death, is dedicated to his memory. Surely this circumstance colored Der Ling's memories, if such they are, of Cixi weeping as she played with toys of the long dead Tongzhi Emperor, who had died close to the same age as Thaddeus Raymond, toys now stored in the dusty sheds of Mukden, as Der Ling's own imperial antiques would one day collect dust in a Los Angeles warehouse.

The Der Ling of this book is far more pensive than the one writing of court experiences of almost a quarter century earlier — the book ends with Cixi listening to court musicians in a garden as Der Ling recites poetry to her. "Silence, soothing and tranquil, settled over the Summer Palace," runs the last sentence of the book, "as the lengthening shadows deepened into night." To underscore that she truly hailed from a lost world, for a frontispiece for *Imperial Incense* her brother's photograph of her and Cixi, taken on a snowy Peony Hill, was rendered by the fine American artist Bertha Lum into a kind of poignant cartoon sketch. A cartoon eunuch shields the women from cartoon snow with a cartoon umbrella that looks about to tip over. Der Ling looks far more stereotypically Chinese than she did or was, and Cixi recalls a pert little girl given her mother's gown to dress up in. The genius of the painting is that this is how Der Ling saw the old lady who, at the same time, she could also imagine poisoning her way to power.

It is in Der Ling's final book, *Son of Heaven*, put forth as a biography of the Guangxu Emperor, that she reached her nadir as a historian even as she showed marked improvement as a fiction stylist. "During my years at Court as a Lady-in-waiting to the Empress Dowager," Der Ling writes in the preface to this book, published in 1935, "it was my privilege to know Kwang Hsu well and get from him at first hand much of his unhappy story and many of his advanced ideas of government." She goes on to write that she hopes that in this biography she will have cleared up any "misconceptions the world has had of this ill-fated emperor of the Manchus . . . a truly great man," yet she writes not a biography but a novel, filled with all the trembling shadows of film noir. Worst of all, in expanding on this last tiny piece of her now distant past, Der Ling traduces the very woman she claimed to have loved by blaming her for the Guangxu Emperor's death, details of which she was in no better position to know than anyone else outside the court circle. Ironically, her image of the Empress Dowager as a two-faced murdering harridan was to join similar Grand Guignol depictions in film and print for the next several decades (from Hollywood's *55 Days in Peking* in 1963 to *The Last Emperor* over thirty years later), and make it difficult, if not impossible, to rehabilitate Cixi as woman or ruler.

When all is said and done, what makes Der Ling a unique voice and personality is not so much who she knew or what she did (or who she thought she was, which differed from year to year), but the self that we glimpse through her accounts of others. The self that could move among the greats of China like one of their own, yet always keep her active, questioning Western-trained mind awake and aware; who, though dressed in the sedate silk robes of an imperial lady-in-waiting could demonstrate the waltz in the red-pillared halls of palaces which had never known

other than the slow ceremonial of coronations and official audiences. The
self who, when tiring of Cixi's overbearing personality and her court's
overbearing etiquette, could escape with Rong Ling to a nearby hill and
sing European opera arias, as if they were back in Paris, strolling along
statued pathways beneath white lace parasols. The self who could look
past the glamor and the grandeur, as well as the myth and legend, of the
Empress Dowager Cixi, and see an ordinary woman who was in most of
the ways that matter no different from other women, because she had a
heart that could love as well as hate, and that quality which only two men
(Sir Robert Hart and the artist Hubert Vos) ever saw in her but which
many of the women who came to like her admired most: an abiding
love for beauty. Beauty was Der Ling's passion, too, although unlike the
dowager, who had had to learn to face reality, the ideal was all Der Ling
wanted to, or could, see.

Most of all, Der Ling had the keen ability, often seen in those who
move on the margins of society, to stand outside herself, to freely turn
and look back at what she saw, and see that self for what it was: a woman
of contradictions, of passions and prejudices, of unresolved identity —
a woman who, despite the training toward freedom of such teachers as
Isadora Duncan and her own father, remained unfinished and incomplete,
whose love for the country of her birth, like Cixi's love for her Summer
Palace, blinded her to the expenditures required to maintain the fantasy.
In a very real sense, Der Ling was lost to the China that most intrigued
and inspired her the moment she found more temporal, immediate
happiness in European gowns, dancing in sheer Isadoran sheaths before
men she did not know, driving her own car and turning Chinese tradition
on its head with gleeful abandon.

Der Ling's whole life became a stage for a dance of opposites which
she never reconciled — curiously enough, not so much the opposites
of East and West, in Kipling's imagery, but of the conservative minds
of the old century versus the progressive ones of the new. China and
America caused reactions in Der Ling which were, in effect, reflections of
reflections. In China, Der Ling could not resist dancing the Charleston
and bobbing her hair, leading American tourists through the old palaces
and marrying an American; in America, the one country where she
could get away with it, she dressed in her court gowns, ludicrously signed

herself "Der Ling of the Manchu Dynasty," and lectured like an ordained expert on the Byzantine ways and wiles of the Empress Dowager Cixi and imperial China. Somewhere between the Jazz Age flapper and the jade-fringed court lady was a woman who spent her life searching for who she really was. In negotiating her balancing act, Der Ling lost her equilibrium. She knew that the China of painted scrolls and bell-hung temples and the China of starving peasants, oppressed women and vicious government were not the same thing, but she, too, was drawn to the dream of China that kept the Empress Dowager Cixi tightly gripping the reins of government long after any sensible ruler would have dropped them. Again and again Der Ling returned to that dream, through all eight of her books, until by the last one, she had conflated her experiences to the point where it is impossible to tell what happened on the ground and what only happened in the pleasantly cloudy spaces where imagination and wishful thinking do their best (and worst) work. The world became for her, in the end, a mirror image, in which she watched all those around her, and herself, enacting actions and reflections of actions, never sure which was real, and never clear whether it really mattered very much in the end whether or not they were.

Mirrors, in fact, play a major role in the most penetrating self-analysis Der Ling ever committed to paper — a moment in her perception of herself that may be likened to the Empress Dowager's first fascinated yet perplexed glimpse of her photographed image. In the final chapter of *Jades and Dragons*, Der Ling seats herself in her favorite corner of her favorite Beijing hostelry, the Hotel des Wagons-Lits' mirrored dining room, and watches the arrival of the guests she has invited, all of whom she has skewered throughout the foregoing chapters — except for one.

As the guests file in, a woman at Der Ling's table turns to her and babbles questions about each person in the childish form of English with which Westerners in Asia often addressed "the natives." Did Der Ling know many people in Beijing? Der Ling asides to her reader that there were probably a few ricksha coolies whom she had yet to meet, but tells the woman she knows no one. She abases herself to no avail because the foreign lady does not listen but begins to recite her own litany of vicious Beijing gossip, singling out one woman for particular venom. This woman was one the foreign lady had never met — in fact, there she was now, sitting across the room, recognizable from her cerise-colored gown and her sleek black hair, which considering her age everyone knew must be dyed. So proud! the woman sneered. Sits all alone! No wonder — she was rumored to be the worst gossip in gossipy Beijing.

"I must admit," writes Der Ling, after the foreign lady leaves her, clucking at the woman in the red dress, "I was interested in this mysterious character to whom the stranger referred," and with great reluctance got up to leave, only to find that the woman in the cerise gown was also departing the dining room. Their eyes met as they drew together side by side. Der Ling was about to speak to her when she disappeared, "right into the wall, where the mirror merged with the woodwork."

"Now let me see," Der Ling says, "have I overlooked anyone?" None, she suggests but does not say, except herself.[6]

The End

Notes

Preface

1   In his book on Chinese history, art and customs, *Chinese Potpourri* (1950), Der Ling's close friend James Zee-min Lee writes: "During the war in 1943, Der Ling gave Mandarin lectures at the Berkeley University, California, when one morning while crossing the campus to attend class she was fatally struck down by a hit-and-run-truck" (p. 328). This is the only account to state just what Der Ling was doing the morning of the accident and to describe her work at U.C. Berkeley. A stage and film actor who had played opposite everyone from Greta Garbo to Paul Muni, Lee had starred in one of Der Ling's own English-language plays, *Saving the Throne*, produced (she says) in Shanghai's Carlton Theatre. Lee's book features photographs of Der Ling and the Empress Dowager which Der Ling has inscribed, in English, to the author; one inscription refers to him as "my brother," hinting at the closeness of the friendship. The *Time Magazine* obituary quote derives from the issue of December 4, 1944.

2   Los Angeles County records, last will and testament of Thaddeus Cohu White, March 17, 1952 (codicil February 19, 1953) and death certificate, State of California; Alameda County records, coroner's inquest for Elizabeth Antoinette White (No. 822), November 28, 1944, and death certificate, State of California.

3   Han Suyin, *A Many-Splendored Thing*, p. 99.

Chapter 1

1   Sir Robert Hart, edited by John King Fairbank, Katherine Frost Bruner and Elizabeth MacLeod Matheson, *I. G. in Peking*, letters 1143 and 1252.

2   Ibid., letter 1252.

3   Der Ling, *Kow Tow*, pp. 222–223.

4   Pamela Kyle Crossley/author correspondence, 2002–03.

5   Mark Elliott, *Manchu Way*, p. 75; Pamela Kyle Crossley, *A Translucent Mirror*, p. 90.

6   Pamela Kyle Crossley, *A Translucent Mirror*, p. 91 and pp. 120–122; and Crossley/author correspondence, December 11–12, 2002.

7   Der Ling, *Imperial Incense*, p. 105, and p. 28, where she describes her brother Xunling as heir to his father's ducal title; Mark Elliott, *Manchu Way*, p. 334; Lydia Dan, "The Unknown Photographer," *History of Photography*, 1982; Der Ling, *Two Years*, p. 158; Tony Scotland, *The Empty Throne*, pp. 60–61, and Zhu Jiajing's *Historical Inaccuracies in the Books by Der Ling and Rong Ling* (1982), in which he declares that Yu Keng's title of "Lord" (*guoje*), as described by Der Ling, was neither inherited by nor bequeathed upon him, and that he was not a member of the imperial clan (*guizu*). Zhu probably only read Der Ling's memoirs in Chinese translation, in which Chinese equivalents for some of the terms she used (like "Lord") were rendered into terms that do not always match the original English.

8   Mark Elliott, *Manchu Way*, p. 65 and p. 352; Pamela Kyle Crossley, *Orphan Warriors*, p. 87; and Pamela Kyle Crossley, *A Translucent Mirror*. Hanjun participated in the examination system along with Manchu and Mongol bannermen, under a quota called *hezi hao* or "allied category": *Orphan Warriors*, pp. 89–90.

9   Der Ling, *Kow Tow*, p. 23.

10   Ibid., p. 1.

11   Ibid., p. 8.

12   Sir Robert Hart, *I. G. in Peking*, letter 1143.

13   Der Ling, *Kow Tow*, pp. 34–35. Der Ling describes her father as wearing the ruby button, but as he was still a third-grade official (out of nine possible grades), his button should have been sapphire, not ruby. In addition, the animal on his rank badge would have been a peacock, not the first-class stork. As will be addressed in a later note, Der Ling was apparently not as familiar with the various symbols of Chinese official rank as she presents herself to be.

14   Ibid., p. 88.

Chapter 2

1   Sir Robert Hart, *I. G. in Peking,* letters 800 and 814; Arthur W. Hummel (ed.), *Eminent Chinese*, p. 523. It is surely a factor in the Hubei uprisings that the province was second only to the large coastal province of Guangdong for its large number of Western missions (a total of fifteen in the 1898 map provided in Mrs. Archibald Little's *Intimate China*, p. 207).
2   Sir Robert Hart, *I. G. in Peking*, letters referred to above. Judging by his visual and auditory troubles, it is possible that Yu Keng was suffering from type 2 diabetes. *Vide infra.*
3   Der Ling, *Kow Tow*, pp. 61–79.

Chapter 3

1   Der Ling, *Imperial Incense*, p. 189.
2   Der Ling, *Kow Tow*, pp. 88–95. Though Headland's *Court Life in China* says that Manchu daughters had to be registered at age fourteen to fifteen, Crossley says that such registration was not necessary for either Manchus or Mongolians, and we must remember that *hanjun* were not required to register their daughters for palace service.
3   Der Ling, *Kow Tow*, p. 93.
4   Mrs. Archibald Little, *Intimate China*, p. 192.
5   See Donald Keene, *Emperor of Japan: Meiji and His World 1852–1912* (hereafter *Meiji*), pp. 474–483.
6   Der Ling, *Kow Tow*, p. 111.
7   Mrs. Archibald Little, *Intimate China*, pp. 318–319.
8   Der Ling, *Kow Tow*, pp. 115–118.
9   Ellen LaMotte, *Peking Dust*, pp. 15–20.
10 Lin Yutang, *Imperial Peking*, pp. 28–29.
11 Lao She, *Beneath the Red Banner*, p. 105.
12 Der Ling, *Kow Tow*, pp. 123–124.

Chapter 4

1   Der Ling, *Kow Tow*, pp. 127–128.
2   Marina Warner, *The Dragon Empress*, p. 71.
3   Arthur W. Hummel (ed.), *Eminent Chinese*, p. 382.
4   Der Ling, *Kow Tow*, p. 137.
5   Ibid., p. 141.
6   Edward Thomas Williams, *China Yesterday and Today*, p. 317.

7   Arthur W. Hummel (ed.), *Eminent Chinese*, p. 247.

8   Der Ling, *Kow Tow*, pp. 141–142.

Chapter 5

1   Baroness Shidzue Ishimoto, *Facing Two Ways*, p. 5.

2   Ibid., p. 17.

3   Der Ling, *Kow Tow*, pp. 145–146.

4   Ibid., pp. 146–147.

5   Ibid., p. 157.

6   Ibid., pp. 151–153.

7   Ibid., pp. 158–159.

8   Ibid., pp. 163–165.

9   Yu Keng evidently also understood French, though Der Ling paradoxically records his disavowal of it when asked about it by the Guangxu Emperor during a visit to court years later. See Der Ling, *Two Years*, p. 241.

10   Der Ling, *Kow Tow*, pp. 181–182.

11   Ibid., pp. 185–187.

12   Ibid., pp. 199–200.

Chapter 6

1   Baroness Shidzue Ishimoto, *Two Ways*, pp. 58–59.

2   Der Ling, *Kow Tow*, p. 201.

3   Ibid., pp. 203–204.

4   Donald Keene, *Meiji*, p. 551.

5   Baroness Shidzue Ishimoto, *Two Ways*, p. 63.

6   Der Ling, *Kow Tow*, pp. 208–209.

7   See Jonathan D. Spence, *God's Chinese Son*.

8   Sterling Seagrave and Peggy Seagrave, *Dragon Lady*, p. 39.

9   Jonathan D. Spence, *God's Chinese Son*, pp. 51–65.

10   Sterling Seagrave and Peggy Seagrave, *Dragon Lady*, p. 108.

11   Wu Yung, translated by Ida Pruitt, *The Flight of an Empress*, p. 194.

12   Arthur W. Hummel (ed.), *Eminent Chinese*, pp. 470–471.

13   *Eminent Chinese* states that Li refused to go ashore during his stop in Japan — he had crossed from Vancouver, British Columbia.

14   Agreeing with Wu Yung, to whom Li described this coffin, see Wu Yung, *The Flight of an Empress*, p. 189 and *Eminent Chinese*, p. 470.

15   Li could be very strict with his servants. Li's American secretary William Pethick once told American artist Cecile Payen of witnessing Li fall by

accident as one of his valets helped him through a narrow door. According to Pethick, Li looked up from the floor at the cringing servant and said, "I will throw you into boiling lard when we get home." Cecile E. Payen, *The Century Magazine*, January 1901, Vol. LXI, No. 3, pp. 453–468.

16 Sterling Seagrave, *Soong Dynasty*, pp. 68–85.

17 Der Ling, *Kow Tow*, p. 230.

18 Ibid., pp. 314–315.

19 Luke S. K. Kwong, *A Mosaic of the Hundred Days,* p. 207.

Chapter 7

1 Sue Fawn Chung, "The Image of the Empress Dowager Cixi," in Paul A. Cohen and John E. Schrecker (eds.), *Reform in Nineteenth-Century China* (Cambridge, MA: East Asian Research Center, Harvard University, 1976), pp. 101–110.

2 Der Ling, *Lotos Petals*, p. 21.

3 Mrs. Archibald Little, *Intimate China*, pp. 411–412.

4 Sterling Seagrave and Peggy Seagrave, *Dragon Lady*, p. 234.

5 Ibid., p. 205 *ff*. Also see Sue Fawn Chung, "The Image of the Empress Dowager," *supra.*

6 Béguin and Morel, *The Forbidden City*, p. 89.

7 Der Ling, *Two Years*, p. 5.

8 Der Ling, *Old Buddha*, p. 241.

9 Ibid., p. 242.

10 Der Ling, *Kow Tow*, pp. 258–259. Der Ling translates "ermaozi" as "secondary hairy ones," but the more figurative meaning of this term, per Stephen Wadley, refers to the way hair changes color with age (in other words, black going to gray or white). "So *èrmáozi* are people who are no longer fully Chinese — 'salt and pepper' Chinese." Wadley, private correspondence, January 2004.

Chapter 8

1 The apartment house at 4, Avenue Hoche now houses the Union française des Industries Petrolières, including a number of other petroleum trade associations.

2 Der Ling, *Kow Tow*, pp. 266–267.

3 Ibid., p. 266.

4 A Roman Catholic, Ching-Ch'ang had served as Minister to France from 1895 to June 17, 1899. He should have returned to China immediately

after Yu Keng began his tour of duty, but remained in Paris and then in Switzerland for another couple of years, understandably fearful of returning to Beijing during and after the Boxer Uprising for two obvious reasons: his religion and the fact that one of his staff was related to Shoufu, a proscribed member of Kang Youwei's circle. See Sir Robert Hart, *I. G. in Peking*, letters 1237, 1242 and 1243.

5   Vincent Cronin, *Paris on the Eve 1900–1914*, pp. 14–15.
6   Ibid.; and Nigel Gosling, *The Adventurous World of Paris 1900–1914*.
7   Der Ling, *Kow Tow*, pp. 277–279.
8   Paul A. Cohen, *History in Three Keys*, pp. 228–229.
9   Der Ling, *Old Buddha*, pp. 238–239.
10 Seagrave concludes in his biography of Cixi that the real begetter of the use of the Boxer groups as a "secret irregular force" came from the conservative military commander, General Li Peng-heng; again, like Tuan, Li was probably as interested in diverting Boxer wrath from the Manchu dynasty as he was in scouring China of foreigners.
11 Der Ling, *Two Years*, pp. 123–124.
12 B. L. Putnam Weale [Bertram Lenox-Simpson], *Indiscreet Letters from Peking*, p. 19.
13 George Lynch, *The War of the Civilisations*, p. 106.
14 Ibid., pp. 106–107.
15 Der Ling, *Kow Tow*, pp. 289–290.
16 Sterling Seagrave and Peggy Seagrave, *Dragon Lady*, p. 340.
17 Ibid., p. 343.

Chapter 9

1   Cecil E. Payen, *Century Magazine*, January 1901, p. 457.
2   Ibid., p. 455.
3   Der Ling, *Kow Tow*, pp. 291–292.
4   *New York Times*, December 2, 1900.
5   Lao She, *Beneath the Red Banner*, p. 171.
6   Cecil E. Payen, *Century Magazine*, January 1901, p. 468; and Wu Yung, *The Flight of an Empress*.
7   Wu Yung, *The Flight of an Empress*, p. 72.

Chapter 10

1   Peter Kurth, *Isadora*, pp. 70–78.
2   Eliza Ruhamah Scidmore, *China: The Long Lived Empire*, p. 5. A pioneer

woman journalist born in America, Scidmore is credited with having introduced cherry trees to Washington, D.C.

3 Der Ling, *Lotos Petals*, p. 239.

4 Nigel Gosling, *The Adventurous World of Paris 1900–1914*, p. 75.

5 Der Ling, *Lotos Petals*, p. 234.

6 Ibid., pp. 236–237.

7 Ibid., pp. 241–242.

8 Ibid., pp. 243–244.

9 Ibid., pp. 249–250.

Chapter 11

1 Nigel Gosling, *The Adventurous World of Paris 1900–1914*, pp. 13–14.

2 Cornelia Otis Skinner, *Madame Sarah*, pp. 110–111.

3 Ibid., p. 269.

4 Der Ling, *Lotos Petals*, p. 173.

5 Ibid., pp. 177–178.

6 Bernhardt's affectionate, motherly regard for Der Ling is all the more intriguing when we compare it with her quite opposite feelings for the exquisite Japanese actress Madame Sadayakko, who had played the Comédie Française during the Paris Expo to packed audiences and was often called the "Japanese Bernhardt." "*Atroce! Abominable!*" Bernhardt is recorded as having snapped to a friend who had asked her for her opinion of Sadayakko and her fellow actors. The same friend remembered her describing the Japanese troupe as "A pack of monkeys!" Even more intriguing is the rumor, reported by Sadayakko's biographer Lesley Downer, that Bernhardt sat incognito in the Comédie Française to watch the ex-geisha perform. See Lesley Downer, *Madame Sadayakko*, p. 176.

Chapter 12

1 Sir Robert Hart, *I. G. in Peking*, p. 1303.

2 Eliza Ruhamah Scidmore, *China: The Long Lived Empire*, pp. 133–134. Writing of the period just before the "Hundred Days" of summer 1898, Scidmore says: "Only one Manchu noblewoman of the court circle has been educated in a foreign country in foreign ways, and has permitted her daughters to be taught on the same lines, and orders were given this Manchu family to devise and take charge of the changed ceremonies of the Empress Dowager's court. Before that family could reach Peking, the crash came; reaction reacted; the coup d'état fell; the reformers fled for their lives." This

reference can only be to Louisa and her daughters. Also see Sir Robert Hart, *I. G. in Peking*, pp. 1328–1329.

3   Sir Robert Hart, *I. G. in Peking*, p. 1335; Der Ling, *Lotos Petals*, p. 302; and *New York Times*, March 30, 1903.

4   Sterling Seagrave and Peggy Seagrave, *Dragon Lady*, p. 415: the painter Hubert Vos was escorted into the Empress Dowager Cixi's presence by Zaizhen in 1905 and found that he could not communicate with the prince because he spoke only Chinese.

5   In 1899, Sir Robert Hart was describing Yu Keng as having vision and hearing problems, which he does not attribute to age. To have such age-related problems, Yu Keng would have had to be much older than Der Ling tells us. On the other hand, the symptoms he developed seem to accord more with a gradually deteriorating case of type 2 diabetes, which left untreated can cause both blindness and loss of hearing, and may have developed as Yu Keng increasingly ate a Western rather than Asian diet. (Type 2 is especially prevalent among Asians who have immigrated to the United States.) Identified in medieval times as an illness, diabetes was never properly treated until insulin was discovered in 1921. The disease could be one of the reasons why Yu Keng was so adamant that he be treated by his foreign doctors in Shanghai after his return to China in 1903. I thank Dr. Dennis Cunniff for his advice in this medical guesswork.

6   Der Ling, *Lotos Petals*, p. 71. Like her sister Rong Ling, whose nickname was Nellie, Der Ling also had a nickname — Venie — which was used with close friends. She very rarely inscribed her books with this name.

Chapter 13

1   Aisin-Gioro Puyi, translated by W. J. F. Jenner, *From Emperor to Citizen*, p. 210.

2   Der Ling, *Two Years*, pp. 4–5.

3   Ibid., pp. 7–8.

4   Sterling Seagrave and Peggy Seagrave, *Dragon Lady*, p. 549, note on "The Yu Keng family."

5   Edward J. M. Rhoads, *Manchus and Han*, p. 272.

6   Der Ling, *Two Years*, p. 8.

7   Sterling Seagrave and Peggy Seagrave, *Dragon Lady*, p. 251; Sarah Pike Conger, *Letters from China*, pp. 40–42; Derling, *Kow Tow*, p. 98.

8   Der Ling, *Kow Tow*, pp. 54–55.

9   Der Ling, *Two Years*, p. 12.

Chapter 14

1   Der Ling, *Two Years*, p. 12. Rong Ling claims in her memoirs that Louisa and her daughters received a "crash course" in court etiquette at the home of Prince Qing.

2   Jonathan D. Spence, *Gate of Heavenly Peace*, pp. 9–11.

3   Der Ling, *Two Years*, p. 13.

4   Numerology played a powerful role throughout Chinese culture and art, with certain numbers assigned more auspicious powers than others.

5   Der Ling says fourth rank, but this rank called for lapis lazuli buttons, not crystal. She also gets her father's button wrong, sometimes giving him the second-rank coral instead of first-rank ruby; in fact, Yu Keng seems not to have risen higher than the third rank, which would permit him to wear the sapphire button.

6   Beijing Summer Palace Administration Office, *Summer Palace*, pp. 25–28; Der Ling, *Two Years*, pp, 14–15.

7   Sterling Seagrave and Peggy Seagrave, *Dragon Lady*, p. 124.

8   Mary M. Anderson, *Hidden Power*, p. 21 and pp. 307–311.

9   Isaac Taylor Headland and Dr. Headland, *Court Life in China*, p. 102, for description of Louisa; and for Der Ling's observations, see *Two Years*, p. 15. On a visit to the Summer Palace, Lady Townley seems to have seen Der Ling and Rong Ling in their velvet gowns, but gives details too insufficient to date exactly when the sighting took place. We may assume it occurred prior to Cixi's order that Louisa and her daughters be given Manchu court clothing to wear. "I was present when for the first time public opinion forced [Cixi] to permit two of her Ladies-in-Waiting to appear before her in European dress . . . They were dressed alike in crimson broché velvet, with European shoes on their tiny feet. They looked most awkward as they curtsied in place of kotowing. The Empress was cold at first, but curiosity overcoming her annoyance and no foreigner besides myself being present, she gradually softened towards them. Before very long she was seated on a divan between them trying on a Parisian shoe on the Imperial foot." Cixi did try on Der Ling's French shoes on Der Ling's first visit to court, but the latter mentions no foreign woman being present, and it is likely Lady Townley was present for another trying-on session. Cixi seems to have also been curious to touch and examine Lady Townley's clothing, per the latter's account. See *The Indiscretions of Lady Susan*.

10 Katherine Carl, *With the Empress Dowager of China*, p. 125.

11 Der Ling, *Two Years*, pp. 16–17.

12 Ibid., p. 17 and p. 159.

13 Isaac Taylor Headland and Dr. Headland, *Court Life in China*, p. 202 and Der Ling, *Two Years*, p. 18.

14 Der Ling, *Two Years*, pp. 18–19.

15 Sir Robert Hart, *I. G. In Peking*, p. 1304 and p. 1311.

16 Der Ling, *Two Years*, p. 20 and p. 138.

17 Ibid., p. 20.

18 Isaac Taylor Headland and Dr. Headland, *Court Life in China*, p. 166.

19 Wu Yung, *The Flight of an Empress*, p. 203.

20 Der Ling, *Son of Heaven*, p. vii and "Pu-Yi, the Puppet of Japan," *The Saturday Evening Post*, April 30, 1932, p. 70.

21 Der Ling, *Two Years*, pp. 24–25.

22 Ibid., pp. 42–43.

23 Ibid., p. 28.

24 Ibid., pp. 27–28.

25 Ibid., p. 35. See Han Suyin, *The Crippled Tree*, p. 165, where the author describes food sent with her father on a trip to Europe.

26 Cixi was very fond of pork, particularly enjoying the rind cut into strips and fried into a dish called "Tingling Bells." Wu Yung confirms Der Ling's account of this with his similar descriptions of Cixi's eating habits on the road to Xian. See Wu Yung, *The Flight of an Empress*.

27 Der Ling's description in *Two Years* of where she, her mother and sister were lodged at the Summer Palace refers to a two-story building located to the right of where Cixi slept, and a courtyard away from the Hall of Jade Billows, where the Guangxu Emperor lived, beyond which was another courtyard containing a residence for Guangxu's wife, Longyu. The Hall of Happiness in Longevity is described by Der Ling as the Empress Dowager's primary residence, which it was, containing not only sitting rooms but a bedroom. However, the only building located to its right was the Porch of Nourished Clouds (*Paiyundian*), which according to Arlington and Lewisohn, was "used as a residence by Court ladies" (see *In Search of Old Peking*, p. 287). Because Der Ling describes being able to open a lake-facing window and look out at the lake under the dawning light of morning, it is hard to see how she could do this from the Porch of Nourished Clouds; whereas there is more logic to obtaining this view from a pavilion to the west of the Lodge of Propriety in Weeding.

Chapter 15

1 The Yuanmingyuan was first begun in 1709 by the Kangxi Emperor, itself built on the ruins of a Ming prince's garden; see Marina Warner, *The Dragon Empress*, p. 73.

2   Sterling Seagrave and Peggy Seagrave, *Dragon Lady*, pp. 132–133.

3   The banner system as a whole, as sent up hilariously by novelist Lao She, was one in which bannermen were virtually forced into lives of unemployed, unemployable dole-drawers, and was a system that was easily taken advantage of. Lao She describes cripples unable to serve in the army, who hired his fit young cousin to pass all the equestrian tests required to enter military service and then assume the rank he had won for them and the emoluments that came with that rank, or widows who drew the pensions of several different dead bannermen relatives, all draining the imperial war chest with far greater rapacity than any spending project Cixi could create. See Lao She, *Beneath the Red Banner.*

4   Philip W. Sergeant, *The Great Empress Dowager of China*, p. 123.

5   Sterling Seagrave and Peggy Seagrave, *Dragon Lady*, p. 181.

6   Juliet Bredon, *Peking*, p. 302.

7   Der Ling, *Two Years*, pp. 48–54.

Chapter 16

1   Der Ling, *Two Years*, p. 95.

2   Ibid., pp. 57–58.

3   Der Ling, *Imperial Incense*, p. 233.

4   Adrian Levy and Cathy Scott-Clark, *Stone of Heaven*, p. 28. It should be noted that the authors have confused Der Ling with a Princess Yu of the imperial family, p. 219.

5   Der Ling, *Lotos Petals*, pp. 261–264.

6   Der Ling, *Imperial Incense*, p. 67.

7   Ibid., p. 68.

8   Der Ling, *Two Years*, p. 114.

9   Der Ling, *Two Years*, pp. 68–69; Der Ling, *Kow Tow*, p. 92.

Chapter 17

1   Der Ling, *Two Years*, p. 75.

2   Ibid., pp. 77–78.

3   Ibid., p. 260 and p. 78.

4   Der Ling, *Imperial Incense*, pp. 200–201; Der Ling, *Two Years*, pp. 279–282.

5   Beijing Summer Palace Administration Office, *Summer Palace*, pp. 100–101.

6   L. C. Arlington and William Lewisohn, *In Search of Old Peking*, p. 287, for confirmation of the clay village in miniature.

7   Der Ling, *Two Years*, p. 82.
8   Ibid., pp. 83–84.
9   Ibid.
10 Su Hua Ling Chen, *Ancient Melodies*, p. 174.
11 Der Ling, *Two Years*, p. 87.

Chapter 18

1   Der Ling, *Two Years*, pp. 95–100; Sarah Pike Conger, *Letters from China*, p. 228.
2   Der Ling, *Two Years*, pp. 95–108.
3   Ibid.
4   Ibid.
5   Ibid.
6   Ibid.
7   Ibid.
8   Ibid.
9   Ibid.
10 Ibid.
11 Ibid.
12 Ibid.; Der Ling, *Lotos Petals*, p. 251. See "Empress Dowager Cixi: Her Art of Living," English section.
13 Katherine Carl, *With the Empress Dowager of China*, p. 176.
14 Isaac Taylor Headland and Dr. Headland, *Court Life in China*, pp. 118–128; see also Eliza Ruhamah Scidmore, *China: The Long Lived Empire*.
15 Der Ling, *Two Years*, pp. 104–108.
16 Ibid.

Chapter 19

1   Der Ling, *Two Years*, pp. 112–113.
2   Ibid., pp. 110–111.
3   Ibid., pp. 116–119.
4   Frank Ching, *Ancestors*, p. 348.
5   Der Ling, *Two Years*, pp. 126–128. Cixi's fascination with Buddhist monastic structure seems to have influenced to a certain degree her choice of Der Ling for her favorite; in most monasteries, the monk whose job it was to welcome guests had under him a "young, quick-witted" monk called *zhaoke* whose job it was to entertain the guests face to face and make them comfortable in their strange surroundings. This, rather than the role of "first lady-in-waiting" that

Der Ling assumed for herself in retrospect, was much more aligned with what Der Ling actually did for the dowager at court. See Nan Huai-Chin, *Basic Buddhism: Exploring Buddhism and Zen*, p. 184.

6 Der Ling, *Two Years*, p. 129.

7 L. C. Arlington and William Lewisohn, *In Search of Old Peking*, p. 243.

8 Der Ling, *Two Years*, p. 132.

9 Juliet Bredon, *Peking*, pp. 80–82.

10 Der Ling, *Two Years*, p. 134.

11 Isaac Taylor Headland and Dr. Headland, *Court Life in China*, pp. 105–106. Dr. Headland does not name Louisa and her daughters specifically, but the descriptions of them are accurate, and the incident seems to have happened at the time Cixi returned to the Forbidden City, Der Ling's first time there.

12 Der Ling, *Two Years*, pp. 137–138.

Chapter 20

1 *The Indiscretions of Lady Susan*, pp. 86–98.

2 Sterling Seagrave and Peggy Seagrave, *Dragon Lady*, pp. 407–409.

3 Der Ling, *Two Years*, pp. 140–141. In his critique of Der Ling's *Son of Heaven*, Zhu Jiajing claims the author was incorrect to describe a party at one of the imperial palaces with such mats stretched over the courtyards, insisting this was not a practice of members of the imperial house. Zhu's criticism is in direct contradiction to Katherine Carl's recollection of just such matting being used to cover a courtyard for the Guangxu Emperor's birthday party at the Summer Palace, see Katherine Carl, *With the Empress Dowager of China*, p. 60. Zhu also claims that Cixi never took a train ride except when she returned from Xian in 1902, which is not true; she also took a train when she went to visit the Western Tombs in spring 1903.

4 Der Ling, *Two Years*, pp. 143–144.

5 Lin Yutang, *My Country and My People*, p. 157.

6 Der Ling, *Two Years*, p. 192.

7 Ibid., p. 157.

Chapter 21

1 Sarah Pike Conger, *Letters from China*, pp. 247–248.

2 Ibid.

3 Froncek, Thomas, *The Horizon Book of the Arts of China*, p. 204.

4 Katherine Carl, *With the Empress Dowager of China*, p. xix.

5 Sarah Pike Conger, *Letters from China*, pp. 247–248.

6 Der Ling, *Two Years*, p. 195.

7 Ibid., p. 194.

8 Ibid.

9 Ibid., p. 198.

10 Ibid., p. 200. Interestingly, this aspect of Der Ling's relationship with Cixi was delineated perfectly, and with some humor, in Li Hanxiang's 1976 film, *The Last Tempest*. Li has Cixi comment to Li Lianying, when the actress playing Der Ling assents quickly to fulfill the old lady's request: "This kid will do anything I ask."

11 Ibid., pp. 203–204.

12 Ibid., pp. 204–205.

13 Sterling Seagrave and Peggy Seagrave, *Dragon Lady*, pp. 409–410.

14 Der Ling, *Two Years*, pp. 206–208.

15 Ibid., p. 210. The next to last reference to this portrait that I can find occurs in an April 20, 1937 article in the *Los Angeles Times*: "A year ago, the Princess went to Peking and brought back with her twenty-five packing cases of belongings . . . [including] a painting of the former court lady herself, as a girl of 18 in Paris." The painting was included in the catalog for the 1953 auction of Der Ling's objets d'art, but its whereabouts now are unknown.

16 Der Ling, *Jades and Dragons*, p. 189.

17 Der Ling, *Two Years*, p. 210.

18 No author contemporary with the events except for Katherine Carl has ever given young Xunling proper attribution for these photographs; only with Lydia Dan's 1982 unpublished article, "The Unknown Photographer," and her 1984 published letter in *History of Photography* (Vol. 8, Number 4, October–December 1984, p. 345), and then Sterling and Peggy Seagrave's *Dragon Lady*, published in 1992, was Xunling given his due. Ironically, even Der Ling deriders like Edmund Backhouse and J. O. P. Bland used Xunling's photographs without attribution. The dowager had in fact been photographed before Xunling came to court: one of the foreign ladies standing on the city wall, watching Cixi's return from Xian in April 1902, snapped a photo of the short, silk-clad dowager waving toward the camera with her handkerchief, a smile on her face. Whether Cixi knew she was being photographed, given her total inexperience of cameras at the time, is debatable. See Béguin and Morel, *The Forbidden City*, p. 88.

19 The photographs of the Meiji Emperor and Empress Haruko were made in 1872 by Raimund Baron von Stillfried-Rattonitz. Interestingly, the oldest existing daguerreotype in Japan depicts Shimazu Nariakira (1809–58), daimyo of the Satsuma clan, who sat for a camera in September 1857.

The photograph of King Rama IV (Mongkut) of Siam and wife Queen Debsirindra, from 1856, can be found at the Smithsonian Institution, Department of Anthropology, cat. #E4003, NAAI #1735. The photographs of King Louis-Philippe and Queen Amélie are kept in the Archives Nationales de Paris. The photograph of Queen Victoria and Princess Victoria (not the future King Edward VII, as noted in the caption) can be seen on www.btinternet.com/~sbishop100/vic23.jpg. The image of young Duleep Singh can be seen on www.duleepsingh.com/gallery.asp. I thank Oliver Rost, François Velde, Chris Pitt Lewis and Richard Lichten for pointing me to these examples.

20 Der Ling, *Two Years*, pp. 218–219, and Lydia Dan, "The Unknown Photographer," unpublished article, 1982. In the film *The Last Tempest* (*vide supra*) Der Ling has a cameo role, anachronistically in 1898, in which she is shown not just as Cixi's translator and favorite — dressed in trailing evening gowns and white gloves and shooing foreign ladies off the dowager's thrones — but also as court photographer, a role she never served. According to Lydia Dan, when Rong Ling was leaving her Beijing house in 1931, she was apprised by a servant of a couple of crates of Xunling's glass negatives; and whether because the boxes were too heavy to move easily, or because she shared the family's alleged disdain for Xunling's "lack of ambition" and belief that this lack signaled "stupidity," she ordered him to throw the crates away. The servant disobeyed the order and, Dan believed, sold the negatives to a Mr. Yamamoto, who owned a photo studio in the city. Yamamoto then made prints from these negatives, though he did not claim them as his own work. Dr. Shiou-yun Fang (University of Edinburgh thesis, 2005) believes Yamamoto gave the two cases of negatives to Der Ling or T.C. — it is just as possible they purchased them from him. Soon after 1931, cheaply produced prints of Xunling's famous photos of the Empress Dowager and her court began to appear in little cloth-bound booklets, one of which is in the author's possession.

21 Der Ling, *Two Years*, pp. 222–223.

Chapter 22

1   Der Ling, *Two Years*, p. 266.
2   Katherine Carl, *With the Empress Dowager of China*, p. 4.
3   Ibid., p. 6.
4   Sarah Pike Conger, *Letters from China*, p. 270.
5   Der Ling, *Two Years*, p. 230.
6   Ibid., pp. 230–231 and *With the Empress Dowager of China*, p. 6.

7 Katherine Carl, *With the Empress Dowager of China*, p. 10.

8 Der Ling, *Two Years*, p. 232 and *With the Empress Dowager of China*, p. 11.

9 Ibid., p. 31 and pp. 27–28.

10 Ibid., p. 115.

11 Der Ling, *Imperial Incense*, pp. 182–185; Rumer Godden, *The Butterfly Lions*, p. 16 *ff.*

12 Katherine Carl, *With the Empress Dowager of China*, pp. 53–56.

13 Ibid., p. 161.

14 Ibid., p. 194.

15 V. R. Burkhardt, *Chinese Creeds and Customs*, p. 32.

16 Der Ling, *Old Buddha*, pp. 315—316 and *Two Years*, p. 248.

17 See Tsao Hsueh-chin, *A Dream of Red Mansions*, Vol. II, Chapter 64.

18 In 1999, Liu Qi, a "director of chronicles" of the City of Changzhi, Shanxi province, published a book in Chinese titled *Cracking the Mystery of Cixi's Youth*. According to this research, based on interviews with farmers from the area, and "38 pieces of evidence" in all, Liu Qi claims that Cixi was actually born the daughter of a farmer named Wang, who sold her at age four to another farmer, by name Song, who then sold her as servant to the bannerman Huizheng of the Yehonala clan. The young girl's beauty and intelligence impressed the family to such degree they adopted her as a Manchu and had, so the story goes, no qualms about presenting her in the imperial concubine roundup as one of their own rather than as a child of Han farmers — something that would have been considered a criminal act, as only Manchu and Mongolian girls were eligible to be not only chosen as concubines and wives but even presented for such choosing. While intriguing, the story needs much more rigorous investigation in and out of China before taking its place alongside facts on the life of the Empress Dowager.

19 Sterling Seagrave and Peggy Seagrave, *Dragon Lady*, pp. 61–62.

20 Der Ling, *Two Years*, pp. 250–253.

21 Ibid.

22 Ibid.

Chapter 23

1 Der Ling, *Imperial Incense*, p. 204.

2 Wu Yung, *The Flight of an Empress*, p. 141.

3 Der Ling, *Imperial Incense*, pp. 250–251.

4 Ibid., pp. 236–239. According to the catalog for the Palace Museum exhibit, "Empress Dowager Cixi: Her Art of Living," Cixi used her face massager to blend in a powder made up by court doctors from sixteen herbs, which

was devised to help remove the freckles to which she was disposed. Called *yurongsan*, this mixture was a favorite of Cixi's which she used every day.

5   Sterling Seagrave and Peggy Seagrave, *Dragon Lady*, p. 144.

6   Der Ling, *Imperial Incense*, pp. 205–206.

7   Ibid., pp. 210–211.

8   See the early picture in *With the Empress Dowager of China*, compared with the one taken in the winter of 1903 on Peony Hill with Der Ling, her sister and mother; see Der Ling, *Two Years*. The dowager is noticeably more aged and tired in appearance.

9   Der Ling, *Lotos Petals*, p. 96.

10 Der Ling, *Two Years*, pp. 263–267.

11 Ibid.

12 Ibid., pp. 315–316.

13 Der Ling, *Two Years*, p. 161 and pp. 371–373; Juliet Bredon, *Peking*, p. 135; and Fei Shi, *Guide to Peking*, photo of "The 'Foreign Palaces'" at the Forbidden City.

14 Ibid; Katherine Carl, *With the Empress Dowager of China*, p. 196.

15 Der Ling, *Two Years*, pp. 284–285.

16 Der Ling's informal butterfly robe was donated to the Metropolitan Museum of Art in New York City by Mr. and Mrs. George Miller in 1970. It is composed of silk and silk wrapped with gold on a satin ground and measures 58 inches from sleeve end to sleeve end and 82 inches in height.

17 Der Ling, *Two Years*, pp. 286–287.

18 Katherine Carl, *With the Empress Dowager of China*, pp. 196–198; a photograph of Cixi standing in front of the richly decorated Hall That Dispels the Clouds, with Der Ling, Rong Ling, Louisa and court ladies, seems to date from this birthday celebration; see Der Ling, *Two Years*.

19 Katherine Carl, *With the Empress Dowager of China*, pp. 198–199.

20 Der Ling, *Two Years*, pp. 300–301.

21 L. C. Arlington and William Lewisohn, *In Search of Old Peking*, p. 100.

22 Der Ling, *Two Years*, pp. 301–302.

23 In his *The Flight of an Empress* [1936], p. 68, magistrate Wu Yung, who greeted Cixi on her flight to Xian and served her in exile, notes that Li Lianying was last in the line of carts streaming out of Beijing, placing the chief eunuch in a unique position for impromptu escape.

22 Der Ling, *Two Years*, pp. 313–314.

25 Ibid., p. 318 and Pierre Loti, *Last Days of Peking*, pp. 106–107.

26 Der Ling, *Two Years*, pp. 320–321.

27 Ibid., pp. 321–322.

28 Ibid.

29 Ibid.

Chapter 24

1 Sterling Seagrave and Peggy Seagrave, *Dragon Lady*, p. 549.

2 Der Ling, *Imperial Incense*, pp. 94–97.

3 Sterling Seagrave and Peggy Seagrave, *Dragon Lady*, p. 421.

4 Katherine Carl, *With the Empress Dowager of China*, p. 290.

5 Der Ling, *Two Years*, p. 332.

6 Ibid., pp. 323–324.

7 Ibid., p. 325.

8 Ibid., pp. 325–327.

9 Der Ling, *Imperial Incense*, pp. 264–265.

10 Edmund O. Clubb, *Twentieth Century China*, pp. 32–33.

11 Katherine Carl, *With the Empress Dowager of China*, p. 302.

12 Ibid., pp. 287—289 and *Two Years*, p. 346

13 Der Ling, *Two Years*, p. 346.

14 This photograph can be seen in Katherine Carl, *With the Empress Dowager of China*, after p. 304.

15 Katherine Carl, *With the Empress Dowager of China*, pp. 297–299; Der Ling, *Two Years*, pp. 347–348.

16 Der Ling, *Two Years*, pp. 347–348.

17 Katherine Carl, *With The Empress Dowager of China*, p. 235.

18 Der Ling, *Two Years*, p. 355.

Chapter 25

1 Der Ling, *Two Years*, pp. 350–351.

2 Der Ling, *Kow Tow*, pp. 316–317.

3 Der Ling, *Two Years*, p. 375.

4 Der Ling, *Kow Tow*, p. 318.

5 Der Ling, *Two Years*, p. 375.

6 Der Ling, *Kow Tow*, pp. 319–320.

7 Der Ling, *Two Years*, pp. 375–376.

8 Ibid., p. 378; Wu Yung remembered Cui being "fierce" and "haughty;" see *The Flight of an Empress*, p. 70. According to one legend of the murder of the Pearl Concubine, Cui was one of the eunuchs who pushed her into the Forbidden City well traditionally pointed out as the site of her death. The entire story has been discredited in modern times, not least because the well traditionally supposed to be the site of the Pearl Concubine's death is too small to admit an adult body. In addition, Na Genzheng, great grandnephew of Cixi and currently an official at the New Summer Palace, claimed in

an interview from August 2004 that his grandfather, son of the Empress Dowager's younger brother, witnessed the Pearl Concubine's suicide, and deplored the way the Empress Dowager had been "framed" for this and other alleged acts. See Richard Spencer article, www.royalarchive.com, August 4, 2004.

9   See Zhu Jiajing, *Historial Inaccuracies in the Books by Der Ling and Rong Ling*. Rong Ling used her title — Princess Shou Shan — in her 1930 book, written in English and published in Beijing, on the love affair between the Qianlong Emperor and his Muslim concubine, Xiangfei, the so-called "Fragrant Concubine" (*vide supra*). The book was dedicated to a "Princess Tsai Tao, in memory of happy days at the imperial court." I have not found a princess so-named among the daughters of princes of the Qing imperial house, but there was a Prince Zaitao, fifth son of Prince Chun, whose wife Rong Ling may have been referring to. She did not use her title in her memoirs of the court published in 1957. Der Ling's title was possibly, like her sister's, also tagged to some feature of the Summer Palace. The author owns an embroidered panel designed by Rong Ling and signed "Shou Shan."

10   Der Ling, *Two Years*, pp. 378–380.

11   Stella Dong, *Shanghai 1842–1949*, p. 73.

12   *Britannica World Language Dictionary*, 1960.

13   Enid Saunders Candlin, *Breach in the Wall*, pp. 41–42.

14   As of 2003, this record, placing White with the Battery "A" Light Artillery, derives from White's gravestone in Los Angeles National Cemetery, and has not yet been verified by the U.S. Department of Veterans' Affairs.

15   Lo Hui-men (ed.), *The Correspondence of G. E. Morrison*, p. 524.

16   Der Ling, *Kow Tow*, p. 321.

Chapter 26

1   Edward J. M. Rhoads, *Manchus and Han*, p. 187.

2   Ibid., pp. 173–210; also for quote from British missionary J. C. Keyte.

3   Sterling Seagrave, *Soong Dynasty*, p. 181.

4   Ibid., pp. 202–203.

5   Harry Hussey, *My Pleasures and Palaces*, p. 264.

Chapter 27

1   Sterling Seagrave and Peggy Seagrave, *Dragon Lady*, p. 412.

Chapter 28

1   Given the fact that Vos served on the jury at the International Exposition in St. Louis, where Katherine's portrait of Cixi was exhibited, he may well have wondered whether a better likeness could not be taken of this almost legendary woman, and felt he was the man for the task. As can be seen from the results, he was not mistaken.

2   Sterling Seagrave and Peggy Seagrave, *Dragon Lady*, pp. 414–417.

3   Ibid.

4   Ibid., p. 428.

5   Ibid., pp. 434–435.

6   Der Ling, *Old Buddha*, pp. 312–313. In her *Saturday Evening Post* article on Puyi, Der Ling states categorically that "Even Kwang-su's death was tragic, as he was poisoned." See *Saturday Evening Post*, April 30, 1932, p. 70.

7   Sterling Seagrave and Peggy Seagrave, *Dragon Lady*, p. 436.

8   Der Ling, *Old Buddha*, pp. 328–330.

9   Isaac Taylor Headland and Dr. Headland, *Court Life in China*, pp. 343–347.

10 Ibid.

11 Der Ling, *Old Buddha*, p. 335; Arthur W. Hummel (ed.), *Eminent Chinese*, p. 299.

12 Philip W. Sergeant, *The Great Empress Dowager of China*, pp. 306–308.

13 Daniele Varè, *The Last Empress*, pp. 283–284; this description is based on the so-called diary of Li Lianying, which never existed except in Edmund Backhouse's head. Varè is the source for the Bennet quote from the *London Illustrated News*.

14 Der Ling, *Old Buddha*, pp. 334–335.

Chapter 29

1   Lydia Dan, "The Unknown Photographer," unpublished article, 1982; see 1930 Census for New York City, Manhattan, Assembly District 10, Wentworth Hotel. I am indebted to Kathie Klein for sharing information and photos of the *Fu Lu Sho* game with me.

2   Sterling Seagrave and Peggy Seagrave, *Dragon Lady*, p. 440; Eliza Ruhamah Scidmore, *China: The Long Lived Empire*, pp. 127–142.

3   Ibid., p. 445. J. O. P. Bland and Edmund Backhouse, *China Under the Empress Dowager* [hereafter *CUED*] was reissued in January 2004 by Trubner and Co. of London, without notes indicating its many errors and/or deliberate falsehoods, thereby helping perpetuate the usual crude and evil image of the dowager.

4   *CUED*, pp. 477–478.

5   1929 Chautauqua lecture brochure.

6   Lady Dorothea Hosie, *A Portrait of a Chinese Lady*, p. 267.

7   Yi-tsi Feuerwerker, "Women as Writers in the 1920's and 1930's," in *Women in Chinese Society*, pp. 149.

8   Ibid., p. 158.

9   Han Suyin confuses Rong Ling and Der Ling by describing Rong Ling as having "written a book on the Empress [Dowager], a book which had been sold in England and America," see Han Suyin, *The Crippled Tree*, p. 401.

10 Han Suyin, *The Crippled Tree*, pp. 403–406. Madame Dan had another, warmer side, according to Hilda Hale's memoir *Indomitably Yours*. Mrs. Hale, whose husband ran the Cook's Tours office in Beijing, knew Rong Ling and visited her palace; Rong Ling also attended the Hales' wedding in Kobe, Japan. Mrs. Hale writes of how Rong Ling took in starving ex-palace eunuchs — artisans, musicians, servants — after the dynasty's fall in 1912, defraying expenses by offering their needlework and tickets to special musical and dance performances to select foreign tourists. She occasionally danced herself, and told Mrs. Hale she could not survive without her daily opium pipe. (Source: *Indomitably Yours*, and a handwritten note about "Princess Shou Shan" [Madame Dan] from Mrs. Hilda Hale, in the author's possession.)

Chapter 30

1   Fei Shi, *Guide to Peking*, p. 23 and advertisement page I.

2   Ellen LaMotte, *Peking Dust*, pp. 13–14.

3   Ibid., pp. 14–15.

4   "Our Escape from Peking with Our Treasures for the University of Oregon Museum," excerpts from letters written in November 1924 by Gertrude Bass Warner, see http://libweb.uoregon.edu/speccoll/photo/warner/escape.html.

5   From author correspondence with Luke S. K. Kwong, professor of history, University of Lethbridge, Alberta, Canada, October 31, 2002.

6   Der Ling, *Old Buddha*, pp. xi–xiv.

7   Der Ling, *Jades and Dragons*, pp. 223–224.

8   *Los Angeles Times* article, "Men in U.S. Best Lovers," March 21, 1930.

9   Der Ling, *Jades and Dragons*, pp. 243–244.

10 *Los Angeles Times* article, "Chinese Women 'Go Hollywood' Princess Finds," July 22, 1929.

11 Ibid., p. 247.

12 Kate Buss, *Studies in the Chinese Drama*, p. 46.

13 Ibid., pp. 48–49.

14 Der Ling, *Jades and Dragons*, p. 249.
15 Letter in private hands.

Chapter 31

1 *Los Angeles Times* article, ""Chinese Here Fete Princess," February 9, 1928; correspondence with Gretchen Mittwer (2003); and *New York Times* obituary for Thaddeus Raymond White, April 5, 1933.

2 *Los Angeles Times* article of February 9, 1928 mentions that a scale model of the proposed Forbidden City replica was displayed at the Los Angeles Chamber of Commerce. In the inaugural issue of *Fortune* magazine (February 1930), a tongue-in-cheek article on the private lives of island-owning Americans relates a story according to which Der Ling and T.C. leased the miniscule Mexican island of Golondrina off the southern California coast in 1927 and staffed it with a female court of retainers and dancing girls, supervised by a palace guard of ex-Marines who in turn were commanded by T.C. When not dressing up in Manchu court garb, Der Ling and her ladies were doing the Charleston. The *Fortune* article shows the sort of exaggerations and elaborate falsehoods that surrounded Der Ling in America, and which still get reprinted in such books as Thurston Clarke's *Searching for Paradise* (2001), where the story is rehashed without comment.

3 Iris Chang, *The Chinese in America*, p. 26.
4 Ibid., p. 51.
5 Ibid., p. 83.
6 Ibid., p. 141.
7 *Los Angeles Times*, "Chinese Princess on Way Here to Make Home," May 27, 1929; *New York Times* obituary for Thaddeus Raymond White, April 5, 1933.
8 Der Ling, *Lotos Petals*, p. 9.
9 Ibid., p. 20 and p. 71.
10 Ibid., pp. 10–11. A *New York Times* society column item from July 1931 mentions that Der Ling and Thaddeus were dinner guests at the Park Avenue apartment of Mr. and Mrs. Russell Law, along with the Earl and Countess of Gosford and a Prince Demidoff. Perhaps this was the occasion in question.

Chapter 32

1 Der Ling, *Jades and Dragons*, p. 82. The woman whom Der Ling mentions in this passage from *Jades and Dragons*, who referred to her as "a so-called Princess," also asked her to review a manuscript "begun after a residence in Peking of exactly two weeks." This sounds very like Ellen LaMotte's *Peking*

Dust, which does refer to Der Ling, not mentioned by name, as a "so-called princess," and does reflect the author's impressions after a short stay in the city.

2   Ibid.

3   Hugh Trevor-Roper, *The Hermit of Peking*, p. 17.

4   Ibid., p. 34.

5   J. O. P. Bland and Edmund Backhouse, *China Under the Empress Dowager*, pp. 251–252.

6   Der Ling, *Jades and Dragons*, pp. 82–83.

7   Ibid., pp. 83–84. Also see Mrs. Archibald Little, *Intimate China*, p. 370.

8   Der Ling, *Jades and Dragons*, p. 84.

9   J. O. P. Bland and Edmund Backhouse, *China Under the Empress Dowager*, p. 98; Seagrave/author correspondence, September 19, 2003. A search of Bland's diaries from the years 1900–10 (located in the Fisher Rare Book Library, Toronto) showed no mention of Der Ling.

10 Sterling Seagrave and Peggy Seagrave, *Dragon Lady*, p. 449.

11 See Bland papers in the Fisher Rare Book Library, University of Toronto, letters of J. O. P. Bland and Sir Reginald Johnston, April 20 and 24, 1935; Trevor-Roper/author correspondence, October 21, 2002.

12 Der Ling, *Old Buddha*, p. 300. Also see Der Ling's recollections of first meeting the infant Puyi and his mother at the Summer Palace. *The Saturday Evening Post*, "Pu-Yi, the Puppet of Japan," April 30, 1932, p. 70.

13 *The Saturday Evening Post*, "Pu-Yi, the Puppet of Japan," April 30, 1932, pp. 13–77. It is possible that Der Ling's involvement in the Mukden antiques sale may have brought T.C. into the project as partner or manager, and given rise to the story editor Lo Hui-men heard (referred to on p. 524, *The Correspondence of G. E. Morrison*, Vols. I and II; see Chapter XXVII *supra*) that T.C. was involved in illegal sales of Mukden palace treasures.

14 Ibid.

15 Ibid.

16 See Bland papers in the Fisher Rare Book Library, University of Toronto, letters of J. O. P. Bland and Sir Reginald Johnston, April 20 and 24, 1935; Trevor-Roper/author correspondence October 21, 2002.

17 Ibid.

18 Daniele Varè, *The Last Empress*, pp. viii–ix.

Chapter 33

1   Aisin-Gioro Puyi, translated by W. J. F. Jenner, *From Emperor to Citizen*, p. 194.

2   Ibid., p. 195.

3   Ibid., p. 212.

4   Brian Power, *Puppet Emperor*, p. 157.

5   Philip Van Rensselaer, *Million Dollar Baby*, pp. 9–10 and 17–19.

6   See David C. Heymann, *Poor Little Rich Girl* and Philip Van Rensselaer, *Million Dollar Baby*.

7   Philip Van Rensselaer, *Million Dollar Baby*, p. 114 and *New York Times*, January 20, 1934.

8   Philip Van Rensselaer, *Million Dollar Baby*, p. 114.

9   David C. Heymann, *Poor Little Rich Girl*, pp. 98–99.

10 Ibid., pp. 109–110.

11 *Los Angeles Times*, "Noted Princess from China to be Prudence Guest," March 13, 1935.

12 David C. Heymann, *Poor Little Rich Girl*, pp. 115–121.

13 *Los Angeles Times*, "Court Life Described by Chinese Princess," May 29, 1935.

14 *Los Angeles Times*, "China Calls to Princess," August 19, 1935.

15 *Los Angeles Times*,"Chinese Author Goes to Peping," September 3, 1935 and "Princess Der Ling Will Return from China," November 14, 1935.

Chapter 34

1   Edmund O. Clubb, *Twentieth Century China*, p. 218.

2   Harry Hussey, *My Pleasures and Palaces*, pp. 321–337.

3   Iris Chang, *The Chinese in America*, pp. 218–221.

4   "History of Old Chinatown Los Angeles," reprinted from *The Los Angeles Chinatown 50th Year Guidebook* (June 1988), available at http://oldchinatownla.com/history.html.

5   Der Ling, *Lotos Petals*, p. 98.

6   *Los Angeles Times*, " 'Rice Bowl' Party to Aid Chinese," June 14, 1938.

7   *Los Angeles Times*, obituary for Der Ling, November 23, 1944.

8   *Los Angeles Times*, "Der Ling Antiques to be Displayed," August 1, 1941; and *The Chinese Art Collection of the late Princess Der Ling*, presented by Thaddeus C. White (catalog), post-1944.

Legacy

1   Harry Hussey, *My Pleasures and Palaces*, pp. 356–357.

2   I am indebted to Sterling Seagrave for information about Pettus and the California College; information on Pettus can be found via Claremont College's Web site.

3   The thirty negatives were sold to Ernst von Harringa of Los Angeles (1899–1961), whose widow later made the negatives' existence known to *Arts of Asia* magazine, which published two previously unknown images of Cixi. One of them shows not only one of the few shots of the dowager smiling, but also of usually dour Chief Eunuch Li Lianying smirking in an engagingly natural way. *Arts of Asia* Magazine, September–October 1979 (p. 122). Most of these negatives were eventually sold to the Freer Gallery of Art/Arthur M. Sackler Gallery, where they remain today. Thaddeus White's 1952 will indicates that the "bulk of my estate . . . consists of a collection of Chinese art objects which are stored in the warehouses of Bekins Van and Storage Company, Beverly Hills, California, and the All-American Van and Storage Company, of Hollywood, California . . ." His executor, Citizens National Bank of Los Angeles, was directed in the event of White's death to "sell and dispose of the said property of my estate only at such time when, in the opinion of the said Executor, a sale of my property, or any portion thereof, can be made to the advantage of the estate and with as little sacrifice as possible."

4   James Zee-min Lee, *Chinese Potpourri*, p. 328.

5   Thaddeus Raymond was interred at the White family plot in Sag Harbor, New York. (*New York Times* obituary, published April 6, 1933). It is possible that Der Ling's account of the Mukden trip is actually a conflation, for reasons we do not know, of the trip to the Western Tombs. Even Zhu Jiajing, who declared that the Mukden trip never occurred, could not find anything unprovable in the rest of Der Ling's narrative. (He is also incorrect to state that Cixi never made another train trip after her return from Xian in 1902.) See his *Historical Inaccuracies in the Books by Der Ling and Rong Ling*, supra. Lady Townley claims she was allowed by the dowager to take the imperial train back to Beijing from the southern city of Paoting Fu, where Lady Townley and her husband Sir Walter visited her on her way back from the Western Tombs in spring 1903. See *The Indiscretions of Lady Susan*, p. 96.

6   *Jades and Dragons*, pp. 280–287.

Family Tree

Mr. Pierson m. Chinese woman
merchant from
Boston in
Shanghai

Lord Yu Keng m. before 1874 **Louisa Pierson**
(posthumous name Lang-shih)
Minister to Japan and France
Secretary of State, Board of
Foreign Affairs in Beijing
Treasurer of Hubei Province
d. May 1905

b. Shanghai
Lady-in-waiting at the court
of the Empress Dowager Cixi
(1903–1905)

Xunling
(1874–1944)
engineer, director
of the imperial
electrical plant at
the Summer Palace,
photographer of the
Empress Dowager
Cixi; had a daughter,
Li-Li; adopted
surname Xu after
1911 revolution;
d. 1943

Xinling
engineer, worked with
the imperial railroads;
had at least one son;
adopted surname Xu
after 1911 revolution

Der Ling
(Elizabeth
Antoinette)
writer and lecturer;
b. June 8, 1885
Beijing/Tianjin
d. November 21, 1944
Berkeley, California
m. May 21, 1907
Thaddeus Cohu White,
diplomat and
entrepreneur;
had a son, Thaddeus
Raymond, b. 1912,
d. New York, NY,
April 1933

Rong Ling
("Nellie"), known as
Madame Dan
m. General Dan
Paochao; mistress of
ceremonies to wife of
Republican president
Li Yuanhung;
adopted a daughter
(Lydia Dan)

Bibliography

Note: Where possible, I have acquired private translations of Chinese sources. I have also made every effort to render proper names into pinyin, with the deliberate exception of the names of Der Ling and her sister. Where I am unable to locate pinyin equivalents for names given by Der Ling, I have left them without change.

Aisin-Gioro Puyi, translated by W. J. F. Jenner, *From Emperor to Citizen: The Autobiography of Aisin-Gioro Puyi*. Beijing: Foreign Languages Press, 1965.

Almanachs de Gotha (annuaire diplomatique), 1897 (Japan) and 1900 (France, Germany).

Anderson, Mary M., *Hidden Power: The Palace Eunuchs of Imperial China*. New York: Prometheus Books, 1990.

Arlington, L. C. and William Lewisohn, *In Search of Old Peking*. Peking: Henri Vetch, 1935.

Arts of Asia Magazine, September–October 1979 (p. 122).

Backhouse, Edmund and J. O. P. Bland, *Annals and Memoirs of the Court of Peking*. New York: Houghton Mifflin Co., 1914.

Béguin, Gilles and Dominique Morel, *The Forbidden City: Center of Imperial China*. New York: H. N. Abrams, 1996.

Beijing Summer Palace Administration Office, *Summer Palace*. Beijing: Zhaohua Publishing House, 1981.

Bland, J. O. P. and Edmund Backhouse, *China Under the Empress Dowager*. London: William Heineman, 1910.

Bredon, Juliet, *Peking: A Historical and Intimate Description of Its Chief Places of Interest*. Shanghai: Kelly and Walsh, Ltd., 1931.

Burkhardt, V.R., *Chinese Creeds and Customs*. Hong Kong: South China Morning Post, 1955.

Buss, Kate, *Studies in the Chinese Drama*. Boston: The Four Seas Co., 1922.

Cammann, Schuyler, *China's Dragon Robes*. New York: The Ronald Press Co., 1952.

Candlin, Enid Saunders, *The Breach in The Wall: A Memoir of the Old China*. Macmillan, 1973.

Carl, Katherine, *With the Empress Dowager of China*. New York: The Century Co., 1905.

Chang, Iris, *The Rape of Nanking*. New York: Basic Books, 1997.

———, *The Chinese in America*. New York: Viking, 2003.

Chen, Su Hua Ling, *Ancient Melodies*. New York: Universe Books, 1988.

Ching, Frank, *Ancestors*. London: Harrap Limited, 1988.

Chow Chung-cheng, translated by Joyce Emerson, *The Lotus Pool*. New York: Appleton-Century-Crofts Inc., 1961.

Clark, Thurston, *Searching for Paradise*: New York: Random House, 2001.

Clubb, O. Edmund, *Twentieth Century China*. New York: Columbia University Press, 1964.

Cohen, Paul A., *History in Three Keys: The Boxers as Event, Experience, and Myth*. New York: Columbia University Press, 1997.

Cohen, Paul A. and John E. Schrecker, eds., *Reform in Nineteenth-Century China*. Cambridge, MA: Harvard East Asian Research Center, Harvard University, 1976.

Collis, Maurice, *The Motherly and Auspicious*. New York: G. P. Putnam's Sons, 1944.

Conger, Sarah Pike, *Letters from China*. Chicago: McClurg and Co., 1909.

Cronin, Vincent, *Paris on the Eve 1900–1914*. New York: St. Martin's Press, 1990.

Crossley, Pamela Kyle, *Orphan Warriors: Three Manchu Generations and the End of the Qing World*. Princeton, NJ: Princeton University Press, 1990.

———, *The Manchus*. Cambridge: Blackwell Publishers, 1997.

———, *A Translucent Mirror: History and Identity in Qing Imperial Ideology*. Berkeley: University of California Press, 1999.

Dan, Lydia, "The Unknown Photographer," (1982), unpublished article in collection of the Freer Gallery of Art and the Arthur M. Sackler Gallery Archives.

———, letter published in *History of Photography*, Vol. 8, No. 4, October–December 1984.

Dan, Rongling, "Princess Shou Shan." In *Hsiang Fei: A Love Story of the Emperor Ch'ien Lung*. Peiping: Yu Lien Press, 1934.

Der Ling, The Princess, *Two Years in the Forbidden City*. New York: Moffat Yard and Co., 1911.

———, *Old Buddha*. New York: Dodd Mead and Co., 1928.

———, *Kow Tow*. New York: Dodd Mead and Co., 1929.

———, *Lotos Petals*. New York: Dodd Mead and Co., 1930.

———, "From Convent to Court," *Pictorial Review*, January 1931, pp. 4 and 54.

———, "Pu-Yi, The Puppet Emperor of Japan," *Saturday Evening Post*, April 30, 1932, pp. 13, 70, 74, 77.

———, *Jades and Dragons*. New York: The Mohawk Press, 1932.

———, *Golden Phoenix*. New York: Dodd Mead and Co., 1932.

———, *Imperial Incense*. New York: Dodd Mead and Co., 1933.

———, *Son of Heaven*. New York: Appleton/Century, 1935.

Dong, Stella, *Shanghai 1842–1949: The Rise and Fall of a Decadent City*. New York: William Morrow and Sons, 2000.

Downer, Lesley, *Madame Sadayakko: The Geisha Who Bewitched the West*. New York: Gotham Books, 2003.

Earle, Joe (ed.), *Splendors of Imperial Japan* (catalogue). London: The Khalili Family Trust, 2002.

Eastman, Lloyd E., *Throne and Mandarins: China's Search for a Policy During the Sino-French Controversy 1880–1895*. Cambridge, MA: Harvard University Press, 1967.

Eldridge, Mona, *In Search of a Prince: My Life with Barbara Hutton*. London: Sidgwick and Jackson, 1988.

Elliott, Mark, *The Manchu Way: The Eight Banners and Ethnic Identity in Late Imperial China*. Stanford, CA: Stanford University Press, 2001.

Fang, Shiou-yun, "History of the Photographs of Empress Dowager Cixi taken by Xunling." Appendix of thesis, "Images, Ideas, Reality," University of Edinburgh, 2005.

Fei Shi, *Guide to Peking and its Environs Near and Far*. Tientsin: The Tientsin Press, Ltd., 1924.

Folsom, Kenneth E., *Friends, Guests and Colleagues: The Mu-fu System in the Late Ch'ing Period*. Berkeley: University of California Press, 1968.

Froncek, Thomas, *The Horizon Book of the Arts of China*. New York: American Heritage Publishing Company, 1969.

Gaan, Margaret, *Last Moments of a World*. New York: Norton and Co, 1978.

Godden, Rumer, *The Butterfly Lions: The Pekingese in History, Legend and Art*. London: Macmillan, 1977.

Goodrich, L. Carrington and Nigel Cameron, *The Face of China, As Seen by Photographers and Travelers 1860–1912*. Millerton, NY: Aperture, 1978.

Gosling, Nigel, *The Adventurous World of Paris 1900–1914*. New York: William Morrow and Co., 1978.

Graham, Dorothy, *Through the Moon Door*. New York: J. H. Sears and Co., 1926.

Hale, Hilda, *Indomitably Yours: An Account of My Kaleidoscopic Life*. Privately printed. Victoria, BC; no date.

Han Suyin, *A Many-Splendored Thing*. Boston: Little Brown, 1952.

Han Suyin (Rosalie Chou), *The Crippled Tree*. New York: G. P. Putnam's Sons, 1965.

Hart, Sir Robert, ed. John King Fairbank, Katherine Frost Bruner and Elizabeth MacLeod Matheson, *The I. G. in Peking: Letters of Robert Hart, Chinese Maritime Customs 1868–1907*, Vols. I and II. Cambridge, MA: The Belknap Press/Harvard University Press, 1975.

Headland, Prof. Isaac Taylor and Dr. Headland, *Court Life in China: The Capital, Its Officials and People*. New York: Fleming H. Revell Co., 1909.

Heymann, C. David, *Poor Little Rich Girl: The Life and Legend of Barbara Hutton*. New Jersey: Lyle Stuart Inc., 1983.

Hodges, Graham Russell Gao, *Anna May Wong: From Laundryman's Daughter to Hollywood Legend*. New York: Palgrave Macmillan, 2004.

Hosie, Lady Dorothea, *Two Gentlemen of China*. London: Seeley, Service and Co. Ltd, 1926.

———, *A Portrait of a Chinese Lady and Certain of Her Contemporaries*. New York: William Morrow and Co., 1930.

———, *The Pool of Ch'ien Lung*. London: Hodder and Stoughton, 1948.

Hummel, Arthur W. (ed.), *Eminent Chinese of the Ch'ing Period (1644–1912)*, Vols. I and II. Washington DC: United States Government Printing Office, 1943.

Hussey, Harry, *My Pleasures and Palaces*. New York: Doubleday, 1968.

Inn, Henry (ed.), Prof. Shao Ching Lee, *Chinese Houses and Gardens*. New York: Hastings House, 1950.

Ishimoto, Baroness Shidzue, *Facing Two Ways: The Story of My Life*. New York: Farrar and Rinehart, 1935.

Johnston, Sir Reginald, *Twilight in the Forbidden City*. London: Victor Gollancz, 1934.

Keene, Donald, *Emperor of Japan: Meiji and His World 1852–1912*. New York: Columbia University Press, 2002.

Kidd, David, *Peking Story: The Last Days of Old China*. London: Aurum Press Ltd., 1988.

Koo, Madame Wellington, with Isabella Taves, *No Feast Lasts Forever*. New York: Quadrangle/New York Times Book Co., 1975.

Kurth, Peter, *Isadora: A Sensational Life*. Boston: Little, Brown and Company, 2001.

Kwong, Luke S. K., *A Mosaic of the Hundred Days: Personalities, Politics, and Ideas of 1898*. Cambridge, MA: Harvard University Press, 1984.

LaMotte, Ellen N., *Peking Dust*. New York: The Century Co., 1919.

Lang, Olga, *Chinese Family and Society*. Hamden, CT: Archon Books, 1968.

Lao She [Shu Qingchun], translated Don Cohn, *Beneath the Red Banner*. Beijing: Panda Books, 1982.

Lee, James Zee-min, *Chinese Potpourri*. Hong Kong: The Oriental Publishers, 1950.

Levy, Adrian and Cathy Scott-Clark, *The Stone of Heaven: Unearthing the Secret History of Imperial Green Jade*. Boston: Little Brown and Co., 2001.

Lin Yutang, *My Country and My People*. New York: Reynal and Hitchock, 1935.

——, *Imperial Peking: Seven Centuries of China*. New York: Crown Publishers, 1961.

Little, Mrs. Archibald, *Intimate China*. London: Hutchinson and Co., 1901.

Liu Qi, "Cracking the Mystery of Cixi's Youth," on-line version: www.tydoo.com/suwu/lishi/cxss.htm.

Lo Hui-men (ed.), *The Correspondence of G. E. Morrison*. Cambridge: Cambridge University Press, 1974.

Los Angeles Times, "Chinese Here Fete Princess," February 9, 1928.

——, "Chinese Princess on Way Here to Make Home," May 27, 1929.

——, "Chinese Women 'Go Hollywood' Princess Finds," July 22, 1929.

——, "Men in U.S. Best Lovers," March 21, 1930.

——, "Noted Princess From China to be Prudence Guest," March 13, 1935.

——, "Court Life Described by Chinese Princess," May 29, 1935.

——, "China Calls to Princess," August 19, 1935.

——, "Chinese Author Goes to Peiping," September 3, 1935.

——, "Princess Der Ling Will Return from China," November 14, 1935.

——, "Secret Culinary Success Told by Chinese Princess," April 20, 1937.

——, "Tons of Articles to Leave This Week for War-Torn Country," October 20, 1937.

Loti, Pierre, translated by Myrta L. Jones, *The Last Days of Peking*. Boston: Little Brown and Co., 1902.

Lum, Bertha, *Gangplanks to the East*. New York: The Henkle-Yewdale House Inc., 1936.

Lynch, George, *The War of the Civilisations*. London: Longmans Green and Co., 1901.

Mailey, Jean, *The Manchu Dragon: Costumes of the Ch'ing Dynasty 1644–1912* (exhibition catalog). New York: The Metropolitan Museum of Art, 1980.

Moats, Alice-Leone, *The Million Dollar Studs*. New York: Delacorte Press, 1977.

Nan, Huai-Chin, *Basic Buddhism: Exploring Buddhism and Zen*. York Beach, ME: Samuel Weiser, Inc., 1997.

National Anthropological Archives, Smithsonian Institution, James Zee-min Lee's lecture brochure (pre-1944), with preface written by Princess Der Ling.

New York Times, "Says Powers Waste Time," November 15, 1900.

———, "Observations of the Chinese Minister in Paris," December 2, 1900.

———, "The New Chinese Minister," March 30, 1903.

———, "Tribute to Clemenceau: Princess Der Ling Gives Her Recollections of Him," November 24, 1929.

———, "An Evening in the Palace of the Mings," November 15, 1931.

———, "The Microphone Will Present," April 3, 1932.

———, "Fellow-Writers Praise Mrs. Buck," January 21, 1933.

———, "Thaddeus R. White: 20-year-old Son of Chinese Princess Dies of Pneumonia," April 5, 1933.

———, "Exotic Pomp Marks Beaux-Arts Ball," January 20, 1934.

———, "Geographic Theatre Gives First Show: Princess Der Ling Tells of Her Experiences at the Court of the Late Empress," January 22, 1934.

———, "Farley Sees Air Lines to Europe and to East," October 16, 1934.

Palace Museum Beijing, catalog for exhibit, "Empress Dowager Cixi: Her Art of Living."

Paludan, Anne, *Chronicle of the Chinese Emperors: The Reign-by-Reign Record of the Rulers of Imperial China*. London: Thames and Hudson, 1998.

Payen, Cecile E., "Besieged in Peking. The Diary of a Visitor at the United States Legation," *The Century Magazine*, January 1901, Vol. LXI, No. 3, pp. 453–468.

Power, Brian, *The Puppet Emperor: The Life of Puyi, The Last Emperor of China*. New York: Universe Books, 1988.

Preston, Diana, *The Boxer Rebellion: The Dramatic Story of China's War on Foreigners that Shook the World in the Summer of 1900*. New York: Walker and Co., 1999.

Priest, Alan, Curator of Far Eastern Art, The Metropolitan Museum of Art, *Imperial Robes and Textiles of the Chinese Court* (exhibition catalog). Minneapolis, MN: The Minneapolis Institute of Arts, 1943.

———, *Costumes From the Forbidden City* (special exhibition program). New York: The Metropolitan Museum of Art, 1945.

Pruitt, Ida, *Old Madam Yin: A Memoir of Peking Life 1926–1938*. Stanford, CA: Stanford University Press, 1979.

Rawski, Evelyn S., *The Last Emperors: A Social History of Qing Imperial Institutions*. Berkeley: University of California Press, 1998.

Rhoads, Edward J. M., *Manchus and Han: Ethnic Relations and Political Power in Late Qing and Early Republican China 1861–1928*. Seattle: University of Washington Press, 2000.

Ruoff, E. G. (ed.), *Death Throes of a Dynasty: Letters and Diaries of Charles and Bessie Ewing, Missionaries to China*. Kent, OH: Kent State University, 1990.

Scidmore, Eliza Ruhamah, *China: The Long-Lived Empire*. New York: The Century Co., 1900.

Scotland, Tony, *The Empty Throne: The Quest for an Imperial Heir in the People's Republic of China*. London: Viking, 1993.

Seagrave, Sterling, *The Soong Dynasty*. New York: Harper and Row, 1985.

Seagrave, Sterling and Peggy Seagrave, *Dragon Lady: The Life and Legend of the Last Empress of China*. New York: Knopf, 1992.

———, *The Yamato Dynasty: The Secret History of Japan's Imperial Family*. New York: Broadway Books, 1999.

———, *Gold Warriors: America's Secret Recovery of Yamashita's Gold*. Bowstring Books, 2002.

Sergeant, Philip W., *The Great Empress Dowager of China*. London: Hutchinson and Co., 1910.

Seton, Grace Thompson, *Chinese Lanterns*. New York: Dodd Mead and Co., 1924.

Skinner, Cornelia Otis, *Madame Sarah*. Boston: Houghton Mifflin, 1967.

Spence, Jonathan D., *Ts'ao Yin and the K'ang-hsi Emperor: Bondservant and Master*. New Haven: Yale University Press, 1966.

———, *The Gate of Heavenly Peace: The Chinese and Their Revolution, 1895–1980*. New York: Viking, 1981.

———, *God's Chinese Son: The Taiping Heavenly Kingdom of Hong Xiuquan*. New York: W. W. Norton Co., 1996.

Spector, Stanley, *Li Hung-Chang and the Huai Army: A Study in Nineteenth-Century Chinese Regionalism*. Seattle: University of Washington Press, 1964.

Strand, David, *Rickshaw Beijing: City, People and Politics in the 1920s*. Berkeley: University of California Press, 1989.

The Palace Museum, *Life of the Emperors and Empresses in the Forbidden City 1644–1911*. Beijing: China Travel Tourism Press (no date).

Thorp, Robert L., *Son of Heaven: Imperial Arts of China* (exhibition catalog). Seattle: Son of Heaven Press, 1988.

Townley, Lady Susan, *The Indiscretions of Lady Susan*. New York: D. Appleton and Company, 1922.

Trevor-Roper, Hugh, *Hermit of Peking: The Hidden Life of Sir Edmund Backhouse*. New York: Knopf, 1977.

Tsao Hsueh-chin and Kao Ngo, translated by Yang Hsien-yi and Gladys Yang, *A Dream of Red Mansions*. Beijing: Foreign Languages Press, 1978.

Van Rensselaer, Philip, *Million Dollar Baby: An Intimate Portrait of Barbara Hutton*. New York: G. P. Putnam's Sons, 1979.

Varè, Daniele, *The Last Empress*. New York: Doubleday, Doran and Co., 1938.

Vollmer, John E., *In the Presence of the Dragon Throne: Qing Dynasty Costume (1644–1911) in the Royal Ontario Museum* (exhibition catalog). Royal Ontario Museum, 1977.

———, *Decoding Dragons: Status Garments in Ch'ing Dynasty China*. Eugene, OR: Museum of Art, University of Oregon, 1983.

Warner, Marina, *The Dragon Empress: The Life and Times of Cixi Empress Dowager of China 1835–1908*. New York: Macmillan, 1972.

Weale, B. L. Putnam [Bertram Lenox-Simpson], *Indiscreet Letters from Peking*. New York: Dodd Mead and Co., 1907.

Wei, Katherine and Terry Quinn, *Second Daughter: Growing Up in China, 1930–1949*. Boston: Little Brown and Co., 1984.

Wei, Tao-Ming, Madame, *My Revolutionary Years: The Autobiography of Madame Wei Tao-ming*. New York: Scribner, 1943.

White, Thaddeus C., *The Chinese Art Collection of the Late Princess Der Ling* (catalog for auction of Der Ling's belongings, post-1944, at 928 North La Cienega Boulevard in Los Angeles).

Williams, Edward Thomas, *China Yesterday and Today*. New York: Thomas Y. Crowell Co., 1927.

Wolf, Margery and Roxane Witke (eds.), *Women in Chinese Society*. Stanford, CA: Stanford University Press, 1975.

Wong Su-ling and Early Herbert Cressy, *Daughter of Confucius: A Personal History*. New York: Farrar Straus and Young, 1952.

Wu Yung, translated by Ida Pruitt, *The Flight of an Empress*. New Haven: Yale University Press, 1936.

Yen, Liang, *Daughter of the Khans*. New York: W. W. Norton and Co., 1955.

Zhou Jianren/Zhou Ye, *An Age Gone By: Lu Xun's Clan in Decline*. Beijing: New World Press, 1988.

Zhu Jiajing, "Deling Rongling suo zhu shuzhong si shishi cuowu" (*Historical inaccuracies in the books by Der Ling and Rong Ling*), *Gugong bowuguan yuankan* (Palace Museum Journal), Beijing, No. 4 (1982), pp. 25–42 (translated by Willow Zheng).

Index